STILL JOUI
ON

By Debbie Fletcher

2

Football Grounds Visited

1 – St. Andrews – Birmingham City

2 – Baseball Ground (Demolished) – Derby County

3 – Wembley Stadium – Old (Demolished)

4 – Villa Park – Aston Villa

5 – Portman Road – Ipswich Town

6 – Goodison Park – Everton

7 – Vicarage Road – Watford

8 – Kenilworth Road – Luton Town

9 – The Valley – Charlton Athletic

10 – White Hart Lane (Demolished) - Tottenham Hotspur

11 – The City Ground – Nottingham Forest

12 – The Dell (Demolished) – Southampton

13 – Ashton Gate – Bristol City

14 – Goldstone Ground (Demolished) – Brighton & Hove Albion

15 – Carrow Road – Norwich City

16 – Molineux – Wolverhampton Wanderers

17 – Mainc Road (Demolished) – Manchester City

18 – Highfield Road (Demolished) – Coventry City

19 – Anfield – Liverpool

20 – Elland Road – Leeds United

21 – Roker Park (Demolished) - Sunderland

22 – Old Trafford – Manchester United

23 – The Hawthorns – West Bromwich Albion

24 – Victoria Ground (Demolished) – Stoke City

25 – Selhurst Park – Crystal Palace

26 – Filbert Street (Demolished) – Leicester City

27 – Ayresome Park (Demolished) – Middlesbrough

28 – Highbury (Demolished) – Arsenal

29 – The Vetch Field (Demolished) – Swansea City

30 – Upton Park/Boleyn Ground (Demolished) – West Ham United

31 – Meadow Lane – Notts County

32 – Gay Meadow (Demolished) – Shrewsbury Town

33 – Turf Moor – Burnley

34 – Fellows Park (Demolished) – Walsall

35 – Loftus Road – Queens Park Rangers

36 – Brammall Lane – Sheffield United

37 – Hampden Park – Scotland

38 – De Vijverberg (Holland) – De Graafschap

39 – Puyenbeke Stadion (Belgium) – SKN Sint-Niklaas

40 – Oosterpark Stadion (Holland) (Demolished) – FC Groningen

41 – NAC Stadion (Holland) (Demolished) – NAC Breda

42 – Boundary Park – Oldham Athletic

43 – Craven Cottage – Fulham

44 – Home Park – Plymouth Argyle

45 – Ninian Park (Demolished) – Cardiff City

46 – Plough Lane (Demolished) – Wimbledon

47 – Leeds Road (Demolished) – Huddersfield Town

48 – Manor Ground (Demolished) – Oxford United

49 – Brunton Park – Carlisle United

50 – Ewood Park – Blackburn Rovers

51 – Blundell Park – Grimsby Town

52 – Fratton Park – Portsmouth

53 – Oakwell Stadium – Barnsley

54 – Eastville Stadium (Demolished) – Bristol Rovers

55 – Boothferry Park (Demolished) – Hull City

56 – The Old Den (Demolished) – Millwall

57 – Elm Park (Demolished) – Reading

58 – Valley Parade – Bradford City

59 – Sealand Road (Demolished) – Chester City

60 – Springfield Park (Demolished) – Wigan Athletic

61 – Burnden Park (Demolished) – Bolton Wanderers

62 – Gresty Road – Crewe Alexandra

63 – Prenton Park – Tranmere Rovers

64 – Brisbane Road – Leyton Orient

65 – Griffin Park (for demolition) – Brentford

66 – Millmoor (abandoned) – Rotherham United

67 – Deva Stadium – Chester City

68 – Glanford Park – Scunthorpe United

69 – Bootham Crescent (Demolished) – York City

70 – Adams Park – Wycombe Wanderers

71 – Twerton Park – Bristol Rovers

72 – Bloomfield Road – Blackpool

73 – John Smiths Stadium - Huddersfield Town

74 – Vale Park – Port Vale

75 – Riverside Stadium – Middlesbrough

76 – Britannia Stadium - Stoke City

77 – Banks Stadium – Walsall

78 – Memorial Stadium – Bristol Rovers

79 – Millennium Stadium – Wales

80 – St. Mary's Stadium – Southampton

81 – St. James Park – Newcastle United

82 – Etihad Stadium – Manchester City

83 – Stadium of Light – Sunderland

84 – Madejski Stadium – Reading

85 – Keepmoat Stadium – Doncaster Rovers

86 – Zahed Sports City Stadium (Abu Dhabi) – United Arab Emirates

87 – The New Wembley Stadium – England

88 – Pride Park Stadium – Derby County

89 – Cardiff City Stadium – Cardiff City

90 – KC Stadium – Hull City

91 – Hillsborough Stadium – Sheffield Wednesday

92 – Autotech Stadium – Solihull Moors

93 – Aggborough – Kidderminster Town

94 – JJB Stadium – Wigan Athletic

95 – New York Stadium – Rotherham United

96 – Amex Stadium – Brighton & Hove Albion

97 – Vitality Stadium – AFC Bournemouth

98 – Academy Stadium – Manchester City Women

99 – Macron Stadium – Bolton Wanderers

100 – Stadium MK – Milton Keynes Dons

101 – Stoke Gifford Stadium – Bristol City Women

102 – Meadow Park – Boreham Wood (Arsenal Women)

103 – Camp Nou (Spain) – Barcelona

104 – Estadio Heliodoro Rodriguez Lopez – CD Tenerife

105 – The Northcourt – Abingdon United (Oxford United Women)

106 – Wheatsheaf Park – Staines FC (Chelsea Women)

107 – The Hive Stadium – Barnet FC (London Bees Ladies)

108 – Pirelli Stadium – Burton Albion

109 – Deepdale – Preston North End

110 – The New Den – Millwall

111 – Rossett Park – Marine FC (Everton Women)

112 – Jonny Rocks Stadium – Cheltenham Town

113 – Bracken Moor Stadium – Stockbridge Park Steels (Sheffield United Women)

114 – Farley Way – Quorn FC (Leicester City Women)

115 – London Stadium – West Ham United

116 – Kingsmeadow – Chelsea Women

117 – Liberty Stadium – Swansea City

118 – Avenue Stadium – Dorchester Town (Yeovil Town Ladies)

119 – Rush Green Stadium – West Ham United Women

120 – Technique Stadium – Chesterfield (Sheffield United Women)

121 – King Power Stadium – Leicester City

122 – Shenley Lane Community Association – Northfield Town

123 – Trevor Brown Memorial Ground – Boldmere St. Michaels

124 – The Valley Stadium – Redditch United (Women)

125 – Sixfields Stadium – Northampton Town

126 – The Tottenham Hotspur Stadium – Tottenham Hotspur (Women)

127 – Weston Homes Stadium – Peterborough United

128 – Chigwell Construction Stadium – Dagenham & Redbridge (West Ham Women)

129 – Rowheath Pavilion (Birmingham) – Crusaders Women

130 – RICOH Arena – Coventry City

131 – Central Ground – Sutton Coldfield FC (West Bromwich Albion Ladies)

132 – Illey Lane (Previously Bartley Green FC) – Bustlehome FC

133 – Dickens Heath Sports Club – Leafield Athletic Ladies

134 – Keys Park – Hednesford Town

135 – Estadio Antonio Domínguez Alfonso (Tenerife) – CD Marino

136 – The Bolt New Lawn – Forest Green Rovers

137 – Cadbury Recreation Ground - Cadbury Athletic

Introduction

I have been privileged enough to have traveled to many football grounds during the last fifty years as I watched my team Birmingham City home and away and along the way I have visited various other stadiums with England, England Women and Birmingham City Women. I attended other games too as I strove to explore new stadiums in various areas of England and the rest of the world.

I have been lucky enough to visit some amazing stadiums be they large or small and I have gathered some fantastic experiences along the way. I wanted to share those experiences and I have attempted to describe my first experience of each ground I have visited along with my favourite visits along the way. Some grounds I may have visited only once whereas others may have been on several occasions.

There was a period of seventeen years when I lived abroad whereby I could not get to as many games as I had previously until I returned to the UK in 2014 to embark on my football journey once again. It has been, and still is, a fantastic journey and one that I wanted to share with those who may be interested in our football pilgrimage. I give you my football journey so far.

Ground 1 – St. Andrews 24th March 1973 – Division One - Birmingham City 3 Coventry City 0

On Saturday, 24th March 1973 my friend Sue and I set out for St. Andrews to watch Birmingham City take on Coventry City in a local derby in the old first division which is now know as the Premier League. It was to be my first ever football game and a big journey for two 11 year olds who had to get three buses to get to St. Andrews

I don't remember a lot about the journey or the match really but I do remember the atmosphere and the feelings it inspired. When I first set eyes on the stadium I was overawed. It looked so big! I stood outside St. Andrews on the Coventry road and gazed up at the KOP sitting regally at the top of the grassy bank that it sat on. I saw the Blues fans inside that had already gone through the turnstiles and were now climbing up the steps towards the entrance to the terraces at the top. I remember paying my money and squeezing through the old turnstiles and climbing the many concrete steps to the top of the old KOP terracing. We had got there early and the terracing looked massive while it was filling up. I thought the pitch looked so green. On the terracing the atmosphere was unbelievable! I was completely overwhelmed. It was fantastic – I was well and truly hooked! The whole stadium looked so big to me, and the noise was incredible.

It was still early but the ground seemed full already and the fans (as always) were in fabulous voice. It was the first time I heard the Blues anthem 'Keep Right On', and it was belting out so loud and so proudly. I fell in love with the club and the supporters that day. Sue and I were brave little souls and we stood at the heart of the KOP, in the middle, just to the left of the halfway fencing and just in front of the refreshments block at the back. In fact we were so small at the time that the guys lifted us onto a concrete shelf, about six inches wide and about 2 foot high that surrounded the refreshment stand, so that we could see.

I remember looking across the top of all those heads and seeing a sea of swaying blue and white. There were 34,775 inside St. Andrews that day and it seemed like every one of them had at least one scarf either around their necks or tied to their wrists. At the time the KOP and Tilton were terracing, with the old seated railway end behind the goal and the seated main stand situated opposite the massive KOP terrace. I had a blue and white bar scarf tied proudly around my wrist as this was the style at the time.

When Blues scored I remember throwing my arms in the air, whilst trying to keep my balance and catching my scarf on the barbed wire on the top of the refreshment stand! One of the guys had to untangle it for me. I am sure I did that a few times over the years. The fans on the KOP were swaying back and forth like a tide and I loved it when they did 'Knee's up mother brown' and everyone jumped up and down until they all surged forward with a few getting squashed or getting wrapped around the crash bars. No one seemed to get hurt though and they soon came back to where they had previously been standing, or thereabouts! The odd pie would get dropped and a few drinks spilt but it was all good fun and added to the atmosphere.

Seeing my heroes run out onto that lovely green pitch was such a thrill, as it still is. I was so excited that day and although I don't remember much about the game I remember that I thought Blues played fantastic in their royal blue shirts as they beat Coventry City 3-0 with goals from Bob Hatton, Bob Latchford and Gordon Taylor. I soon caught on to the songs and sang my heart out for the entire time I was there, despite trying to stay on the six inch shelf I was balancing on. I did fall off a few times though but was always caught by the guys beneath us who seemed to look out for us. I came out thinking

Birmingham City were the best team in the world. The sound of 'Keep Right On' and 'Shit on the Villa' were ringing in my ears for days afterwards. I was learning fast that we really hated the villa! Mind you, I had already gathered that from school!

Leaving the ground was fantastic too, being amongst the tide of people marching down the steps towards the waiting football special buses that were always waiting to take everyone back to the city centre. I remember the long line of Double Decker buses and how we would all queue to get on one, and when the bus was jammed full then the queue would move on to the next one. The bus would then head for town with the bluenoses singing at the top of their voices and the buses seemed to sway with the singing. There would be Blues scarves hanging out of every window. All the way back to town I could see the Blues fans on both sides of the road as well as in the road and it was like a continuous sea of blue and white. It was fabulous and I couldn't wait to go back again. That was me hooked for life!

I have been to so many games at St. Andrews since then with all of them being special to me and with several special memories. One of those was back in May 1980 when Blues played Notts County in the old second Division when a draw would be enough to see Blues promoted and I had decided to stand on the Tilton that day and the ground was packed. The game finished in a 3-3 draw with fantastic celebrations at the end of the game when the tide of fans carried us onto the pitch to join the festivities. A great day.

One of my very favourites was the League Cup Semi Final Second leg game against West Ham United inside a packed St. Andrews in 2011. These days the Stadium is of course all seated with the KOP and Tilton stands joined by a rounded corner and a new high stand behind the goal with the top tier being quite high up and the lower tier being split between home and away fans and is called the Gil Merrick stand (the old railway stand). Along the opposite side of the pitch to the KOP is the old main stand which still has character despite looking slightly out of place these days. This is where the dugouts are situated.

I was really excited about the semi final 2nd leg in 2011 against West Ham as we set off for St. Andrews. Stephen (my nephew) had come over from Leicester where he was at university and my sister Annette came with us too. It was packed outside the ground and we had to walk up from the traffic island and there was loads of trouble and police were everywhere. When we arrived at the stadium it was like a throwback to the 80's as Blues and West Ham fans battled it out while the police ran around with riot shields and were being quite heavy handed in trying to separate them. Some of these clashes were in the car park so we just headed into the ground and took up our places on the KOP/Tilton corner which was already packed.

It was a fantastic atmosphere, the best I had known for many years and everyone was standing! It was absolutely buzzing. As two of us were in the back row of the KOP/Tilton corner (the other one was on the KOP) we all squeezed in together. A couple of Bluenoses passed me and said that they had brought my book (Truly Blue) for their dad. That pleased me as the whole point of my book was to share my memories and try to get the passion back into football.

The game got underway and we were stunned and devastated when West Ham scored from a cracking 25 yard shot which beat Ben Foster and put West Ham 3-1 ahead on aggregate (0-1 on the night). Blues now had a mountain to climb. We never stopped singing though and Blues were giving their all. Zigic came on for the second half and he seemed to make quite a difference to our performance. Blues should have had a penalty when West Ham's Wayne Bridge handled the ball but we were awarded a corner instead. The corner went straight to Lee Bowyer who powered a shot into the net and St. Andrews exploded as we all celebrated and we were filled with renewed hope as it was now 1-1 and 2-3 on aggregate.

Blues were on fire now and with the partisan crowd behind them they were throwing everything at West Ham. Then in the 79th minute Roger Johnson powered in a header to make the aggregate score 3-3 and the place went completely bonkers! I was so happy as we jumped around and fell over seats, it was fantastic! In the last minute of the game Craig Gardener hit a cracking long range shot which the West Ham keeper got his fingertips to and diverted onto the post as we came so close to winning it.

The game went to extra time and with only 4 minutes in, Craig Gardener repeated his shot from the same distance which was hit with so much power that it flew into the net and St. Andrews went crazy! Unbelievable scenes all around the Stadium as we realised what had happened and that this remarkable comeback could mean a trip to Wembley! Blues saw out the remaining minutes and scarves all round the stadium were waved as everyone sang an incredibly loud 'Ka sa ra sa ra whatever will be will be, we're going to Wembley, ka sa ra sa ra'.

When the final whistle sounded it was absolutely amazing - the best night at St. Andrews for many many years and Blues were in our first major Cup Final at Wembley for 50 years.

Another amazing event took place in 2020 when Blues were the away team at St. Andrews and it would be the only time I would be an away fan in our own stadium as we were drawn away against Coventry City. It meant that

Birmingham fans became the ones to hold the record of the largest number of away fans inside St. Andrews with over 9,500 present!

Everyone was looking forward to the FA Cup tie against our tenants Coventry City because of the novelty value of being away in our own stadium. Considering we were only getting crowds of about 7,000 for home ties in the FA Cup there was suddenly thousands wanting tickets and complaining about missing out. Blues would have over 9,000 tickets and me, June, James G and James H had tickets in the Olympic gallery above the away section. On the day of the game me, June and James met up with the others in our usual spot despite this now being the Coventry 'home' end and we watched as some double decker buses arrived with Coventry fans on. There were a lot of other Bluenoses around the 'home end' too. We then headed round to the away end (with our new half half scarves due to the special occasion) so see what it was like.

Terry, Nigel, Charlie and Harry were in the lower Gil Merrick while me, June, James and James headed up into the Olympic gallery. It was already filling up and the view was fantastic! Blues had the Gil Merrick Stand and the whole of the Main Stand while Coventry had the KOP and about a third of the Tilton. The atmosphere was brilliant. It was strange seeing the scoreboard being operated by Coventry and with their own tannoy people too. The Message on big screen thanked Blues for helping Coventry (letting them use our ground and saving their skin). It was also strange seeing Blues warming up in our away kit and coming out of the away dressing room/tunnel.

The teams came out for kick off and the noise from the Bluenoses was fantastic. There were some great songs and banter. Blues sang 'you're supposed to be at home' and Coventry responded with 'you're supposed to be away'. We sang 'you've got no home' and 'we saved your club' - to which they applauded. The best banter of the day was when Blues sang 'who's the wanker in my seat?' and Coventry fans responded with 'we're the wankers in your seat' to which we laughed and applauded them. Great stuff.

Unfortunately the football was rubbish as both teams looked afraid to lose and although Blues were slightly the better team we have could have lost it late on as Coventry missed a sitter. The game finished 0-0 and so we had a replay which would involve us changing ends as we would then be at home and Coventry fans would now have the novelty of being in the away section of the stadium they called home this season. Bizarre eh. On a positive note Blues fans now held the record for the largest away following at St. Andrews. You couldn't make it up could you!

Ground 2 – Baseball Ground – 1st February 1978 – FA Cup 4th Round - Derby County 2 Birmingham City 1

I raced home from school on the Monday lunchtime to catch the FA cup draw. I waited nervously by the radio and then I heard it. Derby County versus Birmingham City. That's it, I thought, I have to get to this game, this has to be my first away game. I began trying to talk my mates into coming with me and eventually a couple of them agreed. I was so excited and off we went to the ticket office to buy tickets for the away end at the old Baseball ground in Derby.

Finally the day of the Derby game arrived. It was Saturday, 28th January, four days after my birthday and I was so excited. I met up with my friends and we set off for New Street station to catch one of the many football special trains that were travelling to Derby that day. The train station was starting to fill up with Bluenoses and we joined the queue for tickets for the special. That was when it all started to go wrong. It was announced that the Derby v Birmingham City game had been called off due to bad weather! I was devastated. Especially as the game would now be played midweek on a school day. The other girls were upset too and said that they would get their tickets for the game refunded, as they would not be able to go. Me, on the other hand, was determined to go still – even if it meant bunking off school and going on my own. I had looked forward to this for so long that I could not give up.

I told my mom when I got home and when she saw how determined I was she said I could come out of school early to go to the match. She was really worried about me going on my own though, but I reassured her that I would be okay. The replay was now on the 1st February – midweek.

I ran all the way home from school that day and got changed in record time. Mom had arranged for my Nan to take me to town to the station and to put me on the train! So off we set, my Nan and me. We arrived at the station and purchased my ticket for the special with no problems. Football fans were not allowed to get on the specials through the station, we had to queue outside the station at the side door where the police would keep an eye on proceedings. As we walked to the queue my Nan spotted a group of girls and to my embarrassment, took me over to them and asked if I could stay with them as I was alone and would they look out for me.

It was nice of my Nan and I made friends with them and stayed with them for the trip. It was a massive queue by the time the doors were opened and we surged through and onto the waiting football special. There were a few football specials on that day and the one I was on was packed with singing fans. The bluenoses were sitting everywhere, on the seats, on the tables, in the luggage racks and standing in the aisles. It was brilliant. 'Wembley – Wembley' was being sang loudly throughout the journey along with 'Keep Right On', 'Shit on the Villa' and other favourites.

The train pulled into Derby station and immediately everyone streamed off en mass. The noise was deafening in the confined space of the station as the bluenoses sang 'the Brummies are here!' at the top of our voices. People just stopped in amazement and watched the flow of fans as we swarmed up stairs and out of the station to the waiting police escort. The police were waiting in numbers and immediately moved to the front of the fans and to either side and attempted to lead us towards the ground in some sort of order. It was non-stop singing – it was great. I have always thought that away games are better for the atmosphere of the visiting Blue army and this day was when it all began for me. I was as overwhelmed as all the people we passed who stopped what they were doing in amazement to watch the blue army as it passed by in full voice. We passed the odd Derby fan too and they immediately encountered some verbal abuse from the blue army. It was an invasion. I was so impressed.

The ground was a bit of a disappointment. It was a right shed. It was smaller than St. Andrews and just looked tatty and old. We were led into the away end, which was on the one side and included the corner, which contained a massive floodlight in the middle of it. A bit crap I thought at the time. Our end was the lower terracing underneath a seated stand with the top stand jutting out over the top of most of us. There was 31,995 inside the Baseball ground and the away end was packed and due to fact that I am not that tall, it was difficult at times to see some of the match. The blue army sang our hearts out, and I thought that we out sang the home fans. Could have just been me being blue eyed thought! The Derby fans were in good voice too and the game was exciting.

During the game I began to smell smoke. The Blues fans started singing 'Derby County's burning down!' to the tune of London town is burning down, and I looked behind to see that the refreshment stand was on fire! Never a dull moment following the Blues eh.

The match was always going to be a close encounter with Derby just shading it and beating us 2-1 with Keith Bertschin scoring for Blues. When Blues scored the Bluenoses went wild and I got an accidental punch in the face – what a day. I was okay though and still managed to jump up and down to celebrate the goal. Shame we lost though. I have always loved the FA Cup, as most fans do, so I was feeling a bit disappointed on our walk back to the station. We had the usual police escort back and at one point the Derby fans taunted us with a rendition of 'were going to Wembley – your not', but they soon ran when some Bluenoses broke free from the escort and chased them down the road to lots of cheering from the rest.

We continued to sing and stormed into the station and onto the waiting football special in full voice. The train journey back was fun with everyone singing and we got back into Birmingham late in the night. I had to ring my dad and explain why I was out late and get him to come and pick me up from the station. I don't think he was too impressed to be honest, but I had enjoyed my first away game immensely despite our defeat and was really looking forward to my future away travel. I was hooked. The match programme that day was a newspaper, which was somewhat unusual and the only match programme I ever had that was this format.

Derby's Baseball Ground was also me nephew Stephen's first away game. I had been taking Stephen to St. Andrews since he was 5 years old and I decided that Derby would be a good first away trip as it wasn't too far away. Derby County were flying high at the top of the table at the time and on the 20th April 1996 at the age of six Stephen experienced his first away match. We went in my friend Julie's car and I chatted away about the game to Stephen during the journey. I bought him comic's etc for the journey as it is hard to keep a six-year-old entertained for long periods! Once in Derby though we parked up and with his hand in mine I led him towards Derby County's old baseball ground. It was quite funny as we approached the ground and I asked Stephen what he thought of the ground, as it was his first away ground and he looked up at me and replied 'it's a shed!' Julie and I laughed; he had been spoiled having St. Andrew's as his home ground!

The away end was packed with Bluenoses and Stephen loved it. Blues fans sang throughout the game and as Derby had already been promoted to the Premiership they were singing 'going up, going up going up' to which the Blues fans were replying 'you're coming straight back down, you're coming straight back down!' There was a player playing for Derby who had a hairstyle whereby all his hair was in sort of dreadlocks sticking up and throughout the game the Blues fans were singing 'he's got a pineapple on his head, he's got a pineapple on his head' etc, which I though was really funny. They sang the same song over and over throughout the game and I read in a newspaper years later that this had really affected him and ruined his career! I think it took off a little bit really and all the other fans sang it to him wherever he played at. I still think it was really funny and so did Stephen. Derby went 1-0 ahead and when Gary Breen scored our equaliser the Blues contingent went wild and I lifted a celebrating Stephen high into the air as we went mad. It was a great day and Stephen really enjoyed his first away game. At least he got a better result than I had for my first away game at the same ground years before.

Like most old grounds though, the Baseball Ground did have its own character. In total I saw three games at this ground with the other one being in October 1983 when Birmingham City beat Derby 3-0 in the first leg of the second round of the Milk Cup (League Cup) with 13,114 in attendance. At least I saw Blues win there (1 win, 1 draw and 1 defeat).

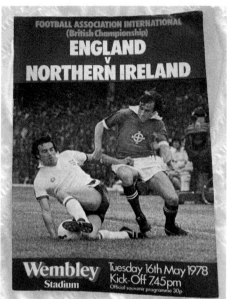

FOOTBALL ASSOCIATION INTERNATIONAL
(British Championship)
ENGLAND
v
NORTHERN IRELAND

Wembley Stadium

Tuesday 16th May 1978
Kick-Off 7.45pm
Official souvenir programme 30p

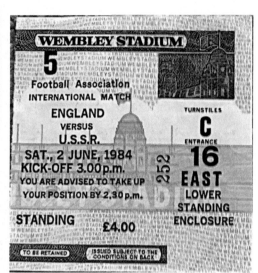

WEMBLEY STADIUM

5

Football Association
INTERNATIONAL MATCH

ENGLAND
VERSUS
U.S.S.R.

SAT., 2 JUNE, 1984
KICK-OFF 3.00 p.m.
YOU ARE ADVISED TO TAKE UP
YOUR POSITION BY 2.30 p.m.

252

TURNSTILES
C
ENTRANCE
16
EAST
LOWER
STANDING
ENCLOSURE

STANDING £4.00

TO BE RETAINED   ISSUED SUBJECT TO THE
CONDITIONS ON BACK

WEMBLEY STADIUM

No ticket genuine unless it carries
a Lion's Head watermark below

Football Association
INTERNATIONAL MATCH

ENGLAND
VERSUS
WEST GERMANY

WED., OCT. 13, 1982

KICK-OFF 7.45 p.m.
YOU ARE ADVISED TO TAKE UP
YOUR POSITION BY 7.15 p.m.

722

TURNSTILES
H
ENTRANCE
54
WEST
UPPER
STANDING
ENCLOSURE

STANDING £4.00

TO BE RETAINED   ISSUED SUBJECT TO THE CONDITIONS ON BACK

Ground 3 – Wembley Stadium (Old) – 16th May 1978 – England 0 Northern Ireland 0

It was in the same year – 1978, that I made my first trip to the twin towers of Wembley. On Saturday, 16th May 1978 I set off for London to see my first England international at the home of football. It was a really nice day and I was out of bed bright and early and I excitedly ran around the house, eating breakfast and getting ready for the trip ahead. I had my new England scarf all ready and I was soon on my way to New Street Station to catch the train to London. England were playing Northern Ireland in the home championships that were a regular thing at the time.

This was when England, Scotland, Wales, Northern Ireland and Republic of Ireland all played in a competition each year in a sort of mini league. It was eventually stopped due to trouble between rival sets of supporters. Emotions would always run high in these games, especially between England and Scotland. I think it came to a head the year when Scotland fans invaded the pitch at Wembley, taking away the goal posts and tearing up most of the pitch to take home with them.

The train was full of England fans on their way to the game and everyone was in good spirits, downing cans of larger and singing England songs. It was great. It was strange for me to be amongst fans wearing red and white rather than blue and white but I easily became part of them and have continued to proudly wear the white and red of England ever since.

Everyone who has ever walked down Wembley way will have his or her own memories and they will stick in their minds forever as do mine. It was fantastic getting off the train and seeing the seething mass of white and red swarming down Wembley way as one towards the great twin towers in the distance. The sight was magnificent. I didn't much enjoy coming out of the station though. It was through an underpass, which was jammed with fans and a bit claustrophobic to be honest, and a little frightening. But once we were out and onto Wembley way it was great. The noise and the singing was amazing. Wembley looked so impressive as I got closer and I wandered around the stadium, stopping at various stalls to buy food and of course a programme. I remember buying sausage and chips in a tray and eating it as we walked around, watching everyone and looking for our entrance. It was a carnival atmosphere and I was really enjoying it.

I found my way to an entrance and pushed through the turnstile into the long corridor/tunnel that ran all around the inside of Wembley, below the terracing. There were more stalls inside selling food and drink including beer in bottles. I remember that a bottle of skol was really expensive at the time and the only choice of alcohol available. I know I was only sixteen but I admit to drinking the odd alcoholic drink on occasions.

My ticket was for the lower terracing just behind the goal, so I made my way up the steps and out onto the terrace. What an awesome view it was inside Wembley itself. It looked massive and the sound inside was amazing, even though it was still early and the stadium was only half full. There was a real buzz around the place and the fans were already in full voice.

As kick off time got closer and the stadium filled up the noise level went up another notch and the singing was brilliant. I have always loved Wembley, it had such a great tradition and it certainly lived up to its reputation. I don't remember much about the game, probably because I was so overwhelmed by the occasion. I seem to remember that it finished 0-0. I remember the white shirts of England and the green shirts of Northern Ireland running around on the green of the pitch. After the match finished, when we had applauded our boys off the Wembley turf we headed back down the steps and joined the sea of fans swarming out of the ground and back up Wembley way towards the local train station. There was a bit of a crush going through the subway that led to the station, which I have to admit I found frightening. I thought I was going to get crushed and was glad to get to the other side still in one piece. However, I was soon safely back on the train and on my way back home to Birmingham feeling tired but satisfied with the fabulous day I had had.

My favourite trip to the old Wembley Stadium was in the 1995 Auto Windscreens Shield Final as Blues took on Carlisle United. On the day of the Final Wembley was a sea of blue and white. I had never seen or heard anything like it before. Three quarters of the ground was the blue and white of Birmingham with about 20,000 Carlisle Utd fans at the other end. It was awesome seeing 55,000 Bluenoses inside Wembley waving flags, banners and scarves. 'Keep Right On' was sang like I had never heard before, in was fantastic. Barry Fry led the team out and onto the pitch amongst a crescendo of noise from the Blues fans. Blues were top of the league and in the cup final at Wembley, life was very good. There were 76,663 people inside Wembley, a record attendance for the competition. In fact there were more for the Birmingham City v Carlisle game that there had been at the League cup final between Liverpool and Bolton a few weeks before.

The game was full of chances but neither team seemed able to score and it finished 0-0. This meant extra time and the first time in a final that a golden goal could decide the match. This meant that the first team to score a goal in extra time would win the game. It was nerve wracking. So into extra time it went and before long the ball was crossed in as Blues attacked the end in front of their supports and there was Paul Tait to head the ball home. Wembley

23

Stadium erupted as 55,000 Bluenoses celebrated wildly. Paul Tait, a Bluenose himself, ran towards the Blues fans and lifted his shirt to reveal a T-shirt, which read 'BIRMINGHAM CITY SHIT ON THE VILLA!' Brilliant! The camera's got a lovely shot of it and it was plastered across the back pages of all the papers the next day. Yes, Paul Tait got fined but he became a real Blues hero that day and it must have been worth every penny of his fine! In fact when he ran out for the next home game at St. Andrews he received a standing ovation!

I was on my seat celebrating and I couldn't believe I had just seen Birmingham City win at Wembley! I was so overcome. As the Birmingham City team made their way up the Wembley steps and then lifted the Trophy I was so proud. This moment was what being a Birmingham City fan was all about. The likes of Manchester Utd and Liverpool will never know what it feels like as they win things so often that they take it for granted. It was a fantastic experience and one I wouldn't have missed for anything. Blues still had the second division championship in their sights too; all in all it was a great time to be a Bluenose.

We were all so excited as we boarded the bus to take us back to Birmingham and we continued to celebrate as we headed home. However, with so many Bluenoses having travelled from Birmingham, the traffic heading away from Wembley towards Birmingham was more or less at a standstill. At one point we were stuck in traffic so long that loads of the lads got off, crossed the road into the local off licence and stocked up on beers for the long journey back. It took us six hours to get home! We were so happy though that none of us complained. It was a fantastic day out and one that will live in my memory forever.

I loved the old Wembley Stadium and in total I saw six games there. I saw England lose 2-1 to West Germany in October 1982 in a friendly and two years later I saw England lose 2-0 in June 1984 to a very good USSR team, also a friendly game, and they were applauded off at the end of the game. We had waited around inside Wembley after the Russia game to avoid the crush at the tube station and we were lucky enough to bump into ex England player Trevor Brooking who signed our match day programmes. Then in March 1985 I saw England beat Ireland 2-1 in a friendly game at Wembley.

In 1989 I moved to Liverpool to live and do my midwifery training and during this time I headed back to Wembley with my Scouse friends to see the only ever FA Cup Final that I have been to as Liverpool beat Sunderland 2-0 to lift the trophy. In total I saw four England games (2 wins, 2 defeats) one FA Cup Final and one EFL Cup Final. Great days out!

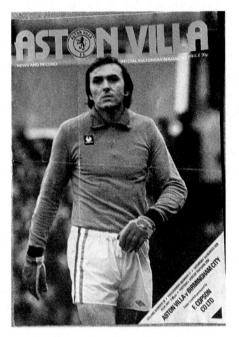 

Ground 4 – Villa Park – 3rd May 1979 – Division One - Aston Villa 1 Birmingham City 0

My first trip across the City to see Blues play our arch enemy was certainly not the best visit that I have ever made. I travelled across the city to Villa Park to see us lose to the only goal of the game. It was the first time I had seen us lose to the Vile, and I must admit I took it very badly as I always do. I wasn't impressed with Villa Park on my first visit there; but then again I wouldn't be really due to my intense dislike of them. At the time the away end was just open terracing behind the goal at the Witton end with no roofing. The new seated stand was not built then. The Holte End was a large terrace situated behind the other goal and housed the home support. The Bluenoses sang throughout and the away end was heaving with swaying blue and white clad supporters. It was great. I am pretty sure that we out sang them, and each time 'shit on the villa' rang out (which was a lot!), it seemed to echo around the ground. The attendance that day was 42,419 with thousands of Blues supporters crammed onto the Witton terrace. Far more away fans than they 'allow' these days and it created a brilliant atmosphere.

And so I headed home with a heavy heart. I went quietly to my room and didn't talk to anyone for days.

One of my favourite trips to the dark side was on the 22nd August 1987 and remains a fond memory to this day. I was really looking forward to this game as always and I had a couple of mates who were Villa fans so we planned to go to the game together although to separate ends of the ground! We all met up in town and decided to head to Villa's main pub, the Holte which was situated just outside the home end of the ground. Most of us were Bluenoses and only two were Villa fans so we zipped up our jackets to cover our colours following pleading from our Villa mates and headed into the pub.

Once a few drinks were consumed I suggested to my Villa mates that I undo my jacket as I was getting hot, much to their horror. This egged my mate Deb on, and she said that she would chalk her nose blue from the pool table nearby if I would unzip my jacket and show my colours as I was wearing a Blues shirt. Despite the now growing panic from my mates, I agreed and Deb chalked her nose blue and I unzipped my jacket. It didn't take long for us to be noticed and just as a few newspapers were thrown at us as we stood proudly on the seats arms aloft, a load of Blues fans arrived and all hell seemed to break loose. Most fans spilled outside and it wasn't long before the police arrived and we had lost sight of some of our mates in the mayhem. Two of my Bluenose mates and I headed towards the Witton terraces - the Blues end.

It was buzzing inside on the terraces amongst the away support and having consumed quite a few drinks beforehand, my friends and I were in a great mood. Blues were massive underdogs for this game but the Blues end was packed solid. Scarves were being waved and 'shit on the villa' rang out loudly as well as our anthem 'Keep Right On'. It was a brilliant atmosphere and it was fantastic when Ian Handysides belted the ball into the net right in front of us to put Blues in the lead. Our end erupted and I was quite literally swept off my feet and I ended up on the floor, as did my mate. I felt a strong pair of hands on my waist and I was swept back to my feet in an instant and I carried on with my celebrations. I got some lads to help me onto the crash barrier and for a little while I balanced there holding onto someone's hand for support and proudly waving my Blues colours. It was brilliant, and the Blues fans were in heaven.

Then, unbelievably right in front of us, Tony Rees smashed the ball into net for Blues second goal – 2-0! Once again the Blues end erupted and I found myself on the floor once again before the same pair of hands found my waist and lifted me to my feet again. I was so happy and we celebrated like mad things, everyone hugging everyone else, including people we didn't even know. It was at times like these when being on the terracing felt fantastic and to this day I wish they would bring back a terraced area as it would bring back the atmosphere that is sadly missing these days. And so it was 2-0 at half time and we sang our hearts out. The score remained the same and when the final whistle went the Blues end went wild before heading back into town for a night of wild celebration. Villa had been big favourites that day with Blues not given a chance and this made our victory that much sweeter. The town was Blue and White!

Another favourite game at Villa Park was in the Premier League in February 2004 on one of my trips back to England as I lived in Abu Dhabi at the time. I was so looking forward to this game as I had not seen Blues play Villa live for over 17 years. I was also really nervous as I could not stand the thought of losing to them. The game had been made a noon kick off to avoid trouble and for live TV viewing, and this does tend to take the edge of games. Not this match though!

Annette, Steve, Stephen and I were inside a pub in Harborne at around 10am even though pubs didn't open till 12 on a Sunday. We popped into McDonalds to pick up breakfast first and saw a couple of vile fans in their drab colours. They looked in our direction and we glared back. Then it was round the back of one of the pubs that was only letting in Bluenoses of course, and pre match drinks began. We met the usual crew such as Brendan, Graham etc and chatted to them whilst downing beers.

As we had left it a bit late we decided to get a taxi to Villa Park and five of us piled into a black cab and off we set. As we approached the away end at Villa Park the roads became really busy, so with the ground in sight but the taxi stuck in traffic, we disembarked and walked the rest of the way to the ground. Steve told me to keep quiet with all the villa fans around but you know me. I remarked to Stephen, 'can you smell something?' and he innocently replied 'like what?' to which I answered 'smells like shit!' Stephen laughed but the others looked around worriedly.

Once inside the ground the atmosphere was brilliant. Just as I had remembered and the Bluenoses were in full voice with 'shit on the villa' being sang at full blast by the 3,000 Blues in the away end. The blues end behind the goal was packed and everyone was standing and singing. Annette and Steve had tickets away from us but when we got to our seats there was a few empty next to us and everyone remained standing anyway so I made a mental note to get Annette and Steve to come and stand with us for the second half.

The match got under way and Blues just never got started. They looked awful in the first half and it was no surprise when Villa took the lead. The Vile fans were going wild as we looked on in despair. Before half time it was 2-0 to Villa and Blues had just not turned up. Losing is bad enough in the local derby but when the lads on the pitch do not put in the effort then it makes it worse. The Villa fans were enjoying it and it was obvious that they were confident that they had already won the game. The games not over yet though, I thought.

Blues came out with all guns firing in the second half and were unlucky on a number of occasions. It didn't seem like it was going to be our day though but the Bluenoses never stopped singing. Then Forsell scored a cracking goal right in front of the Blue army and the away ended exploded with celebrations. Annette and Steve were now standing next to us and Annette, Stephen and I all jumped around madly, hoping that perhaps we could get something out of this game. I just did not want to lose today and I just could not bear that thought.

The game reached the 90 minute mark and the 4th official held up the board informing us that there would be 4 minutes of injury time. My heart was in my mouth by now and the Villa fans were taunting us and celebrating their win. In the 93rd minute Clinton Morrison got the ball just on the edge of the area and as he ran into the penalty area he unleashed a shot that their keeper dived to his right to save but he only parried the ball to the onrushing Stern John with the goal at his mercy. Time seemed to freeze as well as everyone in the ground and my heart stopped as I fully expected him to blast it over but to my utter delight he blasted the ball into the top of the Villa net! Yeeeeessss, 2-2 in the last minute of stoppage time.

Stern John pulled his shirt off and ran to the ecstatic Blues end and was mobbed just as he reached us. This had all happened right in front of us and I lifted Stephen in the air as Annette jumped on me from the other side. Everyone was jumping on everyone else – it was unbelievable, it was like we had won. Instantly a chant went up from the Bluenoses '2-0 and you fucked it up, 2-0 and you fucked it up!' Brilliant! The Villa fans looked absolutely gutted. They could not believe it, their faces were a picture as they looked totally defeated. Then the Blues fans started singing 'beat the Blues you're having a laugh, beat the Blues you're having a laugh!'

When they interviewed our Finish striker Forssell after the game, he said it was "incredible celebrations, just like we had won the league or something". I was over the moon as I watched the Villa fans stream out silently and the Blues fans leaving the ground singing 'Beat the Blues, you're having a laugh, beat the Blues, you're having a laugh'. The trains leaving Aston were silent apart from the singing Bluenoses. Someone remarked that you could tell who were Bluenoses as they couldn't wipe the smiles from their faces. What a brilliant day, and we went on to Harborne to celebrate our win in the Stores pub. I could hold my head up high as we still had bragging rights in the city and I could head back a very happy girl.

I have other happy memories too including the time Blues won 3-0 in March 1986 which I thoroughly enjoyed. I have had bad times too but you cannot beat the second city derby's.

I have visited Villa Park sixteen times over the years with Blues (3 wins, 2 draws, 9 defeats) with my last visit seeing Birmingham City Women beat Villa Women 1-0 in front of a crowd of over 8,000. I also once saw Juventus beat Villa 2-1 in the UEFA European Cup Quarter Final in March 1983 when my Dad got us free tickets in the away end. I went into the North Stand wearing my Blues badge (as did others in there too) to cheer on Juventus.

Another visit came in the FA Cup Semi Finals on 8th April 1990 when Crystal Palace beat Liverpool 4-3. I lived in Liverpool at the time and I got tickets in the Liverpool contingent on the Holte End and took my sister with me. It was an exciting game but there was another crush when we were trying to get out after the game. The gates remained closed but the fans at the back were not aware of this and they continued to push forward whilst the rest of us were getting crushed. It reminded me of Hillsborough only the year before and people shouted this down to those at the front to open the gates. Happily they saw sense and opened the doors and disaster was averted. So all in all not an awful lot of happy memories from my visits to Villa Park but those that were good were very good.

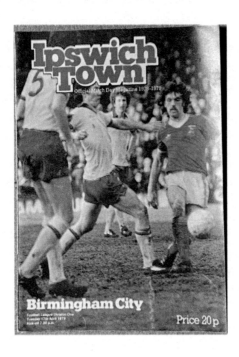

Ground 5 – Portman Road – 17th April 1979 – Ipswich Town 3 Birmingham City 0 – Division One

My first trip to Ipswich was on a Tuesday evening in April 1979 and was such a long time ago now that my memories were mostly of the long distance travelled and the old style terraces that we stood on. In all honesty Portman Road does not seem to have changed much over the years apart from going all seater when all other grounds also had to do so following the Hillsborough report. It's not a massive stadium but it does still hold some of its character and familiarity from years gone by. I remember standing on the away terrace with the home fans next to us separated by fencing that was very high and there was lots of banter and gesticulation between the two sets of supporters. Blues fans sang loads and despite the narrow defeat I enjoyed the trip.

I clearly remember the first time I took my nephew Stephen to Ipswich for his first visit. It was May 1997 and even though it was quite a long way to Ipswich

I had decided to take Stephen with Julie, Emma and I. I had patiently explained to him that there might not be many Blues fans at Ipswich unlike what he was used to seeing because of how far away we were travelling.

However, after a four hour journey involving a few comic's and a bit of entertaining for Stephen including a stop off, we arrived in Ipswich and parked up in a car park jam packed with Bluenoses! Stephen looked on in amazement and as we headed into a pub just opposite the train station packed with Blues fans, he turned to me and said 'I though you said there wouldn't be many Blues fans?' I had to laugh, especially as we looked out of the pub window and hundreds of Bluenoses were streaming out of the station having obviously just got off a train from Birmingham.

I saw Alan in the pub and we all had a couple of pints and caught up on Blues news. As I came out of the toilet I found Stephen standing outside the men's. 'What are you doing?' I asked and he held his hand open revealing a pound coin saying 'I'm the lookout!!' I had to laugh as I led him back to our friends. He was made up with his pound and off we headed to the ground. I blamed Stephen for our constant trips to the toilet during the game but really it was the few pints of cider I had consumed in the pub! It was a good atmosphere amongst the travelling Bluenoses and I got to swing Stephen about again when we scored as the match finished 1-1.

Another good trip to Portman Road was in April 2019 and it was an early morning for the Ipswich trip as I was getting picked up by June at 8am to get the coach from St. Andrews which was due to leave at 9am. It was great to see the gang again and we had 6 official coaches heading to Ipswich for the game. We stopped on the way at the services at Cambridge and although it should have only been for 30 minutes we ended up waiting a further 30 minutes for one of the Blues stewards and therefore we were late leaving. We all found this quite frustrating especially as we were looking forward to heading to the great chip shop in Ipswich that Terry and Nigel went to last time they were there. Hence I gave up the idea of a pub and agreed to join the lads, as did June.

When we arrived it was nice and sunny and we walked into the centre to a lovely chip shop called 'the Ipswich Chip Shop' and it was lovely. There was a nice seated area inside and once we had all obtained our chips, fish etc, which James very kindly paid for (thanks James) we sat down and tucked in. I had run across to the shop to get beers and when we came out and opened our cans (Nigel's was a bottle so the chip shop man opened his bottle with a spoon!) it was hailing! Hence we spent about 5 minutes under cover drinking before braving the weather and heading to the ground.

When we arrived at the ground we went over to see the Bobby Robson statue and had photos taken by it. As we left Nigel tapped the statue and said "sorry Bobby but we've got to send you down today' and we all smiled and headed to the away end. If Ipswich failed to win today their relegation to League One would be confirmed and they currently sat bottom of the Championship. It must have been made even worse as their rivals Norwich were top of the table. Inside there were 1,700 Bluenoses and we were looking forward to the game.

The teams came out and Blues were playing in yellow with blue shorts as was expected and we started really well. Ipswich looked a poor side and it didn't take long for Blues to take the lead and the away end celebrated. 'Your going down' rang out and 'we'll meet again'. Blues also sang 'there's only one Mick McCarthy' - a reminder to the Ipswich fans that they should have been more careful of what they wanted as they had been comfortably under McCarthy till they all complained that his football was boring and called for him to be sacked. We also sang 'minus points and we're better than you!'. Bluenoses were singing a lot and the team were playing well but not putting our chances away. This did worry me a bit but as Ipswich were so poor I couldn't see them getting back into it as Blues went in 1-0 up at half time.

I was wrong though as Blues conceded in the first half and it was 1-1. I was beginning to dread the first 5 minutes of the second half as this seem to be when we conceded most of our goals. Ipswich had their tails up now and Blues were now very poor. We gave the ball away so much and defended poorly. It seemed we were now just sitting back and trying to hang on. Blues did create more chances but again we failed to take them. Blues fans had gone a bit quieter now but did sing 'we're Birmingham City, we're sending you down' and 'we've got the Monk, Super Garry Monk, I just don't think you understand, Harry spent the lot, Cotterill lost the plot, we've got super Garry Monk!'

The final whistle sounded and the game ended 1-1 which meant that Ipswich were relegated and some of their players dropped to the ground in despair. Blues sang 'ka sa ra sa ra, whatever will be will be , your going to Shrewsbury!' to the departing Ipswich fans. At least the hail had stopped and we headed back to the coaches.

We had a brilliant trip back as we laughed and sang all the way. Very funny when a Bluenose mooned at some Ipswich fans who were making gestures as us. June put some 80's top of the pops on and we sang and laughed. Great fun. Another great trip following the Blues.

Over the years I have been to Portman Road on twelve occasions all of them following Birmingham City. I have seen just two wins, (2-1 in January 1984 and 1-0 in September 1985) four draws (all 1-1) and six defeats. It is another old ground with its own character that I quite like to be honest. Sadly the away end lets it down due to the small concourse with very few ladies toilets leading to massive queues at times, especially when leaving the stadium before boarding the coaches back to Birmingham.

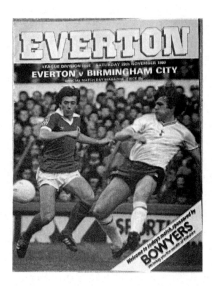

Ground 6 - Goodison Park – 28th April 1979 – Everton 1 Birmingham City 0 – First Division

In April 1979 I was off to Liverpool to see Blues take on Everton at Goodison Park. This would be my first trip to Liverpool and my first to Everton's ground. I set out early once again and boarded the train at New Street to Liverpool Lime Street. We soon arrived in Liverpool, another station with lots of character about it, and we got a local train to somewhere near Everton and walked down the street by Stanley Park towards the away end at Goodison Park. There were lots of fans milling around the ground outside and as we approached there was a bit of trouble between Blues fans and Everton fans just outside by the pub known as the Blue House.

The police soon came between the rival supporters and led the Blues fans into the nearby away end which was a terraced section behind the goal. I followed them inside and we were on the terracing behind the goal, and there were already quite a few Bluenoses inside happily singing and chanting. I was impressed with Everton's ground, one side seemed to be quite high and although it looked a bit old it did have a certain character. I remember some girls dressed up in old-fashioned dresses passing our end with baskets of Everton mints, which they proceeded to throw into the crowd for the fans. Needless to say the Blues fans immediately returned them with amazing accuracy!

Blues did not have a good record against Everton at Goodison and although we played well we suffered a 1-0 defeat. The Blues fans sang our usual songs and we came away in good spirits as we always did. It had been a good trip despite the result. On our way back to the station I looked across at Liverpool's ground just across Stanley Park and thought it looked quite impressive.

In the 1981 season I again made a trip to Liverpool to see Blues take on Everton at Goodison Park for the first match of the new season. It was a lovely sunny day and I popped into the cake shop that my mom worked in on the way to get the bus to New Street Station to catch the train. Have a nice time she said as she handed me sausage rolls and cakes for the journey. After a pleasant journey to Liverpool on a train full of Bluenoses, beers and food, we disembarked at Lime Street Station and headed off towards Everton. As usual there were loads of Blues outside the away end and they were already enjoying banter with the Evertonians as the local police tried to intervene.

Inside the ground I was quite optimistic. Blues won a corner and after I jinxed them by remarking to Julie that we never score from a corner – sure enough the ball was in the back of the net! We had scored – brilliant! The Blues end erupted and we were swept one way and then the other. However, Blues being Blues we then conceded three goals and lost our first game of the season by 3-1. Oh well, there was still a long way to go I thought. On the way back to the train station we were cutting through a piece of wasteland when some scousers started throwing stones at us! We soon chased them away as they were only about 7 or 8 years old – cheeky sods!

In January 2000 I was visiting from Abu Dhabi, where I lived at the time, and it was going to be difficult for me to get to Liverpool as I couldn't hire a car as I wouldn't be around to return it because I was flying back to Abu Dhabi the next morning. Happily my brother Neil kindly offered to drive us up there for the game against Everton. Sue and Nicola also came and they dropped me and Stephen at the ground while they went shopping in the city centre. This was going to be an exciting match as it was against premiership opposition. It was Stephens first time inside Everton's ground and I think like me, he wasn't too impressed with the old stand that the Blues fans were situated in just to the side of the goal. There was another stand which came over the top of us and the seats were wooden and old.

34

The Blues faithful were in good voice though and we had travelled in large numbers. A lot of fun was had and lots of songs were sung, especially aimed at the scousers. 'Stand up if you robbed your car' got a laugh from the scousers as did 'hey scouser, I wanna know where's my DVD?' Blues also sang 'my garden shed is bigger that this' with regards to their ground.

Blues gave a great account of themselves but were robbed by two very dubious penalties losing 2-0. I still had faith though because I felt we were much better than our premiership opposition on the day and were extremely unlucky to lose with the score somewhat flattering them. It was quiet as we headed out and I don't think the Everton fans realised just how many Blues fans were amongst them in the streets outside as every time they taunted the odd Blues fan many more Blues would appear and skirmishes kept breaking out and the Everton fans would run off down the road where another skirmish would then break out. The police soon arrived in force but they couldn't quite fathom out what was happening as once they arrived at a fight it would stop suddenly and then break out further up the road. Once they arrived at that skirmish it would stop and again start in another place! It was like a comedy sketch, and I don't think they knew what hit them.

As we arrived back at the car, Neil and sue could see all the flashing blue lights down the road and asked Stephen if he was okay as he was still only young and he bravely answered 'yes, we always fight when we lose!' I must admit I had to laugh. Then it was off back to Birmingham and for me to prepare to fly back to Abu Dhabi again.

In December 2009 I was travelling with Stephen (my nephew) and Brendan, Marie, Sam and Liam and we were heading to Liverpool by train. It always seemed funny arriving at Lime Street due to the fact that I lived in Liverpool for nine years and did my midwifery training there. I also made a lot of friends in Liverpool and enjoyed my time in the city.

On arrival in Liverpool we set off for Wetherspoons to get pre-match drinks and something to eat. However, despite the fact that the pub was half empty, the jobsworth behind the bar refused us service because we had children with us (Brendan's children were not especially young though and would not be drinking alcohol). So we went into the pub next door which was much nicer and friendlier and we all had drinks and meals all round. It was Wetherspoons loss though, as we spent a lot of money on food and drink and we had a nice time before we left to head to a pub closer to the ground to meet up with the others.

We got a taxi to take us to the Taxi Club not far from Goodison Park where we met up with Ron, Graham and Craig and enjoyed drinks and some good pre match banter before heading off in the pouring rain for the short walk to the ground.

The atmosphere amongst the travelling Bluenoses was great inside the ground and we were all enjoying the fantastic run that Blues were on at the time and we were all feeling pretty positive. The game got underway but it wasn't long before Everton scored, not that it stopped our singing which went on in abundance. I really loved the Scott Dann song which was sang to the tune of 'Gold' by Spandau Ballet, and went 'always believe in Scott Dann, he's got the power to know, he's indestructible!' brilliant.

Then Blues won a free kick on the edge of the box and up stepped Seb Larsson to score the equaliser and send the Bluenoses into mass celebration. It was brilliant! The away section made so much noise and I loved it when we sang 'we are invincible! we are invincible! we are invincible !' It was now 1-1.

Some of the songs were so funny and even the players seemed to be enjoying them. Blues sang 'channel five on a Thursday night!' – this being a reference to the Europa League being shown on a Thursday night and Blues aiming for a European place. We sang to the Everton fans 'we're going to Italy - you're going to Coventry!'. This was sang several times, again with reference to our chance of Europe and their chance of relegation (Everton were in the bottom half of the table).

The Blues contingent were absolutely buzzing! It was one of the best atmospheres away from home that I could remember for a long time. Great sense of humour the travelling Blues fans have and I was so proud to be back amongst them again. It was also quite cool when we sang 'we're gonna win the league!'. And of course we also sang 'stand up if you robbed your car' and 'sign on' (to the tune of you'll never walk alone) to the scousers as usual.

As I headed back to my seat at half time I bumped into my mate 'Ballie' who I used to play football with at Birmingham City Ladies and whom I hadn't seen for over twenty years! We were both delighted to see each other and Ballie informed me she was now living and working in Liverpool, although she still had a flat in Birmingham. She commutes at weekends whenever she can make it to see the Blues. I was over the moon to see her and after exchanging hugs we said we would try to meet up at the Taxi Club after the game as that was where I was going with the others for a drink before we headed back to Brum.

It was raining on the way back to the club but once inside it was warm and we met up with Graham, Craig and Ron again and celebrated our away draw. We had a few laughs as always and then we headed back to the station and had a quick drink in the station bar before boarding our train back to Birmingham. It had been a fantastic day out.

Over the years I have visited Goodison Park on eight occasions and I have seen four draws and four defeats. I have yet to see Blues win there.

Ground 7 – Vicarage Road – 17th November 1979 – Watford 1 Birmingham City 0 – Second Division

My first trip to Vicarage Road was to see Blues take on Watford in the old Second Division and it was by football special and as always I was looking forward to another new adventure. We had another enjoyable train journey with lots of singing on our packed train and we disembarked in Watford to a crescendo of noise from the travelling Bluenoses. "The Brummie's are here!" announced our arrival and we were soon escorted on our walk to the ground by the awaiting constabulary.

It didn't take long and I quite liked the character of Watford's stadium with the one stand having a funky roof with several dome like structures creating a bit of a wave affect. Us away fans were on a terrace behind the goal and there were quite a few of us present. As always we sang a lot throughout the game but sadly Blues lost 1-0 and we trooped off back to the stadium to head home but still singing our hearts out. Despite the result it had still been a good day out to yet another new ground for me and I knew I had many more exciting trips ahead of me as I was still very young.

In April 2015 we had another nice trip to Watford by coach and went to a nice pub just up the road called 'Odd Fellows' which was already full of Blues fans. It was another lovely sunny day and when we got in the away end we saw Chris Kamara in the outdoor commentary box. This resulted in loads of songs being aimed at him - especially as he was reporting back on sky sports news live - 'Chris Kamara is a Blue! He hates Villa!' was greeted with a smile and a finger to his lips. 'Kammy, Kammy give us a wave' was also directed at him. Great fun. The match wasn't as good as our banter with Kammy though and Blues lost 1-0 to a good Watford side on their way to the Premier League. Their fans created a good atmosphere too with all their yellow and black flags.

In March 2023 I was really hoping that Blues might be able to continue our good run of form in our next away trip to Watford, who were on their fourth manager of the season despite being around the play off places, but I didn't expect much to be honest. Always the optimist though and I headed to St. Andrews to get the coach in good spirits. June and I met Taff in Morrisons, across the road from the stadium, to have brunch/lunch in their restaurant. It was a nice meal too with June and I enjoying the breakfast brunch whilst Taff tucked into fish and chips.

Once on the coach we were joined by Charlie and Nigel and it was a full contingent of us despite it being a midweek away journey. It would be a new ground for Nigel and Charlie. The coaches headed straight to Watford's Vicarage Road Stadium without a stop and we arrived in plenty of time to head for the nearby pub that I had visited previously. It was a nice little pub with a beer garden called 'The Odd fellows' and we were soon enjoying our drinks in the beer garden where we were joined by my nephew Stephen who still lived in London with his wife Alice.

It was nice to see Stephen as I had not had chance to see him all season at an away game as this was Blues first trip to a ground in or around London this season but there would be a few between now and the end of the season. After a nice catch up we all headed off towards the stadium and while Nigel and Charlie headed into the chip shop Stephen and I headed off to get my hat from the coach as it was cold. However, we reached the stadium only to discover that the coaches had vanished and so I would have to put up with the cold.

The others joined us and we headed into the stadium where Stephen was dismayed to discover that there was no alcohol on sale. There was another great midweek turnout from Blues fans as over 1,800 had made the trip and they were in excellent voice. My favourite song of the evening was aimed at Watford's fourth manager of the season – Chris Wilding as Bluenoses sang 'you're getting sacked in the morning' which did make me laugh.

Somewhat disappointingly Blues were really poor in the first half against a very fast Watford side and we were 2-0 down by halftime and it really could have been six down. In the second half Blues looked a completely different team and it really should have been 2-2 as Scott Hogan missed a one on one with the goalkeeper and put it wide, whilst Austin Trusty failed to convert another great chance. Against the run of play Watford then scored a very lucky goal on the break as the ball rebounded off the keeper onto a Watford player and into our net for 3-0 and it was game over. Despite the first half I didn't think Blues deserved to lose and our fans got behind the players and sang their hearts out.

I enjoy my trips to Watford but I have yet to see Blues win there. I have visited on eight occasions and I have seen one draw and seven defeats. Not good really.

Ground 8 – Kenilworth Road – 24th November 1979 - Luton Town 2 Birmingham City 3 – Second Division

My first visit to Kenilworth Road was November in 1979 and apart from becoming all seater, the ground hasn't changed much at all since. I was astounded to discover that the turnstiles into the away terraces were part of a terraced house in the middle of the street and if it wasn't for the floodlights that were in place at the time you wouldn't know there was a football ground there at all.

Amazingly, once through the turnstiles we were stunned to discover that we had to climb stairways that took us over neighbouring gardens to get into the away stand. I thought it had loads of character and although it was small and old looking, I really liked it. It's a bit like a tardis (Dr Who). I quite liked the tiny stand running along one side of the pitch that housed glass fronted boxes and was really small. It made for a great atmosphere amongst the away support as we sang our hearts out on the terraces and it was made even better by a good 3-2 away win for the Blues. We all left really happy and I had enjoyed my experience of Kenilworth Road.

In January 2020 Blues visit to the bottom club in the Championship attracted a lot of interest for away tickets. This was mainly because many Bluenoses had not visited this ground before and Luton were planning to move to a new ground the following season and so it would be a last chance to visit. I had been before but many years ago in the 80's and I was really looking forward to a trip back in time. As it was a really small ground the away allocation was small with only around 1,000 tickets going to Blues and the demand for these tickets was huge.

All of my 'Blues family' wanted to go, especially Nigel and Charlie who had never been before. I had no problems getting tickets for me, June, James G and Steve as we were all Platinum travel members and I even managed to get one for Terry as he was in the high end of the Gold travel members but unfortunately I couldn't get tickets for James H, Nigel and Charlie so they would be unable to attend.

On the day of the game we met up at St. Andrews and boarded the coaches to Luton and were joined by Taff and Ryan too. It was a great trip to Luton and we all hoped we could get our season back on track. The area around Luton's Kenilworth Road Ground is really built up and just off a main road that resembles the Coventry road in Birmingham with all its Asian shops selling fruit and saris.

Arriving at Luton's ground was like being in a Harry Potter movie as our coaches pulled up in a small street of terraced houses and in the middle of this was the entrance to the ground through turnstiles disguised as a terrace house. Brilliant! Right next to this turnstile was a secret door to a bar! Unfortunately we didn't discover this till after the game when Harry Potter (Baz) told us he had been in there! It got better once we were through the turnstiles as we then went up the staircase that took us above the back gardens of the terraced houses and into the tiny ground. I thought this was really cool and just as I remembered from my last trip in the 80's. I do love the old grounds - proper football grounds.

There were loads of Bluenoses already inside as we watched out team practicing and we were really close to the pitch. As I watched them warming up at our end I saw keeper Lee Camp boot the ball towards the halfway line and to my amusement it hit an unsuspecting Harlee Dean full in the face and knocked him flying. As Lee Camp looked around innocently I fell about laughing which took me some time to get under control.

The game got underway to a crescendo of noise from the away end and it took only 4 minutes for Blues to take the lead as Lucas Jutkiewicz scored to send us wild. Blue smoke filled the air and we all jumped about in celebration. There were a couple of bookings before the halftime whistle went but Blues went into the break leading 1-0 and we dared to dream. Into the second half and somewhat disappointingly Luton managed to grab an undeserved equaliser in the 62nd minute and my heart sank. We really needed a win today. Blues rallied though and Craig Gardener scored a cracking goal right in front of the

Blues end just 7 minutes later and more blue smoke and wild celebrations ensued and the players ran to celebrate in front of our fans. Brilliant.

Luton came back at us but Blues held firm and we continued to attack them. The only setback came when Harlee Dean received a second yellow card for a foul in the 86th minute and was sent off. Blues dug in deep and when the final whistle sounded Blues had a good 2-1 away win and we certainly celebrated in the Blues end. The trip home was an extremely enjoyable one!

In August 2021 I made what was to be my favourite trip to Kenilworth Road so far. I had been really looking forward to the trip to Luton as it was a small ground but with plenty of character. The coach journey was good with lots of catching up and banter on the way. Once we arrived the coaches parked up on a street of terraced houses that resembled Coronation Street and one of these houses contained the turnstiles into the away end. We all decided to head into the ground to see if we could get some food and drink inside.

We squeezed through the old turnstiles and it was like going back in time. The toilet blocks looked they were built in the 1800's and had never been modernised. There was a small refreshment trolley just a few feet from the turnstiles and they had hot dogs and drinks (beer or dark fruit cider) ready to sell but unfortunately the new 'card payment only' system was not working which effectively meant that it was impossible to purchase anything. Great, I thought, as we headed up the stairs above the local back gardens and into the away end.

June and I headed to another outlet in the far corner where their card machines were working and we joined the queue in the hope of obtaining food. We were soon at the counter and were approached by a Bluenose who was unable to obtain food as his card wasn't working and they couldn't accept cash and so June very kindly took his cash and got him a cheeseburger. June got a pie for herself and I opted for a chicken and mushroom pie and a coke, to which they immediately confiscated the lid. Great, I thought, it's too fizzy to drink all at once and now I would risk getting it kicked over when I put it down.

We made our way to join the others who had taken up a spot next to an iron pillar which meant I had to climb over the seats to get to them. June looked like she was enjoying her pie and I set about trying to eat mine. I soon discovered there was absolutely no chance of this as the bottom of the pie was as hard as concrete and would never yield to a knife left alone my attempts to break it! With a sigh I climbed back over the seats with a bit of help and headed back to the food hut to trade my concrete pie for a Cheeseburger. Happily the trade off went well and I was soon climbing back over the seats to join the others.

The cheeseburger looked quite nice and indeed tasted really nice too. Two bites in and I again let out a sigh as I spotted that the programme seller who had finally made an appearance on the edge of the pitch at the front of our stand, and I quickly wrapped up my cheeseburger and climbed back over the seats to head towards him – I kid you not! This also meant using contactless payment again for the hefty price of £3.50. I found it sad that we couldn't use cash and wondered what the world was coming to. Baz was just in front of me purchasing several programmes and exchanging banter with me and the seller at the same time.

This now meant that I had a programme in one hand and a cheeseburger in the other as I managed to again climb over the seats without ending up on my backside, although it was a close call on this occasion with June helping to steady me as I accidentally booted the bloke behind me. I finally tucked into my cheeseburger and the players were soon out onto the pitch for kick off.

The Bluenoses were in great voice today and the singing never stopped throughout. Luton's executive boxes were right next to the away contingent and literally at pitch level. One of these nearby boxes held a group of lads who were enjoying their drinks in their little outside balcony and were obviously Luton fans looking for a bit of banter with the Blues fans. No problem there as the Bluenoses immediately responded with the largest lad becoming the focus of their attention. It was pretty friendly and funny though to be honest. Especially when he lifted his top to show his belly to cheers from the away end. Even funnier was when he disappeared into their box as Bluenoses sang 'we want our fatty back' and he reappeared and raised a pint of beer in explanation to cheers from the away end who responded with 'we love you fatty, we do'. He was obviously loving it and when they sang 'fatty, fatty, give us a wave' he happily obliged and waved.

The game kicked off and Blues were attacking the opposite end and we were in all Blue today. Luton had started the season well and Blues keeper Sarkic made a good double save early on which proved to be important when Bela crossed for Marc Roberts to give Blues the lead with only 7 minutes gone and the away end went mental with Blue smoke filling the air as flares were let off. One such flare landed only inches away from us and didn't exactly help the cough I already had (I had taken a lateral flow test and it was negative for Covid). I immediately put my mask on, which helped, as did June but it was quite amusing as several Bluenoses were attempting to kick it away and failing miserably whilst the stewards watched in amazement and thick blue smoke engulfed us. It was eventually thrown onto the pitch where the stewards also failed to put it out for quite a while as we continued with our goal celebrations.

The singing from the away end continued with gusto as Keep Right On was belted out along with 'fatty, fatty what's the score?'. 'Bowyer, Bowyer give us a wave' saw manager Ian Bowyer respond with a dutiful wave each time it was sang. The afternoon got even better when Scott Hogan looped a header over the Luton keeper to make it 2-0 after 26 minutes and we again exploded in celebration, although without the Blue smoke this time. Blues were playing really well and Tahith Chong was on fire and was unlucky not to get on the scoresheet and at half time Blues led 2-0.

The second half started as the first half ended with Blues again looking good and from a Luton corner, just 2 minutes into the second half, Chong sprinted 50 yards before being tackled (looked a penalty) and the ball ran to the on running Scott Hogan who fired home to make it 3-0 to Blues and the away end erupted. 'Scotty Hogan is a Blue, he hates Villa!' rang out loudly followed by 'Chong, Chong will tear you apart again!' I must admit he looks absolutely class.

With the game virtually won and Blues looking comfortably in charge, Bowyer brought Chong off to rest him and amazingly he was even applauded off by the Luton fans too. Blues were passing the ball around with ease to cheers every time a Blues player touched the ball. A loud rendition of 'we're Birmingham City, we're taking the piss!' was belted out and as if to confirm this Gary Gardener who had just come on as a substitute, then curled a cracking shot over the keeper to make it 4-0 and some crazy celebrations ensued. We had not seen such a big away win for a long, long time and us Bluenoses were enjoying it no end.

'We're Birmingham City, we're taking the piss' continued to be belted out and the atmosphere was brilliant. We could see the Blues players sitting on the bench with big smiles on their faces and they even joined in with some of our clapping as we sang. 'Chongi, Chongi give us a wave' which resulted in a smile and a wave from Chong as did 'Hogan, Hogan give us a wave' which saw Scott give us a wave and a smile. Life was good.

The icing on the cake came with 2 minutes remaining as substitute Chuks Aneke scrambled Blues fifth goal and the celebrations well and truly began as Luton fans, that hadn't already left, headed for the exits to 'time to go' from the Bluenoses who were in heaven. The final whistle sounded to confirm an amazing away win, Luton Town 0 Birmingham City 5 and the players headed to the away end to be greeted by a spine tingling rendition of Keep Right On. Even the remaining Luton fans applauded the Blues players for their outstanding performance. It had been the best Blues performance I had seen for a long long time and one I had been waiting to see for many years.

After the game Lee Bowyer said it was the best performance he had ever witnessed from any of his teams. Bowyer said "some of our passing was excellent, maybe, 15-20 passes without them touching the ball. Then people coming off the bench and scoring, today ticked every box you want. This is a whole performance and it was outstanding."

We had a very enjoyable journey back to Birmingham after a fantastic away day out. I do quite enjoy my trips to Luton. I have visited on seven occasions and seen three wins, two draws and two defeats.

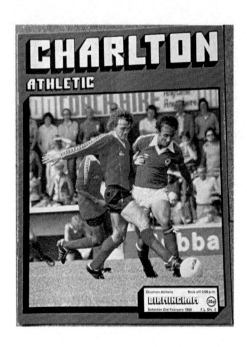

Ground 9 – The Valley – 2nd February 1980 - Charlton Athletic 0 Birmingham City 1 – Second Division

My first trip to The Valley was in February of 1980 as we travelled on the football special train for a day out following Blues. I remember being very impressed by the two massive terraces, particularly the large terrace that stretched along the length of the pitch and resembled our very own KOP but without the roof if I remember correctly. There were loads of Bluenoses there and it was a great atmosphere, especially as Blues won 1-0 and we all headed back to Birmingham very happy indeed.

In November 1984, we again travelled to London to see Blues play at Charlton Athletic. I was looking forward to this match as Blues had just got a player called Tony Morley on loan, and I thought he was quite an exciting player and so I was looking forward to seeing him play in Blues colours. We arrived early and ventured round to the player's entrance in time to see the players arrive. This was quite exciting to see our heroes arriving and once they were inside the ground we then headed into the Blues end. This was the old Valley ground before its current refurbishment and although it was old looking I quite liked the large terracing along the side of the pitch, which was very much like our Kop terracing.

It was quite sad when we visited again a few years later when that section of terrace was closed and run down with weeds and stuff growing through the concrete. It was quite a big ground I though, for what I considered not to be a very big club. The game got under way and my initial excitement was tempered somewhat by a 2-1 defeat but at least our new loan player Tony Morley scored a goal for Blues and gave us something to cheer.

In October 1999 I was again off to London to watch Blues take on Charlton at The Valley. Julie was the driver with Emma, Stephen and I travelling with her. It was a nice day and before long we were parking up not too far from Charlton's end of the ground. It was a bit intimidating when I got out the car in my Blues shirt and found myself surrounded by red shirts! It didn't help that Julie and Emma had Blues red away shirts on! Thanks girls.

We joined the red mass heading towards the ground with me standing out like a sore thumb in my Blue shirt. Just before the ground we stopped at a chippie, where I once again found myself surrounded by red shirts and getting some very funny looks indeed. I decided not to hang about trying to retrieve the vinegar from the Charlton fans and headed off towards the ground with my chips in hand.

As we arrived at the turnstiles, chips still in hand, and the policeman informed me I couldn't take my own food inside. I informed him that it wasn't mine and it was in fact Julies! "Ah a smart one!" He replied – "go on then" he said as he gestured with his thumb towards the entrance. So inside we went and the minute we got inside Julie managed to drop her tray of chips on the floor. Nice. We should have known at that point that it wasn't going to be our day. We had really good seats and the atmosphere was great amongst the Bluenoses who had travelled in great numbers.

Unfortunately Blues lost 1-0 and it was off back to the car amongst that bloody sea of red again! A few days later Julies face was circled in a photo in the newspaper from that very match with me sitting next to her! It was a name the fan competition in which the person in the circle contacted the magazine and won a year's supply. Brilliant!

In 2019 I enjoyed a great visit to The Valley. Despite Blues away form this season I was still really looking forward to the trip to Charlton and as was then the norm when we played in London we had booked tickets for the train to Euston and we were meeting Stephen on our arrival. It was a long journey with several stops and we arrived at Euston at 11.25 and got the tube to London Bridge. As we came out onto the main road I heard singing and looked across the road to see loads of Blues fans outside The Old Kings Head pub and immediately decided to join them. Stephen had already arrived in London

Bridge but had come up the other side and was waiting in an empty pub but he quickly drank up and joined us.

The atmosphere was brilliant on a lovely sunny day with Bluenoses both inside and outside of the pub and they were already making a lot of noise singing their hearts out and of course I joined in. A few Croatian Blues fans arrived to join us with a large Croatian flag and they also joined in the singing and dancing. Amidst this a blue smoke bomb was set off and the alleyway looked brilliant with a blue hue as the blue smoke filled the air. The blue smoke soon made its way into the pub through the open windows and set the fire alarm off. This prompted cheers and a rendition of 'is there a fire drill.' Very funny. A little while later the same happened again and the alley was again filled with blue smoke. It was absolutely brilliant and we all really enjoyed it.

After a couple of drinks we made our way towards the nearby Shard and caught the overground train to Charlton for the match against a Charlton team currently second in the table and unbeaten at home in 20 games. Having lost our last 3 away games 3-0 I would happily have settled for a draw and I just hoped for a better performance. The atmosphere amongst the 3,200 Bluenoses inside the stadium was amazing and the noise levels were stunning as song after song rang out.

I was amazed to see that 16 year old Jude Bellingham was making his starting debut especially as it would be his 4th game in 2 weeks having played 3 games for the England U17 team for whom he scored and was named best player. Great to see him playing though and the Bluenoses happily sang his name. Blues played much better today and went in level 0-0 at half time and the second half would see Blues attacking the away end where we were in such good voice. Charlton's manager was ex Blues player Lee Bowyer and the Blues fans sang such a loud version of 'Bowyer, Bowyer give us a wave' and he actually looked over and waved at us. We all fell about laughing and sang 'there's only one Lee Bowyer!' Followed by 'who put the ball in the Arsenal net?' (Lee Bowyer was in the Blues team that beat Arsenal at Wembley to win the League Cup in 2011).

Just 7 minutes into the 2nd half Maxime Colin went on an amazing run before passing to Mbrati who ran into the box and pulled the ball back into the path of Jude Bellingham who calmly fired it into the net to give Blues the lead and the away end completely erupted with several blue smoke bombs emitting their blue smoke into the air. Jude Bellingham was engulfed by the Blues players as he ran to the away end and 'Jude Bellingham!' rang out followed by 'Jude Bellingham - he's one of our own!'. Brilliant scenes.

There was a funny incident in the second half when an extra ball made its way onto the pitch from the direction of the benches and the game was stopped. The referee headed to the Blues bench and asked manager Pep who threw the ball on. Pep said he didn't know and the referee said if he didn't tell him then he would get a booking and Pep said "okay I'll take the booking" and the referee showed him the yellow card. In the meantime Charlton manager Lee Bowyer had walked over towards the Blues bench (they are a long way apart at Charlton!) and had thrown the ball at the Blues bench. The referee (to an increasing crescendo of noise from the Blues fans in anticipation) then walked over to Lee Bowyer, spoke to him then produced a red card to cheers from the away end. As Lee Bowyer made his way to the dressing room the Blues fans sang 'there's only one Lee Bowyer'. Very funny!

Blues held out for a fully deserved and brilliant 1-0 away win which ended Charlton's 20 game unbeaten run. The Blues players came over and celebrated with us fans and more smoke bombs which ensured that the air was full of blue smoke as we enjoyed one of our best away days for quite a while. Brilliant, we enjoyed every minute before heading back to get the train back to London Bridge then Euston then home. What a fantastic away trip.

I have visited The Valley on seven occasions up to 2024 and I had seen two wins, one draw and four defeats.

Ground 10 – White Hart Lane - 15th February 1980 – FA Cup 5th Round – Tottenham 3 Birmingham City 1

It was brilliant to be in the hat for the fifth round of the FA cup in 1980 and when the draw sent us to White Hart Lane to play Tottenham Hotspur I was really excited. So on the 15th February 1980 I set out clad in my blue and white to new street station to board the train bound for London. I travelled with my sister in law Sue and we set out early, which meant getting the normal intercity train to London and not the football special. With drinks and sandwiches packed, we settled comfortably on the train and began chatting avidly about our chances of getting to Wembley this year.

We arrived early and got on the underground to seven sister's tube station. This was my first experience of the London underground. It seemed really noisy and busy but the tunnels and the underground maps of the various lines that ran throughout London intrigued me. On our arrival at seven sisters we headed up the stairs and out of the station and onto the main road that led up towards White Hart Lane. We decided to walk up to the ground to have a look around and then we went for a drink as we were very early. The pub on the way up the road looked good, so we decided to head back there after a look round the ground. It was always good to visit different football grounds, as most fans know. White Hart Lane looked interesting, and after locating the away end we then headed back to the pub.

As we were really close to the ground we left it late before we left the packed pub to head up towards the ground and that turned out to be a big mistake. As we approached the ground we saw thousands of Blues fans standing outside the away end singing and drinking. I thought they were just waiting to go in, but when I got closer I discovered that the ground was full and the turnstiles had been closed! I was gutted! There were 50, 000 people inside and at least 3,000 Blues fans locked out. After travelling all this way, no one was going anywhere, and all the Blues fans remained outside throughout the game singing and listening to the noise from within. Whenever there was a goal scored someone inside would shout out to us all with who had scored, although it was easy to know when Blues scored because we heard our end erupt and we could see the Bluenoses inside the ground jumping around – so we all celebrated outside too! Everyone was jumping up and down, jumping on each other and running around celebrating when we scored our goal. It must have looked strange really with so many of us outside.

Unfortunately, Blues lost the game 3-1, and at the final whistle the fans started pouring out. There was already lots of police around due to the fact that there was a lot of football violence around this time, but I don't think they were helped by the fact that a milk float passed by the Blues fans as the Spurs fans came out of the ground. It really kicked off and there were milk bottles flying everywhere. I don't think the spurs fans knew what hit them really (apart from the milk bottles), and the police were just as surprised. I decided to leave them to it as glass rained down everywhere, and we made our way back to the tube station to head back to Euston to catch the train back to Birmingham.

I couldn't believe that after travelling all that way, we had not even got inside the ground. Paying at the turnstile had its advantages but I wouldn't be making that mistake again. It was my own fault though for staying in the pub too long, but I hadn't anticipated the vast amount of fans, especially blues fans that travelled to the match. Blues have always had good away support though and it was always great fun to travel with them. It was still a good day out though despite not getting inside the ground and Blues losing. Over the years I travelled a lot and got quite used to the regular away travellers. It became like a second family.

I went back to White Hart Lane the following season on January 10th 1981 and this time I get there early and finally gained entry into the ground.

So, we arrived in London and disembarked at seven sister's tube station with plenty of time to spare. This time however, we only stopped briefly in the pub, downed our beers in record time and headed up to the ground and we gained entrance into the ground and I was able to look around another football ground with lots of character. I must admit I really miss the terraces nowadays. There was such a fabulous atmosphere standing on the terraces which some people will never be lucky enough to experience now. I count myself extremely lucky to have experienced this fantastic period in football history. Bring back the terraces and we will bring back the atmosphere. By all means keep some seats for the prawn sandwiches, but give us back the terraces and we will bring back the atmosphere!

I liked White Hart Lane when it had terracing, particularly the 'shelf' which was like terracing in sections. The away end was behind the goal with the terracing at the front and seats above and behind us. At the time the home fans were in the seats above us and we were occasionally treated to a beer shampoo. I guess it all goes in one way or the other though, and it was their beer! There were not as many people inside the ground as there had been for our previous cup-tie against them last year with only 24,909 present. As usual though the Blues contingent were in good voice and 'Keep Right On' rang out loud and proud. The game wasn't too bad but unfortunately ended in defeat by the odd goal with Blues going down 1-0. Oh well, there was always next time, so we set off back to seven sisters tube station trying to remain optimistic.

I did see Blues win at White Hart Lane though on a visit in February 1984 when a single goal saw Blues take all three points in a (old) First Division game as we ran out 1-0 winners. It was a great trip and turned out to be my last one to this stadium.

Over time I visited White Hart Lane on five occasion and I saw only one Blues win, one draw and three defeats. It was sad to see White Hart Lanes demolished to make way for a new stadium at the end of the 2016-17 season after 118 years of history to make way for the building of a new stadium. Tottenham were relocated to Wembley Stadium until their new stadium was completed.

Ground 11 – The City Ground – 20th August 1980 – Division One – Nottingham Forest 2 Birmingham City 1

I had a good summer of 1980, happy in the knowledge that Blues would start the new season in August back in the First Division (top flight) and I had turned eighteen in January, had been in full time work at the same company for two years and was intent on going to every game of the coming season, home and away.

In our first away game of the 1980/81 season Blues were away at Nottingham Forest and it would be my first trip to the City Ground in Nottingham. I travelled by the football special again, from New Street Station, which was, as usual, packed with Bluenoses. There was the usual singing and chanting, with fans sitting on tables, and standing in corridors drinking beers. I would sing and chat with various people as we journeyed onwards, watching the countryside passing by through the windows. It was great to hear people's stories of the games they had been to and the journey's they had been on. I would vow to travel and follow the Blue boy's wherever they went. I thought the journey was the best part of following your team away from home, there was so much fun to be had.

When the train arrived in Nottingham Station, the Bluenoses poured off the train and headed towards the waiting police escort, singing at the top of our voices. It was so loud, and announced our arrival, as it was meant to do, in dramatic style to all those within earshot! We were met by the police, and the hundreds of us that had just disembarked, were surrounded and escorted towards the ground. It seemed like a long walk along various roads before we saw the ground. I remember crossing a large bridge and looking at the floodlights of the City Ground on one side and the floodlights of the older looking ground of Notts County on the other side. I know I saw Trent Bridge cricket ground at some point too, but I can't remember where. I remember that they are all close together though.

The City Ground was on the edge of the river and the waiting Forest fans were singing songs threatening to throw us in the river. They were immediately answered by the travelling Bluenoses with several gestures inviting them to try! The ground itself was interesting, as I thought most grounds were around this time. I always loved going to a new ground, and still do in fact.

I've been to the City Ground lots of time since, but I think on this first occasion that the away fans were situated along the side of the ground, close to the pitch. The singing at away matches is always great, and so it was today at Forest with the Bluenoses giving the Forest faithful loads of stick. There was loads of Blues there and we sang our hearts out for the Blues. I thought the ground was slightly better than Derby but not as good as St. Andrews. I bought a programme, as I enjoyed collecting them, as well as reading them during the game, and it cost twenty-five pence! Football was affordable to the normal supporter in those days.

Despite Frank Worthington scoring for Blues, we lost the game 2-1, but being Blues fans we were never too down. Keep Right On, rang out loudly as the game finished and we clapped our lads as they came over to applaud us for our support. Blues had played well, and fought hard, so we had no complaints as we filed out towards the police escort that would lead us back to the station to get the football special. As was usual around this time the Blues faithful were kept inside the ground for about 15 minutes to allow the home supporters to leave the ground first. The weather was nice, so the walk back was pleasant with lots of singing and the odd fight breaking out as a few Forest fans turned up to taunt us and a few Blues broke away and joined them for a scuffle before the police intervened. Then we were back at the station and onto the train back to Birmingham. The singing and chatting carried on all the way back home with everyone in good spirits. We were happy to be back in the First Division and still full of hope. It was a good day out really, and as usual when I got back to Birmingham, I picked up the Pink Sports Argus, fish and chips and headed home.

In January 2010 Blues had been drawn away at Nottingham Forest in the FA Cup and I was really looking forward to this trip. We arrived in Nottingham with plenty of time to spare and I texted Stephen to tell him which pub we were in. We met up with Graham and Craig in the pub and soon after we were joined by other Bluenoses. It was predominantly a home pub and before long it was full of red shirted Forest fans. I was in my usual Blues colours and had to make my way through a sea of red to get to the toilets. No problems though, I made it there and back in one piece! Mind you, I did have Graham as a bodyguard!

During the time we were in the pub I could see the snow coming down outside in large flakes and it was sticking! By the time we left the pub everywhere was white and I was worried that the game would be called off. It was getting really cold too. The walk to the ground warmed me up somewhat, although the snow was still falling and I was glad I had a hat and scarf on. Once inside the ground it was buzzing. There were more that 4,500 Bluenoses in the away end and the atmosphere was brilliant. It was a real old fashioned cup atmosphere and despite the cold the Blues fans were singing their hearts out.

The match got underway and Blues had quite a few chances, even hitting the bar, but we just couldn't score. Then Forest were awarded a penalty and their fans celebrated loudly. Up stepped the Forest player to a crescendo of whistles and boo's from the Blues end and he dispatched it high into the stands to wild celebrations from the Bluenoses – myself included. That certainly warmed me up! The game finished 0-0 and now meant a replay at St. Andrews in two weeks time but I was due to head back to Abu Dhabi.

We managed to squeeze Stephen into the car and we dropped him back at Nottingham station for him to catch his train back to Leicester. I gave him the rest of the sandwiches and packed lunch that mom had made me for his train journey back.

In December 2014 we set off for the early kick off game at Nottingham Forest on a freezing cold day. At least it turned out to be very worthwhile and enjoyable as Blues scored 3 goals in a ten minute spell just before half time which put us 3-0 up. Forest did pull a goal back but Blues held on for a great 3-1 win and achieved the double over Forest that took us up to 14th in the table.

In August 2019 it was a lovely sunny day when we headed to Nottingham after parking our cars at St. Andrews school because of Coventry playing their home game at St. Andrews. We arrived early in Nottingham and we headed to the chip shop where Terry very kindly paid for our chippie meals. We then purchased some ciders from the nearby shop and we all headed back towards the away end. Somehow a wasp managed to fly into Nigel's mouth as he was drinking his cider and despite quickly spitting it out it managed to sting him - twice! We couldn't help but laugh as he seemed okay apart from spluttering and sticking his tongue out but he did have a red mark on his tongue. He went straight to the first aid when we got inside the away end. They gave him a massive lump of ice to stick in his mouth the sight of which caused us to laugh some more.

I saw Hoppy (ex Blues player) on the way in and he came over to say hello. The concourse was heaving with singing Bluenoses and it was quite tricky making our way through them without getting a beer shampoo. It was brilliant seeing everyone in such good form and having a great time. There was some pretty wild dancing going on. We had all had bets on what away kit would be worn today and me, June, Taff and Nigel were delighted to see that we were correct and the players were in yellow shirts just as we were. Cool.

The atmosphere in the Blues end was great as usual and the singing was top notch. Our end was a mass of blue and white with a splattering of charcoal from those wearing the new away shirt which I still thought was a bit dull to be honest but apparently it had been voted the best away shirt in the Championship. Pep played the same team as the previous Saturday but today we just didn't seem to know what we were doing and a poor display saw us lose 3-0 and it could easily have been 6 or 7 had Forest not missed a lot of chances as we defended poorly. Blues didn't seem to pose much of a threat due to only Jutkiewicz being up front on his own with no wingers and our defenders trying to be both full backs and wingers.

It was awful to watch and I couldn't see where the goals would come from. I found it all very depressing as we seemed to be back to the Zola days but the football was worse and unless things changed and the new players gelled then I could see us getting relegated. Early days yet though and I would try to remain optimistic although I was already finding it hard. We trudged back the our coaches and headed home. It was a fun journey back though as we made jokes about Nigel's wasp encounter and laughed all the way home over it. We were definitely 'buzzing'.

I have visited the City Ground on fifteen occasions and have seen two wins with the last being 3-1 in December 2014 and 2-1 in August 2000. I have seen four draws and nine defeats with the heaviest being 5-1 in April 1984 which I remember clearly as the away contingent sang 'we want six'. Typical of Blues humour at the time.

Ground 12 – The Dell – 30th August 1980 – Division One - Southampton 3 Birmingham City 1

This was the furthest trip so far for me and I was really looking forward to heading to the south coast, especially as it was August, and the weather was really nice. So, off we headed to the station for the long trip south. Mom had made me some sandwiches for the train journey and we had purchased a few cans for the trip too. I can't remember how long the journey was, but it was relaxed and as always, the train was full of bluenoses. It wasn't a football special because of the fact that it was a long journey and not as many fans were expected to travel. Blues fans, however, had different ideas and the train was pretty full. Everyone was in good spirits and we arrived in plenty of time and made our way to the ground. We popped into the pub just outside the ground for a couple before the game, and it was full of bluenoses in full voice. Great!

We left the pub in good time to get into the ground which, I have to say, did not look very impressive from outside. It was the old Southampton ground known as The Dell. What an awful ground it was for the away fan. Inside was even worse, I remember thinking that it was the worst football ground I had ever been inside, or for that fact would ever be inside (until Swansea that is!). The main problem was the fencing. The away fans were given one end of terracing behind the goal and apart from it being really small the fencing was really big and everywhere you stood the view seemed to be obstructed. There was also a floodlight inside our end as well, which also obstructed the view. The home end was very interesting though as it was a terraced area which was wider one end than the other. One side was much higher than the other and sort of sloped from one end to the other and looked a bit odd. At least it had character though and was quite unique.

As an away fan, I have to say the end they gave us and the view was crap. The ground was so small that there was a block of flats that could clearly be seen inside the ground and the people living there must have had a great view on match days. They could clearly be seen watching the game from their windows. Mind you, at least most football grounds had character about them in those days. The Blues end was packed, especially as it was so small, with no roof on I might add. Luckily, though, the sun was shining, because if it had been raining, we would have all got soaked.

The game got under way and despite Frank Worthington scoring for us again, Blues lost 3-1. It didn't stop us bluenoses from singing and giving the opposing supporters some stick though, and we left the ground a little downhearted but still optimistic. Once again the players came over and applauded the Blues faithful for our support and we applauded their effort in the game.

The trip to The Dell that really stands out is the big relegation match at the end of the 1982/83 season when Blues needed a win to stay up. With one game left we were fifth from bottom and just one point clear of the drop zone.

Therefore, we set out on our travels to Southampton with hope in our hearts. The girls and I travelled by car to Southampton with some lads that we knew. It was a nice journey, very picturesque and we stopped about half way in a nice village or town and had a quick drink in a nice country pub. We were all really nervous and really excited as we really believed we could win again and stay up. We had a good team with fighting spirit who played with heart, unlike some of the players we have now. Once we arrived in Southampton, after parking the car, we headed to the pub just across the road from the Dell and stood on the step watching the fans wandering past and heading in and out of the pub.

Just as we were preparing to drink up and head into the ground, the Blues team coach drove past, much to our delight. We waved at the lads with one hand, whilst trying to look girly and hiding our drinks behind our backs with the other hand. Classic! Then we were off towards the ground and we were soon settled in the away end behind the goal. The away end, as I have said before, is pretty crap at the Dell, but today they had given us the entire end and it was soon choc a bloc with Blues fans. Some fans were sitting on the walls at the back and there were also Bluenoses sitting on the roof of the refreshments. The view of the pitch was really poor but we were full of hope and excitement and the singing was really loud and we swayed forwards and backwards. It was a lovely sunny day and when the teams ran out onto the pitch we cheered and waved flags and scarves in the air.

The match got underway and a severe case of nervousness set in and I began to ponder the outcome. Half time it was 0-0 and as the second half got under way Blues were now attacking the goal in front of the massed Blue army. As the game drew towards the end there was a bit of a scramble in the Southampton goal mouth in the 87th minute and Mick Harford was on hand to blast the ball into the top of the net and the fans went wild! I jumped on my mates and the wild celebrations began. We were staying up!

As the final whistle went the celebrations really began and we headed out amongst mass celebrations. We decided to head out of Southampton and stop at a pub on the way for our celebrations, which we did. Everywhere we looked there were Bluenoses celebrating. It was brilliant! In a final twist Luton had won 1-0 at Maine Road and sent Manchester City down in the third relegation place. We were safe for another year though and I was more than happy.

Over the years I visited The Dell on six occasions before it was demolished. I saw only one win, but what a massive iconic win it was and it will stay in my memories forever. The remaining five games ended in defeat and I never saw a draw played out there between Southampton and Blues. Great memories though. The Dell was demolished in 2001by a Portsmouth demolition company and it is now a housing estate.

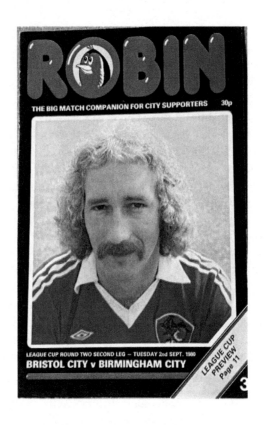

Ground 13 – Ashton Gate – 2nd September 1980 – League Cup 2nd Rd 2nd Leg – Bristol City 0 Birmingham City 0

My thirteenth ground came about when I decided to make the trip to Bristol for the second leg of the league cup game with Bristol City. Again, it would be another new ground for me. I don't remember a lot about this trip, but the ground itself was okay if not a bit worn looking and we held them to a 0-0 draw, which meant that Blues were through to the next round of the League Cup because we had beaten them 2-1 at our ground, and so went through on aggregate. I was really excited because I love the cup and I was always dreaming of seeing Blues at Wembley! It was funny because it was the smallest crowd I had ever been in. There were only 7,000 in the ground, and a lot of them were Bluenoses on the away terrace and as always we were in good voice.

In September 2008 myself, Stephen, Annette, Steve and Lee set off for Bristol in Lee's car in the hope of arriving early and getting a pre match drink. It was a fun drive as we were in good spirits and Steve had bought a bag of bottled beers as it was his birthday. Lee had remarked that the kids were quiet in the back! I then sang several Blues songs, driving Lee mad in the process. I even sang 'front end, front end give us a song'. Lee told Steve to sing something but the front end remained silent despite my taunts.

The traffic wasn't too bad either and just before six we arrived in Bristol. Steve was navigating and had about a hundred pages of instructions from the Internet by which he directed Lee to a nice little pub set back off the main road just next to the Ramada Hotel. As we drove up a small road to the pub at the top I couldn't help but notice all the parked cars were facing us. I pointed this out and asked if perhaps it could be a one way street. Steve replied that it wasn't as he had walked up the road previously! We all burst into laughter at his words – WALKED up this way! Lee dropped us at the pub and then went to park the car just down the road.

It was a lovely little old pub with just a few locals inside and no Bristol City fans to be seen. There was a small beer garden out front, to which we headed before deciding it was too cold and heading back inside just as Lee arrived from parking the car. We had a great time in the pub chatting amongst ourselves and downing several pints – except Lee who had to stick to water due to the fact that he was driving.

At just after seven o'clock we drank up and headed for the ground. As we got close to the ground the traffic became heavy but luckily we spotted a parking space outside a boarded up pub not too far from the ground. We arrived in the ground about five minutes before kickoff and the Blues end was buzzing! The away end was behind the goal and was unreserved seating, which was brilliant. All the Bluenoses were in great voice, around 2 – 2,500 of us I reckoned. Only problem was the seats had no backs to them but no problem tonight as the entire Blues end were on our feet throughout the game.

It was a brilliant atmosphere and after only five minutes Larsson put the Blues in front and we erupted in wild celebrations. I jumped on Annette and Stephen and we danced about madly. Then to our delight Jerome put us 2-0 up after about 25 minutes to more wild celebrations! The Bluenoses were in full voice and 'Keep Right On' rang out loudly on a number of occasions and also several renditions of 'were Birmingham, we're Birmingham, we're Birmingham City!' The Bristol City fans were silent and it wasn't too long before Blues began singing 'no noise from the tractor boys'. It was a brilliant first half.

As the second half kicked off we had moved to the corner section and had seen several other Bluenoses that I know. I was surprised by the arrival of two Osama Bin Laden's, a horse and Rodney from only fools and horses. I love when Blues fans come in fancy dress to away games; they looked brilliant and stood behind us. Dave from Made In Brum took a quick picture of them, which included Steve, as he does resemble Del from only fools and horses!

Blues didn't play quite as well in the second half but could still have been further ahead but for a bit of luck before we made a mistake leading to the ball dropping to a Bristol player who planted it straight into the empty net 2-1. With ten minutes to go the Bristol City fans began heading out and the Bluenoses began singing 'time to go, time to go, time to go' song. The game was never in any doubt, though and it finished with another away win for Blues and we were still in second place in the table. Brilliant.

Back to the car and we were soon on the way back to Birmingham. I sang all the way back home much to the amusement or perhaps annoyance of the others? I did several renditions of 'were Birmingham' a few 'Keep Right On's' and several other old ones. I think Lee was probably relieved when I got out at my moms, although he did say it was a top night and he had forgotten how much fun travelling away could be.

My favourite trip to Bristol came on the final day of the 2016-17 season when Blues needed a win to stay in the Championship. I woke really early on the morning of the Bristol City game with the excitement/ nervousness of what lay ahead. This was Blues most important game since the last great escape at Bolton three years before and today would be just as nerve wracking due to a dramatic turnaround in form of the two teams below us. Blues had to win – no doubt about it. If Blues drew or lost then we would need Nottingham Forest or Blackburn to draw or lose and to be honest I thought they would both win because that's the sort of luck Blues have. No pressure then!

Because of the early kick off time of 12:00 the coaches would be leaving St. Andrews at 8.30am from the Main Stand car park because the KOP car park was being used by those going to church. Yes us fans came second once again. To top it off the coaches were late leaving again, wether this was down to poor organisation by the stewards again, or the fact that we had to wait ages to get the gates to the car park open due to the wrong key being sent, I don't know.

The coaches did finally get away though at 8.37am and we were on our way. It was me, June and James on coach one heading to Bristol. There were loads of Blues coaches (around 15 – 20) and we were all told to meet at the Bristol services to meet the police escort who were planning to escort all the coaches to the ground. This was mainly because there was a 10K Run through Bristol happening on the same day and many of the roads were closed. We met the police escort and were soon on our way through the back roads with the police motorbikes stopping traffic and taking us straight through. The coaches parked at the usual place on the industrial park and we had quite a walk over the railway lines and on to the away end of the stadium.

I was impressed to see that an outdoor bar had been set up near the away turnstiles which was selling beer and cider. Fabulous! I had a nice cold Thatchers cider (when in Somerset eh) as we watched the other Bluenoses arrive, many in fancy dress. I had on a long blue wig, face paint and a pair of massive blue sunglasses. I said Hi to Batman and we headed into the stadium.

Inside the stadium the away end was buzzing with over 2,600 Bluenoses on their feet and in full voice. There was a mixture of nerves and excitement in the air, although it was probably mostly nerves to be honest. The game got underway and Blues looked up for the fight. However, news soon reached us that Blackburn were leading 1-0 at Brentford – not what we wanted to hear as this meant that only a win would prevent Blues from being relegated to League One. Then it was 2-0 to Blackburn and I became even more nervous. This was not good.

Blues fans sang continuously and got behind the team and in the 16th minute Che Adams turned his man and fired the ball past the Bristol City goalkeeper – 1-0! The away end erupted as we all celebrated and some of the tension lifted. A new song was born and was belted out with passion 'we've got Redknapp, Harry Redknapp, I just don't think you understand, he saved us from the drop, he'll take us to the top, we've got Harry Redknapp'

As the match went on and we sang our hearts out, more news kept coming in. Nottingham Forest were leading Ipswich 1-0. Then in was 2-0 and Blackburn were 3-0 ahead. As ninety minutes approached, Forest were winning 3-0 and Blackburn 3-1. This meant that Blues had to win and as the fourth official held up his board showing six minutes of injury time we all knew that a Bristol City goal would send us down to League One.

Bristol City were now relentless in their attacks on the Blues goal in their attempt to send us down (and we will never forget this Bristol City!) and those six minutes were probably amongst the most stressful six minutes of my life! I could hardly bear to watch. It was awful and my nerves were wrecked. Even their goalkeeper came up for their corners! Then the sound of the final whistle rang out and the roar of celebration and relief in the Blues end was deafening.

Strangers hugged each other, barriers were climbed and many surged towards the pitch and some of the barriers collapsed under the strain as police and stewards tried in vain to keep the celebrating Blues fans off the pitch. The players had sprinted the length of the pitch, jumped over the barriers and dived into the mass of celebrating Blues fans!

Harry Redknapp came over and punched the air in celebration before appealing for calm as the barriers collapsed. Calm? No chance! He then went around the players hugging them and someone got a Blues scarf to him which he proudly put around his neck. The players were now in a group and bouncing around singing 'we are staying up!' Craig Gardener, who had been celebrating with the fans, noticed this and ran and dived on top of them. Fantastic celebrations and I was privileged to be part of it all.

I have visited Ashton Gate on nine occasions and seen 5 wins (2008, 2017, 2019, 2020 and 2023), 2 draws and 2 defeats. Quite a lucky ground for Blues and I always enjoy my visits there.

BIRMINGHAM CITY

Seagulls fly with British Caledonian Airways

Ground 14 – Goldstone Ground – 13th September 1980 – Division One - Brighton 2 Birmingham City 2

The next ground that I visited was the Goldstone Ground which was home to Brighton and Hove Albion from 1902 to 1997 when there owners sold the ground (to become a retail park) meaning that Brighton had to travel 70 miles to ground share with Gillingham for 2 years. Brighton then played at Withdean Stadium (an athletics stadium) just 2 miles north of the city centre until their new stadium the AMEX was built in 2011.

Back in 1980 it was the old Goldstone Ground where I was headed. I was really looking forward to this because of Brighton being a seaside town. We set out on the long trip south very early and in doing so, arrived in Brighton with time to look around and see the beach. It was great, we had been really excited on the trip, and had sandwiches and various extras's that my mom had put together for the long train journey. By the time we arrived in Brighton station we had finished off the lot, plus the beers we had packed. Brighton station was a bit different because all the trains finished there; it's sort of like all the railway lines just ending at a wall. It has a nice sort of character about the place. There were a lot of people around though, and we headed out and down the road towards the beach and the pier.

The beach was quite nice, with pebbles at the top but the sea was quite a long way out when we got there. I could see the old Victorian pier that was now abandoned and cut off now that the connecting walkway had collapsed. It must have been very impressive in its heyday. We walked onto the beach and when we turned around to look back at the town, I noticed that someone had spray painted – 'BIRMINGHAM CITY' in rather large letters on the sea wall. I had a bit of a giggle at that. Obviously some Bluenoses had arrived before us! Then we had a little look around the shops before calling into a small pub for a pint before catching a bus with 'Hove' on the front, and heading towards the ground.

Brighton's old Goldstone ground was quite open, but the weather was nice and there were quite a few Bluenoses present. Even though the ground was a bit old it had character and I quite liked it to be honest. Probably because it was a seaside town, and I have always liked being by the sea. The Blues faithful sang our hearts out as usual and we came away with a respectable 2-2 draw, so everyone was happy. There were a lot of police waiting outside the ground for us, and they insisted on putting everyone on the many coaches that were outside waiting! Despite us insisting to them that we had come on the train, the police were having none of it and insisted on putting us onto a coach! It took us ages before we were able to get off again and head back towards the train station. It was a good laugh though and a great day out by the seaside.

I was back again the following year and I had yet another great visit to the seaside in November 1981. It was a bit colder than our last visit and we had a look around the town this time as well as visiting the beach to see the sea obviously. The game was just as entertaining and ended in a draw once again only it was 1-1 on this occasion.

In total I visited the Goldstone Ground on five occasions between 1980 and 1986 with three of them in September, one in October and one in November. I'm guessing that even back then they didn't want us Bluenoses visiting during the warmer months. I saw 2 draws and 3 defeats and I never saw us win there but it never stopped me enjoying the visits. The ground was sold off and the last game played there was in 1997 with Brighton having to play at Gillingham's ground (70 miles away) for the next 2 years before returning to Brighton to play at Withdean Stadium (athletics stadium). The Goldstone Ground was demolished and a retail park built in its place.

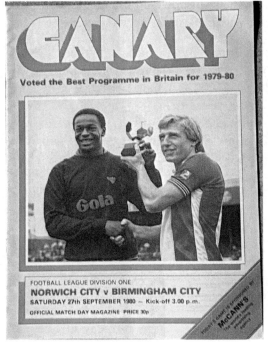

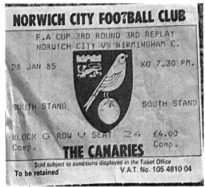

Ground 15 – Carrow Road – 27th September 1980 – Division One – Norwich City 2 Birmingham City 2

The next match meant a journey to Norwich, another place that would be a new experience for me. This seemed like the longest trip so far to me as it took such a long time to get to and involved a lot of travelling through the countryside. It was a very pretty and pleasant trip thought. The ground was okay and we popped in the pub on the corner, not too far from the ground for a couple of pints before the game. It was a small pub with a good atmosphere, and there were a few bluenoses also in there with the same idea, enjoying a pint.

Inside the ground there were plenty of Bluenoses, despite the distance, and all were in good spirits on the terraces singing loudly. We were on a terrace section behind the goal next to a seated area which ran along the side to our left and housed more Bluenoses. There were 13,801 inside Carrow Road that day. It was quite colourful with all the yellow and green of the Norwich City fans, and we took great pleasure in singing 'I can't read, I can't write, but that don't really matter, cos I'm a Norwich City fan and I can drive a tractor!' Quite fun really and good banter with the Norwich fans. It was a good game too, and ended in a 2-2 draw with goals from Alan Ainscow and Frank Worthington. A nice trip out, but a long journey home when you are tired and weary.

In 1985 Blues played Norwich, which turned into a marathon in the FA Cup and involved a couple of trips to Carrow Road to see replays, which were common at this time. Blues had been draw at home against Norwich City and I, personally was quite hopeful. Well, as hopeful as you can be, being a Bluenose. The tie proved to be a relay and after a 0-0 draw at St. Andrews I was planning my long trip to Norwich on the eve of my birthday. I had booked the day off work and we had arranged to go with Alan, Julie's uncle, and some of the lads. It was a long trip but quite nice as it was through the countryside and we chatted avidly amongst ourselves as Alan drove. We arrived in Norwich early and headed to a pub, not too far from the ground where Alan had been before and suggested it as a good place for pre match beers.

Once again the game ended in a draw, this time 1-1 which meant that there would now be another replay at St. Andrews in a few days time. Anyway, as it was my birthday the next day, we headed back to the pub after the game for a few more drinks before heading back. This proved to be a big mistake for me, as I drank way too much, due to the fact that it was my birthday in a couple of hours. It was a very very long journey back. Alan had a bit of a joke with the barmaid before the game, telling her that if we drew and came back he would bring chocolates!

And so it was that three days later we again played Norwich and surprise surprise drew again! 1-1 and Blues lost the toss, which meant another trip to Norwich for a fourth game against them! Alan again drove us and we went back to the same pub, where Alan presented the barmaid with a large bag of maltessers as promised! We had seat tickets this time but soon climbed over the railings and onto the terrace to join the Bluenoses singing and chanting in the away end.

The game was really frustrating as most of the decisions were going against us and we were beginning to feel victimised by the referee, to which we aimed our verbal opinion. I was chatting to one lad who said he was getting sick of the bad decisions by the man in black and if it continued then he was going to get on the pitch and tell him himself! I told him I would happily come on with him and contribute my opinion if needed! Then, unbelievably, the referee gave a penalty to Norwich! The Blues fans were up in arms and the lad I had been talking to earlier was now scaling the fence and onto the pitch.

In my drunken state of mind I decided I was going on too, but luckily for me I only got half way up the fence before Alan pulled me back. By this time the lad was now in the centre circle, finger pointed, giving the referee a piece of his mind. He was at it for ages before the police came on and escorted him from the pitch. I thought it was hilarious, as did the rest of the Bluenoses! However, it proved to be the turning point in the match and we were robbed 1-0 and our Wembley dreams were over for another year. We also had a very long trip home to look forward to as well! Time for more beers.

I have visited Carrow Road on 12 occasions and I have not had a lot of enjoyment when it comes to results apart from in November 1996 when I got to enjoy a 1-0 away win which sent me home very happy for a change. I witnessed 4 draws and 7 defeats with the worst being a 5-1 loss in September 1982. Not a very lucky ground for us really.

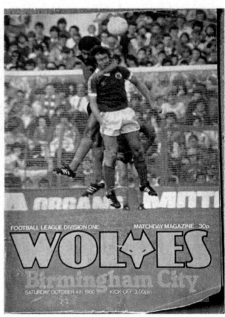

Ground 16– Molineux Stadium – 4th October 1980 – Division One – Wolves 1 Birmingham City 0

Next was a nice local trip to Wolverhampton for the local derby with Wolverhampton Wanderers. I was really looking forward to this, especially as the atmosphere at local derbies was always brilliant. You can't beat a bit of rivalry. As it was only about twenty minutes by train from the city centre, we had a few drinks in Birmingham before the setting off for the match. Around this time we would drink in the likes of Edwards No 7, Boogies and others around that area, as they were 'Blues' pubs. Other times we might pop into the Midland hotel, the Yard of Ale etc. Or sometimes we would just go into the station bar, inside new street train station.

Anyway, we set off on one of the many trains that passed through Wolverhampton, and enjoyed a short but sweet journey on a train packed with Bluenoses. When we arrived at Wolverhampton, the police were waiting for us and we set off on the short journey to the Molineux ground with half of us on the pavement and the other half in the road. There seemed to be thousands of

Blues and it wasn't long before some Wolves fans appeared and attempted to attack the Bluenoses before being chased back up the road. This happened a few times before they gave up and fled in various directions. I could see the ground and the floodlights in the distance.

This was my first time to Molineux and I was thoroughly enjoying it. The ground looked impressive, and we were led onto the terracing for the away fans that was behind the goal next to, or part of a grassy bank to the one side. We were given a fair amount of terracing though, and soon proceeded to fill our end and the singing and chanting began in earnest. As it was a local derby there was a lot of singing and banter from both sets of supporters, which always adds to the occasion. Our end was a mass of blue and white and I remember looking around at all the gold and black of the Dingles (wolves' fans!). I had my programme proudly tucked into the back pocket of my jeans, as everyone seemed to do at the time, and took up a good position on the terrace.

The atmosphere was electric with 22,777 inside the ground but unfortunately Blues lost by the only goal of the game. This in turn, let to quite a bit of fighting outside, although most of it was just wolves fans confronting the departing Blues fans, only to get chased back down the road again for their trouble. I just watched it all in wonder, laughed a bit, and headed back to the station with the others. It wasn't long before I was back in new street station and heading towards the bus stop to board a bus back to my mom's to pick up my usual fish and chips and the pink sports Argus.

In 1996 I met someone connected with Wolverhampton Wanderers and they had said that they would get me tickets when Blues next played at Molineux. I was surprised and pleased to discover that they had two tickets for me in one of the executive boxes which was really kind of them. So Julie and I headed to the match and took our place in the executive box amongst the others also in our box. It was a really nice change with nice food available and an outdoor balcony where we could sit and watch the match whilst also enjoying the atmosphere.

We were situated just behind the Wolves fans and we got some funny looks as we celebrated each of Blues two goals. Unfortunately Blues lost the game 3-2 but it had been a nice day out and the Blues fans had sang their hearts out. I must admit I did miss being amongst the Blue army even though Julie and I created our own atmosphere, much to the dismay of the Wolves fans!

A really good trip to Wolves came in 2017 on a Friday as once again we were being shown on live TV. At least it was only a short trip to Wolves and we went in a hotel bar by the train station for a pre match pint, then walked up with the arriving Bluenoses to the stadium. It was buzzing inside the away end and it was a carnival atmosphere as 2,151 made the short trip. Blues started well and were playing some good football even though we were playing with only Adams up front and when the Wolves keeper dropped the ball at the feet of Kieftenbeld he fired home and the away end exploded in celebration. A couple of bottles were thrown down at us from the Wolves fans above up but they were returned ten fold in response. 'Always shit on the old gold and black' rang out as the Wolves fans looked despondent.

It got even worse for the Wolves fans when ex-Wolves David Davis curled home a shot to make it 2-0 to Blues and he ran to the Blues fans in celebration and the away end erupted. It was brilliant and I jumped around in celebration. I prayed we could hold out, especially when Paul Robinson got a straight red for allegedly punching a Wolves player (later rescinded). Wolves did manage to pull a goal back once Blues were reduced to 10 men but we held on for a 2-1 win and the celebrations began. It was a happy journey back to the car and Blues moved up to 13th. It made a change to win in front of the cameras as we usually lose and to win in a Derby game was even better. I was very happy.

Over the years I have been to Wolves on 11 occasions and witnessed 4 wins (2-0 in 1984, 2-1 in 1996, 3-1 in 1998 and the 2-1 in 2017), 4 draws and only 3 defeats.

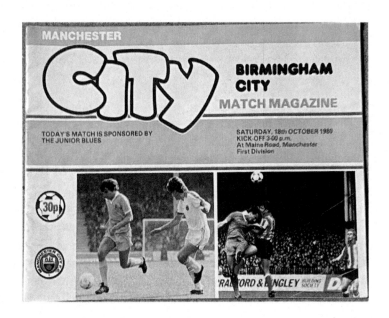

Ground 17 – Maine Road – 18th October 1980 – Division One – Manchester City 0 Birmingham City 1

Saturday 18th October 1980 saw us head to Manchester to see Blues take on Manchester City at Maine Road. We were being driven to the station by my friend Pam's dad and as we were driving along the Bristol Road I remembered that the tickets for the match were still at home so we had to turn around and go back to fetch them! It was thanks to Pam's Dad who asked 'you have got the tickets haven't you?' to which I replied 'What tickets?' before realising he meant match tickets and I had, in fact, forgotten them, much to my horror. Good job we hadn't gone too far really. Once we finally arrived at New Street station, complete with tickets, we soon found our train and settled down for the journey north.

When we arrived in Manchester we were unsure which way it was to the ground so we asked a couple of Blues fans the way. They were Julie and Debbie, who over the coming games became good friends. Julie and I are still very good friends to this day. So we all headed off together towards Maine Road for the game. Outside there were loads of police on horseback and I found it very difficult to get passed them as they made a line, squeezing all the away fans into the turnstiles. It wasn't very nice with the horses slobbering everywhere and I thought I would get crushed by one of them. It put me off horses for life, I can tell you!

There were the usual hostilities between the two sets of fans outside the ground and once inside the chanting continued. Both sets of supporters were standing on the terrace along the side of the pitch, with us Blues fans having one third of it and the corner and the Mancs having the rest with a large fence and a line of police separating us. The official attendance was 30,041. The four of us stood together on the terracing and before long a bit of missile throwing commenced and I was very narrowly missed by a flying object that actually brushed my hair as it sped past, hit a crash barrier and bounced back landing at my foot. It was a cylinder type object with a three-inch spike poking out of it – very, very dangerous! If it had been an inch closer it could have done some serious damage to me. I was all for lobbing it back at the Man City fans as they had thrown it in the first place (only for a split second), but Pam picked it up first and took it to a nearby policeman.

It was a big ground and the side terracing reminded me of our own KOP at St. Andrews, although not as good of course! I did like Maine Road; it was a nice ground to travel to. The atmosphere inside was good and the Blues were having in great voice and were singing the usual war songs and giving loads of stick to the neighbouring Man City lot. Keep Right On rang out loud and clear as usual and the fans swayed like a big blue wave. It was great, and to make it even better Archie Gemmill, our little Scot, scored the only goal of the game from the penalty spot giving us a very good 1-0 away win. The Blues end erupted in a massive celebration and we taunted the Man city fans with chants of 'one-nil, one-nil!' It is brilliant when we win away, it seems to give you that bit more satisfaction.

At the end of January 1982 I was again heading off to Manchester City again. We arrived in Manchester and the most memorable part of the day was when I was the only person inside Maine Road insisting that we would still come back and win when we were 4-0 down. Ever the optimist eh! The girls looked at me as if I was a compete nutter! Mind you, Blues did get 2 goals back and the game finished 4-2. I was mauled by a horse on the way out, as the police tried to keep the Blues and Manchester City fans apart. They are bloody massive and they scared the life out of me. I don't like horses to this day thanks to the Manchester police.

My last game at Maine Road before it would be demolished was in Blues first season in the Premier League in 2003 and I was lucky that Steve managed to get me a ticket as the demand for tickets for away games was massive for our first season back in the top flight. I travelled to the game with Stephen and this time we travelled on the coaches from the St. Andrews Tavern. It was great, a couple of drinks and a bacon buttie in the St. Andrews Tavern before we left and then we were on our way.

It was a really nice day and before we knew it we were arriving in Manchester and we were soon inside the ground. We were sitting next to a couple of Steve's mates who had got the tickets for us and I soon got chatting to them and they gave me some chocolate that they had bought with them as he worked in Cadbury's. Stephen soon ate his as the match got underway. The 2,000 Bluenoses sang loudly but the Manchester City supporters were silent and soon the Blues fans were singing 'it's just like being in church, it's just like being in church'.

After gaining no response from the Mancs, the Bluenoses turned our attention to their new signing Robbie Fowler who had done nothing up to now so we sang 'what a waste of money' to him. I should have known that this would come back to bite us on the bum as he bloody scored the winner right in front of us as the Mancs now taunted us with chants of 'what a waste of money'. Oh well, can't win them all and off we headed back to catch the coach having lost the game 1-0.

Maine Road closed for good in 2003 and was demolished in 2004 and is currently a housing estate. The only sign that it existed is the marking of the centre spot inside the housing estate. Over the years I visited Maine Road on 7 occasions in 1980 (won 1-0), January 1982 (lost 4-2), November 1982 (drew 0-0), 1984 (lost 1-0), 1985 (drew 1-1), 1996 (lost 1-0) and I made my last visit in 2003 (lost 1-0). In total Blues Won 1, lost 4 and drew 2. Overall I quite enjoyed my trips to Maine Road and it reminded me of Coronation Street.

Ground 18 – Highfield Road – 15th November 1980 – Division One – Coventry City 2 Birmingham City 1

On the 15th November 1980, I set out for my first visit to local neighbours Coventry City. I was really looking forward to this as Coventry is not far from Birmingham on the train and it was a lovely sunny day. Blues were 9th in the first division at this point in the season and Coventry were below us in 13th so it should be a good game. I set off early to get the local train which ran regularly to Coventry and I was soon disembarking at Coventry station. As expected the train was jam packed with Bluenoses who were also keen to get there early. So off we headed out of the station and after asking directions headed in the general direction instructed whilst also following the majority of Bluenoses who were also heading towards the ground. We had a nice walk by a park and it was so warm that I had taken my cardigan off and carried in over my arm. Somehow, however, I managed to lose it by the time I had gotten back to the station after the game! I loved that cardigan too.

We found the ground okay and it looked quite nice from outside with lots of early Bluenoses milling around drinking beer from cans. With that idea in mind we headed for the nearest off licence and obtained some cans before heading

76

back to the ground and consuming them sitting in the sunshine outside watching more fans arrive for the game. As kick off approached we paid our money and squeezed through the turnstiles into the ground. I bought a programme, which cost me thirty pence, and it was a nice colourful programme with Sky Blue v Birmingham City across the front cover. It had a picture of a Coventry player in the sky blue kit that had the black and white lines running down each side of the front of the kit into the shorts. I bet a lot of people remember that kit, I do. I think it was the kit they had on when I went to my very first game a few years back. There was an advertisement inside the programme for the new madness album called 'absolutely madness'. I wonder how many people remember that?

Inside the away fans were on the terracing behind the goal up to and on the corner and as the end had no roof on we were basking in the sun. I quite liked Coventry's ground, Highfield Road, it had a bit of character, and despite no roof the Blues fans singing rang out loud and clear. However, despite Alan Curbishley scoring for Blues we lost the game 2-1. It didn't stop us singing though and we poured out of the ground at the final whistle and headed back to the station down but not out. We still had lots to play for.

The most memorable of my trips to Highfield Road came on the last game of the season on the 15th May 1982 and it was a day that would stay long in my memory. There was only one result that could keep us in the first division, and that was a win. Anything less and Blues would be relegated. No pressure then!

It was a lovely sunny day when we headed off to get the train to Coventry, and there were Blues fans everywhere when we disembarked at Coventry Station. It was really hot, and everyone, me included were in football shirts with our arms bared to the sun. It was a lovely walk up to the ground where we obtained beers and sat on walls outside drinking them before it was time to head inside the ground. This time I was sitting in the seats with the Blues fans to the side of the goal and there were 5000 Blues fans inside the ground (not counting the ones in the home sections).

The atmosphere was electric with excitement and of course, fear of relegation. It was bloody nerve wracking. I was so nervous that I felt sick, but we sang our hearts out and 'Keep Right On' could be heard for miles. It was a party atmosphere as the players ran out onto the pitch, with Blues playing in their away colours of Yellow shirts, black shorts and black socks. There were balloons and cheering as Blues fans wanted to enjoy the occasion as much as possible and we hoped it wouldn't be our last in the first division.

The match got underway and as time ticked on without a goal the stress became unbearable. My stomach was in knots, as I am sure was the case with all the other Bluenoses who refused to sit down and stood for the entire game. Time was ticking by and with about five minutes left on the clock it was beginning to sink in that we were about to be relegated. I felt sick. The fans were beginning to get a bit subdued but we kept singing in the hope that a miracle could happen and save us. Just as the tears were beginning to form in my eyes, the ball was crossed into the Coventry penalty area right in front of us and the big yellow and black shape of Mick Harford rose to meet it and the net bulged – GOAL!!!!!!!

Unbelievable! The crowd went wild, the noise was incredible and as Mick Harford was mobbed by yellow shirts on his way over to the crowd, the Blues fans were over the hoardings and onto the pitch to celebrate. Only those of us that were there that day can truly know the depth of our feelings. We went mad, jumping on strangers, climbing over seats to get onto the pitch and crying with relief. It took a while to clear the pitch for the game to restart, but there were only seconds remaining. We had to be safe. With Blues fans all around the edges of the pitch at our end, the game managed to restart but before long the final whistle went, 1-0! The Blues end erupted!

It was like a home game and we invaded Coventry's pitch in great numbers to celebrate with the players. No one could keep us off and I am sure nobody really cared as we were celebrating in style. I could not believe it, one minute I had thought we were down and the next we were saved, what a feeling. It felt like we had won a championship. The players were carried to the tunnel shoulder high by the Bluenoses, and they looked just as happy as we felt! It was such a beautiful sunny day and it will be engraved in my mind forever. What a fantastic day! This was one of the many 'Joys' that I have experienced being a Bluenose.

Birmingham finished in 16th position in division one and meant that we would be looking forward to playing in the first division again come August. I was relieved and happy and convinced that we could do much better next season.

My next two trips in April 1983 and March 1984 also ended in 1-0 wins to Blues. Great stuff! I saw 2 defeats with one of them taking place on my birthday on 24th January 1982 in the FA Cup 4th round as Coventry ended my dreams for another year with a 3-2 loss. It was mostly good memories though especially the great escape in 1982. Overall I saw 5 matches at Highfield Road with 3 victories (1982, 1984 & 1985) and just 2 defeats.

Highfield Road became Englands first all seater stadium in 1981 but months later Leeds fans ripped hundreds of seats out and in 1983 Coventry returned some standing. In 1989 it became an all seater stadium once again following the Hillsborough report. Highfield Road saw it's last game played in April 2005 and was demolished in 2006. It is now a housing estate with just a plaque to commemorate where it once stood.

Ground 19 – Anfield – 2nd December 1980 – League Cup ¼ Final – Liverpool 3 Birmingham City 1

My boyfriend Graham had decided that he would drive us up to Anfield for my first game there as he had also got cup fever and wanted to see the game. He still had his spitfire sports car, which meant that only the two of us could go as it only had two seats. The game was on Tuesday night, 2nd December and Graham picked me up from work early and we took the country roads up to Liverpool, not the motorway, so that we could stop somewhere nice on the way up. We arrived in Liverpool with time to spare and parked the car on the middle section of the duel carriageway not far from the away end, just next to Stanley Park. Lots of cars were already parked up on this grass section so we figured (wrongly I add) that it would be okay to park here too.

So, with the car parked we headed to the pub on the corner, near the Anfield Road end of the ground, called The Arckles. Inside the pub there were Bluenoses and Liverpool fans and everyone seemed to mix okay and the atmosphere was friendly, even though it was the Blues fans who were singing quite loudly. We had a few drinks and then headed across the road and into the away end. Blues had half of the Anfield Road terracing behind the goal, with fencing, half way along separating us from the Liverpool fans.

The atmosphere was fantastic and the ground was packed. Thousands of Blues had made the trip amongst the 30,236 that were inside that day and they sang their hearts out. There was a lot of rivalry between the supporters inside the ground and a few missiles flew backwards and forwards between the two lots of supporters in the Anfield Road end.

We were standing near a crash barrier and a girder that supported the roof, and at one point a bottle that had been thrown our way hit the girder and smashed and some of the glass fell onto us. When I put my hand to my head there was a bit of blood, but not too much to worry me or make me miss the game! Liverpool seemed to be getting hit just as hard though and a few casualties were taken out of the crowd and led away. One person from the Liverpool contingent had to be carried on a stretcher high above the heads of the crowd and passed over the iron fences onto the pitch to the sound of 'one-nil' from the Blues lot. It was packed on the terraces and the fans swayed and sang, it was great.

Blues went into the game with the incentive of knowing that we were the last team to beat Liverpool on their own ground. It turned out to be a really good game but we were to rue our missed chances as Liverpool took theirs and were rather lucky to beat us 3-1. I took heart from our performance as I really felt that we were robbed and should have come away with a win. Liverpool looked relieved to snatch the third, just five minutes from time. The Bluenoses were not dejected due to the fact that we had played so well, and totally out sang the Kop. Blues had even sang 'where's your famous Kop?' and 'you're supposed to be at home'.

Graham and I headed back across the road and back into the pub for a quick drink before we headed back, and to allow the traffic to die down a bit. We got talking to some Liverpool fans who were quite honest with us and said that they thought they were lucky to beat us and that we were the better team on the day. I found their honesty quite refreshing and remember it to this day. Their fans went up in my estimation that day. Their keeper Ray Clemence had made some first class saves and it was good to see that the Merseyside press praised Blues performance and admitted that we gave Liverpool a fright. In the team talk in the following home programme at St. Andrews the manager Jim Smith, praised the marvellous following of Blues supporters who encouraged the team and were a credit to the club.

After a couple of drinks we headed back to the car only to find that the local constabulary had put a bloody parking ticked on our car plus several other cars that had been parked on the grass. I am convinced it was only the away fans that got the tickets though! There was no sign saying you couldn't park there. Oh well, that just about completed our night so we set off home to Birmingham out of the cup but proud of our performance.

In 1995 I lived in Liverpool and I had arranged to meet Julie before the FA Cup replay as she was travelling up for the match amongst the 9,000 other Bluenoses that had tickets. I didn't live far from Anfield, so we walked from mine to the Arkles pub by the away end. There were Blues fans everywhere and the atmosphere was brilliant. Once inside Anfield the atmosphere was electric and Blues had the whole of the Anfield Road Stand behind the goal and half of the Kemlyn Road Stand along the side of the pitch. It was an amazing sight with so much of Anfield being a sea of Blue and White. All the singing was coming from the Bluenoses and I must admit feeling a lump in my throat. I was so proud to be a Birmingham City fan that day inside Liverpool's ground as we out-sang our Premiership opposition.

There were 9,000 Blues fans amongst the 36,275 inside the ground and when the teams ran out onto the pitch there was an almighty roar to meet them. Once the match got underway Blues gave a good account of themselves and were not about to become pushovers as Alan Hanson had suggested after the game at St. Andrews. It was really quite amusing as the 9,000 Bluenoses gave many loud renditions of 'Alan Hanson – what a wanker, what a wanker!' I remember he said after the game that he would never make comments like that again! It was sang really really loud and must have been heard on live TV!

Blues went behind somewhat unfortunately to a deflected shot before half time and I must admit we felt a bit hard done by. Mind you, we were two divisions below our mighty opponents! The second half got under way and the Bluenoses continued to sing our hearts out for our lads. Then an amazing thing happened right in front of us. Ricky Otto got the ball and from just outside the penalty area he curled a wonderful shot into the top corner of the Liverpool goal! The Blues end of the ground erupted.

It was a brilliant goal and we were in heaven! As the stunned Liverpool fans looked on Blues fans took the roof off the stadium with our wild celebrations. All those Bluenoses that were there that day will remember that feeling as the ball hit the back of the net - forever. What a night. The game went to extra time and then finished 1-1 meaning penalties. It also meant that Alan Hanson would have to eat his words!

Blues, however, have a terrible record when it comes to penalty shoot out's having lost many important games in the dreaded penalty shoot out in the past. The run continued as all of our players missed their penalties and although a couple of the Liverpool players also missed, Blues went out of the FA Cup losing 2-0 on penalties. I was determined not to be disheartened though, especially as Blues had given a good account of themselves against Premiership opposition two divisions above them. After all, Liverpool had failed to beat us home and away during both games.

We had quite a journey when we visited Anfield in 2007 when I travelled with Annette and Steve by train. When we arrived at Lime Street Station Steve had decided that we should get the soccer bus that ran directly to the ground as he said it would be the only way we could get back after the game, so we got a local train to Sandhills station and headed for the soccer bus. I must admit I did not enjoy this part of the journey one bit, as it was not much fun being the only person on a Liverpool football special bus with a Blues shirt on I can tell you! It didn't help much when Steve's phone rang and he chatted away loudly with a broad Brummie accent. Annette and Stephen had been pretending they didn't know me at this point and now we all pretended we didn't know Steve!

I had already obtained my programme for the game whilst queuing to board the soccer bus, and we soon got off the bus by Stanley Park and headed for the Blue House on Steve's instructions. As we were walking past a pub full of Liverpool fans called the Abbey, Steve saw two of his mates Craig and Graham, who informed him that the Blue House was closed so we went into the Abbey for a pre match drink or two with them. As this was one of Liverpool's main pubs I don't think the Liverpool fans were too impressed by having us gate crashing their party in a Blues shirt, but I lived to tell the tale. It was full of Reds with not a single Bluenose in sight, not a comfortable place to be for me really. I downed a few pints though and was comforted by the fact that I was next to the door should a quick exit be required!

I had to laugh when Craig and Graham went to the bar and ordered two 'wicked's' and the barmaid asked red or blue? The pub went quiet as everyone awaited their reply and I thought ooooh! Especially when they answered Blue!

At twenty to three we left the pub and headed through Stanley Park towards the Anfield road stand where we had tickets for the away section. There was still loads of people milling around outside and we headed through the turnstiles and into the ground. Our seats were great, they were right at the front in row two and we had a great view. The sun had come out as well, and the Bluenoses were in full voice. 'Keep Right On' rang out loud and proud as always. The Liverpool fans were silent and remained so for most of the game, only singing once. Blues were singing 'it's just like being in church'.

As always the Bluenoses created the atmosphere and it was quite funny when they began singing 'you're on a day trip from Belfast' to the scousers. We also sang 'sign on, sign on, with pen in your hand and you'll never work again!' to the tune of you'll never walk alone, several times quite loudly.

The game kicked off and we all got quite excited. Especially when the ball came flying in the direction of my face, very fast, but luckily hit the edge of the boarding just missing the head of a steward who jumped a mile! He recovered quite quickly and with a smile I said 'I nearly shit myself then!' Stephen, who was sitting next to me had also ducked and laughed before admitting that he nearly shit himself too.

Blues were playing quite well in defense and when a Liverpool player blasted over the fans sang 'fucking useless!' They also sang, 'we'd forgot that you were here' when the scousers finally sang. There were also several renditions of 'shit on the villa' and when Liverpool finally bought on their expensive signing Torres, all the Blues fans sang 'who are ya? Who are ya?'. Even the stewards smiled at that. The Blues fans certainly kept the stewards busy, and they had to move into the crowd a few times, you could see from their faces that they wished they had avoided this shift! The Blues fans sang 'get a proper job, get a proper job' to the tune of where's your mamma gone. We had a laugh at half time as my sister and I headed to the toilets. We were both singing 'I hate villa more that you!' to each other from adjoining cubicles.

The Blues did really well, and if McSheffrey had done better when we caught them on the break, we may even have snatched a win, but a draw was an excellent result. Liverpool had never beaten us in the premier league under Rafa Benitez. We had a good recent record against the scousers and we were jubilant when the final whistle went. Blues broke into a chorus of 'were gonna win the league, were gonna win the league, and now you're gonna believe us!' Quality! The players came over to applaud the Bluenoses and we rewarded them with a loud rendition of Keep Right On and applauded our players for their effort.

It was great leaving the ground as all the Bluenoses were still singing loudly and all appeared in good spirits. We headed in the opposite direction to the other bluenoses towards the soccer special back to Sandhills to get the train back. There was a queue for the soccer bus back to town and we joined the end, I promptly zipped up my jacket in the hope of avoiding getting my head kicked in. Before long we were on the bus and we sat quietly until we arrived at

Sandhills station where we boarded the local train back to Liverpool Central station.

Once back in Liverpool Central we wandered outside as we couldn't decide whether to eat in Liverpool or carry on to Chester to eat. As we left the station two Blues fans ran past us singing 'sign on, sign on, with pen in your hand and you'll never work again!' They were laughing but I'm not sure if they were just having a laugh or running from scousers – it was really funny anyway. We had a bit of a laugh at that before deciding that we were better heading back to Chester for food, because at least we would have got the worst train journey over with and could relax a little bit.

We returned back to Central station and boarded the train to Chester via about two hundred stops! Forty minutes later we arrived in Chester station and after zipping up my jacket and hiding my shirt, we left the station and went into the Town Crier pub across the road from the station. The pub had filled up since we had left and there was now a hen night partying in there. Never mind, we ordered food and beer and sat down to enjoy our visit. It was quite busy in there now, and after enjoying our food we drank up and headed back to the station to catch the train back to Crewe. The train arrived shortly and we boarded.

Before long we were back in Crewe and after asking the staff we were informed that the train to Birmingham was not for another 45 minutes, so off we headed out of the station to try to find a supply of alcohol for the rest of the journey. Once we had replenished our stocks from the local garage, we headed back to the station where there were now lots of Bluenoses waiting to get the train back to Brum. One bloke was asleep on a bench in a bizarre position and lots of Bluenoses were taking pictures on their mobile phones and laughing. I had to laugh when someone said 'that's how Blues fans get a bad name!'

It wasn't long before the train pulled up at the platform and we pilled on board. The journey was brilliant and the singing and drinking began in earnest. Both ends of the carriage were singing 'we hate villa more that you!' to each other as well as doing a few renditions of Keep Right on. The lads sang quite a few funny songs that I had not heard before including a song about Liam Ridgewell and a song about Steve Bruce being a Zulu.

Suddenly the train stopped and one of the fans standing was bashed against the wall. Next thing we knew the driver appeared and asked 'did one of you lot pull the cord?' to which the reply was 'I don't even know where the fucker is!' We all laughed as the driver pointed out where it was. 'I know where it is next time then' was the reply. Someone said 'that's it, blame the football supporters!' I don't know who pulled the cord but it wasn't anyone in our carriage.

As we journeyed on someone pointed out that we were about to pass through Wolverhampton and instantaneously a chorus of 'always shit on the old gold and black' to the tune of always look on the bright side of life, broke out. It was really funny. As the train pulled into New Street station, Keep Right On was belted out at full volume to announce our arrival and it sounded brilliant.

We disembarked and as we all headed up the stairs into the Station everyone started singing 'were Birmingham, were Birmingham, were Birmingham City!' really loud and it echoed around the station, alerting the waiting police, amongst others, that the Blues were back in town. All those in the local station pub looked around and the police arrived from everywhere to make sure we left peacefully. It had been a great day and a great result and as we headed for a taxi back home I contemplated the adventure I had just been on. 9 hours of traveling, 8 trains, 2 soccer special buses full of scousers – what a day! Next time I vowed to take the direct route and not the long way round! I think we all went home happy.

I visited Anfield a lot during my time living in Liverpool but with Birmingham City I vis 8 times seeing 5 defeats and 3 draws. My worst trip was a 5-0 defeat in 1986 and the most enjoyable was probably the 2-2 draw in 1981.

Ground 20 – Elland Road – 26th December 1980 – Leeds United 0 Birmingham City 0 – First Division

My first trip to Elland Road was on Boxing Day in 1980 and we traveled on the football special train on a cold winters day. I remember standing on the terrace to the side of the pitch and the Bluenoses were in good numbers and good voice. There was a lot of banter between the two sets of fans and the game was entertaining but finished goalless. I enjoyed the trip though and we made it back to the station safely too.

It was off to Elland Road to take on Leeds Utd on a cold December day in 1984. Leeds fans had quite a reputation at this time, not unlike our own supporters so it was always going to be billed as being a bit of a battle between the supporters of both teams. However, we decided to brave the football special, which was extremely lively, and it was a very enjoyable trip to Leeds. We didn't know whether it was safer to stay with the police escort, with the risk of ambush or whether to try and slip away, which was also risky as we had on Blues colours and would be alone. Anyway, we decided to stay with the escort, and after a couple of attempted ambushes with Blues running at the approaching Leeds fans, the police prevailed and we arrived safely at the ground.

It was a bit of a misty day though and once inside the ground the view across the pitch was obstructed somewhat by the fog. It was difficult to see the other goal (we were situated along the side towards one end) and it was only when I saw the Blues player's running back towards us with their arms in the air that we realised that we had scored! Wayne Clarke scored the only goal of the game and we came away with a good 1-0 away win. During the game someone in the Blues end shot a flare right into the middle of the main Leeds end and their fans scattered in panic, much to the amusement of the Blues contingent. The police came into our end in an attempt to find the flare gun but to no avail, the Leeds fans, however, where now very annoyed and threatening to get us outside. It didn't help that the Blues fans just laughed and gestured back to them to have a go!

After the game the police kept us locked inside for a while in the hope that the Leeds fans would go home and we could safely be taken back to our train. Or was it for the Leeds fans safety? Anyway, before too long we were led out and back to the station where we were hoarded onto the special to make our trip home. However, various scuffles kept breaking out and the train would start up only to travel for a couple of minutes before the cord was pulled and it would stop again. It took over an hour just to get out of Leeds! I think a couple of windows were broken and everyone was pretty fed up by the time we finally got our journey under way properly! Once we were underway though, the Blues fans continued our celebrations and sang and chatted all the way back to Birmingham.

In February 1996 Thousands of Bluenoses made the trip to Leeds for the League Cup Semifinal second leg and the away end was packed. I must admit the new stand at Leeds looked very impressive and was so big. There were 35,435 inside Elland Road and the atmosphere amongst both sets of supporters was fantastic. The Bluenoses never stopped singing throughout the game despite going down 3-0. Our players did put up a fight and I think the scoreline somewhat flattered Leeds.

We already knew that the other finalists would be Villa and we had been desperate to meet the old enemy at Wembley. However, once we knew this dream had slipped away the Blues fans belted out 'we hope you the beat the villa!' to the Leeds fans who in turn applauded us loudly all round the ground. Bluenoses then broke into a rendition of 'shit on the villa' which the Leeds fans also joined in and soon the entire stadium were singing 'shit on the villa'. I must admit it sounded brilliant with both Blues and Leeds fans singing it at full blast. It gave me a right laugh despite heading home disappointed.

In October 2015 the trip up north was enjoyable but I couldn't believe how run down Elland Road had become. It looked really old and worn. We were right outside the away end and I headed to the programme booth to purchase my match day program. I got chatting to a Leeds fan who said he liked what we had done with our badge (club crest) for this season. It was done to celebrate

140 years. I agreed with him that it was very impressive but that I hoped it really was only for this season as we all love our ball and world club crest. In fact our normal badge had gained a place in the list of the top twenty most easily recognised football club crests in the world.

The football federation supporters trust had planned a national protest today about away ticket prices. It was known as 'Twenty's Plenty' in a bid to make all clubs charge a maximum of twenty pounds for away fans. This is because of the extra cost incurred traveling to away games and the increasing cost of the Match ticket. In fact today's ticket had cost £35!

Linda (from the Birmingham City supporters club) had been sent a massive banner from the federation which read 'BCFC FANS SAY TWENTY'S PLENTY' and we were due to meet Leeds fans by the Billy Bremner statue for the protest.

We arrived early clad in our Blues shirts and I obtained a Leeds badge for my collection whilst we waited for the Leeds fans and their banner, although they were currently in the pub while we waited for them, it was soon retrieved though and we all United for the protest as loads of people took photos of us. The press had arranged to be there although amazingly there was no mention of the protest afterwards. With all the money involved in the Premier League and Championship I suppose it's not surprising the football clubs wanted it kept quiet. In fact Leeds would not allow the banners to be taken into the stadium and Linda had to return it to the coach before we headed into the ground for the game.

The atmosphere in the Birmingham section was loud and proud and we were all in good voice as usual. There was some great banter with the Leeds fans. There was the usual 'Keep Right On' and also 'we all hate Leeds, Leeds, we all hate Leeds, Leeds'.

The Jimmy Saville song was a new song for me though as the Bluenoses sang 'he's one of your own, he's one of your own, Jimmy Saville, he's one of your own!' I had to laugh a bit later when the Leeds fans sang 'he's coming for you, Jimmy Saville, he's coming for you'. Demari Gray then scored a cracker to put Birmingham 1-0 up and the celebrations in the Blues end were chaotic. 'We're Birmingham, we're Birmingham' rang out loudly. The Bluenoses were on form and when they sang 'you're not famous anymore!' the Leeds fans looked extremely unhappy.

As the game headed into the 90th minute Leeds were desperate to get an equaliser but Blues got the ball to Maghoma who smashed the ball into the Leeds net. 2-0! Mayhem broke out in the away end as the celebrations began in earnest. Meanwhile Maghoma had ran to the Blues end only for the Leeds fans to throw missiles at the celebrating Blues players. To the players credit though they ignored this and continued their celebrations. What a great away win! At the end of the game the players came over to applaud the Blues fans and we sang our hearts out in response. Back to the coaches and a pretty enjoyable trip home. Birmingham were sitting in fourth place in the League table. Happy times.

In September 2018 we were off to Leeds as Blues took on top of the table and unbeaten Leeds Utd. Despite Leeds charging an extortionate £37 Blues had filled the away section and were in good voice. There was some great banter going on between the Bluenoses and the Leeds fans. There were over 34,000 in the Stadium and Blues manager Garry Monk was returning to face one of his old teams.

The game kicked off with Blues playing in our fabulous Yellow away shirts and on 8 minutes Che Adams fired in a shot to put Blues 1-0 ahead and the away end erupted! It left the home fans stunned and we belted out Keep Right On. It got even better on 29 Minutes when Che Adams hit another shot from the edge of the penalty area which found its way into the far corner and it was now 2-0 Blues and unbelievable celebrations in the away end!

Blues fans started singing 'Leeds, Leeds are falling apart again!' and we were all enjoying ourselves although I was still a bit too apprehensive to think we could hang on and get our first win of the season and inflict Leeds first defeat. The singing and banter was brilliant although the Leeds fans were somewhat subdued now. They were giving Garry Monk lots of abuse as was to be expected as he had managed them. I didn't want half time to come as I wasn't convinced we would play as well in the second half.

The second half got underway and Leeds were really physical although Blues held firm until the 85th minute when Leeds got a goal back and proceeded to lay siege to the Blues goal. It seemed that the referee wanted to continue play until Leeds got level as he added 7 minutes of injury time but actually played 8 minutes! Blues held firm though and Goalkeeper Lee Camp pulled off a great save to preserve our lead and the away end erupted when the referee was forced to blow for full time. What a fantastic away win! We had great fun with the departing Leeds fans as we held our scarves aloft and sang 'Leeds, Leeds are falling apart again'. The singing continued as we made our way out of the stadium and back to the coaches. What a great away day and I was really happy on the journey back to Birmingham.

Over time I visited Elland Road on 9 occasions from 1980 to this year – 2024 and I had seen both ups and downs including the recent 3-0 defeat that saw a section of the Blues 'fans' calling for and getting the sacking of manager Wayne Rooney. I had seen 4 wins, 2 draws and 3 defeats. Not at all bad really.

Ground 21 - Roker Park – 7th January 1981 – FA Cup 3rd Round Replay – Sunderland 1 Birmingham City 2

I had seen a bit more of the other girls we met at the Manchester City game, Julie and Debbie. It was on the supporter's coach that we booked for the FA Cup 3rd round replay in Sunderland on 7th January 1981 that all four of us travelled together, probably for the first time. We set off early due to the distance and when we arrived in Sunderland, the coach parked up not far from a beach. It looked nice, and had a small fair but it was a bit cold to be honest. We didn't care though, because we were so excited about the upcoming cup match.

The ground was okay and had a lot of character about it. It had a good feel about it. The Blues fans were on the terracing behind the goal next to the Sunderland fans, who were in good voice for the cup-tie and all around us was a sea of red and white. Our end however, was a sea of blue and white and as usual we were in very good voice singing 'Wembley, Wembley!' at the top of our voices. Once the match got underway the atmosphere was electric and just fewer than 30,000 witnessed a great game.

Keith Bertschin and Tony Evans scored for Blues and we won 2-1 to set up celebrations for the travelling Bluenoses despite the fact that it was very late and we were knackered. We were through to the fourth round of the FA Cup. And boy, did we celebrate! The coaches were extremely lively on the trip back to Birmingham! We already knew who we would be playing in the next round as the draw had been made and we were relishing a local derby away at Coventry City in round four.

Blues were back at Roker Park in the FA Cup for a 4th Round tie in January 1984, just a few days after my 22nd birthday. When the day of the game came round, I was really excited and I was really nervous on the coach journey up north. After a long trip we arrived in Sunderland and parked up near the beach and headed off towards the ground for the game. The Blues fans were situated on the corner behind the goal and it was packed with Bluenoses who were in extremely good voice. The terracing was swaying back and forth and scarves were being waved as 'Wembley! Wembley!' was being sang. Even when Sunderland took the lead the Blues contingent continued to sing, and 'Keep Right On' was belted out loudly. It was the Sunderland supporters who were now singing 'Wembley' and taunting us with 'were going to Wembley, you're not, you're not'.

As the game drew towards the end I began to resign myself to the fact that we were about to go out of the cup whilst being taunted by the Sunderland fans at the same time. The girls were also feeling the same way, but then in the 89th minute as Blues were throwing everything at Sunderland and attacking the goal in front of the travelling Bluenoses, the ball broke in the box and Martin Khul hammered it home! Unbelievable, the fans went absolutely wild and surged forward like a giant wave. I was swept forward in the mayhem, whilst jumping around madly myself and jumping on everyone around us in celebration. I couldn't believe it; we were going to get a replay at St. Andrews, because surely there was not time for Sunderland to reply.

Just as I was back on my feet again I looked up to see the ball being crossed into the area again and Mick Harford got on the end of it and powered it into the back of the net! Yesssss! 2-1 in the 90th minute! The Blues end erupted and once again I was swept off my feet. Within seconds the Sunderland fans that had been taunting us a minute ago were silenced and Blues fans began returning the favour by singing 'we're going to Wembley, you're not, you're not!' It was unbelievable to be thinking, we're out one minute, we have a replay next, then – we have won – we are through! What a feeling, one of the best I have had I think.

It was a fantastic celebration on the way back, we sang the whole way, including at our invasion of the service station at our stop off. Service station stops were always fun due to the fact that you often met up with various other sets of supporters and there was often some banter to be had. As always I began thinking that this could be our year! It wasn't.

Another trip to Roker Park in April 1984 also springs to mind for its part in another relegation battle. With just four games to go we really did need a miracle but we had started looking at those above us in the table and Swansea had replaced us at the foot of the table with Brighton just below us.

Although the odds were stacked against us we not giving up and we travelled up to Sunderland for our next match with a mixture of excitement and fear. We travelled up on the supporter's club coach and parked up by the beach. It was a bit cold but at least it wasn't raining and we soon disembarked and headed past the fair and on to Roker Park. I know Roker Park was supposed to be famous for its atmosphere but it seemed to me that the Bluenoses created the atmosphere that day. Even after twenty minutes when we fell behind we still sang our hearts out and kept the faith. After all, we still had the late show to look forward to.

In the 82nd minute we were rewarded with a penalty and up stepped Noel Blake to rifle the ball into the net to send the Blues contingent into wild celebrations. 1-1 and we were in with a chance. We could hardly believe our eyes when Mick Hartford scored our winner – once again in the 88th minute! Unbelievable, three matches on the trot now that were all won with goals in the 88th minute! The Blues fans were jumping all over each other. We were all celebrating like lunatics in the hope that perhaps a miracle could in fact happen! The coach was buzzing with atmosphere all the way home and 'staying up, staying up, staying up' rang out loudly on the journey home. Happily we did stay up.

I really did enjoy my trips to Roker Park as it was a nice ground with bags of character and good old fashioned atmosphere. I visited on 6 occasions between 1981 and 1986 and I saw 3 wins and 3 defeats with the victories being extremely memorable.

Sunderland's last season at Roker Park was 1996-97 which was also their first ever season in the Premier and they were relegated at the end of the season and moved to the Stadium of Light in 1997. Roker Park was demolished in 1997 and 2 pieces of the Leitch's balcony truss are on display at The Stadium of Light. The area is now a housing estate.

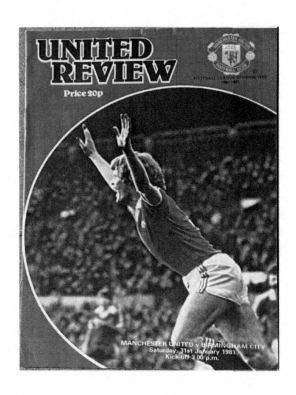

Ground 22 – Old Trafford – 31st January 1981 – Division One – Manchester United 2 Birmingham City 0 – First Division

I was heading off to Manchester for my first visit to Old Trafford, the home of the mighty Manchester United in January 1981. The football special was packed and everyone was on good form, singing, chatting and drinking beers all the way to Manchester. The banter was great and everyone was looking forward to the game and a few beers in the city. Unfortunately, most of us didn't get a few beers as we were met by the local plod at the train station and marched to the ground.

Old Trafford looked very impressive from the outside and we decided to have a wander around to see what their end was like. It was soon made clear that this was not the best idea we had ever had when someone barged into Pam. Due to the fact that we were heavily outnumbered we quickly heading back to our end and the girls soon followed. We did witness the arrival of the team coach however, and as Brian Robson got off, I have to say it was like being at a pop concert as loads of girls were screaming at him! What on earth was that all that about?!

Inside the ground it was very impressive. The away end terrace was behind the goal and it was jam packed with Blues fans by the time kick off approached. The Manchester United fans to our left were separated by a section of empty terrace and fencing and they were trying to incite us by waving 'Brummie Reds' banners. Personally, I thought this was something to be ashamed of rather that flaunting it in such a manner! As kick off approached the Manchester United team came running out of the tunnel onto the pitch and they were met by a really loud rendition of 'who the fucking hell are you' from the Bluenoses. We all found this really funny as we had only just been promoted to the first division and Man Utd were a well-known top team. It was one of those moments in football that you never forget. Priceless!

There were 39,081 inside Old Trafford, but from all the singing you would have thought that it was Blues who were at home. It was great; we sang our hearts out for the entire game despite losing 2-0. Our players came over and applauded our efforts and we applauded theirs in return. The Blues end was packed and everyone headed towards the exits, which were at the end of a concrete tunnel leading away from the terrace and underneath the stand at the back of us.

However, the gates had not been opened and a crush developed in the tunnel with those at the back unaware and still trying to push to get out. I was getting crushed and couldn't breathe then everything went black. Next thing I remember I was lying back on the terracing inside the ground with a policeman who appeared rather worried and he helped me back to my feet. Luckily he had seen me as I was about to slump down and he had been able to get to me and get me back into the ground. What a horrible feeling it had been getting crushed and I was haunted by it for quite a while. It didn't put me off going to games in future though.

As we were making our way back towards the local station a large gang of Man Utd fans came running towards us and chased us towards station. As we ran down the stairs in the station there was one of those old trains, with loads of doors all along the carriages, waiting on the platform. We had been getting a bit worried because it seemed like we were cornered by a much bigger group than us, but then all the doors of the train opened and hundreds of Blues poured off and piled into the Man Utd fans causing most of them to leg it out of the station.

Brilliant! That was a close call. The rest of the trip home was uneventful, but even in defeat we sang and enjoyed the trip. Another great day out following our beloved Blues.

In January 2011 just two days before my birthday I was off to Manchester for our game against Manchester United and I hadn't been to Old Trafford for many years. We traveled up in plenty of time and we were soon settled in a pub called the Quadrant enjoying a pre match drink. It was funny really as a few different people came over to me to ask about my book (Truly Blue) which had just been published. Steve then went about leaving my book 'cards' around the pub. I had a bet at 8 to 1 for Blues to win! We set off to the stadium and it was amazing to see all the changes since my last visit in 1986(I think it had terraces last time I visited) and there was merchandise sellers everywhere.

Once inside the Blues end was packed and in full voice. I was quite shocked as to how quiet the home fans were though. We didn't hear a word from them for the entire time. It was a painful 90 minutes but it was Blues who sang throughout. The usual songs were belted out as well as some amusing ones such as 'your just a ground full of tourists' and 'we support our local team'.

Many United fans had green and yellow scarves which was apparently a protest against their American owner (yes I didn't get it either) and we sang 'are you Norwich in disguise?' and 'Norwich, Norwich give us a song'. We had loads of fun despite the actual game of football as we lost 5-0. It didn't stop us singing and winding up the silent Manchester United fans. '5-0 and you still don't sing' and 'shall we sing a song for you?' We also sang 'we'll see you on the motorway!' Then it was back to the Quadrant for a post match drink while we waited for the traffic to die down.

It was unbelievable that 3,000 Blues fans could out sing 72,000 Manchester United fans. I would hate it if Blues ever became a club like that with thousands coming from other parts of the country and being a tourist attraction. It was a bad defeat for Blues but it wasn't helped that we didn't play Gardener, Jerome and Zigic because of the League Cup semi final being only 4 days away. It was a very different team than the one which had drawn 1-1 with them just 4 weeks ago.

I had a great trip to Old Trafford to watch England Women play in the Euros in July 2022 for the opening game of the tournament which was being staged in England.

The 'European Tour' that we had been planning for ages was finally upon us and Harry, June and myself set off for Manchester on a nice sunny Wednesday morning. We were full of excitement to be off on our travels and we were soon arriving at our Premier Inn in Stockport south where we had booked for our overnight stay. Our rooms would be ready in 30 minutes, we were informed, so we headed into the attached Beefeater for a spot of lunch. A nice way to start our adventures as we enjoyed lunch before checking into our rooms and getting ready for tonight's game.

June and I had bought loads of England gear with us and we were soon dressed in our new England shirts, England wigs, St. George flag tattoos on our face and England capes with 'Come On England' on them. We also had 'England' horns to blow. Harry looked aghast when he saw us but not that surprised as he knows us well by now. By 5pm we were in a taxi on our way to Old Trafford following a photo opportunity with the Premier Inn staff.

It was overcast and really windy when we arrived at Old Trafford and I struggled to keep hold of my cape until we were told by stewards that we had to take it off as it was a flag and it was too big. This was rubbish as, firstly it wasn't a flag, and secondly if it was a flag then it was within the permitted measurements. It wasn't worth the hassle though, so we took it off and set out to find the click and collect to pick up our merchandise.

Amazingly, as we walked around the stadium we saw loads of people wearing capes like ours and flags. Make of that what you want. There were lots of stalls selling unofficial scarves and stuff and I purchased a lovely pink 'England Women' scarf. It was fun walking around the stadium and by the time we had finally found the click and collect and picked up our merchandise it was almost 6.15pm and the players were due to arrive just by where we now found ourselves and so we headed over to wait for their arrival.

There were already loads of people waiting and when the players did arrive everyone stuck their mobiles in the air so that it was virtually impossible to see anything. I did catch the odd glimpse of an England player as they made their way into the stadium though. We then headed towards the donut van where June and I purchased a bag of donuts each and headed into the stadium.

We were in the third tier of the Sir Alex Ferguson stand and boy was it high. I was looking for an oxygen mask by the time we reached level six and it looked like we were only half way up the stairs. We finally arrived at the top gasping for air and immediately headed to the bar for bottles of water. Then it was up to our seats in a scarily steep stand but with a fantastic view of the pitch. The only thing that let it down was the leg room, or should I say lack of leg room. I am only small but my knees would be in the back of the woman in front had she not sat forward for the entire game. God help anyone tall. Considering this is a fairly new addition, I was really surprised by this lack of leg room but then I guess they just want to squeeze as many people in as they can. A sign of the times.

Tonight was the opening game of tournament and the opening ceremony was amazing with loads of fireworks and flames and by the time the players came out they could barely be seen through the coloured smoke that had descended onto the pitch. There were 68, 871 inside Old Trafford and it was a new record for a Women's European match. The atmosphere was great and the noise was tremendous with all the horn blowing. There were loads of families and children which ensured lots of singing, cheering and massive Mexican waves that added to the atmosphere.

England looked nervous to begin with but they took the lead when Beth Mead lobbed the goalkeeper and despite an Austrian defenders attempted clearance via the crossbar it was confirmed by goal line technology and VAR that it was a goal. The stadium erupted in celebration and we got to celebrate again when VAR confirmed it after their goal check. Strange times we live in. I'm not a great fan of VAR to be honest as I think it slows the game down and spoils goal celebrations.

So England were 1-0 up and despite several missed chances and a couple of saves from our goalkeeper, that was how it stayed and we achieved a good opening day victory that put England top of Group A for the time being. We had mistakenly thought that we could walk clear of the stadium and get a taxi. No chance! No taxis available as over 68,871 leaving the stadium ensured that the area was gridlocked and we had to find our way back to Stockport.

All was not lost though as we made our way to the cricket ground nearby and asked a policeman. He sent us to Trafford tram station were we queued with hundreds of others and finally got a tram to Manchester Piccadilly where we got a black cab back to our hotel in Stockport. I was knackered by the time we got back at 00.10 and collapsed into bed. What a great day it had been though.

So far I have made 8 trips to Old Trafford, 1 with England Women and 7 with Birmingham City of which I saw only the 1 win with England and 1 draw and 6 defeats with Blues. I would love to see Blues win there.

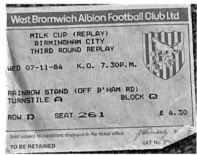

Ground 23 – The Hawthorns – 28th February 1981 – Division One – West Bromwich Albion 2 Birmingham City 2

In February 1981 I was off to neighbours West Bromwich Albion and a venture into the Black Country. I love travelling to away derby games; there is so much banter on the way to and inside the ground. After a few beers we arrived at the ground which seemed to be swarming with Blues fans. I couldn't see many West Brom fans and we headed through the wasteland area towards the away end of the ground. Blues had the entire end and it was highly charged inside. The atmosphere was great and I loved the away terrace as well as West Brom's terraced end behind the goal opposite of us.

The usual derby songs were being sang, including our version of 'I do like to be beside the seaside' which ends with 'fuck off West Brom!' being echoed around the ground. Both sets of supporters were up for the game. It was great when Keep Right On was belted out from a passionate away following. It was a pulsating game too, with Alan Ainscow again scoring and Frank Worthington also scoring to send the Blues contingent into raptures as we came away with a 2-2 draw. I have always wondered how the West Brom fans get home because although their end of the ground empties, you never saw any of them outside. Where did they get to? It was always the same. It is a ground I enjoy visiting whenever Blues play there.

The last game that I was due to attend before the pandemic struck was away at the Hawthorn's and we had planned to meet in town for a drink before heading over to West Bromwich by tram. Sadly that was curtailed just a few days beforehand as the county went into lockdown due to the COVID pandemic and my ticket was to remain unused as the football season came to a sudden halt.

My favourite trip was my recently in September 2022 when I travelled across the city for a televised night game. This time we had booked to travel on the official coaches as we had so much trouble getting home last year when we went by train and tram. It was the four of us who travelled on coach one as there was only one coach going and we were soon at the Hawthorns in plenty of time unlike many others who were stuck in traffic and the kick off had to be delayed. June and I both had pork and stuffing baps outside the ground before heading into the away end where Nigel and I had a cider whilst the others had hot drinks and food. We met Taff inside and we were all looking forward to the game.

The atmosphere was brilliant and the Bluenoses were in great voice as usual. There was plenty of banter between us and the nearby yam yams (Albion fans). Before the kickoff there was a minutes silence in memory of our late Queen Elizabeth the second and it was deeply observed as we were all lost in our thoughts. This was followed by the loudest rendition of the National anthem that I have ever heard as the entire stadium united to sing 'God Save The King' and it sent shivers down my spine, it was extremely moving.

The game got underway and Blues looked good and we took the lead on 14 minutes when Scott Hogan scored and the away end went crazy. We jumped around like mad and taunted the home fans with glee having been on the other on of it last season. Blues were singing constantly and along with keep right on and a few derogatory Albion songs the song of choice seemed to be the new 'Bacuna' one to the tune of 'tequila'.

Albion were gifted the equaliser on 23 minutes when a defensive mistake allowed Jed Wallace to score past Ruddy and the home fans woke up again. We weren't disheartened though and continued to sing throughout. The teams went into the halftime break level at 1-1. The second half saw West Brom coming at Blues a bit more but an amazing move saw Bacuna hit a fantastic ball that curled around the West Brom defenders to the onrushing Scott Hogan who fired a great shot in off the post to make it 2-1 to Blues and the away end exploded in celebration as Scotty and the players ran to celebrate in front of us. It was brilliant!

We were in great voice and the players seemed to respond to it. With 71 minutes on the clock Scott Hogan was fed the ball on the wing and cut into the penalty box before deciding to try his luck from a tight angle and the ball flew into the new for his hat trick and it was 3-1 with the away end in ecstasy. We all went absolutely mental as the players ran to us in celebration. The home supporters were now silent other than aiming gestures at us that we returned with gusto and a smile. This was brilliant.

It was marred somewhat by the poor referee as he awarded West Brom a penalty in the 83rd minute for a foul that was clearly outside the area. This was confirmed after the game and by the match commentators. Up stepped Thomas-Asante, the player who had been coming to Blues but went to West Brom when they lured him with more money, to pull a goal back. Blues fans sang "Brucey what the score?" and "you're getting sacked in the morning!"

Blues held on and the game ended in a great 3-2 away win for Blues. The players all came over to celebrate with us at the end of the game and it was great to see the bonding between fans and players as they joined in with our singing of the 'Bacuna' song. It was great to see Jobe Bellingham dancing around and singing the song with us. As we were leaving at the end of the match we spotted Thomas-Asante warming down and the Bluenoses all sang 'there's only one greedy bastard!' to him. Brilliant.

Over the years I have visited the Hawthorns on 12 occasions and witnessing 3 wins, 2 draws and 7 defeats. Not a happy hunting ground on my trips but I've really enjoyed the victories.

Ground 24 – Victoria Ground – 28th March 1981 - Stoke City 0 Birmingham City 0 – First Division

I remember my first trip the the Victoria ground in March 1981 when we all queued outside New Street Station before boarding the packed football special to take us to Stoke. This was to be another new ground for me and I was really looking forward to it. The football special was rocking on the way up to Stoke and once again I got stuck into the wonderful sandwiches my mom had made for me along with a mini pork pie and crisps.

Soon we were disembarking in Stoke and after announcing our arrival with a loud rendition of 'the Brummies are here!' we were escorted to Stoke City's old ground – known as the Victoria Ground. Our end was behind the goal and it was a large terrace with the seats behind us which were also occupied by Bluenoses. The ground was a fair size and had a certain character about it too. The Blues fans already inside the ground were already in full voice and it sounded like we were at home. Despite the passionate support of our supporters the game ended in a 0-0 draw and we were soon on our way back to the station after our mandatory twenty or so minutes of being locked in the ground.

I have always enjoyed my visits to Stoke as it was an old ground with lots of character and plenty of atmosphere. It always felt a bit like a derby game to be honest. I don't have any memories of any games in particular other than the first trip I made mainly because I never saw any Blues victories. I visited on 7 occasions and saw 3 draws and 4 defeats which were all by just the odd goal.

The Victoria Ground was demolished in May 1997 and the site lay derelict for 20 years before becoming a housing estate named Victoria Park with the streets named after former Stoke players and managers. A nice touch I think.

Ground 25 – Selhurst Park – 11th April 1981 – Crystal Palace 3 Birmingham City 1 – First Division

We were off to London in April 1981 only this time a trip to the Palace – Crystal Palace. We travelled to London by train and it was really good to travel across to Palace on the Underground and we soon found a pub near the ground. I can't remember the name of it but it was nice and we had a couple of drinks before heading to the stadium for the game.

I was looking forward to visiting another new ground and I wasn't disappointed as Selhurst Park was also a bit different and had character. We were situated on the terracing on the side and to the corner of the ground. Blues fans were in full voice and enjoying the banter with the home supporters. The match, however, proved to be a bit of a disappointment and we ended the game losing 3-1 and the train home was somewhat quieter than it was going. I think a lot of the Bluenoses had stayed behind for a night on the town to make up for the disappointment we had just suffered.

On the 29th March 1997 Julie and I were heading to London for another away game at Crystal Palace and Blues were in 19th position in the table. There were loads of Bluenoses that had travelled to Palace for the game and when the teams came running out for the match we all stood and looked on in amazement. There were two teams both wearing Crystal Palace kits! Crystal Palace were in their home kit and Birmingham City were in the Crystal Palace third kit! Bear in mind that this was way before social medial and mobile phones and so there was very little way of finding out what on earth was going on apart from word of mouth.

Apparently, we discovered, the referee had decided that our away kit and our third kit both clashed with the Crystal Palace home kit and so Blues had to play in Palace's third kit in which Palace had never won! Blues then proceeded to show their opponents exactly how to win in that kit and won the game 1-0! Not something that we would forget for quite a while (I've never forgotten it). Quite a good night really and the victory saw Blues move up to 18th place.

I have not travelled to Selhurst Park since 1997 and I am sure there would have been many changes since then. Overall I made 6 trips to Selhurst Park between 1981 and 1997 and I saw 2 wins, 1 draw and 3 defeats with the worst of these being a 6-0 defeat in 1987.

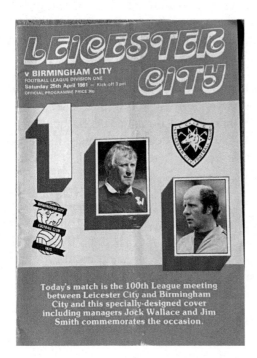

Ground 26 – Filbert Street – 25th April 1981 - Leicester City 1 Birmingham City 0 – First Division

My first trip to Filbert Street in Leicester was way back in 1981 and as was usual at the time we traveled on a packed football special. It was great fun as we sat on the tables with our drinks chatting to various other Bluenoses and joining in with the singing. Once we disembarked at Leicester station we announced our arrival with a loud rendition of "The Brummies are here!" and we were escorted to the ground by an army of police officers.

The ground was old but had lots of character and our away end was terracing behind the goal. I liked the football stadiums around this time as they were all very individual and had character. Each set of fans created their own atmospheres too and today the ground was buzzing with lots of singing especially from the away contingent although, sadly, Blues lost the game 1-0. This didn't stop us singing on the way back though and as was the norm in these days the football special was waiting on the platform when we arrived back at Leicester station taking us back to Birmingham.

I don't have many memories of Filbert Street although I really did like the old stadium and I have visited the same amount of times that I have been to Leicester's new stadium. I visited Filbert Street on 3 occasions between 1981 and 1986 and saw 1 win (3-2 in 1984) and 2 defeats. Obviously it was a very long time ago you lose some memories with age. I still think it had more character than the new stadium though.

Leicester City left Filbert Street in 2002 and Rotherham United expressed an interest in purchasing the Carling Stand and moving it to their Millmoor Ground but this never came about and Filbert Street was demolished in 2003. Part of the site is home to the 'Filbert Village' development as accommodation for students at the nearby De Montford University and University of Leicester.

versus
BIRMINGHAM CITY
Ayresome Park Middlesbrough
1981-82 Season Vol. 2 No. 2

30p

Ground 27 – Ayresome Park – 12th September 1981 – Middlesbrough 2 Birmingham City 1 – First Division

In September 1981 we went on a trip up north to Middlesbrough, and what a trip this turned into! Upon ringing the station the day before I had discovered that there was not a direct train to Middlesbrough that would get us to the game in time for kick off and so we would have to change twice to get there and five times to get back. And it set off at 6.30am. We would also have to leave the game 5 minutes early in order to catch the last train back! What a bloody pain eh! It meant I had to leave the house at the ungodly time of 5.30am, and half asleep, with the packed lunch my mom had prepared the previous night, I headed for New Street Station.

There were lots of Bluenoses on this early train and everyone looked tired. We started on our breakfast as soon as the train pulled out of the station. I can't remember where we changed at on the way, but I have a feeling it was Sheffield as I remember a load of Sheffield Wednesday fans milling around. It was a long journey, with us discussing our chances of a win and wondered how we would find the ground once we arrived in Middlesbrough as there were not enough of us to get a police escort and we would be arriving early. In the seventies and eighties almost all football grounds had four large floodlights that could easily be seen for quite a distance so we presumed that once we got out of the station at Middlesbrough we would be able to see the floodlights and head in that direction.

This plan usually worked quite well, however, at Middlesbrough it didn't! As we came out of the station all we could see were floodlights everywhere. I presumed that these were the docks, anyway, we had to set about asking people for directions and as everyone knows, this is not always a good idea when in enemy territory with a Brummie accent! We got away with it until we reached the ground when the enemy asked us the time – retreated and returned with about 200 Boro fans who then proceeded to chase the 50 plus of us waiting outside the ground for the turnstiles to open. Luckily just as the Bluenoses turned around and bravely ran back to shock and confront the Boro fans, the police arrived and saved the day. I must admit though, the Boro fans did look surprised when the small group they were chasing turned round and ran at them like lunatics. They looked like they were about to run when the plod showed up.

Once inside the ground I looked around to survey my surroundings. Aryesome Park looked quite old to be honest, but it did have a certain character. The away section that we had been put in was a corner terrace and the crash bars were not the usual iron bars but were concrete. It was certainly different and as more and more Blues arrived we met other Bluenoses that we were now familiar with due to our regular travelling. We were soon chatting and joining in the singing and banter whilst waiting for the game to begin. I always enjoyed a laugh with the lads and today was no different as we sat on the terracing in anticipation. I saw Lee Pitman as usual and we got chatting whilst we awaited kick off. Before long the Blues were on the pitch and Keep Right On rang out from our section as we sang our hearts out for the lads.

Despite our loud support we were losing 2-1 with ten minutes to go and as much as it pained me, I knew we had to leave to head back to the station to get home. This is the only time I ever left a game before the final whistle. So, off we headed at a bit of a run, to the station to start on our six-train journey home. Never one to be too downhearted we sang a bit on the train before arriving at our first port of call – Darlington. Once in Darlington station we obtained beers for the rest of the journey along with sandwiches etc. The rest of the day passed in a blur of train journeys and stations and banter with various fans as we passed through their territory. I called my mom from York Station and explained that I could be late home, if I got home at all! 'How did you get on?' she asked as usual. 'Drew 1-2' I answered, knowing that she wouldn't take much notice. 'Nice' she said, it always gave me a little laugh.

As we were waiting in Sheffield we had a bit of a run in with the locals but the plod soon arrived and put a stop to it. There were quite a few of them too. Apart from the result it wasn't a bad day out really, although it was very long and by the time I got home I just collapsed into bed.

I only got to visit Ayresome Park on 2 occasions. In 1981 when Blues lost 2-1 and a 0-0 draw in 1985. Middlesbrough left Ayresome Park to move into the new Riverside Stadium in 1995 and Ayresome Park was demolished in 1997 to become a housing estate.

Ground 28 – Highbury – 22ⁿᵈ September 1981 – Arsenal 1 Birmingham City 0 – First Division

I got up full of hope and excitement ahead of the trip to Highbury. Once again I was on the Euston bound train tucking into my packed lunch and downing the obligatory beer or two and discussing our season of ups and downs back in the first division. Every now and again another Bluenose or two would stop by to chat and share their opinions on the Blues and often the carriage would burst into song. This happened with increased frequency once the beer was flowing.

Very soon we were arriving in Euston and everyone had their own plans about what they were doing first and which pubs they were visiting pre match. We got on the underground with loads of the Blues fans and headed towards Highbury to have a look round and find a nice pub for a pre match drink. I liked Highbury; it has something about it and has a lot of character, although they didn't call it the Highbury library for nothing. What it has in character it certainly lacked in atmosphere. No problems though, because us Bluenoses bring enough atmosphere with us. We were standing on the terraces in the clock stand, of which we had been allocated half. With about fifteen minutes till kick off our end was packed and swaying and we were giving the Arsenal fans stationed on the terrace, to the right of us, a lot of banter.

The match got underway and although we played well we lost 1-0. It never stopped us singing though and the players as usual came over to our end at the end of the game to applaud us for our passionate support. Oh well, back to the station and off back to Birmingham.

I made 4 trips to Highbury between 1981 and 1985 and saw 3 draws and one defeat. I never got to see a Blues victory. Arsenal moved out of Highbury in 2006 and 650 luxury apartments were built in its place completed in 2010. Just the exterior of the Art Deco East Stand and West Stand have remained and have been incorporated into the development. The pitch has been turned into a communal garden.

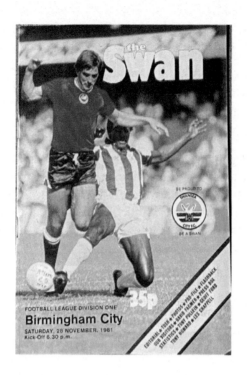

Ground 29 – Vetch Field – 28th November 1981 – Swansea City 1 Birmingham City 0 – First Division

At the end of November I visited another new ground – this time across the border in Wales at the home of Swansea City. I don't remember a lot about the game, which we lost 1-0, but the ground soon replaced Southampton's in my affections as the worst I had visited. The facilities, the toilets in particular were appalling. If I remember correctly Swansea had not long come up from the lower divisions and their ground certainly reflected this. Despite this, I enjoyed visiting a new ground and the usual singing and chanting of the travelling Bluenoses.

In 1994 I was again heading into Wales to play Swansea City at the Vetch Field. Once again Julie drove and my mom had packed us a bit of a picnic for the journey. Once in Swansea we parked up and headed to the ground, only to discover that we had parked right by their main end and had to walk to the other end of the ground to join the Blues fans in the away end. Inside I was once again standing on the terraced end behind the goal where Blues fans had half of the stand with Swansea fans occupying the other half with fencing separating us from them.

It was a nice day and Julie and I sat on the terrace while we waited for the teams to come out and tucked into our packed lunch. Mom had put a couple of peaches inside, so once I had consumed them I lobbed the peach stones over the fence into the Swansea end, much to my amusement. The game soon got underway amid much noise from the Blues fans. It was a really good game and Steve Claridge scored twice to give Blues a well-deserved 2-0 away win.

It was after the game that the trouble began, and it was really tricky getting back to our car safely. We were subjected to some vile abuse from the home fans as we headed back and considering we were just two girls it made it even worse. On this occasion I found the Swansea fans to be complete wankers. Once we got away, Julie and I decided to stop at the services for a bite to eat and we met up with a few other people who had had their car windows smashed by the Swansea fans as they left the ground. Swansea still had to travel to St. Andrews yet and I knew that the Blues fans would be eagerly awaiting them with revenge on their minds.

Over time I saw 4 games at Vetch Field with the majority being enjoyable as Blues won twice, drew once and suffered only one narrow defeat (1-0).

The Vetch Field was abandoned in 2005 and left derelict till it was demolished in 2011 and it is now a park with the centre circle left intact. The only clues that the ground once stood there is an old gate from the East Stand that now leads only to bricked up walls and a rusting players entrance that sits between two houses. There is also an old wall from the ground which sits in the corner of the park.

HAMMER
WEST HAM UNITED F.C. OFFICIAL PROGRAMME

WEST HAM UNITED 35p
VERSUS
BIRMINGHAM CITY
FOOTBALL LEAGUE: Division 1
Saturday 13 February 1982   KICK-OFF 3 p.m.

Ground 30 – Upton Park – 13th February 1982 – West Ham United 2 Birmingham City 2 – First Division

In February 1982 I went in the seats for the first time at a match this season. It was away at West Ham United and Julie, Debbie and I gave in to Pam's wishes and agreed to sit in the seats. We had met up with some of the lads on the Euston train and Brendan had taken us to a Pub by one of the tube stations for a pre match drink. Then it was off to Upton Park, which was nicely situated in what appeared to be an area somewhat like the 'Eastenders' market. Once inside we appeared to have been seated with the West Ham fans and this proved very trying for me as I was sitting next to a girl who was very vocal in supporting West Ham.

This was okay until she started criticising our players and at that point I stood up and words were exchanged before the police spotted the disturbance and the four of us were then led towards the pitch and in the general direction of the away standing area. The away end had spotted this and were singing 'City aggro' quite loudly which amused the life out of me! We were then marched around the pitch towards the away end to cheers from the Bluenoses. Funny! We were then put in with the cheering Blues contingent on the terraced section behind the goal to a round of applause and we soon joined in with their singing and banter.

Quite a good day out really – and we came away with a 2-2 draw. There were a couple of west ham girls making gestures to us through the opening in the fencing, but they declined our invitation to come over and join us in our end.

I visit Upton Park/Boleyn Ground on 4 occasions between 1982 and 1985 and I witnessed one draw (2-2) and 3 defeats with the worst being a 5-0 drubbing in September 1982. It was always a great atmosphere though and a proper football ground.

The Boleyn Ground was demolished in 2016 and has since been converted into 842 posh flats and maisonettes called Upton Gardens. West Ham moved to the City of London Stadium leaving their fantastic atmosphere behind and it is sadly lost with old stadium.

Ground 31 – Meadow Lane – 1ˢᵗ May 1982 – Notts County 1 Birmingham City 4 – First Division

Blues were in serious danger of relegation and we needed to be winning more games when, on 1ˢᵗ May 1982, I made my first trip to Meadow lane, the home ground of Notts County. Although Notts County's ground was near to Forest's ground it was far smaller and older looking. It looked even stranger once inside. Blues were situated on the terrace behind the goal and the opposite end of the ground was very strange indeed. It wasn't like a normal stand; it was just a very high brick wall with executive boxes (of sorts) precariously positioned at the top of the wall. So it looked like there were no fans at that end of the ground.

Anyway, I tried not to get too distracted by this and headed to the refreshment stand at the back of the terracing to see what was on offer. There was a very confused guy behind the counter trying his hardest to understand the Brummie accent of the lads who were trying to order 'some rocks?' I explained to the vacant looking guy in the refreshment stand that the lads were just after sweets and that they were commonly known at the time in Birmingham as 'rocks'.

There were thousands of travelling Bluenoses and we made loads of noise as our boys went on a scoring spree in front of our very eyes. Brilliant! We all came away very happy after beating Notts County 4-1 on their own turf. It was a fantastic away win and great to see four goals scored away. We sang loads of songs and the atmosphere was brilliant.

On another occasion in October 1984 Blues were drawn against Notts County in the 3rd round of the League Cup and after three draws we were drawn to play the second replay in Nottingham at their place. It was the 5th December when I travelled to Nottingham and as much as I usually enjoyed the walk with the escort to the ground it was absolutely freezing and I remember thinking it was the coldest I had ever been. I was convinced my toes had frostbite and were about to drop off! It turned out to be worth the trip and the cold though as Mick Harford scored and Robert Hopkins got two in a good 3-1 win. I may have been cold but I went home happy.

Despite the weird executive box stand I still though it was a proper ground with a lovely open terraced away end and I always enjoyed my trips there. In modern times I have visited the Notts County Social Club near the stadium when we have been playing at nearby Forest and we always get a warm welcome and it is always full of Bluenoses.

I visited Meadow Lane on 7 occasions between 1982 and 1989 and got to witness 3 wins (4-1, 3-1, 3-1), 2 goalless draws and 2 defeats which meant that overall it was a happy place to visit.

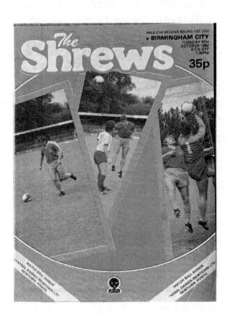

Ground 32 – Gay Meadow – 5th October 1982 – Shrewsbury Town 1 Birmingham City 1 – League Cup 2nd Round 1St Leg

The League Cup draw paired us with Shrewsbury Town and as it was a two-legged affair it meant a nice trip to Shrewsbury for the away leg on 5th October. I was looking forward to this because it was not too far away, a new ground for me and I could imagine it to be a nice little place really. I was proved to be correct, as Shrewsbury was a really nice place to visit.

When we arrived by train it was a nice day, meaning no rain, and it was quite different from the big cities that I was used to. There were Bluenoses milling about everywhere as usual, and we made our way towards the ground to see what it was like. Gay Meadow, as Shrewsbury's ground was called, was situated very nicely next to the big river that ran through the town. It was a really small ground after what I was used to but it looked really quaint. I presumed it wouldn't hold too many though, and once again I was right as the Bluenoses more that filled the allocated away end that we had been given.

Although Blues were given the entire end behind the goal, the terrace was full of Blues fans in the 5,003 attendance that day. The best laugh was the many Blues fans that had climbed up onto the roof (not very high I might add) and although the voice from the loudspeaker begged them to come down there were still a few that remained up there. I was a bit worried about what they would do should they need the toilet thought!

The ground was so small that on several occasions the ball would clear the roof and end up in the nearby river where a man was situated in a small round boat (cant remember what they are called but they are some sort of traditional boat) and he would collect up all the balls. What a fun job. The game ended in a 1-1 draw and as the Blues fans climbed down off the roof, we headed back to a small pub nearby to have a quick drink before leaving Shrewsbury and heading back to Birmingham. It had been a great day out and the Bluenoses had been in great voice as usual inside and outside the ground. They were still singing on the train on the way home. Blues won the second leg 4-1 a few weeks later and progressed to the 3rd Round where they would meet Derby County.

I really did think that it was a lovely ground and I enjoyed all 3 of the visits that I made to Shrewsbury. Blues won there in 1994 (2-0), lost in 1985 (1-0) as well as the draw on my first visit. Gay Meadow was demolished in 2007 and became an estate on a gated community called The Old Meadow with 62 town houses and 117 apartments and gardens which was finally completed in 2015.

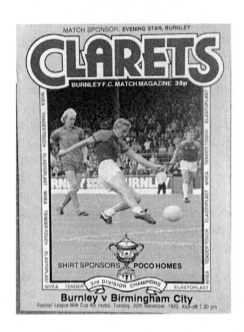

Ground 33 – Turf Moor – 30th November 1982 – Burnley 3 Birmingham City 2 – League Cup 4th Round

In November 1982 Blues were into the fourth round of the League Cup, which I found quite exciting, and the draw was an away tie at Burnley, which I was also looking forward to, as it would be another new ground for me to visit.

We had started travelling to some games by coach around this time and for our trip to Burnley we took the supporters club coach. I remember thinking what a cold day it was and that it was bloody freezing at Burnley. I thought it was the coldest place in the country at the time. The Bluenoses had travelled in numbers as usual and were in very good spirits as we all quite fancied our chances against a lower league side. If you were to look back now though, you would see that our record against lower league sides was not that good really.

Once inside the ground I took in my surroundings. I was very impressed with Turf Moor as it was very similar to our own great St. Andrews in the way that it had a large terraced KOP to one side of the pitch which joined up to a large terrace behind the goal, not unlike our Tilton. The away fans were situated behind the other goal with terracing at the front and seats at the back of the terracing. We sat in the seats for this one and the Bluenoses were in excellent voice exchanging banter with the noisy Burnley fans. It was set up to be a great cup atmosphere.

The game itself would have been enjoyable had we not been robbed and to make matters worse at 2-2 one of our own players managed to put the ball into his own net and we lost the game 3-2. I was deeply disappointed as I thought we were very unlucky to lose. It's always bad to get knocked out of the cup but when you feel it is somewhat unjust then it is even worse. I was not in the best frame of mind on the way home but we still sang a little on the coach on the journey.

In April 2001 I was living in Abu Dhabi but I was on a visit back to Birmingham and was traveling to Burnley in Julie's car with Stephen and Annette. Annette's boyfriend Steve was traveling on the coach with his mates from Harborne and they were going to meet us in Burnley. We had a nice drive up to Burnley and it wasn't long before we found a small pub on the outskirts and made our way inside. There were a couple of Burnley fans playing pool and after a few pints we soon got some banter going with them. Steve found his way to us and not long after we were off to the ground.

   Once inside Steve and Annette, who had left ahead of us, were already there so I set about ringing her to find out where she was sitting as the Blues end was packed. After shouting our seat and row number down the phone, I noticed a whole row of blokes stand up and head to where I was. They all came and stood around me and I discovered they were Steve's mates, Fiddler and Co. I thought it was really funny as did Annette who followed them up not long afterwards. Apparently they asked Annette where I was sitting and then she told them they all just got up and left. Brilliant. It was great to see them and the atmosphere was brilliant.

Blues were singing 'you're just a small town in Blackburn!' to the Burnley fans who seemed to be taking great offense to this. Then it was a chant of 'you'll get it, you'll get foot and mouth!' which seemed to go on for ages and also annoyed the Burnley fans. It was brilliant being amongst the Bluenoses but the game finished in a draw 0-0 and Blues were down to 5th but still in a playoff place. As we headed back to the car we were penned it by police horses for a while as the Burnley fans left. Then the police decided to let us through a few at a time which meant squeezing past the police horse at the front and as Annette passed the horse he snorted white stuff over her. I sang 'you'll get it, you'll get foot and mouth" as we all fell about laughing. Stephen thought it was really funny.

In August 2015 the first away trip of the new season was at Burnley's Turf Moor on the Saturday. Unfortunately these days, television rights dictate what time and when a lot of our games are to be played and because our match was being shown live it would be an early kick off at 12.30. For me this meant leaving the house at 7am to get the coach from St. Andrews that departs at 8am.

It was a cool overcast morning and after a stop at the services we were soon arriving in a somewhat gloomy Burnley. Perhaps it was just the weather? Some of the Blues crew went for a drink in the nearby cricket club, but as it was just under an hour to kick off we made our way into Turf Moor. Once inside we got our drinks and made our way to the back of the stand as the away end began filling up.

Burnley were only relegated from the Premier League the previous season and so I thought this could be a bit of a difficult match for us and I wasn't really expecting much of a result for us. Ever hopeful though I stood at the back amongst the singing throng and cheered as the Blues players came onto the pitch for kick off. I must admit I was pleasantly surprised by how well Blues were playing and the Bluenoses were in full voice, belting out song after song. The locals certainly knew Blues were in town! It wasn't long before Jon Toral hit a fabulous shot that flew into the bottom corner of the net from the edge of the penalty area. The away end exploded and I was amused at the sight of a large crowd of Bluenoses in a pile on the ground as they jumped on each other in celebration. It was wild!

At half time the score was 1-0 to Blues and I made my way down to the toilets. In the second half Burnley equalised with a headed goal from a free kick given away on the left side of the penalty area. I didn't think it was a free kick and neither did David Cotterill who was adjudged to have committed the offence.

Blues hit back with a counter attack that saw Clayton Donaldson brought down in the box and a penalty awarded to Blues. We were delighted in the away end and celebrated accordingly. Up stepped Paul Caddis and he smashed it into the net before sprinting to the celebrating Blues fans – 2-1! As we were jumping around someone set off a blue flare right in the middle of the main Blues section about 10 feet from us and we were engulfed in blue smoke! It did look amazing but did cause a bit of coughing and choking. The stewards and police didn't really know what to do so nobody moved. Usually people scatter – but not us Bluenoses! They did eventually locate the canister once most of the blue smoke had blown away.

However, Blues managed to throw away their advantage, conceding from yet another soft free kick. Admittedly it was a cracking goal that went in off the crossbar but we really have to stop giving away these free kicks. So the game ended in a 2-2 draw and we had to settle for a point – which we probably would have been happy with before kick off. Now though, we were a little disappointed as we headed back to the coaches.

I have made 4 trips to Turf Moor and witnessed 2 draws and 2 defeats. No victories as yet but there is always hope for the future.

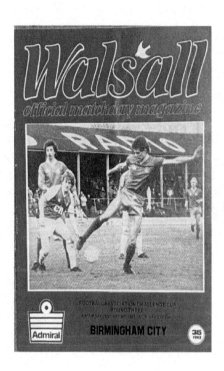 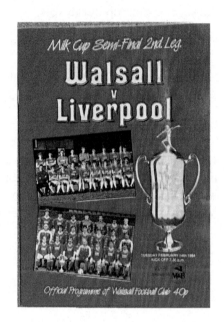

Ground 34 - Fellows Park - 8th January 1983 – Walsall 0 Birmingham City 0 – FA Cup 3rd Round

On the 8th January 1983 I made my first trip to Walsall's stadium just across the city for an FA Cup 3rd round tie. The ground was very small and the terrace occupied by the Blues fans was heaving as we sang our cup songs along with several renditions of 'Keep Right On', and generally enjoyed ourselves. It was a nice little ground though with small terraces at each end of the ground and small seated stands with terraces at pitch side on both sides. It had character.

The game finished 0-0 and a replay was on the cards for the 11th January when we despatched Walsall by a Summerfield goal in a 1-0 win at St Andrews. Blues were in the next round and we drew an away trip to Crystal Palace in the 4th round.

In February 1984 my dad got us tickets for the League Cup Semifinal game at Fellows park between Walsall and Liverpool and as they were free we decided to head over for the sell out game. I had to pick up the tickets from a shop in Walsall (due to my dad's connections there) and it proved very tricky to get out of the local train station as the police were checking that everyone had match tickets. We did manage to talk our way out of the station though and headed to the shop to pick up our tickets.

We then joined the masses inside Fellows Park and enjoyed a great game of football as third tier Walsall put up a great fight against top flight Liverpool. Sadly it wasn't enough to get Walsall to Wembley as they lost this second leg tie by 2-0. It had been an enjoyable trip though.

I visited Fellows Park on 5 occasions with Birmingham City twice, Liverpool twice and Manchester City once. The Blues visits saw a draw and a defeat and I was present at the League Cup Semi Final between Walsall and Liverpool. Fellows Park was demolished in early 1991 although heavy snow, a few months before had caused the collapse of the "Cowshed" section of the stadium. A Morrisons supermarket was built on the site.

Ground 35 – Loftus Road – 19th November 1983 – Queens Park Rangers 2 Birmingham City 1 – First Division

In November 1983 I made my first trip to Queen's Park Rangers and we travelled to the capital by train and disembarked at Euston in large numbers and in great voice. We made our way across to Shepherds Bush by underground and we were soon arriving at Loftus Road home of QPR. Once inside the away terrace behind the goal was packed as everyone swayed back and forth and chanted at the home supporters. It was a bright day too but sadly Blues lost the game 2-1 and we headed home a bit disappointed but having enjoyed a good outing.

In September 2013 there were 14 of us who got the train to London and then the tube to Shepherds Bush where we visited the Wetherspoons before walking to QPR's ground for the game. It was a great atmosphere in the packed Blues end and there was lots of singing despite losing 1-0. Blues fans threw a smoke bomb on the pitch which held up play for 5 minutes while a steward found a bucket of sand and a pair of gloves. Very amusing. After the game we all went back to Wetherspoons before heading back to Euston to get the train back home.

The most exciting game I have ever seen at Loftus Road came in February 2019. It was off to London by train again as Blues took on QPR at Loftus Road, a ground we all hated as the view was shocking with the majority of seats in the upper stand being restricted view - so much so that you cannot see the goal line beneath the stand. They would not give Blues the lower stand although they are happy to allow other teams fans such as Leeds and Sheffield but not Birmingham! There is only one way in and one way out via a very narrow concourse and it was so dangerous. Hence Terry, Nigel and Charlie were not going today. So it was me, June, James and Steve who headed to London to meet Stephen.

We arrived at Euston and got the tube to Shepherds Bush station (Shepherds Bush Market station was closed) and we walked to a pub called The Crown and Sceptre, which was already full of QPR fans but I recognised a few Bluenoses in there too. Me and June ordered Cheesie chips which we then had to eat whilst standing up although a nearby QPR fan let us put our plates on their table and I chatted to him about the match. He reckoned we would get something from the game but I wasn't so sure as QPR were one of our bogey teams. Stephen met us in the pub and it was great to see him again. Barry arrived with a friend so we said hello to him and he had a cheesie chip or two off us. Then it was off to the ground.

It was packed in the away end once we got inside and as I had one of the few unrestricted view seats I could actually see some of the goal line which was in marked contrast to last season. The Bluenoses were in great voice too and I happily joined in. The game got underway and Blues were on fire. The away end erupted when Che Adams fired home on 21 minutes and it was funny to see Bluenoses falling over each other in their celebrations. Five minutes later and Che got his second to make it 2-0 and wild celebrations ensued once again. Stephen and I could hardly believe it. It got even better when Harlee Dean headed in from a corner on 36 minutes and it was 3-0. Unbelievable scenes in the away end as we celebrated an unlikely score line.

Bluenoses were singing our hearts out for the entire time and it was great. Six minutes later the lively Jota curled in a lovely shot which hit the post but the on fire Che Adams was first to react and he fired home the rebound to unbelievable scenes as Blues went 4-0 up before half time! It was crazy! 'Che, Che will tear you apart again!' rang out from the away end. Stephen and I went mental and even the blokes in front of us turned round and hugged us as complete strangers were hugging each other and shaking hands. James did a bit of crowd surfing much to our delight. It was brilliant and I couldn't believe it. We sang 'easy' and 'can we play you every week?'. 'Garry, Garry Monk!' rang out loudly and 'Garry give us a wave' to which he responded by clapping us. The only blip on the horizon was that Blues manage to concede a soft goal from a corner in the last minute before half time to make the halftime score 4-1.

I thought this would now give QPR hope and inspire them in the second half, which it did. QPR scored within 3 minutes of the second half to make it 4-2 and they came at Blues relentlessly. Lee Camp made some good saves as Blues looked like they had imploded and were a different side from the one that was on fire in the first half. It was extremely stressful to watch especially when QPR got a 3rd goal on 80 minutes. It was agony in the away end as we were well aware how Blues were probably the only team who could throw away a 4 goal half time lead to draw or lose. Blues were hanging on and the fourth official put up the board with 4 minute of injury time and I set my stop watch. With only 20 seconds remaining the referee awarded QPR a penalty and my heart sank. The Bluenoses were in stunned silence as their player stepped up to take the penalty and I could barely watch.

Time seemed to stand still and then the player was making his run up before hitting it hard and low to Lee Camp's right but the ensuing celebrations came in the away end as Lee Camp made an unbelievable save and the rebound was cleared! I went mental as chaos broke out all around me amid incredible scenes. The final whistle sounded and the whole of the away end were singing 'Lee Camp! In the middle of our goal! Lee Camp!' to the tune of Madness 'Our House'. It went on for ages as Lee Camp made his way down the pitch to stand in front of us and pump his fist into the air as a massive cheer sounded!

I looked around and though that this had been one of those special games that would be talked about for years and one that I was privileged to have been part of. This was what loving Blues was all about! It had been a very special, although stressful day and we happily left the stadium with 3 precious points as we headed back to the station to go home. Even the fact that the train was packed and we had to stand the whole way home didn't spoil what had been a brilliant day out!

In March 2023 I enjoyed another good trip to Loftus Road, which is my very least favourite away stadium due to the restricted view in the upper tier. I was off on my travels again on the Saturday with a trip to London as Blues took on yet another team with a new manager, this time it was QPR with new boss Gareth Ainsworth. QPR had been struggling of late but had recently won their first game under Ainsworth with a 1-0 win over Watford. However, this had been followed by a 6-1 thrashing by a Blackpool team currently in the bottom three and I was worried that Blues may feel the backlash when we arrived at Loftus Road.

It was an early start for us as the official coaches were due to leave St. Andrews at 9.30 and today it was myself, June, Charlie and Taff making the journey. We usually did the London trips by train but with most of the country constantly striking and the constant cancellations of trains we deemed it unsafe to do so due to the unreliability of it. In fact the trains were indeed on strike on the Saturday of the QPR game. This meant that there were lots of coaches making the trip and I saw five party buses pass St. Andrews as we waited to board our six coaches which left 15 minutes later than advertised. No surprise there but it did mean that we hit traffic and were unable to stop on the way.

The traffic on the motorway was horrendous and was down to one lane at one point and we arrived at Loftus Road just before 2pm. We had been planning to head to our usual pub for this trip but it was a bit too late when we arrived so we headed for the chip shop instead. Today Myself, June and Charlie would be in the lower tier and Taff was in the upper tier so we parted ways and headed into the stadium.

I have to say that in my opinion Loftus Road is the worst away end in the football league if you are in the upper tier with every seat bar the front row having restricted views with supporters unable to view the nearest goal in front of the stand. This is why we held out for the lower tier which would enable us to see the ball go in the net should a goal be scored at our end. It wasn't too busy when we entered the tiny concourse so we were able to obtain pre match ciders and we had the room to enjoy them before finding our seats.

Blues played really well and Tahith Chong scored after only 3 minutes and the away end exploded as 1,800 Bluenoses went wild and a blue smoke bomb landed on the pitch in front of us and blue smoke filled the air. I jumped around in celebration and 'Keep Right On' rang out loud and proud. It was a great atmosphere as Blues fans continued to sing throughout the game as Blues achieved a brilliant 1-0 away win which moved us up to 17th in the league table.

Bluenoses poured out of the stadium afterwards and continued their singing as they marched down the road 'London's a shit hole, I wanna go home', 'we're Birmingham' and 'Keep Right On' were belted out and I had to smile. It was a very pleasant trip back to Birmingham and I was home by 9pm in time to watch the EFL show on TV.

I visited Loftus Road on 12 occasions over the years and I saw 2 wins, 3 draws and 7 defeats. My last but one trip was in March 2023 when Blues won 1-0. I enjoyed that one.

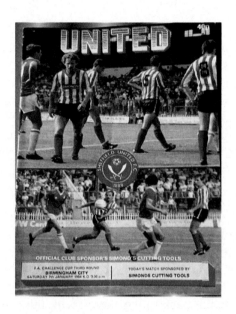

Ground 36 – Brammall Lane – 7th January 1984 – Sheffield United 1 Birmingham City 1 – FA Cup 3Rd Round

My first trip to Brammall Lane was in the FA Cup. The draw for the third round was made on Monday as usual and Blues were drawn to play Sheffield United of the third division at their ground. The cup would make a nice distraction from the league, especially as Blues were currently 19th in the league.

I was up early and soon on my way to Sheffield for the cup-tie. Blues had not won a game since early December with their League Cup win over Notts County but the girls and I were feeling lucky. It was a nice trip on the Shoppers special train this time. It was quite fun really with the shoppers scattered about amongst the Bluenoses on their way to the game and as usual for a cup game there was a carnival atmosphere on the train.

Inside the ground it was packed in the Blues end and the terraces were swaying to the tune of 'KA SA RA SA RA' and 'Wembley, Wembley!' Sheffield Utd were also up for the fight and the match itself was the usual exciting stuff that cup-ties were made of. The game ended in a 1-1 draw and I came away fancying our chances at St. Andrews in the replay in a few days time. I was not disappointed either and our lads dispatched Sheffield Utd 2-0 with goals from Mick Harford and Billy Wright in front of a disappointingly low crowd of 10,888. Perhaps it was because Blues were not doing well in the league, but the FA Cup usually inspired larger crowds than this I thought. I guess times were hard.

On another visit which was on New Years day 1985, complete with hangovers after our New Years Eve celebrations, I headed off to catch the football special to Sheffield for a match with Sheffield Utd. There were hundreds of us on the football special and the police escort to the ground seemed to stretch for miles. Once inside there were thousands of Blues fans on the terrace behind the goal and it took ages in the queues outside to get in! I think this was the game when, by the time we got inside and onto the packed terrace Blues were already 2-0 down.

However, as we took up our spot amongst the heaving mass of blue and white, Blues began the fightback and the goals started to fly in. It was so tightly packed that every time Blues scored the whole stand seemed to shake and we would be carried forward in the surge of celebrating Bluenoses and then carried back again to end up round about where we started. The match finished 4-3 to Blues and was an absolute thriller. Even with my New Year hangover, I was very happy on the march back to the station with the celebrating Blues fans. It was brilliant to win on opposing turf and Blues were doing that a lot this season and I was enjoying it immensely!

In 2009 I was again off to see Blues take on Sheffield United at Brammall Lane. I had arranged to meet my nephew Stephen in Sheffield as he was coming across from Leicester where he was currently attending university there. The game was an early kick off at 12.15. This meant that I would have to leave early and meant that, according to Steve; I would not be able to get a train and that I would have to travel on the Blues supporters coach.

So on a lovely sunny morning I was off to St. Andrews to board the coach and I was traveling alone. It seemed to take a long time to get to Sheffield and as we arrived on the outskirts of Sheffield we were met by a police escort. This motivated the already noisy Bluenoses to break into song and to stand up and bang on the windows whilst in full voice. I was on the phone to Stephen at the time checking his process and he could hear the singing really loudly. 'Sounds great where you are!' he said. Stephen had in fact arrived at the station and was making his way to the ground to meet me.

As we pulled up outside the ground with about 25 minutes to kick off, I called Stephen and asked him where he was. He informed me that he was nearby and he could see the coaches but not me. I told him I was on the second coach and would walk to the front and that was when I spotted him. I could see a sea of red and white coming down the road and right in the centre of them was a lone person wearing a Blues shirt coming towards me. I had to laugh; he has definitely inherited that from me!

We went into the ground, which was a new ground for Stephen, and went for a quick drink before kickoff. To my surprise I discovered they sold Vodka Blue so I got a couple of bottles for me and a pint of Carlsberg for Stephen who was amused by the lad in front who commented on the price of the beer. 'Three pound fifty for a bottle of Carlsberg!' he commented 'it's only a pound in snobs!'

This game was another important match as were all the games at this moment with Blues sitting in second place in the championship and Reading breathing down our necks. The Blues fans were in good voice as usual, apart from a couple of moaners standing behind me in the second half. The whole of the Blues contingent were quite content to stand and as I took my place with Stephen I bumped into Brendon.

As the game got under way it soon became clear that it was not going to be our day and a very disputable penalty cost us the game as Sheffield Utd ran out 2-1 winners. It was a really unjust result but we sang our hearts out and despite the result it was a great day out. I said goodbye to Stephen and gave him some of the sandwiches that mom had made for his journey back to Leicester and told him to enjoy the trip and that I would see him again soon.

The season opener for Blues in August 2021 was a very exciting away game at Sheffield United who would be beginning their season back in the Championship after being relegated from the Premier League. There were 2,500 very excited Bluenoses heading to Sheffield for the 8pm kickoff that was moved to suit Sky TV. I was really looking forward to the trip and seeing the 'Blues Family' after many months apart. Sadly James G could not be with us due to serious health issues which had meant he had to return his season ticket and he would be unable to attend any games at all and we all wished him well and missed him. Charlie and Nigel were looking well and were as happy to be back as we were. Terry was missing as it was a late game but I was sure he would join us for a game soon.

I had a new flag this season with 'WEOLEY CASTLE 1973' (where I live and the year of my first Blues game) on it and 4 Blues crests on (men's crest, Ladies crest, 140 anniversary crest and the old Birmingham Badge) which was brought for me for my birthday and we proudly displayed in on the rear window of our coach for the journey to Sheffield. It was a good trip and we had a great catch up and a nice stop at the services on the way as June and I enjoyed some noodles.

We arrived in plenty of time and stood outside the away turnstiles for a while watching the Bluenoses arriving and joining in their singing and banter with the Sheffield fans who were brave enough to venture out of their 'home' pub on the corner. It was quite funny really as the police looked on with growing concern. The singing was really loud and Lee Bowyer said after the game that he had heard the Blues fans singing outside the ground while the players were warming up on the pitch.

Once inside the away end was buzzing with those inside also in full voice as we took up our seats just behind the goal. We weren't expecting much today against a strong Sheffield side but we were determined to get behind our team and we never stopped singing for the entire game. Blues looked good from the start and new loanee Tahith Chong from Manchester United looked really good and tore Sheffield apart. Blues fans sang 'Chong, Chong will tear you apart again!' really loudly. It was brilliant.

Blues were playing really well and on 19 minutes Jeremie Bela hit a lovely cross into the box which was met by Maxime Colin who's header flew over the Sheffield keeper and into the net to make it 1-0 Blues. The home fans were silent whilst the away end went absolutely mental! I hadn't totally anticipated the sheer magnitude of the celebrations and both June and I were sent flying backwards over the seats whilst several around us seemed to be suffering the same fate. I managed to save us both from hitting the floor, unlike some of the other's, but I knew I would be left with one hell of a bruise on my leg in the morning. Well worth it though and I continued with the celebrations which seemed to go on for ever. It was great to be back!

Happily Blues seemed to be in total control of the game and the match ended with a great 1-0 away win over a very strong team and we never stopped singing. Tahith Chong was named Sky TV player of the match and we all sang 'Chong, Chong will tear you apart again!' while he was being interviewed live for the TV audience. As thousands of Bluenoses streamed out of the away end everyone sang 'we're gonna win the league!' It had been a brilliant day and we headed back to the coaches very happy. Some Bluenoses would have to spend the night in Sheffield as there were no trains back home tonight.

I enjoyed a good trip back as we chatted away at the back of the coach despite being tired and I finally got home to my bed at 1am in the morning happy and too wired to get straight off to sleep. I was daring to hope again.

Ground 37 – Hampden Park – 26th May 1984 – Scotland 1 England 1 – British Home Championship

As the 1983-84 season drew to an end, Julie and I had managed to get two tickets for the Home International game between Scotland and England at Hamden Park in Glasgow, Scotland. We were both really excited as this would be our first away trip with England. The fact that it was in enemy territory across the border made it even sweeter, if not a bit intimidating, and I for one was really looking forward to it. Although it was in the shadow of relegation I managed to pick myself up and look forward to the trip north.

So, on the 25th May 1984, Julie and I set out to board the train to Glasgow, via Preston, at New Street Station. Because it was such a long trip we had to set out very early, and it was still dark when we set off. For some unknown reason, I thought the train would be full of England supporters travelling up to Scotland as well as us, however, it wasn't and I was soon to discover that not that many England fans actually travelled to Scotland for the game.

It was a very long trip despite changing trains and having a little break at Preston station, and Julie and I entertained ourselves with our packed lunches and talk of relegation, the forthcoming season and today's game up in Scotland. The train passed through the Lake District and the view was beautiful, as was the scenery once we entered Scotland. There was lots of green hills, and countryside and it was lovely to see. All in all in was a very nice journey by train and as we arrived in Glasgow's central station I started to become a little apprehensive. The Scots have a reputation for hating the English and I wondered if they felt that way about female England supporters too. Especially as the two of us were travelling alone! Needless to say our scarves were safely tucking away in our bags.

As we disembarked in Glasgow station I immediately noticed that there seemed to be an awful lot of Scotland fans in Scotland football shirts also arriving in the station for the game. Julie and I decided that we should use the toilets before we left the station and as we put our money in the slot and entered the toilets we were followed in by a few 'large' and scary looking women in Scotland shirts. This was a bit worrying, but having kept our mouths closed and scarves hidden, we escaped unscathed. Didn't do much for the nerves though!

After consulting the tourist office and looking at maps and bus timetables, we headed out into Glasgow and caught a bus to Hamden Park. The streets seemed to be filled with Scotland shirt wearing people, including the bus we got on and Julie and I remained silent in the hope that no one would notice that we were in fact the enemy! Getting off the bus and walking up towards the ground I looked around and noticed that every single Scot had at least two flags and a few scarves each. Many of the men wore kilts and had a flag around their shoulders and were waving another one in the air. It looked amazing and I couldn't see another England fan anywhere.

Hamden Park itself looked old but impressive, although nowhere near as impressive as Wembley Stadium. It did have some character though and we made our way inside onto the terracing situated along the side of pitch opposite the seated side. Inside it looked quite big and had terracing around three sides of the ground with seats along one side only. It appeared that the Celtic fans had one end behind the goal while the Rangers fans had the other. I remember thinking that this was a bit bizarre that they didn't all mix together, but Julie and I were to the side just left of the middle.

I noticed that we appeared to be in with the Scotland fans and there didn't seem to be any segregation, apart from around a couple of hundred England supporters who were situated behind one of the goals surrounded by Scots. I found that a bit worrying to be honest with the history between the two teams and countries. Julie and I agreed to keep our England scarves in our bags and our comments to ourselves. There were some scary looking characters around us, I can say!

There was massive fencing separating the various sections, but these were being scaled by more that one Scot wearing kilts! This proved to be entertaining if nothing else. Can you imagine, these big burly men, draped in scarves and at least two flags, wearing kilts and scaling a ten-foot fence! Amazing, and for what end? The atmosphere inside the ground was quite good although not as good as Wembley and with some noise from the couple of hundred England supporters who were being drowned out by the surrounding Scots. At least the English contingent were up for it and were giving as good as they got. Sadly they were quite a distance away from us.

The game got under way and I was finding it extremely hard not to shout my support and cheer for my country. Then, when Tony Woodcock scored, I totally forgot where I was and punched the air and cheered in celebration before noticing that everyone had turned towards us. Quickly lowering my hands I attempted to look innocent. 'You English?' some bloke shot at us. We shook our heads and attempted to get away with it. They let it go at that but one guy started talking to us but he was okay really, whereas I don't think the rest of them would have been. There was a really strong hatred toward the English and it was really noticeable that day. The rest of the England fans were celebrating wildly though and I wished we were in there with them. Mind you, if we were I would have been worried about getting back to the station in one piece!

Scotland then got an equaliser and the game finished 1-1. A bit disappointing but at least it increased our chances of getting back to the station alive. The Home Internationals finished with Northern Ireland as champions, Wales second England third and Scotland finished bottom of the group. Oh well, maybe next year!

As all the fans streamed out, Julie and I jumped on one of the buses going to the Station. Just before we got on, someone asked me the way to the station. Shit, too scared to speak and risk getting my head kicked in, I just nodded in the general direction of the station and he said thanks and headed off. The Scots were clearly looking for any England fans to pick off. We reached the station safe and sound and were soon on board the train back to England. There were a few England supporters on the train back and the journey was just as enjoyable as the outward journey. Julie and I reflected on our day and discussed football in general. Despite the intimidating atmosphere up in Glasgow, I had enjoyed the whole experience and could now proudly say that I had followed England away and at one of the most intimidating of venues.

We arrived back in Birmingham worn out but happy and Julie and I had decided we were going to take some holidays and follow Birmingham on the pre season tour. Happy in this knowledge I headed back to my moms and an exhausted sleep!

Ground 38 – De Vijverbeg (Holland) – 13th August 1984 – De Graafschap 0 Birmingham City 0 – Pre Season Friendly

I was really looking forward to the pre season tour with Blues. This pre season tour was going to be in Holland with one game in Belgium, and I couldn't wait! I had just under two weeks holiday and Julie and I were planning to travel to Holland for the entire tour, which would mean we would spend eleven days in Holland and Belgium.

Our accommodation was booked through Birmingham City football club, so it was part of the official tour, and we hoped that we would be located near the team. The hotel that we were booked in was in Arnhem, so that is where our base would be. It was so exciting when the day came that we were due to set off. It was lovely weather when we arrived and Holland looked lovely on the train journey.

Blues first game was against De Graafschap and we set out early and joined up with several other Bluenoses that we had met coming over plus several others who had made the trip. We were to find that throughout the tour there was about fifty of us that formed the core of our support plus Julie and I. We all bonded and became good friends and due to the fact that it was fifty blokes and only two girls, we were well looked after by the men. So we had a few drinks before the game with the lads before we headed into the ground a little early for the match. While we were enjoying a drink outside the ground one of the players – Robert Hopkins came over and had a chat with us. Julie knew Hoppy from her childhood and he chatted to us for a while before taking a swig of my drink and heading off to get ready for the game.

Drinks could be easily obtained in the ground and the Blues faithful were already in good humour and enjoying more pre match drinks. As is was early a few Blues fans decided to climb the fencing onto the pitch for a game of football with a few of the Dutch fans who also came onto the pitch to play a game against our fans. The Blues fans had bought their own football and a nice friendly game got under way. This was to be reported later in the British press that there was a lot of trouble inside the ground before the game and fierce fighting broke out on the pitch when rival sets of supporters climbed the fences to confront each other. This was untrue! It was a friendly kick about between the two sets of supporters who then climbed back into their respective ends to carry on drinking before the game. It was quite funny really, because the local police were sitting at the back of the terraces with their rifles propped against the wall, enjoying some of the vodka and beer that the Blues fans were consuming and chatting avidly with the Bluenoses!

I had bought a nice De Graafschap silk scarf as a memento and enjoyed watching proceedings and the game, which ended in a 0-0 draw. It was a lovely sunny day and I enjoyed a really good day of banter with the lads, drinking and football. Fabulous! After the game we headed off to have a few more drinks with the lads before setting off back to the hotel. Next time we met up with the lads though, we were informed that some trouble did occur after the game between Blues and some Dutch supporters who were looking for trouble. According to the lads around ten fans ended up in hospital, although only one of these was a Blues fan, and he was soon out and back amongst the travelling support again.

It was not long after this game that we started noticing small posters stuck up on trees, or outside pubs, warning of impending trouble for the last game against FC Breda and threatening violence from the Dutch fans against the Blues fans. Like we were scared! We all just laughed it off to be honest.

Ground 39 – Puyenbeke Stadion (Belgium) – 15th August 1984 – SKN Sint-Niklaas 1 Birmingham City 0 – Pre Season Friendly

Our next match was in Belgium and Jules and I set off from our base for the long trip across the border and into Belgium. We were planning to go to Belgium just for the game, which was a night match, and to travel back afterwards. However, when we arrived we discovered there were no trains back after the game and due to the fact that it was mother's day in Belgium the banks were also closed! We could hardly believe it! We had not bought an awful lot of money with us on the trip to Belgium so we now had to find a really cheap bed and breakfast at the last minute.

Luckily we did find somewhere, although it was a bit of a tip to be honest with two single beds and a small sink to wash in! It was not what we were used to! The rest of the travelling Bluenoses were planning to sleep in the local park and we did receive a few offers to share a bench with us should we wish to join them. We politely declined the offer and decided we would rough it in the bed and breakfast for the night.

We met up with the lads it a fab little pub/bar just outside the ground, which was really nice with a sort of veranda/balcony which we could stand outside on and have a bit of banter. It was right outside the ground and we were able to look over at the ground and watch people arrive. Again it was a small ground but perhaps a bit bigger than the previous two we had visited. It was fun chatting to the lads and they had bought a really big Birmingham City/England flag, which was draped across the railings for all to see. We took some photos of quite a few of us standing on the steps of the pub holding the flag up between us all. It was a great day and one of the lads managed to obtain a roll of tickets from the cellar, which enabled us, all to have free drinks the entire time. They were like the old cinema tickets that we used to have and this is what everyone had to buy to get drinks.

By the time kick off approached we were all a bit the worse for wear and we wandered into the ground saying we were with the Birmingham City team and somehow we managed to get inside without paying! Once inside a couple of the lads tried to climb the floodlights but were pulled down by the local police and thrown out, but after a short while they appeared inside the ground again. I don't remember a lot about the game itself but Blues won 1-0 and we headed back to the pub for a celebratory drink – or two!

A couple of the players joined up with all the Bluenoses outside the pub for a drink after the game, which was fab. Tony Rees and Robert Hopkins came over for a drink and had a bit of banter with the fans. It was really nice when players joined the fans to celebrate, perhaps this helped towards players playing with passion for there clubs unlike today whereby players are more interested in money and playing for the big clubs. Our players at this time gave their all for Birmingham City and that is why we loved them so much. So, after a very enjoyable day, Julie and I headed back to our grotty little bed sit and passed out in exhaustion. On the way we met some Belgium lads and taught them the 'shit on the villa' song, which they picked up rather quickly to be honest.

Ground 40 – Oosterpark Stadion (Holland) – 16th August 1984 – FC Groningen 0 Birmingham City 4 – Pre Season Friendly

Next up was a match against Gronigan, which was a bit of a journey, but we set off in good form as usual and had soon arrived at the small ground ready for the game. Once again we met up with the lads inside the ground this time, as there was a nice sort of clubhouse at the top of the terracing where we were situated. The grounds we visited in Holland were small but sort of nice really. Julie and I had a great time inside this small bar in the ground and just before the game we ventured out onto the terraces. We had already had a little look around the ground when we came in earlier and had enjoyed our little tour.

All the Bluenoses were in good spirits as always, everyone knows what a good sense of humour us Brummies have! The game got underway and it was extremely entertaining as Blues were in good form too and ran away 4-0 winners. The amazing thing was that drink was available throughout the game and we stood on the terraces, plastic glasses in hand, watching the game fully refreshed. And there was no trouble at all! Everyone was probably too drunk to cause trouble to be honest! It was another fun day out watching the Blues and the weather had stayed sunny, making the occasion extremely enjoyable.

The stadium was closed in 2005 and demolished in 2006-7.

Ground 41 – NAC Stadion (Holland) – 18th August 1984 - NAC Breda 0 Birmingham City 0 – Pre Season Friendly

On the day of the last game we set off early and as it was a Saturday game, we found a nice little pub near the ground which was already full of the Blues lads enjoying pre match drinks. It was another lovely sunny day and everyone was sitting either on or at tables outside the pub and the banter was beginning in earnest as the tour and the final match was being discussed. The lads were also discussing the posters threatening the Blues fans with violence at the game. Apparently there were a gang of Breda fans that were going to 'get us' at the game. Like we were worried!

Julie, the lads and myself enjoyed food and drink outside the pub and in due time we set off for the nearby ground and the game. It was an early evening game and we situated ourselves behind one of the goals. As kick off approached the Blues numbers seemed to increase enormously and before long there were hundreds of Blues fans in our end. I wondered what was going on and I got chatting to some of the newcomers who informed me that they were in fact, international hooligans who had heard that the Dutch fans were threatening violence against the Blues and had decided to join in with the Blues. That amused me somewhat.

Before long the game got underway and despite a floodlight failure causing a delay it continued to entertain us. Not long before the end of the game, which finished in a draw, a gang of very young Breda fans made there way towards the Blues end, but after getting the shock of their lives, ended up running their little legs off back to their own end as the Blues lots chased them back. Back on the terraces the rest of the Blues fans laughed at their cheek.

After eleven brilliant days in Holland and Belgium, Julie and I reflected on our great adventure as we packed up and headed back to the Hook of Holland and the ferry trip home. All the lads were also on the same ferry heading back and everyone was absolutely knackered. As we enjoyed our last drinking session together in the ferry bar we exchanged views and some of the lads crashed out in seats to try and catch some sleep. That can be risky when the rest of us are still drinking and a couple of the sleeping lads were covered in newspapers, cigarette butts and one lad had a cigarette placed in his sleeping mouth and his photo was duly taken to show to him when he awoke! And so after a fun packed trip we arrived back on English soil and headed back to Birmingham. It was the sort of thing that memories are made from and a trip of a lifetime for most of us.

The stadium closed and was demolished in May 1996.

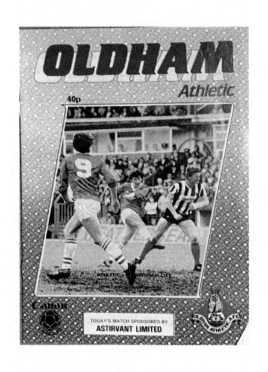

Ground 42 – Boundary Park – 25th August 1984 – Oldham Athletic 0 Birmingham City 1 – Second Division

The 1984 – 1985 season began with an away trip to Oldham, which was a good day out, and Blues came away with a good away win 1-0 to start the season off well. So many Blues fans travelled to Oldham for this game that hundreds of them charged the gates and got into the game for nothing. I was already inside when this happened! I watched as the crowd gathered outside and then suddenly there was a big charge at the exit gate that eventually gave way and loads of Bluenoses surged onto the away terrace. I had to laugh. It was a fantastic atmosphere and when Blues scored our winning the goal the away end went mental. It was absolutely bouncing.

In 1988 I took my mate from Liverpool to the match at Boundary Park with me (even though she was a Liverpool supporter) as it was really easy to get to from Liverpool. We headed to Oldham on the train and my mate got to experience how fantastic Blues away support is. Unfortunately Blues lost 4-0 but I bumped into my mate Julie who I hadn't seen for a while and also my friend Alan.

After the match Alan took us to a nearby sports club for a drink. One thing about Alan is that he always knows a good boozer to go to both before and after matches wherever Blues were playing. The club that we went to this time was a member's only club but somehow Alan managed to get us all in and we had a few drinks and some banter with the locals for a little while after the game. It was really good fun despite the result.

In January 1990 Blues drew Oldham Athletic in the third round of the FA Cup and following a 1-1 draw at St. Andrews, the replay was due to take place at Oldham's ground on the 10th of January. It was an evening game and I asked Angela if she fancied coming too. Angela had some relatives in Oldham, so we decided to head over there early to visit her family.

They were really nice people and one of the lads was an Oldham fan and he was also going to the game. So, after being fed we headed to the pub with him for a few beers before the game. It was a really cold night and I remember thinking what a really cold place Oldham is once we were inside the ground. The game resulted in a disappointing 1-0 defeat for Blues but the Bluenoses had been in good numbers and good voice and 'Keep Right On' was heard loud and proud as usual. Once the game was over Angela and I headed for the local train station and I remember thinking I would die of the cold while we were waiting for the train to take us back to Liverpool where I lived at the time.

I visited Boundary Park on six occasion between 1984 and 1997 and I saw 1 win, 2 draws (both 2-2) and 3 defeats. It's quite sad to see that Oldham Athletic are now a non league team battling it out in the National League (2024). I hope that they return to the Football League soon.

Ground 43 – Craven Cottage – 4th September 1984 – Fulham 0 Birmingham City 1 – Second Division

In September 1984 I headed by train to London for my first game at Craven Cottage to watch Blues play Fulham. I was very impressed when we exited to underground station to find the ground was right next to the river and it had a lovely park by the away end. It was really nice and I liked the big away terrace and the cosy little 'cottage' that was inside the stadium. There was a lot of atmosphere from the home support but the vast Blues travelling support were in excellent voice having visited several London pubs beforehand.

Blues played really well and scored a good goal to take all three points with a 1-0 win. This meant that we headed back to the pubs for a post match drink in very good spirits and eventually headed back to Euston to get a train back to Birmingham. Over the years Fulham has become one of my very favourite away trips.

In November 2015 I was up early and really looking forward to the trip to Fulham as we were traveling by train again and I texted Stephen to let him know what time I thought we would arrive. When we arrived at Marlybone we went on a London Underground adventure that involved four trains and culminated in our arrival at Putney Bridge about an hour later. Stephen was waiting for us outside Putney Bridge station and it was great to see him again. We then had a lovely walk through the park along the riverbank as we headed towards the stadium. We saw boats and rowers in the river and stopped for photos with Putney Bridge in the background. It was damp and overcast but it was still lovely.

After passing a couple of pubs packed with Blues fans we picked up programmes near the ground and I popped into the club shop to get a badge for my collection. Then we followed Baz, for what seemed like ages, to a pub called 'The Crabtree' which, although full of Bluenoses it wasn't as packed as the others pubs we had passed.

I was really hot when we got in the pub after that walk so once we had our drinks we headed to the covered patio area outside. There were Bluenoses there already enjoying their drinks, a few of who I already knew and I had a bit of a catch up. It was great having a catch up with Stephen too and before long the singing began. It started with 'Keep Right On' and we all joined in. It was loud and proud and we all had a great time as we enjoyed our pre match drinks.

Then it was time to head back to the stadium and amazingly the walk appeared shorter than before. Once inside the ground it was swarming with Bluenoses. As everybody stands at away games we managed to get Stephen in with us in the away end so that we could enjoy the game together (his ticket was in the 'neutral area' next to the Blues contingent). The atmosphere was amazing amongst the 4,000 Birmingham fans and song after song rang out.

Craven Cottage, the home of Fulham, was a nice ground with character (sadly lacking from most new stadiums) and we had an amazing view of the Thames from our vantage point in the away end. Blues started the game well and totally dominated. Stephen Gleeson scored a cracker in the 18th minute and the Blues end went wild. Everyone started singing and bouncing and I could feel the stand moving.

Three minutes later cheers broke out again as Clayton Donaldson was upended in the penalty area and the referee pointed to the spot. Up stepped Paul Caddis to smash the ball in the net leading to more wild scenes amongst the 4,000 Birmingham fans plus those in the neutral section. Once again the stand rocked under our feet as the fans bounced in celebration. We were in heaven when Jon Toral scored a fantastic third goal in the 31st minute. Unbelievable celebrations broke out in the away end. The stand was literally shaking. 'Easy! Easy!' broke out and then 'you may as well go home' was sang to the Fulham fans who were looking extremely despondent at this point.

There were cheers at halftime as Blues went into the break with a 3-0 lead. Brilliant! It would have proved too difficult to get halftime refreshments as it was absolutely packed below the stand. It was hard enough getting to the toilets and back. I did see several people that I knew in the process though. Blues were just as good in the second half and Fulham had a player sent off for a second yellow card (in a matter of minutes) in the 49th minute. Fulham did rally a bit though and pulled a goal back in the 66th minute.

This was definitely not a fair reflection of the game though but parity was restored when Clayton Donaldson got our fourth goal in the 82nd minute. The Blues end erupted and Stephen and I jumped around together as the stand shook again. 'All bounce if you love the Blues' rang out. 'Gary Rowett's Blue and white army' followed. Somewhat fortunately Fulham then got a second goal when a lucky deflected pass fell nicely into the path of a Fulham player in injury time. Once again I didn't think that 4-2 was a fair reflection of our dominance but then Solomon-Otabor scored a fantastic solo goal in the 95th minute to make it 5-2 to Blues.

Amazing celebrations broke out in the away end as we celebrated. We had all thoroughly enjoyed this win. Especially as we had been passing the ball about in such style. The Blues fans had been singing 'we're taking the piss, we're taking the piss, we're Birmingham City- we're taking the piss!'

This had definitely been the performance of the season for me. Blues dominated the game and were loudly applauded at the final whistle. The players came over to the away end to applaud the Blues fans and as 'there's only one Gary Rowett' rang out and the man himself turned to wave back and applaud us.

As we all headed back through the park we decided to have a couple of drinks across the river with Stephen before we had to head back to get our train. We crossed Putney Bridge and went into a Wetherspoon's pub called The Rocket, overlooking the Thames. There were several Bluenoses already in there. We took our drinks outside to cool down and watched a fireworks display across the river in the general direction of Fulham's stadium.

Stephen had to head off to meet his friends at a firework display on the other side of London so he headed off. We then headed back across Putney Bridge to get back to Marlybone and our 8.40pm train back to Birmingham. We picked up burgers and pasties etc for the train journey and we were soon on our way home. What a fantastic away day we had enjoyed!

I have visited Craven Cottage 6 times over the years and I have seen 3 wins, 1 draw and 1 defeat which came on my last visit in a totally amazing game in January 2022 that saw Blues lose 6-2 and we didn't play that badly either. Blues Ivan Sunjic scored an absolute screamer in that game too.

Ground 44 – Home Park – 9ᵗʰ October 1984 – Plymouth Argyle 0 Birmingham City 1 – League Cup 2ⁿᵈ Round 2ⁿᵈ Leg

The League Cup draw paired us with Plymouth with the first leg being at St. Andrews. This was duly won 4-1 and then I was really looking forward to the return leg as I had not been to Plymouth before and it would be another new ground for me. Unfortunately it was a night match and with it being so far away it would be quite a long trek and a late return home. With this in mind we booked on the coach, so with a day booked off work, I boarded the coach and we were on our way.

The coach was quite lively and the lads had a few drinks at the stop over and after a fun, if not long journey down south we arrived at Plymouth's ground. It had been a bit of a dull day really and it looked as though it could rain at any time. Although I was 22 years old, I still looked very young so I decided to try the under 16 turnstile to get in for a pound. Julie laughed and said I had no chance, but undeterred, I pulled my Birmingham cap down a little and headed successfully into the ground for a pound through the under 16 turnstile! Great.

Once inside I took in my surroundings. It looked quite old and the away end was terracing behind the goal with no roof! This did not bode well as it looked liked we were in store for rain and I did not fancy getting soaked and having to travel all that way back home soaking wet. As half time arrived the rain duly started so I went over to a steward and told him that I wanted to go back to my seat as I had just popped over to see some mates on the terraces at half time. He asked for our tickets (Julie had joined me as she didn't fancy getting wet either!), which I told him I must have dropped and he duly let us through the fences and round to a nice dry seat with the other Blues fans in the stands. Excellent! The game was quite good too, Blues played well and Wayne Clarke scored the only goal of the game to give us a 1-0 away win and a 5-1 aggregate win to see us through to the third round.

With the game over we headed back to the coach to join the rather wet looking Blues fans that had remained on the open terrace. Everyone was happy and lively and there was loads of singing on the way back. It was quite late when we stopped at the services and everyone poured off for refreshments and toilet breaks. We got back on the coach before most of the others and it was quite funny watching the lads get back on with their arms loaded with various sandwiches they had just acquired and they happily distributed them amongst us. Just what we needed to see us on our way.

The next time I made a trip to Plymouth was on the Saturday before Christmas in 2023 and the game had sold out only hours after the tickets went on sale. Blues would be taking over 1,900 with many going to Home Park for the first time. Although it a return visit for me it had been a long time since my first visit back in 1984 when Blues won 1-0 at a vastly different stadium to that of todays.

Despite the cold weather we were all really looking forward to the trip and we met up at St. Andrews for the early 9am departure to Plymouth. It was a really nice trip and June and the lads all had Blues Christmas jumpers on and looked fab. I can't wear jumpers as I get too hot so I wore my red away top and blue and white tinsel. Once we arrived in Plymouth we all put on our blue and white Santa hats and me and June had our 'Santa is a Brummie' scarves on and we headed round to the away end which was squirreled away down a tree lined alleyway along the edge of a park. It wasn't very well lit either.

We arrived outside the away turnstiles and headed to the outside bar once we had negotiated the searches and the sniffer dogs. Yes that really is how it is at modern day football games. Anyway, we headed to the bar and purchased our Thatchers cider as that was the only cider on offer and we chatted away until we had consumed our drinks then headed into the stadium. We had good seats giving us a good view of the pitch and the Bluenoses were in good spirits. It was a fantastic atmosphere.

Blues played really well and we were really enjoying the occasion. It took only 15 minutes for Blues to take the lead as Jay Stansfield headed home before heading to the Plymouth fans showing his t-shirt that read 'once a red always a red' which was in reference to him and his dad being Exeter City fans, Plymouth's great rivals. Obviously we celebrated accordingly in the away end. We were noisy and jumped all over the place in celebration.

Blues were dominant and we went 2-0 up when Jordan James scored and the away end went crazy. It looked to be a game that Blues would win very comfortably, especially if we took some more of the chances we were creating. However, the Blues players looked a bit too comfortable and when Dion Sanderson was dithering on the ball in a very dangerous position a Plymouth player dispossessed him and scored easily to make it 2-1 just before halftime.

This was extremely disappointing but things got even worse when Kristian Bielik received a straight red card when a Plymouth player actually fell over his foot. What a joke! Blues were now down to ten men and this changed the complexion of the game completely. Blues had been cruising and could easily have gone on to win 4 or 5-1. We were now up against it.

Blues still looked by far the better side though and deservedly went 3-1 ahead when Juninho Bacuna ran through to score in the 62nd minute and the away end exploded in celebration once again. This was absolutely fantastic! We only had to hold on to our lead now and it would be a great away win surely. Then in the 68th minute I remembered that Blues can't defend since Rooney came in and Plymouth pulled a goal back and began to look threatening.

My worst fears came true when more poor defending allowed Plymouth to grab a very unlikely equaliser with only 4 minutes remaining. I sighed. Wouldn't you just know it was going to happen. So what should have be a very comprehensive victory ended in a 3-3 draw. Plymouth supporters remarked that we were the best team they had seen at Home Park this season. It was a shame that we blew it by getting a player sent off. Blues remained 18th in the table and we had a very long trip home following our walk back to coaches down a very dark lane with some (most) of the lights not working.

Hence, I have seen only 2 games, a win and a draw. No defeats is a great record and I have enjoyed my trips there so far.

Ground 45 – Ninian Park – 1st December 1984 – Cardiff City 1 Birmingham City 2 – Second Division

It was a cold December days when we headed to Wales by train for my first visit to Cardiff and we had a very enjoyable journey with our usual pre packed refreshments and beers. There were a lot of Bluenoses on the train and it was great to have a good catch up with them. I was still only young and very much enjoying my away trips with Blues and life was good.

We arrived in good spirits and our singing began as soon as we hit the platform and the awaiting police escort looked less than impressed. We didn't care though and enjoyed our journey to the old looking Ninian Park. The Cardiff fans were even less impressed to see us than the police escort. It was a good atmosphere inside the ground though and there was lots of banter to be had.

Tony Morley scored two goals as we beat Cardiff City in Cardiff. Apart from the fact that the welsh fans can be quite hostile, we had a very enjoyable day out and I got to visit another new ground for me. Again, it was an old looking ground but the Bluenoses had a nice terraced end behind the goal giving us a good view of the game. We sang and celebrated quite a lot really and also got to sing 'Eng er land, Eng er land!' quite a bit. The celebrations continued on our march back to the station after the game and on the train back the Birmingham!

I only visited Ninian Park on this one occasion but it was enjoyable. The stadium was demolished in October 2009 to become a housing estate with the new Cardiff City Stadium built just opposite the site.

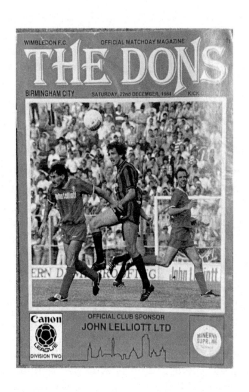

Ground 46 – Plough Lane – 22ⁿᵈ December 1984 – Wimbledon 1 Birmingham City 2 – Second Division

On the 22ⁿᵈ December, just two days before Christmas Blues had an away fixture in London, this time against Wimbledon. The girls and I were really looking forward to this one as it was just before Christmas and we could deck ourselves out in blue and white tinsel – well, I could. It also meant another new ground. At least the rain and snow held off and before long we were standing outside the ground drinking beers and watching people arrive and socialise as we were doing. I had blue and white tinsel round my neck and tied around my wrist and in my hair and was feeling very Christmassy!

After consuming our beers we headed into the ground to have a look around and find a good position to watch the game. Blues were situated on the terrace behind the goal with quite a good view, in what was quite a small ground really, although not bad for a small, relatively new club like Wimbledon. There was no roof though.

As I looked around for any wombles that might appear, I noticed loads of Blues fans coming in dressed in fancy dress. They had made a great effort and everyone looked brilliant! It was really amusing; I remember seeing a John McEnroe impersonator in complete tennis outfit, with wig, headband and tennis racket – on a cold December day! The outfits really were excellent and even the Blues players were impressed. The players duly rose to the occasion and David Geddis scored two goals to make our Christmas complete with a 2-1 win. The Bluenoses were dancing and singing and promptly sang 'jingle bells, jingle bells, jingle all the way, oh what fun it is to see City win away!'

It was a small ground but really nice despite being on an open terrace on a very cold day and I really enjoyed my visit. Sadly I never got to visit again and it remains my only visit to Plough. A nice 100% win rate for me there though.

Wimbledon moved to Selhurst Park to ground-share with Crystal Palace at the start of the 1991-92 season as nothing came of the plans for a new stadium and the board decided that Plough Lane was beyond redevelopment to meet the new FA rules requiring all-seater stadiums. The ground lay derelict until it was finally demolished in 2002. Because they sold their ground at Plough Lane for housing developments Milton Keynes tempted them with a move to their town and they became MK Dons. AFC Wimbledon rose from the ashes and are now back in the football league and have built a new stadium in Plough Lane where the Greyhound stadium used to be.

Ground 47 – Leeds Road – 2ⁿᵈ February 1985 – Huddersfield Town 0 Birmingham City 1 – Second Division

In February 1985 I made my first trip to the old Leeds Road ground to watch Blues play Huddersfield. It was quite a big ground and looked old but like many of the old grounds it had character. It reminded me a little bit of St. Andrews with the large terraces and we were on a large old terrace area designated for the away fans. It felt very open and cold but we warmed the place up with our atmosphere. Blues won the game 1-0 so it was a good trip. I was to travel to Leeds Road again in 1991 to watch Blues again win the game 1-0. Only two trips to the old ground meant that I never saw Blues lose there. Excellent.

Leeds Road had large terraces on three sides of the ground which looked great but made it difficult following the Hillsborough report which stipulated that stadiums had to become all seater. Hence a new stadium was built whilst Leeds Road had a reduced capacity and it was eventually demolished in 1994. Leeds Road had survived a fire, two floodlight pylons being blown down in a gale and the threat of moving to Elland Road as a new club. The site is now a retail park with the only sign of its existence being a plaque in the car park of B & Q.

Ground 48 – Manor Ground – 2nd March 1985 – Oxford United 0 Birmingham City 3 – Second Division

Blues were off to Oxford Utd for a top of the table clash in March 1985 and I was so looking forward to this and had heard other Bluenoses planning for this trip for weeks beforehand. So, on the day of the game, the girls and I boarded the football special and we were soon on our way to Oxford. The atmosphere on the train was brilliant with loads of singing, and after consuming our packed lunch and beers we were soon arriving in Oxford.

There seemed to be Blues fans everywhere and we sang all the way to Oxford Utd's small ground. Once inside the Blues fans were in carnival atmosphere, with chants of 'were gonna win the league' etc. Blues fans were situated on the open terraced end behind the goal, and we had completely filled our end. I thought that Oxford's ground was small but quite quaint. I thought one of the ends along the side with a small stand on its own in the middle was strange and different. There were quite a few Oxford fans present as well as they were on a good run and favourites for promotion. There were 11,584 inside the small ground but the atmosphere was great, just apt for the top of the table clash that it was.

It was a brilliant game and when Blues scored the away end erupted and I was swept off my feet and carried a few yards further on. Our end was swaying like an ocean and 'Keep Right On' was sang loud and proud. There was a gang of Blues lads dressed a bit like the blues brothers in our end. Before long Blues were 2-0 up and I was lifted off my feet again on a massive wave as we again celebrated. I was in heaven when the third goal went in and we came away 3-0 winners in such an important game.

Once again it was great fun following the Blues and life was again enjoyable as a Bluenose. Blues goals were scored by David Geddis and Wayne Clarke, who got two of them. There was loads of trouble as we headed out of the ground and towards the train station as the Blues fans fought with the police and I saw a couple of police vans turned onto their sides. I don't know who was coming off worse to be honest but the Oxford fans were nowhere to be seen. I headed back towards the relative safety of the train home!

I was back at the Manor Ground the following February 1986 for another great trip and once again Blues came away victorious with a 1-0 win. This was to be my last visit there which meant that I had a 100% win record having seen Blues play twice there and won on both occasions.

The last game played at the Manor Ground was in May 2001 and the ground was demolished in 2001. It is now The Manor Hospital which is a private hospital owned by Nuffield Health.

Ground 49 – Brunton Park – 12th March 1985 – Carlisle United 2 Birmingham City 1 – Second Division

It was a long trip in store for us up north to Carlisle as we prepared to take on Carlisle Utd. This would be another new ground for Julie and me and I was again travelling in Alan's car for the long trip. As was usual we sent off early and after a short refreshment break we arrived in Carlisle, parked the car and headed for a pub near to the ground. As it happened the pub we chose was right across the road from the ground and it was a nice little pub to have a few pre match beers in.

I was in my usual excited pre match mood and chatted avidly, sang a few songs enjoyed a few beers and then we were off to join the other Bluenoses on the away terrace inside the ground. Due to the fact that it was such a long way and it was a night game there was not the usual massive Blues away following, but there was still quite a few, never the less, and they were in good voice. Carlisle's ground was really small and there were only 4,099 inside to watch the game.

Probably a good job really as Blues reminded us what it can be like being a Bluenose as we lost 2-1 with Wayne Clarke again scoring for us. It didn't give us much to cheer about on the trip home so we stopped off at local Chinese just before we left Carlisle for a takeaway for the journey. I must admit it was quite a memorable takeaway too, as it was the first time I had had a curry and rice in the same takeaway carton – neatly separated side by side! It was really tasty too, but that could have had something to do with the beers I had consumed earlier! Despite the result I did enjoy my trip and it was another new ground visited

This has been my only visit to Brunton Park up to the present day but I would definitely like to visit again should the opportunity present itself to watch Blues play Carlisle once again so that I could see what changes have been made. From the games I have seen on TV I doubt that much as changed if anything. It did have character though and I would love to stand on those terraces again for old time's sake.

Blackburn Rovers v Birmingham City
Division Two, Saturday, 16th March, 1985. Kick-off 3 p.m.

Ground 50 – Ewood Park – 16th March 1985 – Blackburn Rovers 2 Birmingham City 1 – Second Division

I made my first trip to Ewood park back in 1985 when the stadium showed absolutely no resemblance to the stadium of today. It was old with fenced off terraces and old wooden stands and it felt cold inside. I don't remember too much about that first trip but Blues lost 2-1 in the old second division and so I probably put it to the back of my mind pretty quickly. Today's stadium is completely new compared to what it was in 1985.

In October 2007 I was off to Blackburn to see Birmingham take on Blackburn Rovers at Ewood Park. I had not been to Ewood Park since it had been made all seated. In fact, the last time I had been there it had been to stand on the old terraces, so I was really looking forward to this trip. Also it would be my last game before I had to fly back to my home in Abu Dhabi in the United Arab Emirates, and my niece Nicola was coming with me for her first away trip.

It was a bit cloudy when Steve called to pick us up at 9.15am but at least it wasn't raining. Steve was going to drop us at St. Andrews where we would board the supporter's coaches that were due to leave at 10.15. Nicola and I were really excited and had our packed lunch that my mum had made up the night before for the two of us, along with several other goodies all packed in a carrier bag for the coach.

We arrived in plenty of time, stood in the queue for the coaches and were soon on board and waiting to leave. Nicola had her mini iPod with her and I had a newspaper for the journey. I was wearing my new white away shirt, which looked fab, so I thought. The coaches set off on time and it wasn't too long before we were pulling up at the service station for a forty minute stop. Nicola and I disembarked to use the toilets and saw a few Tottenham fans and a couple of Liverpool fans standing outside the services.

They looked surprised to see so many Birmingham City fans descending on them. It looked quite funny when we came out of the toilets as there were Blues fans everywhere! The shop and restaurants were full of fans wearing Birmingham shirts. It looked great and Nicola was well impressed. We headed back on the coach and spent the rest of the time eating sandwiches, chatting and waiting for the others to return so that we could recommence on our journey.

It wasn't too long before we were being met by our police escort on the outskirts of Blackburn and being led towards the ground. As the coach was pulling into the car park next to the ground, I noticed a nice big pub on the corner with tables and benches outside that seemed to be full of Birmingham fans, so I decided to head over to this pub once we disembarked.

Once Nicola and I were off the coach we headed back up the road and into the large pub called the Fernhouse. The outside area and large car park were already filled with Blues fans and as we headed inside the bouncers directed us to the upstairs bar/function room, which was now being used as an overspill as the downstairs bars were packed with Birmingham fans.

There was a big sign welcoming Blues fans as we entered the pub which had two large bars downstairs with large screens showing the Arsenal v Sunderland game. We headed upstairs into a massive room with a small bar and another large screen showing the same match as downstairs. There were about 20 Blues fans already in there with others coming up the stairs behind us as directed by the bouncers.

I obtained a pint of cider for myself and a coke for Nicola as she was only 15 and we went over by the large bay windows to watch the Blues fans having fun in the car park below us. There was a big Birmingham City flag draped over the wall of the car park which was being held in place by two very large rocks. Nicola and I had a good laugh at that. The Blues fans outside were drinking and singing and generally enjoying themselves as the mounted police looked on nearby. I had a few drinks upstairs, watched the fans and had a chat with the barmaid who kept coming over to chat to me and to enquire about the Blues fans. She was telling me a bit about the Manchester City fans from the week before, who didn't sound a friendly lot at all by all accounts. They had been fighting amongst themselves in the car park when the pub was about to stop serving because of trouble in the ground.

The Blues fans, on the other hand, were just enjoying the day and having a good drink and sing song. As we had got to the pub at just after one o'clock, I was able to have a couple of drinks before we left the pub at about twenty five to three to walk the short distance to the ground. We had electronic tickets which took me a couple of minutes to work out how to use, by which time Nicola had used hers at the next turnstile and was waiting for me inside. There was already a lot of Blues fans in the bar area underneath the stand and I saw a few people I knew and said hello to.

We headed up to our seat behind the goal and the Blues fans were already in good voice and singing abuse towards Robbie Savage. The teams were already on the pitch warming up and Blues were playing in our third kit of red shirts, red shorts and red socks. There were a lot inside the ground but also quite a few empty seats amongst the Blackburn fans. This led to Blues singing 'your grounds to big for you' which was quite funny. They also sang 'it's just like being in church' due to the fact that Blackburn didn't sing much. Blues sang 'you've only got one song' as well as ninety minutes of abuse to Robbie (Judas) Savage, which was highly enjoyable. Nicola and I sang loads, and enjoyed the atmosphere in the away end. Keep Right On was sang loud and proud as usual and when Blues sang 'Brucie – give us a wave', Steve Bruce waved across at us.

The game wasn't quite as entertaining as the Blues fans and when Blackburn took the lead it didn't stop us singing, in fact just the opposite, we burst into a rendition of 'were Birmingham, were Birmingham, were Birmingham City!' loudly. Then, not long after half time we had a perfectly good goal by McSheffrey disallowed. Larsson crossed it in from the goal line and with a player lying at his feet, thereby playing the other onside, McSheffrey tapped it in. NOTHING WRONG WITH IT. Brucie was raging afterwards, especially as Blackburn then went straight up the other end and won a penalty.

At 2-0 down it looked daunting, but give Blues credit, we really came at them and it wasn't long before the ball fell to Jerome in the area and he hit a cracker into the top corner right in front of us. Fantastic, the Blues fans went wild and Nicola and I jumped all over the place. It should really have been 2-2, but somewhat unfairly, it finished 2-1 to Blackburn despite all our attacking. Their keeper kept them in it in injury time by tipping over a Jerome header that was heading for the top corner.

At one point, four Blackburn fans in the end next to us started singing and the whole of the Blues end started singing 'there's only four of you singing, four of you singing, there's only four of you singing'. This gave us a laugh and despite losing it had been an enjoyable trip with the entertainment among the blues fans being perhaps the best part. So, game over, but not too despondent, we headed back to board the coach to head back the Birmingham.

Nicola said she had really enjoyed the trip and would defiantly come again. She was a great little singer and great company. The trip back was uneventful, Nicola listened to her iPod for a while then we chatted and had a laugh as we got closer to home. As the coach passed the vile ground we all sang 'shit on the villa' and had another laugh and before long we were back at the car park at St. Andrews. My brother Neil and his wife Sue came to pick us up and we spent the journey back telling them what a fabulous trip we had just had.

Another good trip was in the FA Cup in January 2023. We arrived early to get the coach to Blackburn due to the large number travelling and today the coaches were leaving from Tilton road. It was disorganised chaos when the coaches arrived and tried to get into some sort of order but we eventually made our way onto Coach 4 and got the back seat and put our flag up. Taff arrived but was on coach 8 and we were told our coach was full. There was one empty seat on the back seat by us just before departure time so we were allowed to call Taff and he came and joined us.

Taff had originally been planning to drive but his son Ryan and 29 of his mates had booked to go on the train hence Taff being booked on coach 8. Unfortunately though, the rail staff were on strike again and the trains weren't running and so Ryan and his mates had to head to Digbeth Coach station. They had to get a coach to Manchester, a train to Bolton and then a train to Blackburn. Fair play to them.

Our coaches arrived at Blackburn's stadium about 12.30 and me, June, Taff, Nigel, Charlie and Liam headed over to the nearby social club and we were soon settled in nice seats with drinks in hand. Nigel noticed that some people in the club had bought chips in and so, after checking with the bouncer if it was okay to do the same, him and Charlie went and fetched chips for us all. They were really dry though, so we didn't eat many. They were so dry I considered pouring cider on them. Obviously I didn't though.

The team was announced and although there were several changes it was still a fairly strong team. I was really pleased about that as I really want to have a cup run. Blues had a strong bench though. We drank up and headed over to the away end to join the 4,000 travelling army. Our seats were down the front, just 6 rows up and the weather was awful and a fine rain blew down on us. A girl in front of us was hit on the head by a stray ball in the warm up and she spent the remainder of the game with a cold compress held to her head.

The game got underway with Blues kicking towards the home end and we were stunned when Khadra fired home to give Blues the lead with only 3 minutes gone and we celebrated accordingly. The Bluenoses were in great voice too and were singing loudly. It was great to hear it following the poor support at Forest Green Rovers in the last round. Sadly Blackburn got their equaliser on 33 minutes from a scrambled goal and then took the lead in the first minute of the second half. My hear sank.

It was looking grim as Eustace made his usual substitutions as he took off our best players and I despaired as he brought on Jordan James with only 2 minutes remaining. I wasn't alone in letting out a huge sigh either and I though 'game over'. Nigel said 'here comes our fucking savour!' with more than a hint of sarcasm.

Amazingly though, that was exactly what he was as Hannibal put a lovely cross into his path and Jordan James fired the ball into the bottom corner in the 91st minute to make it 2-2 right in front of the Blues fans. The away end went completely mental as the players ran over to celebrate with us. There were unbelievable scenes as Blues sang "we're Birmingham City, we'll fight to the end". The magic of the FA Cup! The game finished 2-2 and, as there was no extra time as this stage of the competition, we headed back to the coaches very happy in the knowledge that we would be in the draw for the 5th round on Monday and we would be the only West Midlands team in the draw. It has been a great day despite the weather and we headed home happy.

The draw for the 5th round was made on the Monday and Blues or Blackburn were drawn away to Premier League Leicester City. Following my initial disappointment with this draw I decided it was actually quite good because at least it was away (crap atmosphere at home in cup games), it wasn't too far, it was winnable and we would take a big following. We had to win the replay first though.

I have made 10 trips to Ewood Park over the years and I have seen 4 draws and 6 defeats. I have never seen Blues win there which makes it a bit of a bogey ground for me.

Ground 51 – Blundell Park – 5th April 1985 - Grimsby Town 1 Birmingham City 0 – Second Division

I had another long trip and another new ground to look forward to. This time we were off to Grimsby and we were taking the train. As Julie, Pam, Debbie and I boarded the train we were joined by more Bluenoses including Lee Pitman who sat with us and chatted avidly about 'Blues stuff'. It was a long journey and quite a few refreshments were downed as we all got to know each other and began having quite a laugh.

When we arrived in Grimsby we all stayed together and before long we were all inside the ground cheering on the lads. It was a terraced area behind the goal where we were located and the ground was a fair size for their football Club really. The Blues fans sang their hearts out for the lads and it was a great atmosphere but once again we were disappointed and the game ended in a 1-0 defeat. However, we were still in the mood to enjoy ourselves, so as we headed back to the station we continued to sing and celebrated our victory of out-singing the home supporters.

Once back on the train we were still in party mood, but as our train headed out of Grimsby at a slow speed, we were ambushed by Grimsby fans who had decided to see us off by throwing bricks at the train. It was a big mistake picking on a train full of Bluenoses and the train was brought to an immediate standstill by the pulling of the emergency chain by a few of the Bluenoses. The Blues fans streamed off and chased the, by now petrified Grimsby Town fans across a field and over a fence. It was quite funny to see really as the Grimsby fans had quite clearly not been expecting this and had got the fright of their lives!

Before long, the Blues fans returned the train and after a while we got away again, only to be ambushed again a few minutes along the track. Of course, the Blues fans carried out a repeat of earlier and again chased the remaining few Grimsby fans across more fields and this time they well and truly got the message. However, the train driver was by now fed up and was seen sitting on the embankment with his head in his hands. He told Blues fans that this ambush happened regularly after the games but the Blues fans were the first ones to stop the train and give chase! After much persuasion and promises not to pull the cord again, the driver returned to his cab and the train got underway again. That had been fun. Best part of the trip really!

As boredom set in on the long journey back, we began thinking of ways to enjoy ourselves. With this in mind we decided to see how many people we could get in the tiny British rail train toilet. I think we managed about nine but we were really squeezed in with people standing on the toilet etc. After laughing amongst ourselves as we ran out of air, we decided to wait until someone outside went passed and then file out one after the other. It was really funny to see their shocked face when nine of us calmly filed out of the small toilet. I did say we were bored at this point! We were in very good spirits when we got back so we headed into Boogies in the town centre for a couple of drinks before heading home after a very entertaining day. Who said following Blues wasn't fun eh!

I visited again the following year (1986) with this trip being even better than the last one as loads of Bluenoses traveled, we out-sang the home support and came away with a very good 1-0 win for Blues. A really good day out. I have not been back to Blundell Park since 1986 and I'm sure the ground must have changed an awful lot since then.

Ground 52 – Fratton Park – 13th April 1985 – Portsmouth 1 Birmingham City 3 – Second Division

In April 1985 we headed down south to take on Portsmouth at Fratton Park. Once again we decided to travel by train and it was the same group of us that embarked on the three-hour train journey south. It was another entertaining trip as we all chatted and laughed together, clad in our Blues colours. I personally was full of optimism this season and was enjoying the promotion battle. I don't know which is more nerve wracking to be honest, a relegation battle or a promotion battle! Although I know which I prefer and it's not the former!

Once we arrived at the ground we made our way into the away end which at this time was open terracing behind the goal. As everyone who has ever been to Fratton Park will know, there was no roof on the away end and on most occasions the away fans ended up getting soaking wet and it always seemed to pour with rain when Blues visited. On this occasion however, it was a nice day and there were quite a few Bluenoses that had made the long trip.

It was certainly made worthwhile when David Geddis, our new blonde striker put us ahead. Brilliant! As the second goal by Geddis went in to make it 2-0, I turned around to celebrate with the girls only to be caught in a surge forward – or for me –backwards! I was pinned against a crash barrier and I was very fortunate not to break my back! I would never be doing that again I can tell you! Our day was complete when Geddis got his hat trick – scoring the third goal right in front of us celebrating Bluenoses! The Blues fans went wild and we celebrated for ages, singing the jingle bells song again – 'oh what fun it is to see City win away!' We had been singing it a lot this season. So, after a fantastic 3-0 away win at Portsmouth we headed back to Birmingham very happy indeed.

In 2005 Blues were away at Portsmouth and Neil had said that himself, sue and Nicola would take Stephen and I to Portsmouth and enjoy a day out at the same time. This was great news and I was really happy to travel with them. It was a lovely sunny day too, and we set out early to have the whole day down in Portsmouth. When we arrived we headed to the City centre for a look around before heading to a local pub for a drink. We found a nice city centre pub and were soon joined by other Bluenoses who were also down for the match. Then we headed off to get some food, I fancied chips for a change. Neil had a really nice England top on with a union jack and someone stopped him and asked where he got it from. I thought it was quite funny when he told them he got it in Blackpool. 'Bit far to go really', the bloke replied with a smile.

Just before kickoff, Neil dropped Stephen and me at the ground and they headed off to the sea front. Stephen and I headed into the away end, with no roof, but for once it was a lovely day and we sat down in the lovely sunshine. We were only a few seats from the front and had a great view. Hence we had a great view of Nicky Butt has he got sent off for a foul on a Pompey player right in front of us. I turned to Stephen 'what the bloody hell did he do that for?' as we looked on amazed. Now Blues were really up against it and Portsmouth scored to take a 1-0 lead.

Blues got a corner as the Pompey fans were in full voice. 'This will shut them up' I said to Stephen, and sure enough the ball came across for Jarosik to score our equaliser. We jumped up and celebrated as the away end was a mass of celebration. Even though Blues only had 10 men we played really well for the rest of the game and it finished all square at 1-1 and we were off to meet up with the others for the journey back. We stopped at a small motel on the way back for a drink and a meal and all in all we had had a very nice day out at the seaside.

I was back at Fratton Park in March 2008 and I was really looking forward to the trip to Portsmouth and as it was a night game Stephen and I booked to travel on the St. Andrews Tavern coach. It was a long trip and we had been supplied with refreshments by my mom as always. Once we arrived in Portsmouth we disembarked and headed in the general direction of the ground where we bumped into Alan and his mates. I asked him if he was going to the pub and he said he wasn't but his mate Bob was so I headed off to the pub with Bob.

There were loads of Portsmouth fans in the nearby pub so I kept my shirt covered up until a load of Bluenoses turned up. We were still hopelessly outnumbered though but we enjoyed our drinks in peace and chatted about the game. It was funny being in a pub with Stephen now that he could legally drink and I think this was the first time I had bought him a pre match pint! It didn't seem that long ago since he was 5 years old and I was holding his hand on the way to the matches, now he is so tall that I am only at shoulder level to him!

As kick off time approached we headed off into the ground and took up our seats. Once the match got underway the Blues fans had decided to remain standing for the game as usual and the atmosphere and singing amongst our lot was great. Before long though, Blues were losing 2-0. What a disappointment! Then we started to play better and we pulled a goal back 2-1. Just before half time we scored again 2-2 and the Blues fans began singing '2-0 and you fucked it up!' to the Portsmouth fans. It was really funny and the atmosphere was great even if it was freezing. The half time whistle went and Stephen and I headed off to get a sausage roll.

Unfortunately the second half was not as good as the first and we conceded two more goals which inspired the Pompy fans to sing '2-2 and you fucked it up!' back at us. I admit to finding that a bit funny though, but the game ended in a 4-2 defeat and if was off out into the cold for the long journey home.

Over the years I have visited Fratton Park on 6 occasions and I have seen 2 wins, 1 draw and 3 defeats. The last visit was a shocker in the League Cup in 2019 when we travelled all that way for a midweek night game only to discover that the manager had decided to field the youth team. It was awful and we lost 3-0. On a positive note our young Jude Bellingham made his debut for Blues and he stood out. What a player he turned out to be and we got to watch him grow from a boy into one of the best players in the world and he is Blue through and through.

Ground 53 – Oakwell Stadium – 27th April 1985 – Barnsley 0 Birmingham City 1 – second Division

I made my first trip to Oakwell Stadium back in 1985 and it was and old ground with a large away terrace behind the goal which was filled with Bluenoses in good voice. I don't remember too much about this first trip apart from the cold and the fact that Blues achieved a good 1-0 away win and we all headed home very happy.

In 2009 I made my second trip to Oakwell and I was up early and off to get the coach which, due to the fact that there was only one, it was quickly filling. It was a good journey and we soon arriving in Barnsley. The coach pulled up in the car park near the ground and we were soon disembarking in search of a pub.

Brendon had planned to take us to the local leisure centre next to the ground where, he informed us, there was a very nice pub inside. He was correct and the pub itself was quite big really and very nice. There were a few red shirts already inside when we arrived and as the pub quickly began to fill up with Bluenoses, the red shirts promptly left. I made the mistake of ordering a pint with the lads and then had to keep up with them! We all had a very pleasant time in there and I met some new people.

Then it was off to the ground via a shortcut through a load of bushes. Brendon got stuck as he caught his coat on a bush, which gave me a bit of a giggle. And then it was into the ground, of which Blues had been given half of one end behind the goal with the other end being kept empty. This was great as we just headed to the bars at the empty end and got served immediately. We bumped into other Bluenoses that I knew including Graham and Paul Fiddler from Harborne. Then we went to find a seat and as Brendon headed for empty seats towards the front, I redirected him to the centre of the singing fans as I wanted to sing! And sing I did, encouraging Brendon to join me in full voice, which he did as we belted out 'keep right on' proudly.

Blues played really well, but I was dismayed when Barnsley scored against the run of play. Just our luck, I thought as I headed to the toilets in disgust. I was just returning to my seat when Blues scored and I ran along our row jumping madly on everyone. Brendan and I jumped all over the place in celebration. The atmosphere amongst the Blues contingent was brilliant, although a couple of idiot stewards tried to spoil the party by moving in and trying to drag out anyone who looked to be enjoying themselves too much.

Blues promptly broke into song and sang 'get a proper job, get a proper job'. I smiled and joined in, and before long the local constabulary had a camcorder trained on the singing Blues hoard. Must have been for their collection of all time greats! Blues broke into another chorus of 'you can stick your fucking camera up your arse!' which, again, I found really amusing. So, apart from only getting a draw as the match finished 1-1, I had a really good day out.

In November 2013 we travelled to Barnsley by train and mom dropped me at Selly Oak station to meet Brendan and the others to get the train to New Street and then Barnsley via a change at Sheffield. When we arrived in Barnsley we got a taxi to the 'Dove Inn' where we enjoyed a few pre match drinks. They were serving freshly made pork and stuffing sandwiches and homemade pie and mushy peas. They were even selling match-day programmes in the pub.

We all had a nice time (there was 9 of us) and the pub was full of Bluenoses. We then walked to the ground. It was brilliant. Inside the ground the Blues fans (920 of us) sang throughout the entire match and Blues were 3-0 up after only 37 minutes. The game finished 3-0 and we were all celebrating like mad and a few new songs were born too, I loved the new Caddis song and the Wade Elliott song. Jack Butland was in goal for Barnsley and he got some stick which was a shame really as he didn't want to leave Blues. The Bluenoses did sing 'there's only one Jack Butland' at the end though and he applauded us and gave his gloves to a young Bluenose. Then we were off to a pub by the station before getting the train back to Birmingham.

In February 2020 I made my another trip to Oakwell again on a cold Tuesday night and this time there was four of us as me, June and James G were joined by Charlie. We had our usual meet at Morrisons and then met Charlie at the coaches and we were soon on our way to Barnsley. When we arrived it was really cold, so we headed to the nearby pub in the leisure centre. When we got there we were surprised to see that it was already full and with a queue of Bluenoses waiting to go in. Charlie took one look and said he was heading off to the chippie. The rest of us gave it a few minutes but once we realised they were only letting someone in once someone else came out, and the Bluenoses already inside looked settle, we decided to join Charlie at the chippie.

We found Charlie and once we obtained our chips we stood outside in the cold eating our chips and gravy. And then the freezing hail stones hit us! My remaining chips were quickly dumped in the bin and we made a dash back towards the ground and made our way into the away end. Charlie only had a thin top on and he looked frozen. Even I had my hood up - it was freezing but at least it was dry inside and the Blues fans were in really good voice. There were a lot of Bluenoses here tonight, around 1,500, which was probably helped by the tickets being priced at only £15.

The game kicked off in awful conditions as the storm kicked in and Blues were playing well considering. We sang our hearts out to get behind them. There wasn't many chances though and it looked like it would either end goalless or one goal would win it. That goal came in the second half when Jude Bellingham chased a lost cause but managed to keep the ball in play before crossing to Scott Hogan to fire home right in front of the away end and we exploded in celebration. It certainly warmed us up. What a player Scott Hogan had turned out to be, he only needed one chance and it was in the back of the net. He was on fire at the moment.

The game finished with a great 1-0 away win and we headed back to the coaches really happy and saying that the others had missed two fantastic away trips despite the weather. It was a long cold trip home and I was late to bed but it was worth it.

I have made 6 trips to Oakwell Stadium over the years and I have seen 3 wins, 2 draws and just 1 defeat. It always seems to be freezing cold when we visit but we got a nice big away end behind the goal and it's usually a good trip.

Ground 54 – Eastville Stadium – 24th September 1985 – Bristol Rovers 2 Birmingham City 3 – League Cup 2nd Round 1st Leg

It was time for the League cup again and Blues had been drawn against Bristol Rovers with the first leg away in Bristol. I had never been to Bristol Rovers ground but it didn't look like I would be able to go as it was a night match and there was no way we could get back after the game if we took the train.

To cheer us up and take our mind of the game that day, Julie and I decided to go to Northfield and have a wander around the shops and just as we were about to wander into Woolworth's for a browse we saw a minibus full of Blues fans pull up outside. One of the lads headed for the nearby cashpoint and another headed into Woolworth's. I was gutted that we were going to miss the match so I decided to ask the lads if they were going to the game and if there was room for two more! To Julie's delight and mine they said yes and told us to jump in. This was brilliant and Julie and I jumped in the back of the minibus and after introductions all round we were soon chatting away with the lads.

One of the lads had a massive ghetto Blaster and he had just been into Woolworth's in order to obtain batteries for it as he intended to take it onto the terraces at Bristol. We drank beers and chatted and before long we were in Bristol and headed towards the ground. The lads had decided that they were going to stay overnight after the game so that left us stuck in Bristol with no lift home but I wasn't too worried at this point as I was already looking forward to the game.

There were quite a few Bluenoses on the away terrace and Julie and I soon got chatting to them and joined the singing. I saw one of the lads I had come to know at the away games named Brendan and as luck would have it he had driven down on his own and lived in Bartley Green, which is near to where I live. He said he would be happy to take us back after the game, so with that cleared up I joined in the singing with the background music of the massive ghetto Blaster and looked forward to the game.

Bristol Rovers were in the old third division at the time therefore there were only 4,332 inside the ground but we were treated to a good game of football. Goals from Robert Hopkins, Andy Kennedy and an own goal gave Blues a 3-2 away leg win and we celebrated all the way home in Brendan's car. It had been a surprise trip for Julie and I as we had thought we wouldn't be able to get to the game so both of us were thrilled that we had been to the match and come away with a win. A week later when the return leg came around Blues again beat Bristol Rovers, this time 2-1 and we were through to the next round and we were rewarded with draw against Southampton.

This was my only trip to Eastville Stadium but I really enjoyed the visit. Bristol Rovers moved out of the stadium in 1986 and spent a decade at Twerton Park in Bath. Greyhound racing continued at Eastville stadium though. The old Eastville Stadium was closed in 1997 and was demolished by 1998. It was left derelict till the following year and it was transformed into an IKEA superstore.

Ground 55 – Boothferry Park – 20th September 1986 – Hull City 3 Birmingham City 2 – Second Division

My one and only trip to the now demolished Boothferry Park came in September 1985 and in all honesty I do not remember a lot about this trip other than it was another older ground and was smaller than our own St. Andrews ground. We traveled by official supporters club coach and Blues lost the game 3-2 but it was always great to travel and visit a new ground for myself and friends at this time. I would have enjoyed it immensely.

Boothferry Park took 17 years to build and for 56 years it was the home of Hull City before seeing its last game player there in 2002 when they moved to their new stadium the KC Stadium. The ground was left derelict for many years before demolition began in 2009 with the floodlights being taken down in 2011. The site is now a housing estate with streets named Black and Amber Way, Bunkers Hill Road and Legends Way.

Official Matchday Magazine

London Docklands supports Millwall

Price 60p

Millwall

TODAY'S MATCH
SPONSORED
BY CBS/FOX VIDEO

THE TODAY LEAGUE DIVISION TWO

BIRMINGHAM CITY

SATURDAY, 15th NOVEMBER, 1986 KICK-OFF 3.00 PM

THE TODAY LEAGUE

Ground 56 – The Den (Old) – 15th November 1986 - Millwall 0 Birmingham City 2 – Second Division

My one and only trip to the old Den came back in 1986 and I still remember the trip due to the intimidating atmosphere and the fact that someone offered me a weapon to take into the ground should I need it! That incident alone offers some clue to the reputation of Millwall at the time.

We had travelled to Millwall by train and walked from the underground station en mass with a police escort as usual and headed onto a terraced area behind the goal that had large fences preventing fans from spilling onto the pitch or invading the neighbouring home support. Blue fans were in good voice and had travelled in very large numbers for the second Division game. It was a bit packed in the away end and we swayed backwards and forwards at times and when Blues scored our end went mental. It was brilliant. Especially as Blues scored twice to win the game 2-0. It was a very joyous afternoon and happily we had no trouble getting back to Euston and celebrated the whole way back to Birmingham. I had a great day out.

The old Den was the home of Millwall for 83 years and the site was demolished in 1993 and is now a housing estate. The new Den was just a quarter of a mile away to which Millwall relocated and they remain there to the present time.

Ground 57 – Elm Park – 26th December 1986 – Reading 2 Birmingham City 2 – Second Division

My first trip to Elm Park was on Boxing Day 1986 during a time when I was going to nearly every home and away game with Blues. I remember that the away fans were on a fairly big terrace behind the goal and a large fence preventing the fans from invading the pitch. It was an old ground but did have a certain charm despite the away end having no roof at the time. Happily it didn't rain and Blues scored two good goals to ensure that we came away with a point in a good 2-2 draw. Another good away trip.

On 31st January 1998 with Blues in 7th place we set off for Reading. This was Reading's old ground and it was Stephen's first experience of the old terraces. Blues fans had been given the terraced end behind the goal and Stephen looked on in amazement as he had only ever sat in the seats at games and up to now had never stood on the terraces. Today he would experience it for the first time as terracing was now almost completely phased out in the top divisions of English football.

While Julie and I stood against a crash barrier, Stephen moved down to the front by the fencing at the edge of the pitch whilst I watched him and the game. He seemed to enjoy the atmosphere and the standing and would run up and down to me, then back to the front. Blues were up against it from the start and when we had a player sent off it began to go down hill.

However, Blues held out until we had another player sent off and with only nine men on the pitch we went 2-0 down. The Bluenoses remained upbeat though and even at 2-0 we all sang 'we've only got 9 men, we've only got 9 men', back at the Reading fans. It was not to be our day and we headed back home with yet another new experience under Stephen's belt.

I visited Elm Park on 4 occasions between 1986 and 1998 and I saw 1 win, 2 draws and 1 defeat. Reading moved to the Madejski Stadium in 1998 and Elm Park was demolished and is now a housing estate called Elm Park.

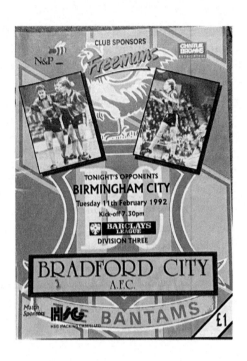

Ground 58 – Valley Parade – 3ʳᵈ January 1987 – Bradford City 0 Birmingham City 0 – Second Division

I travelled to Bradford on a cold January day in January 1987 for my first trip to Valley Parade and it proved to be quite enjoyable. It was a small ground and the away terrace along the side of the pitch was tiny. It was only narrow and it seemed strange being so low and near the pitch. Some away fans were behind the goal in the seats and we were all in good voice in a goalless draw.

On 2ⁿᵈ January 1995, Julie and I headed off to Bradford for a league game. Once again Julie drove there and once we had parked up we headed to a nearby bar in town not too far from the ground. It was a nice bar and I had a couple of beers before we headed to the ground. Bradford City's ground was okay but the little terraced stand that housed the away fans was tiny. It ran along the side of the pitch and the Blues fans were situated to the left goal side. I was still amazed at how small the terrace was; it felt like it was only about ten people deep! The view of the pitch was okay though, if I stood on tiptoe, and the atmosphere amongst the Blues faithful was great.

The game got under way and Julie and I began to think that Blues would never score. Bradford scored and I was beginning to think that it was not going to be our day when Cooper hit a great shot from just outside the area and it flew into the top corner. I must admit that I had been giving Cooper some stick during the match and due to our close proximity I am sure he heard me because when he scored he came running over to where I was standing for his goal celebrations. Point made and great goal! So the game ended in a draw and Blues remained top of the table. A very good away trip.

I visited Valley Parade on 3 occasions between 1987 and 1995 and saw 2draws and 1 defeat. I enjoyed my trips and I will always think of Bradford City's stadium as Valley Parade and not it's present name the 'University of Bradford Stadium'.

Ground 59 – Sealand Road – 17th October 1989 – Chester City 4 – Birmingham City 0 – Third Division

My only trip to Chester's Sealand Road was in October 1989 and I was living in Liverpool at the time. This meant a fairly short train journey to the small stadium in Chester and a rather disappointing defeat for Blues who were currently in the third tier. There were loads of Bluenoses who were in great voice despite the result. The ground was nice but me disappointment meant that I didn't take an awful lot of notice and I was back on the train to Liverpool as soon as the final whistle sounded.

The stadium closed in 1990 and Chester were forced to play their games at Macclesfield for 2 years until they moved into the Diva Stadium in 1992. Sealand Road was allowed to fall into a state of disrepair until it was finally demolished in 1993 and the site now houses the Sealand Road shopping park. The stand roof was made use of by Port Vale for their away enclosure.

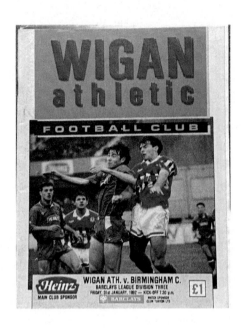

Ground 60 – Springfield Park – 1ˢᵗ December 1989 – Wigan 1 Birmingham City 0 – Third Division

My first trip to Springfield Park was in December 1989 and there were loads of Bluenoses who had made the trip. I remember thinking what an old ground it was with a small seated area on one side and grassy banks/ terraces behind each goal and another seated stand on the other side of the stadium. Sadly Blues lost by the only goal of the game and I could help but think back to when I first saw Blues play Wigan in an FA Cup game back in 1978 when Wigan were just a non league side. That day Blues had won 4-0 and sang 'you should have stuck to Rugby'. Today I wished they had!

In September 1990 I travelled the few miles from Liverpool, where I was living at the time, to Wigan for the match. I remember thinking what a strange place Wigan was as I noticed bouncers in suits outside all the bars early in the daytime and it was impossible to get in to any of them for a pre match drink. Angela and I headed for Wigan's ground (their old ground) and noticed that a social club was attached to the ground. So, I put on my best Scouse accent to get inside only to find, when we did get in that it was full of Bluenoses in full voice singing 'Keep Right On'. This was brilliant and I immediately recognised several people I knew, including Alan and Lee Pitman.

It was great to catch up with everyone again and Lee was amazed to hear the Scouse accent that I seemed to have picked up during my time in Liverpool. Then it was inside the stadium and into the seats to watch the game. The ground was really small with terraces behind both goals, which resembled grass banks to be honest, and a small stand at each side. There were only 3,904 people inside and the game ended in a 1-1 draw with Paul Tait scoring the Birmingham goal.

It was a very enjoyable trip and I had really enjoyed catching up with everyone and the result wasn't too bad as we hadn't lost. I headed back to Liverpool and headed to a local pub for a few drinks.

Springfield Road was demolished to 1999 to make way for a housing estate and Wigan Athletic moved to the new JJB Stadium.

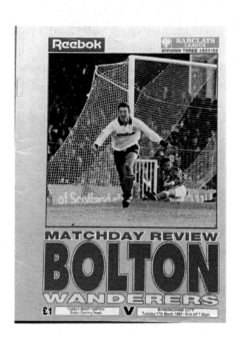

Ground 61 – Burnden Park – 24ᵗʰ February 1990 – Bolton Wanderers 3 Birmingham City 1 – Third Division

I travelled to Bolton in February 1990 for my first visit to Burnden Park for a third division game. It was a really cold day and we traveled up by car for this game and managed to find parking not too far away from the ground. We managed to grab something to eat and then headed to the old looking stadium. The away end was a large open terrace behind one of the goals and had red crush barriers in place with the other half behind the goal being the back of a large building. A bit strange to be honest but the rest of the stadium looked pretty normal with a seated stand with terrace at the front along one side and a large terrace behind the other goal.

It was a good atmosphere as a lot of Bluenoses had made the trip and they sang loads. Sadly our team let us down and we suffered a 3-1 defeat. This meant that the journey home was not as much as when we were on our way to the game. At least I had experienced a new ground and despite the result I had actually enjoyed the trip.

I visited again the following year in the slightly warmer month of April but the game ended in another defeat by an identical scoreline of 3-1. It was another good outing though and at least we remained dry on the large open terrace. It would also be the last visit I ever made. It was always sad to see the demise of a good old stadium with old fashioned character.

The Burnden Park disaster occurred on 9th March 1946 at a FA Cup Quarter Final game against Stoke when a crowd crush sadly resulted in the deaths of 33 people and several hundred Bolton supporters suffered injuries. Fans spilled onto the pitch and the players were taken off the pitch twice. The bodies of those who died were placed along the touchline and covered in coats and shockingly the game recommenced with a new sawdust touchline between them and the players.

It was one of the first stadium disasters and the most deadliest in history until the Ibrox disaster in 1971. There remains a plaque at the Asda store to pay tribute to the fans who lost their lives in the fourth worst football disaster in British history. Fire swept through the ground in May 1998 although tragedy was averted this time.

The ground closed for good on 25th April 1997 and was demolished in 1999 which was two years after Bolton moved to their new home in Horwich which was called the Reebok Stadium. The penalty spot was dug up and planted at the new ground. The site is now an Asda superstore with photos and players above the checkouts.

Ground 62 – Gresty Road – 23rd October 1990 – Crewe Alexandra 1 Birmingham City 1 – Third Division

When we were due to play Crewe away Blues were on their seventh successive draw. I headed down to Crewe from Liverpool, where I was living at the time, and was delighted to meet up with Julie again. Julie informed me that she had bumped into our old friend Debbie with whom we had travelled to away games with in the 1980's and that she was now living in Crewe and was seeing a Crewe fan.

It was a tiny ground but it had character and there were many Blues fans squeezed into the tiny away end. The Bluenoses sang throughout the game but were unable to inspire our heroes and the game finished in another draw, this time 1-1. We were convinced that someone had told the Blues team that if they drew eight games in a row then they would win the pools!

It was a really nice little ground just a stones throw from the main train station and there were a few nice little pubs nearby. I liked the small stands and it was great to stand on the terraces with the partisan Bluenoses. It was easy to get back to Liverpool after the game too and I enjoyed my trip.

In August 2009 I was living in Abu Dhabi and I was back in England for a visit and so after texting Brendan to see if he was going to Crewe (which he was) I was preparing to see my first pre season friendly of the 2009 to 2010 season. Brendan had kindly offered to take me along with him and his son, and he arrived to collect me in Marie's lovely yellow beetle.

The trip didn't take too long and we were soon pulling into a car park not far from the ground in Crewe. We headed for the pub closest to the ground where we found other Bluenoses enjoying a pre match pint or two. It was good to see other bluenoses that I knew or recognised from following Blues. After catching up with a couple of them and chatting to Brendan, his son and Ron, we headed off to the ground just before kick off time.

It was a night game and the Blues fans were situated in the stand along one side of the ground where a few hundred hardy souls were already knocking out a few songs. The game itself left a lot to be desired and ended in a crap 4-1 defeat. Blues fans sang 'I wanna go home, This is the worse trip I've ever been on!'.

Not all doom and gloom though, as us Bluenoses are pretty optimistic and I got to meet even more people that I hadn't seen for a while. The Crewe fans celebrated like they had won the league but they were still pretty much out sang by the entertaining Blues following who never lost faith. I must admit to being a bit worried about the coming season after this showing though. Perhaps we tried to play too much football against lower league opposition? Who knows eh? I met Alan again and we chatted and reminisced about bygone times. He remembered going to Crewe many years ago – I think he said 50 years. I really admired Alan as he was always at every Blues away game that I went to.

So far I have made 3 trips to Gesty Road, currently called the Mornflake Stadium and I have seen 2 draws and 1 defeat. Overall though, I have enjoyed my visits.

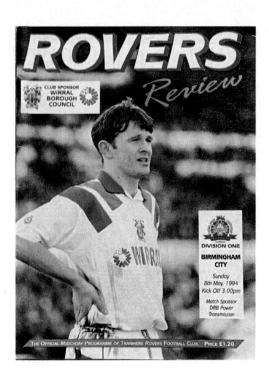

Ground 63 – Prenton Park – 21st December 1990 – Tranmere Rovers 1 Birmingham City 0 – Third Division

My first visit to Prenton Park came in December 1990 and as I was living in Liverpool at the time, it was a relatively short journey across the Mersey. It was a nice afternoon at a relatively small stadium although the away terrace behind the goal did seem quite big. It was packed with Bluenoses though and we sang throughout despite a narrow 1-0 defeat. I remember more about my second visit in 1994 though because is was way more dramatic and saw Blues relegated to the third tier despite winning the game 2-1.

It was in May 1994 that Blues had to win their last game away at Tranmere and rely on West Brom not winning at Portsmouth to stay up. I met Julie at the Rocket Pub just at the end of the M62 in Liverpool and we set off early through the Mersey tunnel and were soon parked up at Prenton Park, the home of Tranmere Rovers. We headed for the pub just across the road from the ground, which was already packed full of Bluenoses in good voice. It was Tranmere's main pub but there was not a Tranmere fan in sight.

It wasn't too long before one Tranmere fan did come in though and he was carried around the pub shoulder high by the Bluenoses who were in good spirits.

He loved it, and told me afterwards that he though the Blues fans were the best supporters he had ever known and that we were great fun. I must admit it was fun inside and everyone was in good voice and we were ever the optimists and hoped we could pull off the great escape. As is always the case at the last away game of the season, many Blues fans had come in fancy dress and there were many amusing costumes to be seen.

Once inside the ground the atmosphere in the Blues end was amazing. Blues had the whole of the terraced end behind the goal and it was absolutely packed with Bluenoses in full voice. It was as though we were playing for the championship not relegation. It was a really good game and as soon as Blues took the lead the atmosphere seemed to go up yet another notch. One of the policemen at the front told the Blues fans that West Brom were losing, so the news soon went around and the whole of the Blues contingent began celebrating. The players looked over and seemed to wonder what was going on. You can imagine our devastation when we were informed that this was not true and West Brom were in fact not losing but winning which would relegate Blues no matter what our score was. It was really awful, Blues won the game 2-1 but it soon dawned on us that we were now down.

When the final whistle went we were stunned. The Tranmere fans came streaming on the pitch from the other end and came running over to us. I don't think anyone in the Blues end had the heart for a fight but to my amazement, the Tranmere fans stopped in front of us and stood and applauded our support. Blues fans applauded them back and despite our disappointment we headed out of the ground to drown our sorrows.

In the car going back through the Mersey Tunnel, it was an amazing sight. Every single car had Blues flags and scarves hanging from the windows and they were all blasting their car horns as they drove through the Tunnel. It sounded absolutely amazing and I was completely overwhelmed. I was (and still am) immensely proud to be a Birmingham City fan. Despite our relegation I, like all Bluenoses, never gave up and I was optimistic that we would be back again as champions the next season.

Between 1990 and 1996 I visited Prenton Park on 4 occasions and witnessed 2 wins, 1 draw and just 1 defeat. The memories stick with me of the time my heart was broken with our relegation in 1994.

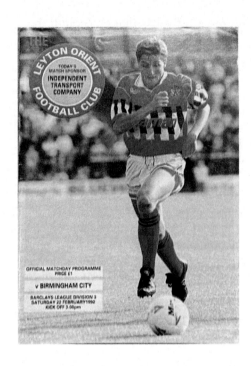

On the programme cover:

LEYTON ORIENT FOOTBALL CLUB

TODAY'S MATCH SPONSOR
INDEPENDENT TRANSPORT COMPANY

OFFICIAL MATCHDAY PROGRAMME
PRICE £1

v BIRMINGHAM CITY

BARCLAYS LEAGUE DIVISION 3
SATURDAY 22 FEBRUARY 1992
KICK OFF 3.00pm

Ground 64 – Brisbane Road – 12th January 1991 – Leyton Orient 1 Birmingham City 1 – Third Division

My first trip to Brisbane Road was in January 1992 and I travelled with Julie as usual. It was a nice ground in London and we stood on a large terrace behind the goal with the other Bluenoses. The game was it the old third division and ended in a 1-1 draw and I must admit that I done have as good a memory of this particular trip as I do of the other 2 visits.

The first game of the 1994 – 1995 season was away in London and Blues started their campaign at Leyton Orient. I had made sure I was not working and I set off for Birmingham from Liverpool to meet up with Julie who would be driving us to Brisbane Road, the home of Leyton Orient. I was really please to be able to stand on the terraces behind the goal with the away support.

There were quite a few Bluenoses there and as usual they were optimistic and in good voice. The ground was an old ground with the majority of the home support taunting us from behind the opposite goal despite being out sang by the Blues fans. Unfortunately the game did not go as plan and despite a Steve Claridge goal, Blues lost the game 2-1 and I headed home somewhat downhearted as I had expected an easy win. I guess I should know better really, being a Bluenose!

Later that season Blues were fourth in the table when I met up with Julie to head back to Leyton Orient for the second leg of the area final of the Auto Windscreens Cup. As usual Julie was driving to London and it wasn't too long before we were parked up and wandering around Leyton Orient's ground looking for a pub for a pre match drink. There were loads of Blues that had also arrived early and were milling around outside. As we were standing outside a local pub enjoying a beer I bumped into one of my old teammates from my days at Birmingham City.

It was great to see 'Ballie' again and we had a great laugh catching up together. Ballie had tickets in the seats amongst the Leyton Orient fans and I had a ticket for the away terrace behind the goal but I said I would look out for her when we were inside for the match. Many Blues fans had also had to get tickets in the Leyton Orient end; such was the demand by the Bluenoses for tickets. Every Bluenose was desperate to see our heroes play at Wembley Stadium.

Once inside Julie and I took up standing positions just behind the goal and the game got under way. It wasn't long before Blues scored, and our end erupted wildly, I jumped on Julie and the entire terrace seemed to come alive like an ocean of waves. I looked across to the side of the pitch where some Blues in the home section were also celebrating, and there in the middle was 'Ballie' also celebrating wildly. The police moved in and they were all herded into our section and 'Ballie' came over to join us.

Blues scored two more goals to much celebration and although Orient pulled two back, the match finished 3-2 meaning that Blues were in the final at Wembley with a 4-2 aggregate win. We all celebrated for much of the night, including on the journey back to Birmingham. It was a brilliant feeling, looking forward to seeing Blues run out at Wembley. I was so looking forward to seeing Wembley way as a mass of Blue and White.

I made 3 trips to Brisbane Road between 1991 to 1995 and saw 1 win, 1draw and 1 defeat. Not sure if I will get to visit again as Leyton Orient are usually in the lower leagues.

Ground 65 – Griffin Park – 9th April 1991 – Brentford 0 Birmingham City 1 – Leyland Daf Cup Area Final

At the end of March Blues played Brentford at St Andrews in the first leg of the Leyland Daf area final and won 2-1 in front of 16,219 which was a record attendance for the competition. Then four days later it was the away leg in Brentford and Julie and I set off from Birmingham in her car to watch the game.

We parked up not too far from the ground and headed to a really nice little pub not too far away and joined the many Blues fans that were already drinking outside the pub. Amazingly Griffin Park had a pub on each of the 4 corners of the ground. It was a really lovely little ground with loads of character and I loved to see the 4 floodlights that loomed over the stadium. We stood on the little terrace area behind the goal that stretched for the whole width of the stadium. It was packed and we swayed with the crowd and joined in the singing.

It was yet another new ground for me, and the Blues were in jubilant form. It was a really good game which finished 1-0 to Blues meaning that Blues won 3-

1 on aggregate and we were now going to Wembley for the first time in our history. We were ecstatic and celebrated for hours afterwards. Fantastic!

In 2015 I had been looking forward to the trip even before it had to be rearranged to enable Brentford to re-lay their pitch following their 4-1 defeat by Oxford on what they deemed a 'poor surface'. I did like Brentford's small ground because of the away terrace section. It was a midweek game and I had booked the day off so I could catch the coach at 3.30pm. It was a pleasant trip down to London, although the M25 was as busy as ever.

The only negative aspect of traveling on the coaches was the lack of a car park at Brentford, meaning that we were dropped off on a main road and had to negotiate our way through side streets and across a narrow bridge (with no lighting) over the railway. It was really easy to get lost. It was much easier years ago when you just looked for floodlights wherever you went.

As we were making our way to the ground we passed a group of locals selling tea and cakes from a table with a big urn on their driveway. Great idea on a cold night and they were a friendly bunch. Once we arrived at the ground we decided to head inside once we had obtained our match program and had to endure a thorough body search on the way in.

It was great to stand on the terrace and we made our way down to the very front to lean on the barrier. It was quite cold really and I was glad that I had wrapped up. Over 1,200 Bluenoses had made the journey and were in good voice as usual. Brentford's ground was quite small and had terraced areas behind both goals. The away end had a seated section above the terrace (also for away fans) and it made for a good atmosphere.

The game got underway and Blues were doing okay. At half time it was 0-0 and I jogged about a bit to keep warm. The second half got underway and the Bluenoses were having a bit of fun at the expense of the Brentford goalkeeper who was now positioned right in front of us and his name read 'BUTTON' on the back of his shirt.

There were shouts of 'Jenson!' and 'hey! Cadbury!' It took me a while to get the Cadbury one but when I did I was reduced to giggles. However, the comment that I found the most amusing was from a posh voice that kept shouting 'Benjamin! Benjamin!' He was then shouting 'Benjamin, stand there on the Penalty spot Benjamin!' 'Let it in Benjamin! Let this one in Benjamin!' It was really funny. I should point out though, the goalkeepers name was not Benjamin, it was a reference to Benjamin Button – the character who aged rapidly.

On 71 minutes Birmingham won a corner which was swung into the area and Morrison rose high to head the ball home – 1-0 and we celebrated wildly (as you do on the terraces). Brentford then came back at us and forced a couple of corners. I had to smile when I heard a lone cry of 'why does it always have to be this way! Why can't we just win?' I think we all understood the anguish in that statement.

The ninety minutes were up and the board went up with five minutes of injury time. We all felt extremely nervous when on 94 minutes Brentford won a corner. They took the corner which was then cleared up field to Clayton Donaldson to run onto it and he smashed the ball into the Brentford net right in front of us. The away end exploded! Relief and ecstasy washed over us as we jumped around whilst Donaldson was mobbed by the rest of the Birmingham team. The Clayton Donaldson song rang out loudly. 2-0!

A few seconds later the final whistle blew and Blues were 2-0 winners. We were now 5th in the League. 'Gary Rowett's Blue and White Army!' Echoed around the ground as the players came over to applaud us, this was followed by 'Keep Right On'. Gary applauded our supporters and pumped his fist in celebration. Then it was back down the dark side streets to find our way back to the coaches and I was in full voice as we boarded. What a great night.

I visited Griffin Park on 7 occasions with the majority of them very enjoyable apart from the 5-0 defeat in 2018. Overall I saw 4 victories, 2 draws only 1 defeat. The grounds name referred to the griffin featured in the logo and Fuller's Brewery which at one point owned the orchard on which the stadium was built. The ground was known for being the only English league football ground to have a pub on each corner.

Griffin Park was closed in August 2020 and demolished in 2021 for a housing estate. As of 2023 the developer Ecoworld was proposing a development of 149 flats and houses with 67 car parking spaces and a Central Park.

Ground 66 – Millmoor – 9th March 1991 – Rotherham United 1 Birmingham City 1 – Third Division

My one and only trip to Millmoor, home of Rotherham United came in March 1991 during the time when I was still living in Liverpool and about to start my midwifery training and I was really looking forward to this trip. The first part of my journey saw me drive down to Birmingham to stay at my moms and my sister was also coming to the game with me the next morning.

Annette, Julie and I set out armed with sandwiches and goodies put together by my mom, Julie was driving and it wasn't long before we were parking up not far from the ground in Rotherham. On our way to park the car we had spotted a nice looking pub just down the road by a large island so this was where we headed for a pre match drink. It was nice inside and was full of Bluenoses who had also travelled to the game. I noticed a lad called Tom who I knew from when I lived at home with my mom and hadn't seen for ages. I had a bit of a chat with him and the others as we watched Blues fans playing pool on the nearby pool table.

Before long the Bluenoses began to sing Blues songs and the atmosphere was great. Soon it was time to head up to the ground and we headed out of the pub and up the road towards the ground. The night before I had dreamt that I was being chased by Rotherham fans under a subway and so I insisted on negotiating the traffic across this very busy island to avoid my dream coming true, much to Annette's dismay! We just about made it across the island alive and happily headed to the ground.

I had never been to Rotherham before and once again I was faced with a small ground that did have a bit of character. The away terrace was situated behind the goal and there was already a lot of Bluenoses inside in full voice once we got through the turnstiles. It was a small crowd of 5,028 and a lot of them were Blues but the atmosphere was brilliant as usual. The game finished in a 1-1 draw for which we had to settle for and then it was off to the car and back to Birmingham. Annette and I both agreed that we had quite enjoyed the outing.

Rotherham United were forced out of Millmoor in 2008 after a row over the rent and spent four years at the Don Valley Athletic ground in Sheffield before moving into their new stadium, the New York Stadium, in 2012. They were given 4 years to return the club to Rotherham or face a fine of £3 million pounds and they did manage to achieve this hence avoiding the fine. Millmoor now lies abandoned and decaying although it was used for youth football from 2016.

Ground 67 – Deva Stadium – 10th December 1994 – Chester City 0 Birmingham City 4 – Division Two

In 1994 I was headed to what would be a more local match for me as I was living in Liverpool and it was just across the Mersey in the city of Chester where Blues were to take on Chester City at their new home ground the Deva Stadium. I headed to Chester by local train and before long I was disembarking in the really nice city of Chester. It has a nice little station and just outside, opposite the hotel facing the station is a nice pub to which we headed for our first pre match drink of the day. Soon it was off to the ground and would be another new ground for me.

The ground was really small compared to what I was used to, but it was kind of quaint and I was astonished to find that the travelling Bluenoses had in fact three ends of the ground. The home support were situated in just one stand behind the goal. The other three stands were jam packed with Birmingham supporters; in fact it was more like a home game for Blues! It was brilliant and the atmosphere was fabulous.

The Bluenoses sang throughout the game as Blues coasted to a good 4-0 away win. Each goal was celebrated wildly. When Liam Daish scored his goal he ran towards the celebrating Bluenoses at one side of the ground where a rather long trumpet was passed to him, which he then proceeded to blow into as part of his celebration! It was brilliant and we all loved it, unfortunately though, the referee was not quite as keen and he proceeded to book Liam Daish for his celebrations to loud boos from three ends of the ground. It was a great result and moved Blues up to second in the table and I headed back to Liverpool in jubilant mood.

The Deva stadium, somewhat unusually, is half in Wales and half in England. Chester City FC was wound up in 2010 when they tried unsuccessfully to join the Welsh League. A phoenix club rose from the ashes when supporters formed Chester FC who were officially established in May 2010.

Ground 68 – Glandford Park – 14ᵗʰ December 1994 – Scunthorpe United 1 Birmingham City 2 – FA Cup 3ʳᵈ Round

I headed down to Birmingham to meet up with Julie for our journey to Scunthorpe for the FA Cup second round replay. Julie was driving there in her car so I left mine at my moms and once Julie picked me up, we headed off to Scunthorpe on a very cold frosty night. When we arrived in Scunthorpe the ground was easy to find from the motorway as it could be seen clearly, so we parked up and headed towards the pub that could also be seen just up the road. The pavements were white with ice as we made our way to the pub.

Once inside though, it was a bit warmer and the pub was full of travelling Bluenoses in their blue shirts. Despite the cold, everyone was in good spirits and looking forward to the cup-tie ahead. It was also a new ground for most of us, so that was something to look forward to also. As we headed back down the road towards the ground we were a bit like Bambi on ice as I for one, slipped and slid down the road to the ground. Once inside I looked around and although it was another smallish ground, it was quite nice.

The away end behind the goal was full of Bluenoses despite the fact that it was on a cold winter's night. The atmosphere was great amongst the Blues fans and when Blues took the lead right in front of our travelling support our end erupted. Barry Fry, our manager, jumped in the air and sprinted maniacally down the wing towards the Blues support and we all enjoyed the sight of his celebrations immensely, joining him in his celebrations.

When Blues scored a second the celebrations began in earnest as we sang our 'Wembley, Wembley' loudly. Much had been made of the fact that our keeper had not conceded a goal for quite a while, and it was a shame the way in which Scunthorpe's consolation goal was conceded. As the Blues defence was preparing for a Scunthorpe free kick, the Scunthorpe player took it early into the unguarded goal as the keeper was busy lining up his wall.

The Blues players protested that the whistle had not been blown and they were still getting ready but the referee ignored their pleas. I personally was disgusted, as were the rest of the Bluenoses who felt that the goal should not have been allowed to stand and was in fact – cheating. However, it did not make a difference to the outcome and Blues won the match 2-1 and we headed back to Birmingham celebrating our passage to the next round of the FA Cup. The draw had already been made prior to the replay and Blues had been drawn at home against the mighty Liverpool.

In 2005 Blues had drawn Scunthorpe away in the second round of the League cup but as Stephen was at school I didn't have anyone to go with and so I wasn't planning to travel. However, as it got closer it was getting harder for me to imagine missing it. It was a night match and when I got up early on the day of the game and the sun was shining it was killing me to think of missing it. I decided to ring Alan and see if he was travelling and if he had room in his car if he was. Alan said he was going and he did have room to take me if I wanted to go. I decided I did and headed off to St. Andrews to get a ticket. Luckily there were tickets still available so I purchased one and Alan came by to pick me up before heading off to pick the others up for the trip.

By the time we set off for Scunthorpe the car was full and I had met more new Blues fans that I would be travelling with. We stopped on the way for sandwiches etc and before long we were arriving in Scunthorpe. We stopped at a really nice large pub within walking distance from the ground, which could clearly be seen nearby. There was a sign outside saying no football shirts allowed. Great, I had mine on, so I had to do my jacket right up and it was quite warm inside.

Mind you, before long the pub filled up with Bluenoses wearing Blues shirts! Hence my jacket was soon removed and I joined with the other Bluenoses in a pre match drink. The lads I had travelled with were great and bought me drinks as we all chatted. I looked around and it was a mass of Blue and White with only two Scunthorpe shirts on display. The atmosphere was a happy one and Alan headed off to park the car near the ground as we arranged to meet up with him in the ground after having a couple more drinks.

Then we headed into the ground and Blues had one end of the ground behind the goal and it was now filling with Blues fans that had made the trip. It was a little cold to be honest, but I joined in with the singing and chatted to other Bluenoses as we waited for kick off. The match got under way and Blues were soon ahead with a nicely taken goal be Forsell and we all celebrated. Forsell scored his second before half time and we celebrated again as Blues took a 2-0 lead. At half time I headed to the toilets and when I got back the lads had bought me a sausage roll and said 'get that down yer love' which I thought was really nice of them. They were real gents and looked after me for the whole of the trip.

The match finished with a 2-0 win for Blues and we were in the next round of the League Cup. The trip home didn't seem to take too long even though we were all tired and Alan dropped me home, which was really nice as he lives the other side of Birmingham to me. Alan is one of life's gentlemen and has always looked after me over many years of watching the Blues. He is the most ardent, loyal Blues fan I had ever met.

Glandford Park was built in 1988 at a cost of £2.5 million pounds and was the first new purpose built football league stadium to be built in England for 33 years, since Southend United at Roots Hall in 1955. I visited Glandford park on the two occasions above and enjoyed my visits with a 100% win record. Sadly Scunthorpe are currently a non league side after suffering relegation in 2022 ending a 72 year spell in the Football League.

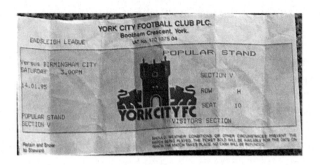

Ground 69 – Bootham Crescent – 14th January 1995 – York City 2 Birmingham City 0 – Division Two

In January 1995 Julie and I headed off to the picturesque town of York for an away match against York City. This would be another new ground for me; in fact I had never even been to York. When we arrived and parked up, Julie and I set out to explore a bit of the town before heading for a pre match drink. York is a lovely place and I really enjoyed what I saw. It was really picturesque and we found a lovely little pub, which we stopped at for a drink. There were a few nice little pubs around and most of them seemed to be filled with Bluenoses enjoying a sing song and a pre match pint.

The ground appeared old inside and the away fans were situated behind the goal and on the corner on a standing terraced area. There were loads of Blues who had made the journey and as league leaders, we were really looking forward to the game. Blues were unbeaten for 26 games, which I think was a record, and we were expecting to make it 27. We were brought down to earth with a bang though.

I think the player's minds were elsewhere and Blues played awful. We never looked liked coming back once Blues went a goal down and when the second went in it was all over. The York fans celebrated like they had won the league as us Bluenoses headed out of the ground disappointed in the performance of our lads. Despite losing our unbeaten run Blues remained at the top of the table so I couldn't really be too downhearted.

This was my one and only trip to Bootham Crescent and I really enjoyed my trip. York City moved out of Bootham Crescent in 2020 and the ground was demolished in 2023 to make was for housing. In 2004 York City were relegated from the football league ending their 75 year spell in the league. They were

203

promoted back into the football league in 2012 but sadly returned to non league status in 2016.

Ground 70 – Adams Park (Wycombe) - 18th March 1995 – Division Two – Wycombe Wanderers 0 Birmingham City 3

In March 1995 Julie and I went on a nice little trip to Wycombe to see Blues take on Wycombe Wanderers. This would be another new ground for me and I was looking forward to the experience. Blues had dropped to fourth in the table and I for one was getting a bit nervous. It would be a disaster to miss out on the one automatic promotion spot after doing so well so far this season. We arrived in Wycombe and after finding a chip shop we had a good look around the ground. Wycombe was a really nice place and as we headed for the ground I admired the nice country feel to it. Once at the ground we headed to the club shop to see what was on offer and I bought a small vintage van with the Wycombe Wanderers crest on the side for my Dad's collection.

The ground itself was really small but nice. It was situated on the edge of a really large hill where people could stand and see into the ground. During the match I could see a few people on the hill attempting to watch the game. I don't know what sort of a view they had though. The Blues fans were situated on terracing behind one of the goals and once again the turnout was superb for Blues. We sang and cheered and thoroughly enjoyed Birmingham's 3-0 demolition of Wycombe. The third goal was superb as a lovely long distance chip over the keeper nestled in the back of the net right in front of the travelling Blues contingent. Although we remained in fourth place we all headed home happy.

My next trip to Adams Park would be many years later when I travelled there to watch Birmingham City Ladies play Reading Ladies as this was also Reading Ladies home ground which they shared with Wycombe. It was on Sunday 4th February 2018.

I had decided to drive to the Reading game as it was being played at Adams Park – home of Wycombe Wanderers. I had visited there many years ago and I was really looking forward to it. On the day Steve offered to drive as I was in work the next day so I agreed and I got to relax and enjoy the trip. It was a nice day and an easy drive down south to Wycombe and when we arrived we saw Harry in the car park. He had come on his own and was therefore delighted to see us so we joined forces and headed into the bar which was already full of the usual Bluenoses.

Harry got me a cider and then the Reading mascot arrived, not sure if it was a bear or a bee, and gave out free copies of the New Panini Euro Women's 2017 sticker album complete with a couple of packets of stickers. Not long before kick off we all headed into the ground for the game. I got my match programme and some chips which I took up to my seat with the other Bluenoses. Our star striker Ellen White was sitting near us as she was currently out injured.

Earlier in the bar we had all agreed that we felt it would be a fiery game with Reading having recently signed ex Birmingham players Jo Potter, Jade Moore and Kirsty Linnet when Notts County folded. Although Blues got the best deal as we captured England international Ellen White from Notts County's demise. A couple of Bluenoses predicted red cards with Jo Potter being the favourite to receive her marching orders.

I was still eating my chips when Charlie Wellings scored in the first minute to put Blues 1-0 ahead so I joined in the celebrations, Chips in one hand and flag in the other. Reading were the dirtiest team I had seen so far in women's football and the predictions were proved to be correct when Jo Potter received a straight red card for hitting a Blues player in the face. To be honest Jade Moore should also have received a red card when she punched a Blues player in the face which was either missed by the referee and linesman or ignored.

To add insult to injury ex Blues Kirsty Linnet went down easily in the box and a penalty was awarded to Reading. It was taken and Blues were pegged back to 1-1 somewhat unfairly I thought. So once again I was disappointed but at least we didn't lose. We all headed back to our cars and back to Birmingham. Another great day out following Blues.

I visited Adams Park on 4 occasions so far. Once with the men's team (a victory) and 3 times with the Women's team (a win, a draw and a defeat) and I enjoyed all my trips to a lovely little stadium.

Ground – 71 – Twerton Park – 29th March 1995 – Bristol Rovers 1 Birmingham City 1 – Division Two

Julie and I were again on our travels this time to Bristol to see Blues play Bristol Rovers. It was a cold day and once in Bristol we headed to a pub close to the ground for a warm and a pre match pint. There were a few Bristol Rovers fans inside and we got talking to a couple of them. I was quite surprised how bitter they were towards us. They called us the big spenders of the league and seemed really jealous and seemed to think that Blues could buy whomever they wanted and would get promotion because of this. Of course Julie and I put them right but there seemed a bit of a hostile atmosphere both in the pub and in the ground afterwards.

It was a new ground for us as our previous trip had been to their old ground and they had now moved to Twerton Park. The ground itself was old and small and the terraced end we were in was a cold and open terrace behind the goal. The match wasn't much to write home about either as Blues conceded a really soft own goal from a back pass that seemed to trickle past our keeper into the net. Luckily Steve Claridge saved our blushes by scoring the equaliser and the match finished 1-1. Blues were now up to third place in the table and closing in on the leaders.

We had both enjoyed our trip and we headed home happy. It was my only visit to Twerton Park in Bath as Bristol Rovers only played there till 1996. The ground is currently home to Bath City FC.

Ground 72 – Bloomfield Road – 4th April 1995 – Blackpool 1 Birmingham City 1 – Second Division

I was still living in Liverpool when I headed to Blackpool for my first visit to the ground in April 1995 and we planned a little overnight stay to complete our trip. We got the train up to Blackpool and headed for a hotel we had booked into then to a pub not too far away where we grabbed lunch and a drink. We could see several Bluenoses already in Blackpool and by the time we headed to the ground there seemed to be loads of us.

We were in the away section at the side of the pitch and the atmosphere was brilliant. Blues fans were in part mood already. It was a small ground but nice and I enjoyed the experience. The game finished in a 1-1 draw and we were lucky enough to have our evening in Blackpool to look forward to. We headed out for a meal and then to a couple of bars and everywhere we went there were Blues fans. Bluenoses had completely taken over the town and tonight Blackpool was Blue! It was brilliant.

One of my worst away trips ever, performance wise, came in April 2022 and was a real low point following Blues. It was a trip we all wanted to erase from our memories the minute we walked out of the stadium and headed home.

The trip to Blackpool was one that we had all been looking forward to since the fixture list had come out and we knew that it would be on a bank holiday Monday. Most of us thought that the police would take one look at this and force the club to change the date but by some miracle they hadn't and thousands had booked accommodation and planned their trip to the coast. Also amazingly, they had given us 3,300 tickets which meant that today Blackpool would be Blue! The party buses had sent 3 coaches on Saturday, 2 coaches Sunday and the rest on the Monday.

Sadly we were travelling on the official coaches as we had seriously thought that the game would be moved. Whilst the party buses left at 8am and were by the sea around 1030, we left at 0938 (should have been 0930) and had a stop (which none of us wanted) and we arrived at 1pm which ensured no donuts for us on the pier.

There were stories of many Bluenose parties and shenanigans over the weekend, one of which contributed to the closure of the Manchester pub for a while. Another involved the donkeys being chased into the sea, although apparently Daisy made a stand and so the Blues fans left her be, ran round her and chased the others into the sea. There was also a photo taken from the Tower of some sand art which read 'Zulu, Blackpool is a shithole' which the locals didn't take very well apparently.

Taff met us off the coach and with only a couple of hours before kickoff we had to choose between the Chippy or the pub and as we were closer to the pub at the time of the dilemma we headed into The Bridge pub. There was a big room at the rear of the pub which was empty when we arrived so we got our drinks and headed in there to be joined shortly by several more Bluenoses. We all enjoyed our drinks before heading to the nearby chip shop only to discover that fellow Bluenoses had been waiting over ten minutes just for a bag of chips so we made an immediate retreat.

We spotted a mass of singing Bluenoses flanked by police heading up the road towards the ground so we joined up with them and added our voices to the singing which was being admired by locals on their doorsteps. Once at the stadium we headed inside and obtained pies and sausage rolls before heading to our seats. Blues fans had the entire stand along the side of the pitch and were in good voice. I raised a smile at 'you can stick your fucking Tower up your arse!' and 'it's just a shit Eiffel Tower'. Very funny.

Sadly the afternoon turned into one of my worst ever watching Blues. It started when we conceded the first goal after only 3 minutes and was followed by the worst performance by a Blues team that I had ever seen in my time watching Blues. The players looked totally disinterested and there was no passion, no heart, they were an utter disgrace (apart from Sunjic who runs his heart out and Lyle Taylor).

Blues were 2-0 down after 14 minutes and 3-0 by halftime. It was so bad that Lee Bowyer only went into the changing room for a couple of minutes and then cut a lonely figure sitting alone on the away bench as he pondered events. It summed everything up right there. The second half was even worse as Blackpool made it 4-0 on 56 minutes and 'we're fucking shit' rang out from the stunned away end and 'we want our club back!'.

Blues made a very brief fight back when Ivan Sunjic scored on 63 minutes which saw Blue smoke bombs lobbed onto the pitch and chants of 'we've scored a goal!' and 'we're gonna win 5-4!' That was soon put to bed when Blackpool scored their fifth goal and 'your not fit to wear the shirt' was directed at the gutless Blues players who looked like they just couldn't be bothered. More blue smoke bombs were thrown on the pitch and a Blues fan ran on the pitch and confronted the Blues players before being tackled and escorted off.

Troy Deeney tried to calm thinks and threw one of the smoke bombs off the pitch and he was greeted with 'your not fit to wear the shirt!' and I have to admit that I agreed wholeheartedly. The sixth goal came in injury time and the referee quickly blew his whistle as he could see the Bluenoses were about to spill onto the pitch in frustration and Pedersen, Roberts and Colin were straight off the pitch and down the tunnel. Some of the players and Bowyer came over to face the venom from the Bluenoses but quickly left. Troy Deeney and Lucas Jutkiewicz stayed longer talking to the fans.

Troy Deeney spent 10 minutes talking to the fans who, like myself, felt that he had made things worse at the club by causing unrest amongst the players and was after the manager's job. We didn't do well when Deeney was in the team. He apologised to the fans but things did not look good at the moment. It was a very dark day.

Lee Bowyer looked absolutely broken in his post match interview. My heart went out to him and I think the majority of Bluenoses could see how much this man cared and how much he was trying. The majority on social media wanted Bowyer to stay and the team and owners to go. I wholeheartedly agreed. Lee said it was his worst day in his football life. He said it was "The darkest day in my whole footballing career. No fight, no desire, no passion. I'm trying to get blood out of a stone."

In contrast, Blues next visit to Blackpool the following season in December 2022 was refreshingly much better and I enjoyed the trip.

Blackpool were given the option of bringing kick off time forward to 1230 to allow away fans time to get home in time to watch Englands quarterfinal game but their answer was 'no, our fans will be home in time'. Very nice Blackpool , thank you for being so considerate. Personally I thought that they had never forgiven us for chasing the donkey's into the sea on our last visit.

Despite the conflict with the England Quarterfinals Blues still took nearly 4,000 fans to Blackpool and the coaches set off at 9am from St. Andrews. There were a lot of coaches going especially with the ongoing rail strikes and some of the party buses were staying in Blackpool till 11pm to allow fans to watch the England games in pubs in Blackpool.

It was brilliant to get back to live football again after the pandemic and we were all looking forward to the trip. Unfortunately Nigel couldn't come as he was really poorly and we wished him well and hoped to return with 3 points to cheer him up. We were joined by his mate Steve on the coach and with Taff also travelling by coach with us it was a full contingent at the back (apart from Nigel). Liam was also on the coach but Stuart was already in Blackpool for a long weekend and he would join us in a pub once we arrived.

It was a nice trip up north and we had a 45 minute stop at the services on the way up and we all enjoyed breakfast/brunch which set us up nicely for our trip to the pub when we arrived. We headed straight to 'The Bridge' pub which was not too far from the stadium and after about 5 minutes they opened up the massive room at the back of the pub and it soon filled up with Bluenoses. Apparently the seafront was a mass of Birmingham fans. Brilliant!

We had a lovely time in the pub before heading back to the stadium for the match. It was cold miserable and started to rain. Inside the ground the 4,000 Bluenoses were in great voice and our team responded by dominating the game against a poor Blackpool side. We started by hitting the post and then had two goals disallowed, one in each half. Not sure why to be honest. It was a game we really should have won but it finished 0-0 and it really was 2 points dropped. Great day out though and we headed home a little disappointed with the result. My favourite song of the game was when Jonathan Leko came on and the Bluenoses sang "If Leko scores we're in the sea!"

I have visited Bloomfield Road on 3 occasions over the years and witnessed 2 draws and 1 (heavy) defeat. I have yet to see us win there although I do enjoy the trip to the seaside.

THE MATCH
OFFICIAL MATCHDAY MAGAZINE

HUDDERSFIELD TOWN v BIRMINGHAM CITY
SUNDAY 6TH MAY 2001: 1.30PM

Ground – 73 – John Smith's Stadium – 6th May 1995 - Huddersfield Town 1 Birmingham City 2 – Second Division

My first and favourite trip to Huddersfield's new stadium came on Saturday 6th May 1995 and Julie and I set out early for our last match of the season. I was nervous and excited at the same time. Knowing Blues as well as I did I was expecting them to fall at the last hurdle as we so often do. But there again we had won the cup at Wembley so perhaps we could also achieve promotion on the last day of the season.

As we headed towards Huddersfield in Julie's car, on a nice day, there were Bluenoses everywhere I looked. Getting closer to Huddersfield on the country roads, we passed several country pubs with beer gardens and all of them were packed with Bluenoses enjoying a pre match pint whilst soaking up the sun. Julie, her brother and myself headed into Huddersfield and made our way to the ground before parking up and heading for a pre match drink. It would take more than a pre match drink to calm the nerves today.

Once inside Huddersfield Town's McAlpine stadium the atmosphere amongst the Bluenoses was fantastic. Huddersfield's ground was a new one and at this time it only had three sides (stands) to the ground with one end behind the goal being completely open with nothing behind it but a car park. Blues had been given the entire stand behind the other goal and it was completely full with noisy singing Blues fans. There must have been about 7,000 Blues fans present, with many in fancy dress, as is traditional for Blues last away game of the season.

Blues fans never stopped singing for the entire time. 'We're gonna win the league' was ringing out loudly as well as our anthem – 'Keep Right On' and flags and scarves were being waved in earnest. Even the home supporters seemed quite impressed by our support. There were many fans carrying small radio's to keep up to date with other relevant games should our plight require it.

The match got underway and Blues were up for it from the start, especially with the vociferous support from the Blues contingent. As time went on I began to get more and more nervous, but then Blues scored. Our end erupted and there really were wild celebrations amongst the Bluenoses. I was so excited but worried at the same time that we would let it slip. Blues second goal settled my fears and I celebrated like someone possessed, jumping all over everyone around me. Mind you, everyone was jumping and hugging each other, including complete strangers, such was the delight. 'We're gonna win the league' was belted out loud and proud and 'the Blues are going up, the Blues are going up!'

It did get a bit stressful when Huddersfield pulled one back but I really felt we could hold on and win. Then the final whistle blew Blues had won 2-1 and were champions! The Blues end erupted into wild celebrations that were unbelievable. 'Champions! Champions!' rang out loudly as the players left the pitch. The home supporters were applauding us and we continued to sing calling for our players to come back onto the pitch to celebrate with us. 'Bring on the Champions!' was being sang really loudly by the Blues fans but after about twenty minutes a tannoy announcement asked for the Blues fans to leave the stadium as the players would not be coming back out onto the pitch.

Blues fans started singing 'we're not going anywhere, we're not going, we're not going, we're not going anywhere!' and the home supporters themselves remained in the ground watching the proceedings with amazement. Forty five minutes later with the tannoy still asking us to leave, Blues fans were belting out 'Bring on the Champions!' to the applause of the Huddersfield support. There was no way, any of the 7,000 Blues fans were going home without seeing our heroes back out on the pitch taking our applause.

About an hour after the final whistle the tannoy again pleaded with Blues fans to leave the stadium as the players would not return to the pitch. At this point all 7,000 Blues fans sat down and started singing 'all night, we're gonna stay all night, we're gonna stay all night, we're gonna stay all night!' I think this was when those in power realised that the Blues fans really would stay all night and the Champions came out onto the pitch. They were still in their Blues kit and had bottles of Champagne in their hands and the celebrations really began. A large union jack with Champions was passed to the players and they happily waved it back at us from the pitch. Ricky Otto was seen hugging a blonde female fan and all the players were celebrating with the Bluenoses —it was brilliant. It was another precious memory that will live on in my heart forever.

Once the players had left the pitch we were now happy to head home. Julie and I headed out of Huddersfield and stopped at a nice country pub just outside Huddersfield with a beer garden full of celebrating Bluenoses. I ordered a pint of cider and called my sister, who was due to meet up with me when I got back to celebrate. 'Don't be late back!' she said to me, 'just one and I will head back and meet you in the Castle Pub' I stated. So after reassuring her and finishing my pint, I headed back to Birmingham and the Castle Pub in Weoley Castle.

In 2001 my trip to Huddersfield brought back fantastic memories of the season that we won the second division championship at their ground. Stephen and I went by car with Julie and Annette went with Steve and his mates on a coach and we met up at the ground. I saw loads of people I knew inside the ground and so did Annette and Steve which meant that they spent the whole of the second half up the back in the bar getting very drunk and did not see any of the second half.

Stephen couldn't work out why they would travel all that way for a match and then spend most of it in the bar. I must admit I could not enlighten him on the matter either. In fact, Steve thought the game finished 1-0 to Blues as that was the score last time he was in his seat! The game did in fact finish 2-1 to Blues and due to a strange set of other results at the last minute Huddersfield were dragged from nearly halfway up the table to be relegated. We were rubbing it in by singing 'we'll meet again, don't know where, don't know when but I know we'll meet again some sunny day' whilst waving to them.

Hence, when we got outside after the game there were a lot of pissed off Huddersfield fans and Julie had parked her car right in the middle of them. So, whilst the other Bluenoses got a police escort we had to head into enemy territory to get to the car. As we passed the Blues coach I saw Martin Grainger on the bus with the door open so I said hello to him and asked if there was any chance of a lift to avoid the angry mob in front of us. 'You'll be okay don't worry' he said to us. Alright for him to say, I though as we headed to the car. It was quite sad really to see the Huddersfield fans as some of them were really devastated. I saw people just sitting behind the wheel of their cars crying. I know how that feels being a Bluenose. But today was a happy day for Blues as we were in the play offs and due to play Preston with the first leg to be played at St. Andrews.

Over the years I have visited what is currently know as the John Smith's Stadium on 9 occasions between 1995 and 2023. I have seen 3 wins, 5 draws and only 1 defeat and I'm pleased to confirm that the stadium now has 4 stands around the pitch.

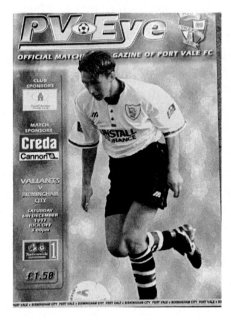

Ground 74 – Vale Park – 29th October 1995 – Port Vale 1 Birmingham City 2 – Division One

My first visit to Vale Park came in October 1995 and as was usual at the time I drove down from Liverpool to stay at my moms in Birmingham and stayed overnight so that Julie could pick me up and drive us to Stoke for the game against Port Vale. It was a pleasant trip and we soon arrived and parked up before making our way to the stadium on foot.

It was an old ground and still had terrace areas at the time as it didn't become all seater until 1998. Bluenoses were on a large terrace behind the goal and they were in great numbers and great voice. I'm sure our support lifted our players as they played really well and scored two good goals to mass celebrations in the away end. We came away with a really good 2-1 away win and I headed back to the car very happy. I had enjoyed my trip very much.

Ground 75 – Riverside Stadium – 29th November 1995 – Middlesbrough 0 Birmingham City 0 – League Cup

The League Cup fourth round draw saw Blues drawn away at Premier league team Middlesborough in November 1995 and it would be my first trip to the new Riverside Stadium which had only opened in August 1995. This would be a very hard tie for Blues as Middlesborough were a strong team and they were doing really well in the Premiership. Blues had slipped down to 5th in the First Division table by the time Julie and I headed to Middlesborough for the cup-tie.

We arrived in Middlesborough in plenty of time and Julie and I managed to park not too far from the ground and near to the centre of town which was where we headed for a pre match drink. Once we had found a nice pub full of Bluenoses we obtained drinks and got down to chatting about our chances. Most people didn't hold out a hope really and Middlesborough were hot favourites to progress through to the next round. I just hoped for a draw and to take them back to our place to be honest.

After a while we headed out towards the ground. Although it didn't look too far away, it was a good walk, which included going through a concrete tunnel/subway beneath the overpass that looked a bit daunting with so many red clad supporters around. We survived though and I must admit, with only one way in and out I did wonder about the safety of the ground. What if ambulances needed access? The only road into the stadium was packed with cars and fans. Seemed a bit dangerous to me, and the ground was on the river edge thereby blocking off access to one side of the ground.

Once inside, Middlesborough's new ground I thought it was much the same as most new grounds these days and I thought it lacked character although it was a nice stadium. The Blues end was packed and everyone in the away end was in good voice. The ground appeared full and the Middlesborough fans sang a couple of times too. The Bluenoses were singing 'where were you when you were shit?' loudly – referring to their recent times in the lower leagues when their support had been much less. It was quite funny really. There were 28,031 inside the ground and Blues did brilliantly to hold on for a 0-0 draw to enable us to take them to a replay at St. Andrews just before Christmas (which Blues won 2-0).

I was happy with the result and I think we all headed back to Birmingham in the same sense of happiness. It had been a long but very good trip. Great to visit a new ground too.

My favourite trip was in October 2021 for a championship game that I was looking forward to despite the very long trip and the fact that it always rains when we go to Middlesbrough. Today was no different and it poured with rain as we waited in the queue for the coaches. It seemed ages till they arrived and then got them ready for us to board. Today it was myself, June, Charlie and Taff making the trip and we had a nice stop at the services where June, Taff and I enjoyed bacon and egg baps. They were really nice.

It was still pouring with rain when we arrived in Middlesbrough and we wisely headed straight into the stadium. Blues started well but it was still goalless at half time. With 8 minutes played in the second half, Marc Roberts scored to put Blues ahead and we all went crazy in the away end as we celebrated and belted out 'Keep Right On'. We were still singing our hearts out when Scott Hogan scored Blues second just 3 minutes later and we erupted in celebrations once again. This was brilliant!

Blues held out to win 2-0 and we sang and danced the entire time and Blues moved up to 14th place and only five points off the play off places. What a great afternoon, apart from the weather, and we even got to see fireworks on our way back to Birmingham.

I have visited the Riverside Stadium on 6 occasions including an evening game when there were only around 400 of us but we still sang our hearts out. It was freezing too. I have witnessed 1 win, 3 draws and 2 defeats.

Ground – 76 – Britannia Stadium – 10th January 1998 – Stoke City 0 Birmingham City 7 – First Division

I was now living in Abu Dhabi and my first trip home would see me visit Stoke City's new stadium. I was so excited being back in Birmingham and I was really looking forward to the trip to Stoke City's new Britannia stadium for the match. Stephen was now eight years old and was also really looking forward to the trip, and so we headed to Stoke once again with Julie driving us. The new Britannia stadium was very nice but once again just like all the other new stadiums being built up and down the country. Blues fans were situated behind the goal and there was already quite a few Bluenoses inside the ground when we arrived. The atmosphere was great and Stephen loved it, as did I.

Blues were playing in our away kit of yellow shirts and black shorts and it wasn't too long before the Bluenoses were singing 'it's just like watching Brazil, it's just like watching Brazil' as Blues raced into a three goal lead. It was brilliant and before long Blues were winning 6-0 and taunting the Stoke fans by singing their 'Delilah' anthem back at them. They were fuming! We however, were enjoying ourselves immensely and at one point I turned to look at Stephen who was gazing at the scoreboard, which read Stoke City 0 Birmingham City 6.

I asked him what he was doing and he replied he was looking at the scoreboard because he couldn't believe it. He was over the moon and once again the Bluenoses broke into a chorus of 'it's just like watching Brazil, it's just like watching Brazil'. There were thousands of Blues fans there and they all began singing 'stand up it your 6-0 up' and all the Bluenoses were already standing. All the seated Stoke fans looked on in despair and the Blues fans then sang 'sit down if your 6-0 down' to the already seated Stoke fans. Quite amusing really.

To add insult to injury for the Stoke fans Blues scored a seventh and completed a 7-0 rout as 'oh what fun it is to see City win away' rang out to the tune of jingle bells, followed by chants of 'easy, easy!' It was a brilliant day out and Stephen and I had a fantastic day.

In December 2009 Stephen and I were going by train to Stoke along with Brendan and we were meeting up early in a pub in the City centre due to it being a early kick off to avoid trouble. Neil (my brother & Stephens dad) gave us a lift into town and we arrived at the pub about 1030am and Brendan and Ron were already inside enjoying a pint. It was soon time to go and we headed off to New Street Station and onto the platform for the Stoke train. It was really cold and everyone looked frozen on the platform, including the many police officers that were also on the platform waiting to join us on our journey to Stoke. A police escort from Birmingham all the way to the match eh!

The train was packed but Stephen and I managed to get seats next to each other whilst the others were scattered about the same carriage. The train was full of Bluenoses on the way to the game. When the train arrived at Stoke we were greeted by several double decker buses to take us the the ground which had been laid on by the police in order to escort us. The Bluenoses were already in good voice and boarded the buses singing loudly, followed by the police.

We boarded the loudest bus and joined in the singing. The Blues were singing 'we all hate Stoke, Stoke, we all hate Stoke, Stoke,...' And the bus was literally rocking. The policeman downstairs looked a bit green and said to the driver 'I could do without this' but he was also laughing as he said it.

All the way to the ground the bus was rocking and the Blues fans were singing loudly and I could see people looking up at the commotion as we passed them. As we approached the ground the ground the Stoke fans heard our arrival and looked on as we taunted them with our singing. It was brilliant. The atmosphere amongst the travelling Blues was really fantastic and I was already having a brilliant day.

Once off the bus we all headed into the ground and met up with other Bluenoses that we knew in the bar under the stands in the away end. Then it was up to the seats for the game. Everyone in the Blues end stood for the whole of the match. I was singing my heart out but I was situated away from the main singers. I vowed to join them for the second half.

The first half ended 0-0 and Stephen and I headed back down to the bar for refreshments and a catch up with the others. We were chatting to Brendan and were amongst the last to leave the bar when the second half got underway. As we headed up the stairs to our seats we heard an almighty roar and the Blues fans were celebrating wildly. Blues had scored and were 1-0 ahead! Stephen and I had missed the goal by seconds but we soon caught on and joined the celebrations.

This time we stood amongst the singers and I proceeded to sing for the entire second half as Blues secured a great 1-0 away win. My favourite song became 'we are unbeatable!'. What a fabulous run we were on and what a great time it was to be a Bluenose! We headed back to the buses and we were escorted back towards the train station with the Bluenoses in full voice and in celebration mode.

Once back at the station Brendan, Stephen and myself managed to escape the police escort and headed into the hotel across the road from the station entrance. We headed into the bar, which was a nice quiet little bar, and ordered drinks. I had a lovely scrumpy cider and Stephen tried it and also had one. By the time we had enjoyed our drinking session and headed back to the station the train had arrived and, after obtaining more beers from the station shop, we boarded for our journey back to Birmingham New Street Station.

My most recent visit was in January 2024 and once again I was looking forward to the trip to Stoke. The coach journey passed okay and we arrived in Stoke in the pouring rain. We disembarked and headed to the food van by the away turnstiles and I was only brave enough to have chips and just like recent visits we all had to consume our food in the pouring rain. It was a relief to finally get inside the stadium and a nice dry concourse.

As is usually the case at Stoke the Bluenoses were in good voice in the sold out away end and our seats were up the back near all the youngsters who filled the aisles rather than find their seats. It was buzzing though. Blues started well and when Jay Stansfield was put through on goal after only 10 minutes he rocketed the ball into the net to make it 1-0 and the away end went crazy. There were bodies everywhere with several of the youngsters in a pile in the aisles. It was really funny to see. They certainly enjoyed themselves as we did in our celebrations.

Blues went into the halftime break leading 1-0 and then won a free kick on the edge of the penalty area with only 4 minutes of the second half gone. Up stepped Juninho Bacuna to curl a beautiful shot over the wall and into the top corner right in front of the away fans and there was an explosion of noise and celebrations as the Bluenoses went absolutely crazy. It was brilliant and I celebrated noisily.

Blues seemed to sit back a bit after going 2-0 up and missed a few good chances and I felt this led to Stoke pulling a goal back after 70 minutes. New loan signing Andre Dozzell came on the 71st minute and he looked okay. Happily Blues held on for a very good 2-1 away win and we were all extremely happy as we headed home. It had been a really good away day, something that had been a rare occurrence so far this season. The Bluenoses had never stopped singing which created a fantastic atmosphere. Tony Mowbray said our away support was 'big, loud and noisy'. He loved it.

Over the years I have visited the Britannia Stadium, or the Bet 365 Stadium as it is now known, on 5 occasions and I have witnessed 4 victories and 1 draw. Happily I have never seen Blues lose here. I really enjoy my visits to this stadium.

Ground 77 – Banks Stadium (Walsall FC) – 8th October 1999 – Division One – Walsall 1 Birmingham City 0

In October 1999 I was back in the UK for a visit and I made my first trip to Walsall's new stadium (well new to me) which was currently known as the Bescot Stadium. It would be a new ground for me and I took my nephew Stephen with me. I had visited Walsall's old ground Fellows Park but not this new stadium which sat just off the M5 motorway which made it quite easy to find. It was a nice new all seated stadium and the Blues fans were situated in the small stand behind the goal. It was a small stadium but quite nice nevertheless. Blues fans were in good voice as usual but unable to inspire our team as we lost the game 1-0. I did enjoy the day out though.

The next time I would visit would be a good few years later when I was living back in Birmingham and I went there to watch England women in a World Cup Qualifier.

On Friday 24th November 2017 a group of us that followed Blues Ladies had tickets for the World Cup Qualifier between England Ladies and Bosnia Ladies at Walsall's Bescot Stadium and I was really looking forward to it. It Would be my first time to watch England Ladies live and I was really excited especially as it was already a sell out match.

I had worked an early shift on this day and as it was a 7.05pm kick off Steve picked me and June up at 5.15pm for the short trip to Walsall's Bescot Stadium. However, the journey turned into a nightmare as it took us 2 hours and 20 minutes due to traffic congestion! There were hundreds of England fans stuck in the traffic leading to the stadium including coaches and mini buses full of excited fans and we were hardly moving.

I rang Harry who was already inside the stadium with Terry and asked if he could get three programmes for us as we were stuck in traffic. The programmes were on sale outside the stadium and the steward would not let him get out to get them. Eventually Sharon managed to persuade them to let her out and she very kindly got us our programmes. We were still stuck in the car on the motorway slip road when the game kicked off and we saw the first goal by Steph Houghton live on our mobile phone as the game went on without us. Lots of empty seats could be seen due to the sheer number of fans still stuck in traffic!

It was proving too difficult to get near the ground so we parked at Morrisons and literally ran the rest of the way to the stadium. We were in the main home end (Tile Stand) behind the goal and arrived in our seats with ten minutes to go to half time. Every seat had a clapper and a fantastic double sided good quality England flag (on a stick). Very impressive! It was great to see the 'gang' as we were among a load of Bluenoses. I had my lovely white England scarf on and my Birmingham City hat.

It was a great atmosphere inside the ground and each stand was a sea of waving England flags. We got to half time with England leading 1-0 and there were still people coming into the ground late. England came out for the second half the way they left off – playing some fantastic football as we looked on in awe and they completely dominated Bosnia.

Nikita Parris scored England's second goal with a header in the first minute of the second half and everyone in the stadium were on their feet. Then on 54 minutes Steph Houghton scored a cracker from a free kick just outside the area to claim her second goal of the game and England's third. England should really have been awarded a penalty not long afterwards when one of our players was rugby tackled to the ground in the penalty area which the referee must have missed as it was so blatant. The referee didn't miss the next rugby tackle in the Bosnia penalty area though and awarded England a penalty in the 83rd minute which Fran Kirby stepped up to score England's fourth and complete the rout.

So overall it was a great 4-0 win and a fabulous night. I particularly enjoyed the enthusiastic Mexican wave which did the whole stadium several times. I also enjoyed the England band and singing along to it. Great atmosphere. England's interim manager Mo Marley commented that she hoped that an expected sell out crowd in Essex next week would prove as noisy as the flag-waving, trumpet-blowing 10,029 fans at Bank's stadium. "It's inspirational" she added "it's freezing cold, it's Friday night and it means a lot of commitment from a lot of parents and school teachers". "But the players absolutely love it. They buzz off the energy round the stadium. You walk out and see that and it gives them an extra 10 or 15%".

Overall England had 80% possession and 31 shots compared to Bosnia's 3 and 12 of those were on target. What a night – what a result! And after taking 2 hours 20 minutes to get to the game we were home in around 20 minutes via the chip shop!

So far I have made 3 visits to what is currently known as the Bescot Stadium and have seen Blues lose just once and England Women win on both of my other visits.

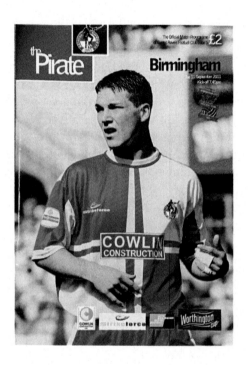

Ground – 78 – Memorial Stadium – 11th September 2001 – Bristol Rovers 0 Birmingham City 3 – League Cup

In September 2001 I was enjoying being home and looking forward to my last match before returning to Abu Dhabi which would be a cup tie against Bristol Rovers away. I was really looking forward to this trip and Neil and Sue were taking us to Bristol for the game. The game was on 11th September 2001 and as I was getting ready for the trip I turned the TV onto sky news only to be shocked by what was unveiling in New York as terrorists flew two airplanes into the twin towers causing them to collapse killing thousands of people. I was in shock. All air traffic was grounded and the skies were silent. I was due to fly back in two days time! So it was in a state of shock that I headed to Bristol for the cup tie against Bristol Rovers that night. It was to be one of only a few games that went ahead that evening.

Neil, Sue and Nicola dropped Stephen and I at the ground and they headed off to shop or get something to eat. Stephen and I headed into the small Bristol Rovers ground and we were soon mingling amongst the thousands of Bluenoses who had also made the trip. Everyone did seem a bit subdued but they soon got a bit of cup atmosphere going. I was pleased to bump into Alan again and I sat by him and we chatted about football and the events of the day. The game got under way and Blues soon raced into a 2-0 lead.

With a few minutes to go to half time Stephen needed the toilet so we headed down towards the toilets that were situated at the back of a little terraced area populated by Blues fans. With a minute to go to half time Stephen asked if he would be okay to go to the toilet or did I think we would score again. 'You will be okay' I replied 'there's not enough time left to score another', so off he went. Within seconds of him going into the toilets Blues scored a third! He'll kill me I thought! As I celebrated he came running out and the look on his face was a picture. He burst into a smile and we both fell about laughing as we celebrated madly. The game finished 3-0 and Blues were through to the 3rd round of the league cup as we headed out of the little ground to meet up with the others to head back to Birmingham.

Two days later I headed to Birmingham International Airport to fly back to Abu Dhabi. The airports were open again but security was red hot causing all flights to be delayed by at least a couple of hours. I was a bit worried about going back to a middle eastern country as I didn't know what the fall out would be like – especially as it was reported that some of the terrorists had UAE passports. I was quite glad of the extra security measures as it made me feel a bit safer about flying even though I was not looking forward to going back. There were only 17 passengers on a large plane that usually carries over 300 and me and my friends from Abu Dhabi who were returning with me enjoying exclusive inflight service and took a carrier bag full of drinks off the flight with us.

My next trip was in July 2019 and I was so excited to be travelling to a Blues away game again even though it was only a friendly game. June couldn't make it and so it was just me and the lads, Terry, Harry, Nigel and Charlie. We had a great trip to Bristol on the official coaches and headed to the local chip shop on our arrival. We had to decide between the pub or the chippie and amazingly the chippie won - although we considered heading to the pub after our chips. We had a lovely lunch sitting at tables outside the Chippie then we headed into the memorial ground to join the other Bluenoses on the away terrace. It was quite sunny now and the Bluenoses were in good voice especially when the tannoy belted out 'sweet Carolyn' and we all joined it. It was really fun.

The teams came out and we sang 'Keep Right On' and applauded them. They were wearing the new charcoal grey away kit, which I must admit I really didn't like as it was dull and boring. I was hoping it would grow on me but I thought it was awful. I had yet to see a team be successful in a grey away kit and that included England and Manchester United. The game got underway and us Bluenoses on the terraces carried on singing and had a bit of banter with the Bluenoses just across from us in the seats as we sang 'we hate villa more then you,' and they responded likewise. We sang 'stand up if you love the Blues' and they duly stood up and then sang back to us 'sit down if you love the Blues'. We all laughed.

Blues then conceded a soft goal to fall behind but it was not long before Pederson scored to restore parity and it was 1-1 at halftime. It was a team of youngsters and they were performing well. In the second half the lively Steve Seddon crossed for Lucas Jutkiewicz to head home and we all celebrated. The Bluenoses in the seats sang 'you only sing when your winning' to us and we all fell about laughing. We were having a fantastic time in the sun. Mind you, I ended up with a very burnt face from the sun! The game finished with a good 2-1 win and a really good performance in the new formation of 3-4-1-2 in front of 1,153 Bluenoses. It was a cracking away trip and I really hoped there would be many more to come.

Two trips to the Memorial Ground and two wins which gives me a 100% win rate here. Great place to visit.

Ground 79 – Millennium Stadium (Cardiff) – 12th May 2002 – Birmingham City 1 Norwich City 1 (Birmingham City win on penalties) – First Division Playoff Final

On a sunny morning on 12th May 2002 we gathered at my mom's getting ready for the exciting day ahead. Sue (my sister in law) brought Stephen over, bright and early and I was pleased to see he had dyed his blonde hair blue for the occasion. He also had on his blues shirt and had bought a Blues flag along with him as well. Annette, mom and myself all had Blues shirts on and I also had a Blues flag. I had bought a crate of Smirnoff Ice for the trip and as Steve pulled up with the mini bus and his sons on board, I loaded the drinks and sandwiches which mom had made and we all boarded. Annette sat up front with Steve, who was driving, and Stephen, mom and I sat together in the row behind them with Stephen ensconced at the window.

We headed off towards Harborne and collected the rest of the lads on the way, and then it was off to Cardiff. We set off really early and it was only about 7.45am when we headed out. Several hisses were heard at the back of the van as the lads opened cans of beer and one voice piped up with 'has any one got a bottle opener?' Much to everyone's surprise I waved a bottle opener in the air and everyone cheered! I then decided to crack open a bottle myself, much to my mom's horror as she pointed out it was only 8am. I reassured her that I would pace myself as I passed Annette a bottle. Stephen informed me that his mom had said he could have some also so I let him have a couple of sips from my bottle, although not entirely convinced that he was telling me the truth!

Everyone chatted and sang on the journey and before long we had reached the 'Welcome to Wales' sign which was by now draped in Birmingham Flags and scarves, no doubt put there by other Bluenoses who had set out before us. I thought this was really amusing and it added to the excitement of the day. By now I had loads of butterflies in my stomach. I needed the Smirnoff Ice to calm me down. Stephen was just as excited also and the two of us soaked up the atmosphere of the day. It was the biggest match that Stephen had ever been to.

Steve had decided to park up just outside of Cardiff at Newport and get the local train into the city centre. This was because of the nightmare of last year's Cup Final appearance when traffic was at a standstill both before the match and out afterwards due to poor arrangements for the final. We parked the van in a side street near the station and headed off to catch a train into Cardiff. As we headed for a subway we spotted three Norwich supporters in their yellow shirts coming out of the subway and after one look at us clad in our Blues gear they did a complete about turn and disappeared rather quickly back the way they had come. I had to laugh at this as did Stephen and Annette.

Once we arrived at the local station we discovered that it was packed with Bluenoses who had obviously had the same idea and we ended up squashed amongst them as we made our way to the platform. Because of the large numbers there were police on the doors to the platforms allowing a few through at a time and we all had to battle to stay together. It was great on the platform where all the Bluenoses were in full voice and I enjoyed joining in. 'were on our way!' rang out loud and clear and it carried on onto the train as we boarded. The train was soon packed and Stephen and I found ourselves sitting in the baggage shelves whilst mom and Annette had to make do with standing. It wasn't too long before we were pulling into Cardiff though and we all surged out as one blue mass.

As we came out the station we were met by an amazing sight. It was blue and white as far as the eye could see. The city centre around the Millennium stadium had been divided into two sides and the Blue half was extremely impressive. There were already thousands of Bluenoses who were happily playing football in the streets and drinking beer either outside the many bars or from cans obtained from the local shops. We headed for the nearest chippie and after consuming chips and gravy we headed to a pub for a drink. All the pubs were packed so after a quick drink that followed queuing for an extremely long time, we decided to head towards the stadium that could be seen from where we were and try to find an off licence.

The Millennium Stadium was really impressive as we walked passed it and crossed the river to find a shop. Once we had obtained beers we headed for the river bank where we chatted in the sunshine and mom dished out the massive bag of sandwiches she had bought with her. The lads were well pleased and tucked in to various sandwiches washed down with cans of beer. I bought a play off final 2002 Birmingham City scarf as a souvenir and we soaked up the atmosphere which was absolutely brilliant. We also took lots of photos and we were soon approached by a reporter who Steve had called over and pointed out our 'Abu Dhabi Blues' St. Georges flag! He asked me how far I had travelled for the game and when I told him I had travelled 3,500 miles he was very impressed and took some photos for the Sunday Mercury the next day.

We headed into the ground early to soak up the atmosphere and due to the fact that the demand for tickets was so high (around 50,000 Blues were there), our tickets were in different areas. I was with Stephen in the lower tier and mom, Annette, Steve and his lads were in the third tier. Blues had the biggest end and the majority of the stadium and it was just a mass of blue and white with a smaller section of yellow and green at the other end. It was brilliant, the noise levels were tremendous. Stephen and I were seated at the back of the stand underneath the second tier and we wondered down to the front to take some photos and look around in total awe at the Blue support.

I felt tears in my eyes and felt so proud and lucky at being able to be part of it. It was a feeling that I just couldn't put into words but it was one of the best days of my life. We had waited 16 years to get here and the possibility of playing in the Premier league was right in front of us. I prayed we could do it. I was so used to disappointment though after the last four years that I was petrified we would miss out again. As I looked up at the many flags and banners, I laughed as I saw one that said 'Beckham bends it like Grainger' – brilliant. For those who don't already know, Martin Grainger was our left back who scored great goals from free kicks. I also saw a massive banner which read 'Goodbye Division One!'

We went to our seats just before the players came out onto the pitch and shared a few words with the people around us. There was a man in front of me who looked at least 80 and had these dark sunglasses on and he kept looking around excitedly and we would share a smile and thumbs up. Then the players came out to a crescendo of noise and once again I could feel tears in my eyes and I felt the emotions of the day. I looked at Stephen and he looked as excited and nervous as me.

The game got underway and the noise level remained pretty much the same as the Bluenoses sang our hearts out. Oh, how I hoped our hearts would not be broken by the end of the match. It was an exciting game and both sides had good chances but 90 minutes ended with the scores still level at 0-0 and another 30 minutes of extra time. It was nerve wracking stuff and not long into the first half of extra time Norwich scored – right in front of our end, we were losing 1-0. We were shocked and our hearts were breaking. I could not believe it. The Blues fans refused to give up though and immediately sang out 'Keep Right On' to spur our team on.

Blues surged into the Norwich half and there was big Geoff Horsefield to smash the ball into the back of the Norwich net – 1-1! The Blues end erupted and everyone was jumping on each other. The old man in front of me turned around with his fists in the air in celebration and a massive smile on his face. I lifted Stephen in the air and everyone else seemed to jump on us too. It was a mad celebration and I can't begin to explain both the joy and the relief that I felt. At least now we still had hope.

As the game carried on we missed a couple of really good chances and Michael Johnson hit the post for Blues right in front of the Blues fans with only three minutes to go. The whistle for full time blew and it finished 1-1. This meant the dreaded penalty shoot and my heart began to sink. We all knew Blues record at penalty shoot outs and in fact I had never seen Blues win in a penalty shootout. I was by now extremely stressed and worried I might have a heart attack!

The toss was made and Blues surprisingly won and chose to take the penalties at our end in front of the Blue Army. Was this a good sign? I debated it with Stephen. Norwich were to take the first penalty and scored putting them in the lead 1-0. Then it was Blues turn and up stepped Stern John as the rest of the Blues team stood huddled with their arms around each other's shoulders. I was a bit nervous as Stern John can often miss chances like this. Behind me someone said 'not Stern John, he's fucking shit that Stern John' as he stepped forward. I could barely look but I am glad I did as the ball smashed into the back of the net! The same voice said 'he's fucking brilliant that Stern John!' much to my amusement, and the Blues fans went wild. It was now 1-1.

Then it was the turn of Norwich again to a crescendo of whistles from the Blues fans behind the goal. The Blues fans celebrated wildly as our goalkeeper Nico Vassen made a brilliant save giving Blues the advantage. Still 1-1. Then it was the turn of Paul Devlin, a true Bluenose and he smashed an unstoppable shot into the bottom right hand corner. 2-1. Then it was the turn of Norwich again and unbelievably Nico Vassen made another great save! Blues fans went wild and Norwich fans heads were now in their hands.

Up stepped Stan Lazaridis for the fourth penalty and he also smashed it into the net! I couldn't believe my eyes, I began to feel that we may actually do it and I joined the others in celebration. Then Norwich stepped up again and they had to score because if they missed then Blues would be promoted! There were whistles from all the Blues fans but despite Nico Vassen getting a hand to it, Norwich scored and it was now 3-2. However, if Blues scored from the next penalty then it would be Birmingham City who would be promoted to the Premier League.

Darren Carter, our 18 year old Bluenose, who had sat in the stand at Cardiff last year to watch Blues in the League Cup final against Liverpool, stepped forward to take the 40 million pound penalty. He asked the referee 'if this goes in are we up?' and the referee replied "yes'. As he stepped up to take it the commentator remarked 'Darren Carter for the Premiership' and our 18 year old hero coolly smashed the ball into the back of the net to set off absolutely wild celebrations amongst both the fans and the players. As he ran towards the Blues fans he was mobbed by Blues players and Andy Johnson was first to get to him and he jumped on his back to be carried to the Blues fans, then it was Jeff Kenna and Paul Devlin that caught up and mobbed him.

By now I was crying and jumping on everyone and the old guy in front of me turned around and took his glasses off and tears were streaming down his face. All around me grown men were crying with joy and it just seemed so right. 50.000 Bluenoses began singing 'we are Premier League, say we are Premier League' and that was when it really hit me. We were back in the top flight after an absence of 16 years! I was ecstatic along with everyone else and we celebrated and sang our hearts out. It was probably the best day of my life and I couldn't begin to describe how I felt. Unless of course you were there and then you would know what it felt like.

Over excited Bluenoses spilled onto the pitch to celebrate and had to be asked to leave the pitch in order for the presentations to be made. Darren Carter looked stunned and Nico Vassen Jumped on a beaming Steve Bruce as he was about to be interviewed. As Darren Carter was interviewed he told how he was sitting up in the stands last year and he couldn't believe he had scored the winning penalty in a strong Brummie accent. He said he didn't think he would be able to sleep for days and it was just unbelievable.

When they came to interview Paul Devlin, also a Bluenose, he was too overcome to speak. Michael Johnson put on a blues jester hat and danced around blowing a horn – classic! Nico Vassen was running around with a 'We're Going Up' flag as 'shit on the villa' rang out from the Blues end. The trophy was bought out onto the pitch and it looked fabulous draped in Blue and White and the fans were going wild as the Blues players did a lap of honour before going over to collect their winners medals. 'Keep Right On' rang out so proudly as the trophy was award to Birmingham City and the fireworks lit up the stadium and the streamers rained down. It was a crescendo of noise as Jeff Kenna lifted the trophy high in the air in a mass of Blue and White. Even Beau Brummie (our mascot) was on the pitch celebrating with the players and fans. Birmingham City were back in the Premier League!

As we headed out of the stadium following long celebrations, we met up with the others and headed back to Newport where we enjoyed a couple of celebratory drinks in one of the local pubs. By the time we headed back to Birmingham the traffic had lessened and we were still in full celebratory mode! We sang our hearts out all the way back to Birmingham and I went to bed a very exhausted but happy person. At last we were in the Premier league and I could not have been any happier.

Ground 80 – St. Mary's Stadium – 23rd August 2003 – Southampton 0 Birmingham 0 – Premier League

In August 2003 I was back in Birmingham and off on a trip down south to see Blues play Southampton at their new St. Mary's stadium. This would be a new ground for me as I had only ever been to their old ground, which had had the worst away end I had ever been in. Anyway, it was a lovely sunny day as Stephen and I set off on the St. Andrews Tavern coach following a bacon buttie and a cider in the pub prior to setting off. As we arrived at the ground the sun was shining and loads of lads had their shirts off and were wandering around in the sunshine drinking beers and eating chips. Stephen and I got off the coach and headed to the nearby chippie van where we obtained chips and cans of pop. It really was a lovely day and there were Blues shirts everywhere.

Once we had eaten our chips we headed into the ground and the Blues end was full as 2,356 Bluenoses had made the trip. The atmosphere was electric and Blues fans were singing loudly and were in good spirits. The noise from the Blues end was amazing and it was as if Blues were at home. Then the players came out to a crescendo of cheers from the Blues contingent.

It was brilliant and once the match got underway Blues played great and really should have won the match. One chance in particular should have resulted in a goal much to the dismay of the Blues fans as it hit the post but some idiot behind me kicked the back of my seat (the whole Blues section stood for the entire game) and my seat shot down hitting me in the backs of my legs. Lucky it wasn't Stephens's seat as he is only young and slim and it could have resulted in some serious harm. As it was I had terrible bruising on both my legs the next day and I never bruise! The match ended 0-0 and Blues were still up in the top half in 6th place.

One of my favourite trips to St. Mary's Stadium was during the Women's Euro's in the summer of 2022. Harry, June and myself were heading back down South for the final Group game against Northern Ireland at St. Mary's Stadium in Southampton. This time Harry was driving and we had booked into the Premier Inn at Fareham where I had arranged to meet my Uncle Haydn and his wife Diane at TGI Fridays across the car park from our Premier Inn.

It was a really good drive down and we were soon pulling onto the car park and checking into our hotel just as Haydn and Diane called to say they were on the car park. It was so lovely to see them and we headed into TGI Fridays for lunch. We had fabulous food and a really lovely catch up and I was so happy to see them again.

Once they left we headed to our rooms and got into our England gear once again before heading back outside to await the taxi we had ordered to take us into Southampton to St. Mary's for the game. Our Uber taxi arrived in about ten minutes and we were approached by some girls who had ordered a taxi ages ago to go the the stadium but it still hadn't turned up and they were desperate to get to the ground as they had pre booked a meal. They spoke to our driver but he couldn't help them so it didn't look good really and we wished them luck as we left.

It took about twenty minutes to get to the ground and we were dropped off right outside the stadium, which was great. There were already lots of fan's milling about and the nearby fan park was starting to fill up. It was a lovely sunny day again and the atmosphere at the Euro's England games was absolutely brilliant. Especially at stadiums like those we had visited so far were we could walk easily all around the outside of the stadium with lots of stuff going on and lots of official merchandise stalls as well as the unofficial merchandise which was also fabulous. June and I got our usual half half scarves both official and unofficial. Today I was tempted by the official replica match ball which had come down in price to £32 and so I purchased one.

We headed to a local food van and June and I had bacon rolls but it wasn't very nice to be honest. I think it was the bread roll that it was on that had a funny taste. It was starting to get busy and was really hot outside so we headed into the stadium. We were seated just near the corner of the 'home' side of the stadium behind the goal and I have to say that so far our tickets had been great with really good views. Right behind us was the BBC TV gantry and we saw both Ian Wright and Alex Scott when they headed up there before the game. Ian Wright stopped several times for photos with the England fans. He seemed really nice and approachable.

The atmosphere was great once again with the sound of all the 'free' clappers being used and the England band belting out songs and chants for fans to join in with. 'England!' was frequently heard loud and proud from the entire stadium again, apart from the small green section on the opposite corner where the Northern Ireland contingent were situated. They did sing at times too though and looked to be enjoying the occasion also.

The game was amazing again as England were on fire and we were treated to another goal fest as England won 5-0 to finish top of the group and qualify for the quarterfinals. England were playing some amazing football at the moment and the TV viewing figures were growing every game with more and more jumping on the bandwagon and enjoying the football on show. It was lovely to hear the crowd singing 'It's Coming Home' with the entire stadium (apart from the Irish) joining in. Fantastic. I was really loving my European tour!

It was great because nobody leaves the stadium before the end of the game with everyone staying to sing and enjoy the experience and the win. Once again we hadn't really planned our trip back to our hotel so we just followed the signs to the train station in the city centre and followed the crowds. Once at the station we took one look at the big taxi queue and ordered a Uber on the app and following a wait of about 15-20 minutes we were in our taxi and on our way back to our hotel and I fell into bed exhausted but excited around 2330. Another fantastic trip.

I have visited St. Mary's Stadium on 3 occasions, twice with Blues – a draw and a defeat and once with England Women – a win. The stadium opened in 2001 at a cost of £32 million pounds and has a capacity of 32,689.

Ground 81 – St. James Park – 30th August 2003 - Newcastle United 0 Birmingham City 1 – Premier League

My first trip to Newcastle was in August 2003 and I was really looking forward to this trip as I had never been to St. James Park in Newcastle and it would be another new ground for me. Once again Stephen and I had booked to travel on the coaches from the St. Andrews Tavern and Neil dropped us at the pub early and we enjoyed our usual bacon buttie and a cider before setting off. As it was a long trip we set off early and made good time, therefore the coaches stopped half way at two pubs situated across the road from each other.

Each coach pulled into one of the pubs car parks and the Bluenoses poured off and into one of the pubs. It was quite funny really as the pubs were only small and in the middle of the countryside, so when loads of Blues fans poured into the pubs the owners were taken by surprise. The pub we headed into had two elderly people behind the small bar and the look on their faces was a picture. They called in the back for help and we had to queue for a while to get our drinks – hence I got two and some crisps and a coke for Stephen. We were both really enjoying the trip so far.

The Bluenoses on our coach were in really good voice on the trip and as we set off again they were singing all sorts of songs such as 'I would rather be a pastie than a pie!' which I admit to joining in. It was great fun, but we encountered some traffic and by the time we had been met by our police escort it was getting near to kick off time. The police stopped all the traffic and rushed us to the ground with their sirens blaring and their blue lights flashing. We had already been boarded and searched by the police when they met our coach and it was quite amusing when one of the coppers said he hoped we beat them as he was a Middlesbrough fan! Of course we gave them some stick as usual.

We arrived at the ground with minutes to spare before kickoff and as Stephen and I ran towards the ground, I dropped my ray ban sunglasses causing them to be scratched. I was well pissed off as they were new and expensive. I just hoped the day would be worth it. Once inside we headed to our seats and as any away fan who has been to Newcastle knows, the away section is at the top of a very high stand and by the time we had dashed to the top I was looking around for an oxygen mask! I was bloody knackered but once inside the atmosphere was brilliant.

There were 2,500 Blues fans who were trying to out sing 50,000 noisy Geordies. It was great. Blues fans having a great sense of humour were singing 'shit ground, no noise' to the amusement of the Newcastle fans. Blues also broke into a chorus of 'my garden shed is bigger than this' to great amusing from the Geordies who were fast warming to us. I sent a text to Craig (Newcastle fan) who was currently off shore, to tell him that I was at the match but I didn't receive a reply.

The match got underway and Blues were playing really well. Before long a Blues player was brought down in the area and a penalty was awarded. It was at the opposite end of the pitch to where we were sitting in the away section be we had quite a good view even though we were in clouds. David Dunn stepped up to take it and it was saved by the keeper but Dunn reacted the quickest to put the ball into the Newcastle net – 1-0 to Blues. The Blues end erupted and we celebrated madly and sang our hearts out.

Just before half time the referee was running backwards and as he put out his arm to indicate a decision he hit our Robbie Savage full in the face knocking him out. As Robbie lay flat out on the pitch Alan Shearer came over to the referee, picked up the cards that had fell from his pocket and showed the referee the Red Card. This was really funny and everyone laughed. Poor Robbie was helped to his feet but even he had a little smile after seeing the funny side. He said afterwards that he was sure many referees would have liked to have knocked him out.

At half time it was still 1-0 to Blues and I texted Craig to inform him of the score and I headed to the bar downstairs. As I was obtaining beers I bumped into Dave and we got chatting about the game and stuff. It was good to see him and he always made me laugh. Then we said goodbye and headed to our seats to watch the second half.

The second half Blues continued to play well and we sang our hearts out in support and in celebration. The game finished Newcastle Utd 0 Birmingham City 1, and it was great to witness such a win in this fabulous stadium. It's always good winning on other teams turf and it doesn't come much better than winning at the big clubs such as Newcastle. As we got outside I couldn't believe how many Blues coaches were lined up along the road. There looked to be about 30 of them and we had to walk along them for ages until we came to ours.

Most Bluenoses were boarding the coaches or getting into cars but I did notice two brave Bluenoses in Blues shirts heading into a pub in the middle of the Newcastle fans. As we headed out of Newcastle the police escort had stopped all the traffic and I noticed loads of Sunderland fans getting out of their cars and they stood with their arms in the air bowing to our coaches because we had just beaten their rivals. It was really funny. We just waved back at them and laughed. On the long trip back to Birmingham we continued to sing and Stephen and I chatted and read our programmes until we arrived back at the St. Andrews Tavern whereby we went inside to await Neil's arrival to take us home.

Another memorable trip was in 2016 mainly because of the atmosphere despite the scoreline. Even though it was getting close to Christmas, over 3,000 Bluenoses headed to Newcastle for the long trip up north on another cold day. We traveled by coach (10 official coaches) and we were impressed by the sheer number of Bluenoses as we arrived at St. James Park. After our very long climb up the stairs to the away end up in the gods (stunning views though) we made our way into the bar area which was quickly filling with Bluenoses in good voice already and we purchased our pre match drinks.

We made our way into the stands and the singing in the away end was incredible. Our anthem was loud and proud and we never stopped singing throughout the game. Unfortunately Blues were awful and Newcastle easily dominated. Bluenoses spent most of the time singing 'we've got the ball' swiftly followed by 'we've lost the ball' and when we did have a shot 3000 Blues sang 'we've had a shot'. It was a very poor performance by Blues as we lost the game 4-0 but the fans were supportive of the team throughout and never stopped singing. As atmospheres go amongst the Bluenoses this was up there with one of the bests despite the result.

Rowett said he was disappointed with the performance saying that "we didn't play enough balls or play with enough quality when we did win the balls. We were too passive at times". After the game the Newcastle fans were full of praise for the Blues fans on social media saying that we were the best group of fans to travel to St. James Park in years and that we were way better than the traveling fans of the Vile. The Newcastle fans loved us.

I have visited St. James Park on only 3 occasions and I have seen Blues win once and suffer 2 defeats but I have really enjoyed each trip. It is always a great atmosphere and a fantastic view.

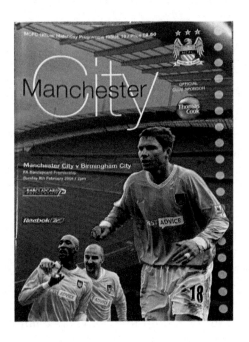

Ground 82 – Etihad Stadium – 8th February 2004 – Manchester City 0 Birmingham City 0 – Premier League

My first trip to Manchester City's new stadium was on the 4th February 2004 as I again headed back to the UK to see my family. This would be my first ever trip to the the City Of Manchester Stadium as it was called at the time before the

Etihad sponsorship. Stephen and I again travelled with the St. Andrews Tavern Coaches and we had a good trip with Blues coming away with a 0-0 draw.

Our goalkeeper Maik Taylor had made a stunning double save and then Blues had missed a brilliant chance to win the game in the last few minutes but a point was good and we were now 10th in the table and looking good.

In December 2005 I was again heading to Manchester and it was a night game and Stephen and I were again travelling on the coach from the St. Andrews Tavern pub. We had a couple of pre match drinks before setting off into what was becoming a very cold night. The trip was enjoyable as always when travelling with the Bluenoses and we were soon arriving in a wet Manchester. I must admit I was quite impressed with the City of Manchester Stadium though I did wonder what on earth the strange looking monument type thing was just outside the ground. I was later to go out with the guy who designed it and he did explain what it was but it was obviously not that memorable as I can't remember what on earth it was.

Anyway, once inside the ground it was really cold but as we downed another pre match drink under the stands with the away Blues support, the atmosphere was brilliant. Blues were singing whilst consuming their food and drinks and it was really loud and echoed underneath the stand where we were congregated before kickoff. The Bluenoses were singing 'shit on the villa' and 'Keep Right On' over and over. It was great. Just before kickoff we made our way up to our seats and I was very impressed with the stadium. Blues had a large section just behind the goal next to the Manchester City fans and the Blues faithful were in good voice despite the cold.

The game got under way and we conceded four goals very quickly really but it didn't stop us singing, much to the amazement of the Man City fans. As the game dragged on and hope began to fade, Jarosik scored a brilliant goal right in front of us and we all began celebrating in the hope it would warm us up and lead to a fight back. Blues fans began singing 'we're gonna win 5-4, we're gonna win 5-4, we're gonna win 5-4!' which was quite funny really. That's one of the things I love about Bluenoses, we have such a great sense of humour even when things are going against us. Even though we lost the game 4-1 I left the ground with a feeling of warmth from the brilliant Blues fans who always make me feel better. Then it was onto the coach and back to Birmingham.

I have only made these two trips to the Etihad Stadium but I did enjoy them despite the defeat. I probably enjoyed the draw more though. The stadium opened in July 2002 at a cost of £112 million and was expanded in 2014-2015 and again 2023-2026.

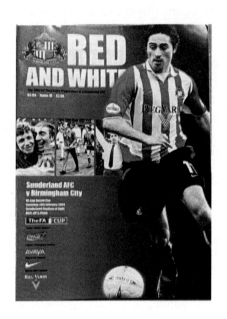

Ground 83 – Stadium of Light – 11th February 2004 – Sunderland 1 Birmingham City 1 – FA Cup

In February 2004 Blues had been drawn to play away at Sunderland in the 5th round and this would be a new ground for me and a first trip to the Stadium of Light. This would be another long trip for Stephen and I and we travelled on the coaches once again. Loads of Bluenoses made the trip and there were 2,429 of us inside the Stadium of Light making loads of noise. The Sunderland support were also noisy but there were large empty sections of seating in the home area.

Sunderland had been relegated the previous season and the Blues fans rubbed this in by singing 'we are premier league!' to them. It was a good game and a great atmosphere and the fact that our manager Steve Bruce was from Newcastle, did not go unnoticed by Sunderland who were big rivals with the Geordies. They sang 'there's only one fat Geordie' to him on a couple of occasions. This came back to haunt them though when Forsell scored a brilliant goal for Blues and all the Bluenoses began singing '1-0 to the fat Geordie!' I thought this was really funny and it certainly wiped the smiles of the faces of the Sunderland fans. However, Sunderland managed to score an equaliser which meant that the game ended 1-1 and would need a reply at St. Andrews to settle the tie.

My most recent trip was in April 2023 and it was a long trip but on a lovely sunny day which meant that the journey was very scenic. We stopped at a service station in Leeds at 1130 where June and Taff wisely decided on a breakfast bap whereas I went somewhat off piste and had a Chinese. It was very nice though and I had been up since 6am so it was like lunchtime really. We rushed back to the coach and continued on our journey.

We arrived at the Stadium of Light at about 1.40pm to be reminded that we were not allowed coins (or vapes or anything that could be used as a missile) and so we left coins on the coach and headed to the stadium. With these rules in mind I got my card out to pay for my match day programme only to be informed it was cash only. This left me scratching my head somewhat but I did have a banknote which I used only to be given coins as change! Unbelievable, I thought as I headed back to the coach to deposit my coins.

Back to the stadium and there were sniffer dogs a plenty around the away entrances and we received a thorough search before entering the turnstiles. Don't believe it when they claim women don't get searched because we do! With there being so many stairs to the away end in the gods, we decided to stop half way and head into the large bar area. Once again there was no 'normal' cider on sale which was very sad and Taff claimed it's due to the increase in the price of normal apple cider (not dark fruit).

Rested and watered we then headed upwards again to our seats. It was a really high section of the stand were the away fans are situated on a balcony with the home supporters below us. It was a cracking view though. We had really good seats and the Bluenoses were in great voice and good spirits. The game kicked off and Blues started brightly. In the 29th minute the lively Chong raced into the penalty area and pulled the ball back to George Hall who fired home right in front of the away end to make it 1-0 Blues!

The away section erupted and Blue smoke filled the air from at least 3 smoke bombs and I watched in horror as another one sailed over the balcony and into the Sunderland fans below. As the blue smoke rose into the air from below there was sheer panic on the faces of the stewards and police who raced to the general area that the smoke bomb was fired from but not really knowing what to do. I continued with my celebrations as the Blues players mobbed young George Hall on the pitch below us.

Sadly George had to go off injured just before halftime and was replaced by Jobe Bellingham. A lapse in defending following Chong losing the ball led to Sunderland equalising in first half stoppage time time. I was quite disappointed by this but was hopeful that we could get a least a point as I felt we were the better team. Unfortunately some very poor defending allowed a Sunderland player all the time and space he needed to fire home a winner for Sunderland and our hearts sank.

Not long before the end of the game Sunderland were reduced to ten men when they had a player sent off for fouling Chong again but Blues couldn't capitalise and we lost 2-1. The police infiltrated the away fans just before the end of the game and made an arrest which was probably the culprit who threw the smoke bomb into the Sunderland fans but it did kick off a bit as they led him and another man away.

It had been a disappointing result but a good trip on a lovely sunny day. Highlight was when the attendance was announced as 37,673 and the Blues fans sang "you're support is fucking shit!"

It was a long long trip back and I was home just after 10pm with an early start for the work the next day and a 12 hour shift to look forward to. It had been a great, but very tiring, day.

I have visited the Stadium of Light on 4 occasions with Blues and I have seen 2 draws and 2 defeats but no victories as yet. Not a happy hunting ground so far. The stadium opened in 1997 at a cost of £24 million pounds and was expanded in 2000. The original capacity was 42,000 and expanded to 49,000 in 2000.

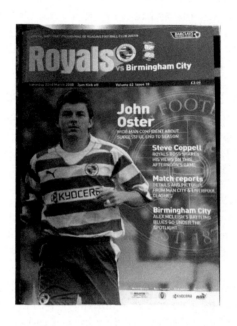

Ground 84 – Madejski Stadium – 22nd March 2008 – Reading 2 Birmingham City 1 – Premier League

I was excited about the trip to Reading despite travelling alone and my mom had made me a packed lunch for the train and Steve had left me a small bottle of wine, also for the journey and my brother Neil had agreed to drop me at New Street station. So after picking up a can of cider, I was soon on board the Reading train and on my way. There were loads of Blues fans on the train

243

chatting amongst themselves, also enjoying a few cans and looking forward to the game. As the train left Birmingham it began to snow! It looked really nice out of the train window but had stopped by the time I got to Reading. Loads more Blues fans got on in Oxford, also loaded up with beers.

As we arrived at Reading station I called Alan's friend who told me that Bob would be in the pub just outside the station, so that was where I headed. The pub was easy to find and was called The Three Guineas. It looked pretty packed with Bluenoses and as I met up with Bob, who was standing outside, he suggested that we head off to Wetherspoons instead. There were two other people meeting up with Bob, a bloke called Paul and his daughter Chelsea, and I soon got talking to them too.

We went into Wetherspoons and Bob and I got a drink, only to discover that they wouldn't serve Chelsea because she was underage – even though she only wanted a soft drink. As the rest of the lads were in a small pub just around the corner, Paul and Chelsea headed off there and we said we would join them when we finished our drinks.

It was quiet in Wetherspoons and as soon as our drinks were finished we headed around the corner and caught up with all the others in a small pub (can't remember the name) which was also full of Bluenoses. A few drinks were downed here and then Bob ordered a taxi to take us to the ground as it was getting very close to kick off time. I hadn't realised the time and when we arrived at the ground Alan was waiting patiently with his nephew in his car outside the ground to give me my ticket. I would be sitting away from my mates in the second row, but after a few beers I didn't really care where I sat so long as it was with the Bluenoses.

I had a great view, although I did think the atmosphere was a bit subdued for Blues. Where had all the singers gone? I think we should go back to having terraced areas again to bring the atmosphere back. However, Blues did give a few loud renditions of 'Keep Right On'. As the match got underway Blues had a few good chances to take the lead, but of course the inevitable happened and Reading scored. Once again, if only we had taken our chances, especially the one that McSheffrey missed when he was through on goal! I felt our defence was at fault for their goal, but Blues launched into a rendition of 'Keep Right On' to try and lift the team.

The game continued and very soon Forssell crossed the ball into the penalty area and Mauro Zarate smashed the ball into the net right in front of the Blues contingent! We went wild in the Blues end and Zarate ran to celebrate in front of the fans and it was right in front of where I was standing – about two feet from the pitch! He was being mobbed by the other player's right in front of us and we were all jumping all over each other in celebration. It was brilliant. I could feel my phone vibrating in my pocket so I pulled it out to answer in and it was my mates in Abu Dhabi, Trish and Tracey, who were watching the game live. 'We just saw you on the telly!' they screamed at me, 'and it stayed on you for a good 30 seconds, unbelievable'. They said I was celebrating like a mad thing, but they know that I always do!

The Blues fans had come alive and found their voices as we danced and celebrated. Blues were by far the better team – surely a winner must come! And come it did, but against the run of play and Reading again took the lead due to poor defending at a set piece. This was certainly becoming a habit this season and I thought that McLeish needed to have a serious look at our defence!

The final whistle sounded and the thousands of shocked Bluenoses headed outside for the waiting special buses put on to take the Reading fans back to the city centre. There were a few seats being kicked and gates being kicked on the way out as Blues fans let out their frustrations. We all know how hard it is at times being a Bluenose! I met up with Paul and Chelsea and we boarded one of the buses. As we headed upstairs the whole bus broke into a loud rendition of 'Keep Right On' which I joined in with.

Before long we were back outside the station and headed to the Three Guineas which was fast becoming full of Bluenoses in full voice. Keep Right On was belting out loudly and the beers were flowing as we all enjoyed the banter before we headed home. One side of the pub was singing 'we hate villa more than you!' to the other side who were also singing 'we hate villa more that you!' back to them. I had a right laugh with the lads and Chelsea and must admit to starting a few songs off myself. In fact, I was enjoying myself so much that I missed my train back! I even got talking to a Reading fan who thought our supporters were great.

So, after a really good time with the Bluenoses in the pub, I headed back to Birmingham on the next train with Paul and Chelsea. The train was full of Bluenoses and after obtaining a few ciders we sang a few songs all the way home. As we came up the steps into New street station we all sang 'Keep Right On' loudly and it echoed impressively around the station. I must admit, the day out itself was a lot of fun, as it always is following Blues away from home, but the defeat was disheartening and it seemed to be the story of our season.

A really good trip took place in June 2018. It was the first away trip of 2018 and was at Reading. I was not particularly confident but hopeful as I knew Blues well. It was me, June, Terry, Charlie and Nigel on the coach heading to Reading and as usual it was late to leave and took the long route which meant that we arrived at the Madejski Stadium at 7.20pm for the 8pm kick off. It was pouring with rain as I met up with Stephen who had travelled from London and we headed into the away turnstiles. Over 1100 Bluenoses had made the trip and were in good voice as usual.

I enjoyed a nice pre match cider and then the game got underway. Blues were in last season's red away kit and started well. Just like the Leeds game everyone was putting in a shift and playing well although Jonathan Grounds did seem to be letting the Reading players fly pass him at times – again. In the 24th minute the deadlock was broken when Jacques Maghoma smashed the ball in the net to put Blues 1-0 ahead and the away end erupted in noise. I looked around for Nigel, who had been telling us how shit Maghoma is, on the way down on the coach, and I shouted 'he's shit isn't he!' and we all laughed.

Blues were now singing 'how shit must you be – we're winning away!' to a lot a of applause from the Reading fans. They replied 'how shit must we be – you're winning away!' which I thought was quite funny. Blues were playing well but it didn't stop me being nervous. We continued to play well and Jeremie Boga, who was having a great game, sent a lovely ball to Sam Gallagher who shot past the Reading keeper to score. He and the rest of the team ran to the away fans as we celebrated wildly. To be 2-0 up was brilliant, although no more than we deserved. Bluenoses sang 'how shit must you be – we've scored more than one!' as the Reading fans looked despondent.

Even at 2-0 I couldn't relax. Blues fans sang 'we want three' to which I joined in. The final whistle went to a roar from the away end and boos from the remaining Reading fans. As we celebrated and sang 'Keep Right On' the players came over to applaud us. Once again though, I was disappointed that our manager Steve Cotterill did not come over to us. We had travelled a long way on an awful rainy night and got behind our team (as always) and it would have been nice for him to acknowledge that. Maybe he was just letting his players take the plaudits.

We celebrated all the way home, singing several songs including the ten German bombers and we all dream of a team of Kieftenbeld's. We also sang 'if I had the wings of a sparrow' as we drove past Villa Park. What a great night despite the weather and our first away win of the season.

I really enjoyed our last away match of the season in May 2019 when we went in fancy dress as is tradition. As much as I was looking forward to the trip to Reading it was also tinged with sadness that such a fantastic season was coming to an end. I loved the last away game because so many Bluenoses adhere to tradition and come in fancy dress.

Because it was so stressful last season June and I had not done the fancy dress - too scared to jinx it but this season we were quite happy to don fancy dress once again. We had decided upon the 2 girls from Abba with June wearing the white Abba outfit (she has brown hair) and I wore the blue outfit with silver stars on the flares and a long white wig (even though I have blonde hair I wanted to get the look right). We both had fantastic 70's style white patent boots with heels that looked brilliant. To top it off we had face jewels and I had blue 'festival' glitter on my face!

We traveled by coaches that left early morning (15 minutes late as always seems to be the case) as it was a 12.30 kick off and we arrived at the Majestic Stadium at 11.00. My nephew Stephen was already there and laughed when he saw us dressed up. We met Adrian 'Taff' who was the only bloke in our group who had made the effort and he looked really cool dressed as a 'blue monk'. We headed to the food vans and got sausage, chips etc, which was really nice although Nigel dropped his sausage on the floor. Then it was into the ground to obtain pre match drinks.

There was a party atmosphere inside the away end as songs were sang and there was some good outfits on show. I liked the 4 men dressed as the Spice Girls, they were really good. I also liked the Beatles in their sergeant pepper outfits, the convicts, the banana's and the baby. Once we were up in the stands we joined in the singing and the game got underway. The Bluenoses then spotted a lad in the nearby Reading end wearing a Vile shirt (yes they really are that obsessed with us) and a loud version of 'Shit on the Villa' rang out. This idiot responded by standing up and gesticulating to the away end and he instantly regretted his actions as loads of singing from the entire away end was directed at him.

He looked embarrassed now but his mate decided to swap shirts with him and put the Vile shirt on and stood up and tried to taunt the Blues end before he was pounced on by the stewards who escorted him from the ground. Many of the nearby Reading fans had applauded him - what a bunch of idiots! They had gone right down in my estimation now, apart from the few who gave him the 'wanker' sign as he was led out.

The game was a typical end of season affair with nothing to play for and it showed. There were a few changes to the team as Garry Monk rested some of his bruised players but they all played really well. The match finished 0-0 and Blues finished the season unbeaten in 7 games. Although the Bluenoses sang a lot at the end of the game as the players came over to applaud our support I had felt that they were unusually quiet throughout most of the game. I was beginning to worry that a lot of the snowflakes and corporate were getting tickets instead of the real fans who sing their hearts out no matter what. I hope we don't lose this support as this is what Birmingham City are all about.

We headed back to Birmingham talking about how much we have all enjoyed this season which even a 9 point deduction couldn't spoil and only strengthened our resolve. Blues finished in 17th place (should have been 14th really!) and easily 12 points clear of the drop despite the EFL trying to send us down. We had been treated to some great football this season and really should have had more points from many of the games we played.

Another good trip was in December 2019. I was looking forward to the trip to Reading on the Saturday and we began the day well with breakfast at McDonalds near to St. Andrews before we boarded the coach. There was a good turnout and we had a nice trip down to Reading and headed to the food stalls near the stadium. To my disappointment the refreshment outlets had changed their menus and didn't look all that appealing as it was all posh nosh and expensive. We finally decided on the hot dogs with the posh herb sausages in them at £5 each and I got one for each of us. They were massive and I couldn't eat all of mine, especially as the lads were taking the piss every time I attempted to take a bite. Biggest and thickest sausages I have ever seen!

Once we had finished our food we headed into the stadium and the away concourse was already full of Bluenoses drinking and watching a Blues goals dvd being shown on the large TV's. We watched for a while then headed up to our seats to join the singing Bluenoses. It was another away sell out and a great atmosphere.

Today Blues would come up against ex Blues player Michael Morrison and Puscas who had been lined up to sign for Blues before Reading stepped in and he amazingly chose Reading! So revenge could be had today I thought. The game got underway and Blues were playing some really nice football, the best we had seen for a long time and it was no surprise when we took the lead on 41 minutes with an own goal by none other than Michael Morrison. He didn't look too upset about it either. The away end exploded and Blue smoke filled the air from a smoke bomb as we celebrated. It didn't last long though as Reading snatched an undeserved equaliser on the stroke of half time.

When the teams came out for the second half Michael Morrison immediately came over to the Blues end and applauded all the traveling Bluenoses and we applauded him back. Blues started the second half well and I felt sure we would get something out of the game if we continued to play this amazing football. Blues won a free kick on 59 minutes and up stepped Jeremie Bela to hit a stunning shot from distance which curled into the top corner and mayhem broke out in the away end as we all went crazy. I couldn't remember the last time Blues had scored from a free kick. It was a cracker and Blues were now 2-1 ahead.

It was amazing watching such sexy football from Blues who were tearing Reading apart and it was no surprise when we added a 3rd goal scored by Gimenez in the 88th minute to make it 3-1 and 'Puscas, Puscas what's the score?' rang out. Unfortunately Reading managed to scramble another goal in the 95th minute which in no way reflected the overall dominance of Blues. The game finished in a good 3-2 win but it should have been more comprehensive as Blues had 57.9% possession. It was a great 3 points that moved Blues up to 15th in the table and we had a very enjoyable coach journey home as we sang and chatted about another great away adventure.

I have visited the Madejski Stadium, now called the Select Car Leasing Stadium, on 9 occasions and I have seen 3 wins, 3 draws and 3 defeats. Not a bad place to visit really and a typical new 'bowl stadium' (or flat packs as I call them). Not an awful lot of character to be honest. The stadium was opened in 1998 at a cost of £50 million pounds (£94 million in 2021) and has a capacity of 24,161.

Ground 85 – Keepmoat Stadium – 14th March 2009 – Doncaster Rovers 0 Birmingham City 2 – Championship

I was excited about to my first trip to Doncaster and I was up early and really looking forward to the day ahead. My mom had packed a bag of food which could quite possibly have fed the most of people on the train itself. This was probably because she knew I would be traveling with Steve! Mind you, Steve duly arrived armed with some sandwiches of his own as well as a few beers for the train.

There were quite a few Bluenoses on the platform waiting for the train which soon arrived and we boarded and found our seats. Beers were duly opened and just before the train departed, one of Steve's mates and his son got on our carriage and sat not far from us. Then we were on our way and the party began. Just before we got to Derby it was announced that there would now be some Derby County fans boarding on their journey to Sheffield. I wondered whether this was to tip off the Blues fans or in the hope of avoiding trouble. There were quite a few Derby fans that got on armed with beers, but there was no trouble and they even asked us who we were playing and wished us well. I suggested that they do us a favor by beating Sheffield Utd, who were also now closing in on us, and we would return the favor by beating Doncaster. This was happily agreed as the Derby fans disembarked and waved farewell to us.

So, following a good journey, we arrived in Doncaster and I promptly zipped up my jacket to hide my Blues shirt and enabled us to slip unnoticed past the waiting police presence at the station and out into the town. Steve was busy on his mobile trying to find out where the others were as the four of us set off into town. Steve's mate and I just wanted to stop at the first pub we saw for a drink but Steve insisted on finding his mates in a pub which proved to be quite elusive. Anyway, we eventually found our way to this pub which was packed with fans of many descriptions watching Liverpool's demolition of Manchester Utd at Old Trafford which was being shown live. It was 2-1 to Liverpool when we arrive but it soon became 3-1 and then 4-1 much to the delight of the neutrals and the few scousers in the pub. The prawn sandwich brigade left with their heads bowed.

The pub was really hot and a bit packed for me and I managed to persuade Steve and some of the lads to head for a pub nearer the ground. Steve had spoken to Brendon who was at the Beefeater near the stadium and he said it was a big pub and there were loads of Bluenoses there. This sounded just my cup of tea and so we ordered two taxis's and before long we were on our way to the Beefeater to join the others.

On arrival at the pub, I was delighted to see it was full of Bluenoses and the atmosphere was brilliant with singing constantly breaking out. There were loads of people I knew in there and I was soon chatting to Brendon near the bar whilst downing another pint of cider. There were also a load of Blues who had drifted outside. I sang quite a bit too and even got a few songs going. It was great and before long it was time to walk the short distance to the stadium which could be clearly seen as we left the pub. As we approached the ground we saw a group of Blues fans who had decided to 'take' the local hill to which the new stadium is named after. They were holding aloft a massive Birmingham City St. George's flag and singing 'Keep Right On'. All the passing Bluenoses, including myself, joined in and it was quite funny.

The stadium itself was quite nice for a new stadium even though it was a little bit small and the atmosphere inside was good. Once inside the Blues end it was free seating, which I really loved because it meant the singers could all be together and made the atmosphere even better. I headed right to the centre of the singers as usual. The Blues contingent were situated behind the goal and were already in good voice. Blues played really well and before long Jerome scored right in front of us Bluenoses and our end erupted. I was jumping about madly as usual as were all the other Bluenoses.

With still some time left to half time Steve decided to go the toilet and said he would get the drinks in and meet me downstairs at half time. Not long after he had gone, Blues scored again and the bluenoses went wild in celebration. 2-0! We were on our way! My phone was vibrating in my pocket and it was Steve asking what I wanted to drink as they didn't have cider. 'Anything vodka based' I replied –'oh by the way Steve, its 2-0!'

So at half time it was 2-0 and I headed down to the bar with Brendon and friends. When I found Steve he was with Paul Fiddler. After a brief chat I headed back to the other lads and handed out a few sandwiches to keep everyone going, and then it was back to our seats for the second half.

The second half was a cruise really as we never looked in any danger of losing and a group of Blues fans did a conga before heading down to the front of the stand to wave flags and sing "Keep Right On'. The stewards looked on in amazement and clearly had no idea what to do. These stewards were okay though and left the Blues fans to their celebrations which was currently being shown live on SKY. Apparently the cameras showed the Blues fans doing the conga and celebrating. It was a great day and we were soon heading to the buses which would take us back to the station where our train would very soon be leaving. I thought we would miss it to be honest, but when we arrived we found that the police had held it back to accommodate us.

We obtained beers for the train in the station and boarded for our journey home. There was a heavy police presence on the train and as much as I tried I could not persuade Steve to sing. No surprise really though as he is not a singer. I decided to venture into the next carriage and see if they would sing and to my delight I managed to get them all singing 'Keep Right On'

On return to our carriage a big group of the lads sang to me 'we love you Blondie, with your long Blondie hair, we love you Blondie, cos you love the blues' it was great, and I immediately decided to go and join them and get them singing. I had a right laugh with them but Steve texted my sister to tell her that I was about to get myself arrested! Mind you, it was quite funny because she immediately called me and my mobile ring tone was the crowd version of shit on the villa and everyone cheered when it rang.

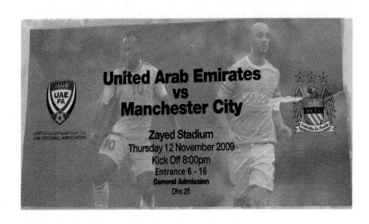

Ground 86 – Zayed Sports City Stadium (Abu Dhabi) – 12ᵗʰ November 2009 – United Arab Emirates 1 Manchester City 0 – Friendly

I was still living and working in Abu Dhabi in the United Arab Emirates when Manchester City came to town for a friendly game at the National stadium and along with some of my friends I decided to attend. Sheikh Mansoor had taken over ownership of Manchester City in September 2008 and now Abu Dhabi had a Manchester City club shop and there was advertisements for them around the city.

My friends and I decided that it would be nice to visit the National Stadium and see an English team take on the UAE national side. I donned my England shirt and we headed to the stadium together. When we arrived there I noticed that there were lots of English supporters with many in England shirts and others in their various club shirts. There were a few Manchester City fans too.

The stadium was nice and quite large and like a bowl with two tiers and a capacity of 43,630. Today there was a good attendance for a friendly game of 26,000 although there wasn't any atmosphere at all unlike games in England. The stadium opened in 1980 and was renovated in 2009 and expanded in 2017.

I was expecting Manchester City under manager Mark Hughes, who was present on the touchline, to easily beat the UAE national team but amazingly the UAE won with a gift of a penalty and they hung on as the game finished 1-0. Obviously I had wanted the English team to win but I wasn't that bothered and I had enjoyed my outing and we headed back into town for a drink.

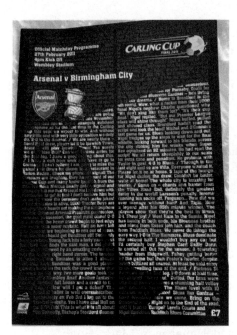

Ground 87 – New Wembley Stadium – 12th October 2010 – England 0 Montenegro 0 – UEFA Euro Qualifier

My first trip to the new Wembley Stadium was in October 2010 to watch England in a Euro qualifying game and I took my mom and sister along with me. As it was a night game we had booked to stay in a hotel near Wembley and got the train down to London on the morning of the game. We checked into our hotel and had a look around the area before returning to the Hotel restaurant for dinner before heading across to Wembley.

The new stadium looked amazing with the big arch lit up under the night sky and Wembley was was busy with England fans arriving for the game. There were merchandise stalls all along the way and I got 2 lovely woollen scarves, one was red with England in white and the other was white with England in red. I gave my mom the white one to wear to keep her warm as it was a bit cold to be honest. I had brought along my ENGLAND flag with the Birmingham City crest on and we had photo taken with me and mom holding the flag with Wembley behind us. It looked great.

We headed into the stadium and wandered around the concourse to see what was available. Our seats were in the lower tier behind the goal and had a very good view. The new stadium looked fabulous although it doesn't have the character of the old Wembley with the twin towers. The big arch looked amazing though.

The game itself failed to inspire really with no goals scored and finishing in a disappointing 0-0 draw. The highlight of the game came when a posh Londoner behind us amused mom with his comment of 'kick him in the nats (nuts)'. Mom couldn't stop laughing as she said "he said that so nicely'. We headed back to our hotel and settled down for the night.

It had been a very nice visit and I had been very impressed by the new stadium. I dreamed of watching Birmingham City play there one day, hopefully in the not too distant future.

My dream was to come true when one of my best trips to the New Wembley came in February 2011 in the League Cup Final. I was so excited to be heading to the League Cup Final despite having to embark on a night flight back to the UK after a 12 hour shift at work (I was still living in Abu Dhabi). Hence I arrived knackered but happy. I had ordered loads of Blues Wembley memorabilia and on day of the match me, Annette and Stephen (my nephew) donned jester hats, giant hands, scarves and flags and made our way to Harborne to get the coach.

I had a blue 'bob' wig on and Steve's brother Eddie fell about laughing when he saw me. I thought I looked cool! I had even painted my nails blue! It was a great trip up to London with music playing - mostly Blues related, and singing and chatting. Stephen had commented on his Facebook status that he was 'just off to London to pick up a cup'. His girlfriend's (she's from London) brother was an Arsenal fan so that could be fun!

We arrived at the pub 'Wards' at 11.15 am and it was already full of Bluenoses as word had gotten around that this was where we were headed. It was fantastic and there were Blues flags everywhere. The landlady had put on hot food (free) for us and it was lovely. Everyone was singing Blues songs and the atmosphere was brilliant. I painted a few faces and James even painted his nose blue. Word and photos reached us via social media showing a large flag which had been put up on the gates at Villa park which said 'while we're at Wembley the City is yours - KRO'. Class!

We set off for Wembley with plenty of time as we wanted to enjoy the pre match atmosphere. There had already been quite a few drinks consumed at this point though as we headed to the nearby tube station. It was fun on the tube as it was mostly Bluenoses with only a couple of Arsenal fans. We sang 'we'll be running round the bullring with the Cup!' Although none of us actually thought we would win the cup with Arsenal being overwhelming favourites. We were here to enjoy our day out. They were under the impression that they only had to turn up though. There was talk of this being their first trophy of the season.

So we arrived on Wembley way in the rain but in very good voice. I was interviewed by TV presenters about the game and I bravely predicted blues would win with a goal in the last minute. I think it was the blue wig that attracted them but I'm not sure the interview made it to the telly as I was probably a little bit tipsy at this point. Then it was into Wembley stadium as we joined the amazing blue army that were already singing their hearts out and I immediately joined in. We were up in the third tier at the corner and had an amazing view.

The teams had already arrived with the Blues players in really nice suits for the occasion whereas the high and mighty Arsenal arrived in track suits to pick up 'their cup'. That was immediately picked up by the pundits who commented on Blues looking the part but Arsenal being a bit disrespectful. The media had been focused on the fact that this would be the first of a possible quadruple for Arsenal and they were overwhelming favourites with the bookies.

When the players came out for kick off the noise was tremendous and it was the loudest version of Keep Right On that I had ever heard and it took the roof off the new Wembley stadium! Even the pundits remarked that the Blues fans were the loudest ever at Wembley! There were 88,851 in attendance and the Blue end was well and truly enjoying the occasion. Although we dreamed of a win we were realistic and we were here to enjoy ourselves and the occasion.

With only 2 minutes gone Bowyer ran through and was brought down by the Arsenal goalkeeper and it should have been a penalty and a red card but the linesman's flag was up for offside so Arsenal were saved. Replays showed the decision to be incorrect as Bowyer was indeed onside! The noise from the Bluenoses at this injustice was immense.

On 28 minutes Blues won a corner which was put into the area by Larsson to Roger Johnson who's header towards goal was headed into the net by Zigic and the Blues end exploded in celebration. We all went absolutely crazy, Stephen picked me up in the air and we were all jumping on each other. We couldn't believe we were 1-0 up against the mighty Arsenal in a Cup Final at Wembley. Incredible!

Of course Arsenal threw everything at us and disappointingly they equalised just before half time with a goal from Van Persie and the red half of the stadium woke up for the first time. Blues fans responded with another very loud rendition of Keep Right On to spur our players on. We were still in this game. Halftime came with the score still at 1-1. In the second half Blues were unlucky when Keith Fahey's shot came back off the inside of the post and as the game went on Blues started to tire and Arsenal threw everything at us but Ben Foster in goal, had a great game which culminated in him winning man of the match for the second time in 3 years at Wembley.

With 7 minutes remaining Obafemi Martins came on to make his debut as he replaced Keith Fahey. It looked to be going to extra time as we entered the 89th minute as Ben Foster made a long clearance which was flicked on by Zigic and as an Arsenal defender and the goalkeeper got in each other's way the ball fell to Obafemi Martins who swept the ball into an empty net. I went absolutely mental as did the entire Blues end as we all jumped on each other amongst unbelievable scenes like I have never seen before. Most of us had tears in our eyes as we realised we may just win the cup! Obafemi Martins ran off and did a string of somersaults whilst the other Blues players tried to catch up with him without getting kicked in the face. The noise was unbelievable as we celebrated.

Blues then defended well for the last few minutes but we could have gone further ahead when Obafemi Martins rounded the keeper but the angle proved to be too tight. Jerome and Ferguson were booked for time wasting before the referee blew and Wembley erupted in celebrations like nothing ever seen before and Birmingham City were the Carling Cup winners 2011 beating Arsenal 2-1.

257

Our first major trophy for 50 years. I couldn't believe it and I was so happy. We were all hugging and singing and crying with happiness. It was a lifelong dream. We all stayed behind for ages as we watched captain Stephen Carr lift that beautiful silver cup with Blue ribbons on it and we watched them parade it before our fans as they popped champagne bottles and drank it from the cup. Such fantastic scenes!

When we eventually headed to the escalators to exit Wembley the noise was incredible as we sang 'we're all going on a European tour!' To the tune of yellow submarine, and 'we won the Cup!' What a fantastic day! It will live long in the memory. We headed back on the tube to and back to the pub where the landlady had laid on more food and the celebrations really began. We drank and sang 'all dance if you won the cup' and 'we're all going on a European tour' for quite a while before climbing back on the coach knackered and headed back to Birmingham. I will never ever forget that day. It will be known as Obafemi Martins Day!

I was lucky enough to experience another fantastic historic day at Wembley Stadium in the Women's Euro Final in 2022 and what a fantastic day it turned out to be!

I was really excited as the final approached although we were a little apprehensive about the train strikes that were ongoing. In fact the train drivers were on strike on the Saturday before the final but happily it didn't seem to affect our trains and June and I easily jumped on a train at Selly Oak station which took us to New Street Station to meet Harry. We then got on an earlier train to Euston to give us more time to get to our hotel and then to Wembley where the gates would open at the earlier time of 2pm for the 5pm kickoff.

We arrived at Euston and immediately got the tube to Brentford where we had booked into a Premier Inn for an overnight stay but it did mean a bit of a walk with our overnight trolleys from the tube station to the hotel. We were too early to check in and so me and June changed into our England gear and applied our face transfers/wigs etc in the toilets before leaving our bags in the baggage room. Then we rang a taxi to take us to Wembley so that we would have plenty of time to obtain souvenirs and food.

It was choc a block around Wembley but our taxi driver did well to take a few short cuts and we were soon disembarking close to Wembley Way. It looked fantastic with a large England presence already there and there was still 3 hours to kick off. It did worry me a bit as there were already large queues at all the official merchandise stalls and I didn't want to miss out on my collections. Sadly though I did, despite queuing I was too late as all the official half/half final scarves were already sold out. I was gutted but at least I did get a programme for the final.

We decided to walk back down to the bottom of Wembley Way to get an unofficial half/half scarf but the good ones with dates on had already gone so we had to settle for and England v Germany one with no date on. I was really disappointed. I was getting hungry by now so we obtained burgers from a nearby food van and enjoyed them in the sunshine as we watched all the fans and media enjoying the atmosphere on Wembley Way. It was a great atmosphere. It was a really hot day too, which was also great as it meant that we hadn't had to wear coats and could wonder around in our England shirts and capes. The wigs were hot though!

I took loads of photos around Wembley and we then headed into the magnificent stadium ahead of kickoff and up to the top tier were we obtained expensive sweets, popcorn and drink. There were amazing views from the concourse up there and we again tried the official merchandise stores but still no scarves. Our seats were almost at the very back of the top tier and the view was amazing. There were already loads in the stadium and it was a sea of red and white with a couple of patches of German fans, although not very many to be honest. Today Wembley belonged to England.

By the time kick off approached there was a record crowd for the Women's Euro's of 87,192 which was also a record for Wembley stadium. To noise was fantastic as "England! England!" rang out around the entire stadium with St. George flags flying everywhere. It was brilliant. The opening ceremony was also fantastic with fireworks, singers and dancers. It was spectacular and I took loads of photos.

The game kicked off and the atmosphere was amazing as the entire stadium got behind England and it was an exciting game but was still goalless at halftime. Once again England manager Serina Wiegman made some very good substitutions especially Ella Toone who had only been on the pitch for six minutes when she ran through to lob the German keeper to put England ahead in the 62nd minute and the stadium exploded with noise. Wembley Stadium went completely bonkers as both fans and players celebrated an absolutely fantastic goal by the Manchester United striker. June and I were ecstatic and celebrated wildly.

England were the better team and I prayed that we could hang on to win the final but Germany grabbed a close range equaliser on 79 minutes to send the game into extra time. I was worried as I didn't fancy penalties and having come so close I couldn't stand the thought of losing to the German's. But with penalties looming England's Chloe Kelly fired home from a corner and Wembley went crazy! The noise was incredible and 'it's coming home' rang out all around the stadium. Chloe took her shirt off and ran off in ecstasy in her sports bra, swinging her shirt in the air with the jubilant England players in pursuit of her. There were celebrations like never before and tears of joy as the final whistle sounded and it was so very emotional.

I was finally witnessing a historic win as England finally won a major tournament after a 56 year wait and it was the Women who brought it home. There were amazing scenes as England lifted the trophy and were crowned European Champions 2022. It was great seeing Prince William hugging the girls after awarding them their winners medals. Over 20 million people had watched on TV or at fanzones and the country celebrated like never before. The celebrations in Wembley went on for a long long time as everyone stayed in their seats and sang song after song with the celebrating players. The England players certainly knew how to celebrate as they did snow angels in the glittering Confetti and swung from the crossbars. It was fantastic and I was so lucky to be there.

June and I had been confident from the beginning that England could do well and we had planned our tournament with military precision that had seen some fantastic trips and culminated it such a fantastic final. The football that we had witnessed had been the best that we had ever had the pleasure to watch and to win a major trophy in England was just so amazing.

We partied for so long that it was late into the night when we arrived exhausted back at our Premier Inn. It was too late for food so we had to raid the vending machine for crisps and chocolate before heading to our rooms. We didn't care though, we had just had the most amazing day and the most amazing tournament ever! Football had come home!

I visited the new Wembley on 4 occasions with the other visit being in May 2017 when I watched Birmingham City Women in the FA Cup final against Manchester City. Once again we stayed overnight in the nearby Holiday Inn and it was a lovely sunny day. Blues took a lot of fans that day and set a new record attendance for the women's FA Cup Final at Wembley but sadly the players looked a little overwhelmed by the occasion and lost 4-1 despite a cracking goal from Charlie Wellings. Disappointing but a great day out.

The old Wembley closed in 2000 and the new Wembley was built on the site of the old stadium and opened in 2007 for the FA Cup Final. It has 90,000 seats and is the second biggest stadium in Europe.

Ground 88 – Pride Park Stadium – 6th August 2011 – Derby County 2 Birmingham City 1 – Championship

It was great to be home for the opening match of the new season in 2011 and I had been really looking forward to the trip to Derby. Me, Stephen and Steve traveled to Derby by train and we got off in Burton and headed to a pub to meet some other Bluenoses. The pub was already busy with Bluenoses and we enjoyed a few drinks before heading back to the station and getting the train to Derby. We were soon inside the stadium and my seat was next to Brendan and his family who had come straight from Manchester airport after returning from their holiday.

Blues took the lead when Curtis Davies scored in the 19th minute and we all went wild in celebration. Unfortunately Derby soon equalised and then scored another before half time. Blues battered Derby but just couldn't score and lost the game 2-1. I was still optimistic though as we had played so well and despite the defeat I had a great day out.

After the game it was kicking off everywhere as the Derby fans tried to attack the Blues fans but they just ended up getting run all over the place. The police didn't know what to do for the best. As we walked up towards the station a group of Derby fans came out of an alley to ambush us but discovered to their horror that there were hundreds of Blues who then chased them back down their alley. Quite funny really. I headed back to moms and early the next morning I sadly headed back to Abu Dhabi.

One of my favourite games at Pride Park was in 2015 although Blues were poor. Derby went 2-0 up and Blues hadn't even have a shot as we approached stoppage time. Quite a few Bluenoses had given up and left before the end and when Blues were awarded a penalty in the 93rd minute those of us that remained celebrated as Caddis made it 2-1.

In the 96th minute Blues won a corner which was scrambled into the net by Donaldson and the away end went completely mental. I forgot my recent abdominal surgery and ended up clutching my stomach after jumping in the air in delight. Painful but oh so worth it! After a poor performance with no shots in normal time Blues managed to grab a fantastic 2-2 draw and boy did we taunt the Derby fans on the way out.

In January 2022 I was back at Pride Park again and it was another bottom three side that Blues were up against as we set out for Derby on a Sunday morning for the 1330 kick off at Pride Park in front of the live Sky TV cameras. There was a large protest planned by the Derby fans about their current situation and it was a sell out due to the Derby fans thinking it could be Derby County's last ever game in the football league. This was because Derby were currently in administration and under threat of being kicked out of the football league by the EFL if they could not prove that they had the funds to continue to pay their staff/players. Other irregularities involving the sale of their stadium amongst other things, had already seen Derby deducted 21 points this season and they currently sat in the bottom three despite doing very well and having already overcome their points deduction and they were picking up points to climb off the bottom.

Prior to the game the EFL granted Derby a months extension but the protest was still going ahead. We arrived at the stadium in plenty of time and headed towards the nearby Subway for a sandwich but we were stopped in our tracks by reporters from Central News requesting an interview about how we felt about Blues current situation with our owners. As much as we just wanted to leg it, we chatted on camera and it was shown on Central News later on in the evening. I texted my sister to tell my mom to watch it and my brother so that he could watch it too.

The queue for Subway was massive so we made do with a burger before heading into the away end. It was buzzing in the away end with the Bluenoses in great voice. The whole atmosphere was brilliant with both sets of supporters in great voice. 'Keep Right On' was amazing loud and drowned out the home support. Both clubs quite rightly felt hard done by the EFL and when Blues fans sang 'fuck the EFL' the Derby fans joined in and the entire stadium were belting it out and I'm sure the microphones all round the pitch were quickly muted! Derby fans applauded the Blues fans and again applauded us when we sang 'We want our club back'.

The game got underway and Blues had the 3 new signings on the pitch and one of them, Lyle Taylor (on loan from Derby's rivals Forest) scored on his debut to give Blues a deserved 1-0 lead. The away end exploded in celebration as Lyle Taylor made his way towards us in celebration whilst being pursued by the rest of the Blues team. There were 6 or 7 flares/smoke bombs with both blue and yellow smoke filling the air. We were engulfed with yellow smoke from a smoke bomb set off right by us. Great scenes though.

Blues were playing really well and a new song was born for Lyle Taylor which was sang to the tune of 'don't you want me baby – by human league' with our version being 'Lyle Taylor baby'. Derby fans were then taunted with 'Lyle Taylor – he's sending you down!'. It was a new look Blues side with speed and skill and a lot of us couldn't believe what we were seeing. Blues started the second half just as well and Scott Hogan scored Blues second in the 56th minute with a great goal that prompted more smoke bombs in the away end and fantastic celebrations. The Derby fans had been quiet since Blues first goal. Blues sang '2-0 down on your big day out!'

Could it be too good to be true, I wondered? Well yes because Lee Bowyer then changed the game completely with his substitutions. First he brought off the amazing Lyle Taylor, who had been tearing Derby apart, and replaced him with defender George Friend and then new boy Juninho Bacuna, who had been absolutely brilliant with his passing, and replaced him with youngster Jordan James and we looked like Blues of old. Blues then sat back and Derby got back into the game with a goal on 87 minutes. Typical. The game was thrown away in the 96th minute, despite only 5 minutes of injury time, when a Derby player scored with a dangerously high overhead kick which nearly took our defenders head off but was allowed to stand. Unbelievable! A previous identical incident by a Blues player had seen a free kick awarded to Derby. Talk about double standards. Poor refereeing again.

The goal should not have stood but I still blamed the substitutions made by our manager that completely changed the game and saw us sit back and defend and we looked a poor side afterwards. I would have settled for a point beforehand but after our initial performance it felt like a defeat as we left with only one point. It wasn't much fun leaving the stadium to the sound of the Derby fans singing '2-0 and you fucked it up' and they were right we had.

I have made 6 visits to Pride Park and have witnessed 1 win, 3 draws and 2 defeats. Pride Park opened in 1997 at a cost of £28 million and a capacity of 32,956.

Ground 89 – Cardiff City Stadium – 4th December 2011 – Cardiff City 1 Birmingham City 0 – Championship

I was up early on the Saturday to head to Cardiff for the away game and Steve picked me up in a taxi to take us to St. Andrews to get the coach. We persuaded the taxi driver to go through McDonalds so that we could obtain breakfast and drinks. I took some plastic 'Halloween' glasses with me so when we stopped at the services we had a nice vodka and coke in them. Once we arrived at Cardiff the 7 coaches were escorted straight to the ground where we met up with Craig, Graham, Mark, Ron, Brendan and Liam inside the stadium and had a nice pint of cider before the game.

It was my first time to Cardiff's new stadium and I thought it was quite nice for a new ground. We had some great banter with the home fans, which can be quite rare these days, and I particularly liked "Swansea are shit but they're better than you!" It was slightly amusing when Cardiff sang '1-0 to the sheep shaggers' when they took the lead. Somewhat disappointingly Blues lost 1-0 and we headed back to Birmingham where I met my sister Annette in the Kings Arms for a post match pint before heading back to moms for a lovely Sunday roast. Unfortunately I lost my beautiful gold Blues ball and world necklace that I had been given for my 18th Birthday so I was really sad about that. It had been made specially for me in the jewellery quarter and was a gift from my mom and dad.

A really good away trip to Cardiff came at the end of the 2016 season. There were 7 official Blues coaches that were due to depart at 8.30am. As we arrived I spotted Jack arriving as a brown beer bottle – very funny. I went as a nun with a long blue wig – hence 'Blue Nun' – the retro wine for those of you who don't remember it. The coach stewards were in fancy dress and looked brilliant. Most of them were dressed as Thunderbirds with a 'where's Wally girl' also. The coach drivers had Gary Rowett masks on – brilliant! There were several Blues fans also in fancy dress including superheroes which included a family of Batman, Batgirl and a Bat child. I particularly liked Laurel and Hardy who were travelling on our coach. They were fabulous.

As usual we were late getting away and late arriving in Cardiff due to us missing the police escort that the other Blues coaches were on time for and had gone on ahead of us. This meant we had to wait forty minutes at the services which was prolonged due to a couple of idiots not coming back on time. We finally arrived at Cardiff City's stadium just before 12 o'clock for the 12.30 kick off. It was buzzing in the concourse below the stands when we entered through the turnstiles into the away end. It was brilliant – there was people in fancy dress everywhere.

I headed to the programme booth whilst Steve headed to the bar and June, James and Jack went to the other bar. Good job I went straight for the match programme as they ran out of them just afterwards. The young girl behind the counter said to me (in a welsh accent) "I've never seen anything like this before, what's it about?" She looked overawed as I explained that it is a Birmingham City tradition to wear fancy dress for the last away game of the season.

The fancy dress clad Bluenoses were in full voice as I made my way to the others to claim my nice cold cider. A few Blues fans did the sign of the cross or bowed as I passed them – very funny. There were 5 or 6 green beer bottles who were leading the singing and soon spotted Jack – the lone brown beer bottle and gave him some stick. They broke into a chorus of "shit on the brown" which I thought was quite funny.

Then a loud rendition of 'Dele Adebola' broke out and I turned to see ex-Blues player Dele Adebola amongst the Blues fans. I think he was heading for his seat but he was being sidetracked by lots of Bluenoses wanting photos with him. Yes we also had a snap with him!

There were some great costumes on display. There was a bloke with a dress and a bright pink wig who looked good, and a great postbox. There were a couple of sheep and a few bananas. As we went up into the stand I saw five sheikhs and a belly dancer – really good! Inflatables were bouncing around the Blues end and these included sheep and penis's – yes you heard correct and no I don't know the relevance of the Willy's either. There were also England flags being waved throughout the away end. There were lots of empty seats around the home sections and their fans were silent but the Blues end was sold out and was in full voice. 'We're Birmingham, We're Birmingham' was being belted out.

The game kicked off and the Blues fans continued to sing. Neither team had anything but pride to play for but that wasn't going to stop us Bluenoses enjoying ourselves. Fun was had by singing 'we hate villa more than you' from each half of the away contingent. A reaction was finally gained following a loud rendition of 'God save the Queen' from the Blues end. The Welsh fans didn't seem to like this as all and a few gestures were aimed our way to which we laughed and returned with gusto.

This enticed loud renditions of 'Enger-land! Enger-land!' With St.Georges flags waving madly, and 'Swing low sweet chariot' was sung. Then followed 'we'll see you in France!' Good clean fun! Blues were playing well and when the ball fell to our Welsh wizard David Cotterill he fired home a shot into the bottom corner. This caused scenes of mass celebration and two blue flares and a smoke bomb in the away end. I was, of course, also dancing around in celebration as

267

the blue smoke seemed to engulf us. '1-0 to the Enger-land!' broke out from the Blues fans. It was great fun.

The lead didn't last long though as Jonathan Grounds cocked up about 2 yards in front of goal as he brought the ball down for a tap in for the Cardiff player. 1-1 but it didn't stop us singing. It spurred the Cardiff fans into life though for about a minute but that was drowned out by a loud rendition of 'Keep Right On'. Our manager Gary Rowett was told after the game that the Blues fans were the loudest at Cardiff this season

The Blues fans also sang 'is this a library?' and other songs and generally had a fantastic time. The match ended with a draw and all the Bluenoses stayed behind to applaud out team as they came over to us at the end. We sang 'We're Birmingham, We're Birmingham' and 'Keep Right On' as the players applauded our support. Gary Rowett did the 'worship' gesture to us as he bowed with his arms raised and we all returned the gesture and sang 'there's only one Gary Rowett!' as he and the players left the pitch.

As we were heading towards the exits the Cardiff team were doing their lap of honour and the Blues fans got to ruin their parade by singing 'who the fucking hell are you?' to them – quite loudly I might add too. Gary Rowett was asked after the game if he was interested in the Burton job, to which he replied '3,000 fans when we have 20,000 at Blues'. He also said he loved when the Blues fans sing 'Keep Right On' and it makes his heart tingle. What a man!

I have visited the Cardiff City Stadium as it is now called, on 8 occasions and have seen only 1 win, 2 draws and 5 defeats between 2011 and 2024. The stadium is very similar to most modern stadiums nowadays and was opened in July 2009 at a cost of £48 million pounds and renovated in 2014. The following renovations the capacity was increased to 33,280.

Ground 90 – KC Stadium – 7th December 2011 – Hull City 2 Birmingham City 1 – Championship

A few days after my first trip to Cardiff's new stadium I was headed to another new stadium with Blues only this time it was off to Hull. I met up with Brendan and Ron at The Old Crown in Bartley Green where Dave, our lift, picked us up just as it was getting cold and dark. The motorway near Hull was closed to high sided vehicles due to the weather as we arrived. Once we had parked up we headed to the nearby social club (the Walton) where we enjoyed a pre match drink.

It was a really windy and cold night as we headed back to the ground. It was another new ground for me and it was quite a nice stadium. We had some good banter with the home fans and there was about 600-700 of us Bluenoses. We were loud though and I enjoyed it when we sang "we came in a taxi and we're louder than you!" Blues went 1-0 up and we all celebrated but after a goalkeeper error we ended up losing 2-1. Very disappointing and we didn't get out of Hull till 10pm meaning that we got home at 1am and it was freezing cold.

In October 2015 it was an early start for the trip to Hull and we were traveling on the official coaches again. We arrived at the services in good time only to see that the party bus was already there and had two coaches this time. This meant six coach loads descended on the motorway services at the same time. It was blue and white as far as the eye could could see. Because the services were now so busy with all the Bluenoses we headed over the bridge and picked up a KFC to take back on the coach with us. It was lovely.

The coach got underway again and it didn't seem too long before we were coming into Hull and we could see the massive Humberside bridge. 'There's the Golden Gate bridge' I said to Steve pointing to the bridge. Not long later we saw the KC Stadium, home of Hull City. I had been to this ground before but it was a new ground for Steve. Once in the car park we headed onto coach one where June and Jake were sheltering from the torrential rain as the turnstiles were not open yet. We persuaded them to join us on a trek to the pub and I led them across the car park to the social club that I went to last time I came to Hull.

I picked up a badge for my collection on the way to the club. It was a nice club the Walton Social Club and well worth the £1 entrance fee. 'Do you think it will be okay for away fans?' Someone asked as we approached. I pointed to a very large Birmingham City flag on display outside and said 'I'd say so yes'.

Inside it was really big and there were loads of Blues fans already drinking in there. We had a couple of drinks and a catch up then headed back across the car park and into the away end. There were around 1,500 Bluenoses that had made the trip and they were in good voice inside the stadium. Hull City's stadium was like most new 'flat pack' stadiums, lacking character but with good unobstructed views.

As usual the Blues contingent stood up throughout and lots of songs were sang. I always love to hear our anthem 'Keep Right On' belted out. My favourite song today (apart from Keep Right On) was 'you know who you are, you know who you are – Hull City Tigers! You know who you are!'. The Hull fans didn't take too kindly to that one.

Blues started well but when Hull hit two goals past us in two minutes in the 36th and 38th minutes we looked shell shocked and never really recovered. When the first goal went in we responded with 'Keep Right On' in defiance but two minutes later we were fearing the worse. The referee was awful again and even though we sang 'we're Birmingham City we'll fight to the end!' the game ended in defeat. The players came over to applaud us and we sang 'Keep Right On', then we trudged back through the puddles to the coaches.

In October 2022 there were three official coaches heading to Hull and it was me, June, Charlie, Nigel and Taff on the back seat of coach 3 and we were looking forward to the match. We all had a bit more confidence in the team now and we all agreed that we felt that Blues had the best midfield in the Championship at the moment and we were not too worried to be missing Dion Sanderson due to suspension today as we had adequate cover.

It was a long journey which included a stop at the services and we arrived at Hull in plenty of time. Today we had caught the end of the massive funfair that they have each year in the adjacent car park and it was now closed off as the funfair workers were busy dismantling the massive rides which included two big wheels! This meant that we were unable to cut across the car park to the Walton Social Club that we always visited and we had to head there the long way.

We paid our pound entrance fee and joined the other Bluenoses already inside although there weren't as many today. I thought this could maybe be because of the 'Tiger Club' which had opened near the stadium where they encouraged away supports to head to for a drink. It could also be down the the train strike which meant that Blues had sold only 1,500 tickets for todays game. I still thought that was a good away attendance though.

Just as we were about to head over to the stadium for the game we received the news that kick off had been delayed till 15.20. This was due to the bizarre circumstances whereby it had been deemed that the goals were too big and two inches had to sawn off and the Hawkeye technology reset before the game could go ahead. Madness!

We headed back to the stadium anyway and joined those already inside and started singing our songs. The game finally kicked off and Blues looked good with Chong, Bielik and Hannibal looking lively in midfield and Bacuna looking good as a wingback for the day. Blues were awarded a penalty on 14 minutes when Bielik was upended in the area and up stepped Troy Deeney to fire home and the away end erupted in celebration.

Bluenoses were in good voice and the songs were great as we taunted the Hull fans next to us. The score remained 1-0 to Blues at halftime and we came out firing in the second half. It took only 2 minutes for Juninho Bacuna to unleash and unstoppable 25 yard shot that flew into the net for a spectacular goal to make it 2-0 to Blues and we went crazy in the away end. Bacuna ran to the away contingent and lifted his shirt to reveal a t-shirt that read 'Tequila' and Bluenoses immediately started singing the Bacuna 'Tequila' song, which he loved, as he was mobbed by his ecstatic teammates.

It was brilliant and Blues were playing really well. The highlight of the day was when the entire away end sang "you're getting mauled by the Brummie's" as they all made mauling actions with their arms. It was really funny. On 74 minutes Chong was through on goal but was brought down as he went round the goalkeeper and the referee had no choice but to point to the spot and award Blues a penalty. We all celebrated and prepared for Troy Deeney to make it 3-0 but amazingly he blasted it way over the crossbar as the Hull fans celebrated a massive let off. We sang 'Time to go' 'Is there a fire drill?' (as they streamed towards the exits) and 'Shall we sing a song for you?'. Obviously this was met by either silence or gestures from their youth who then received a chorus of 'you're going to school in the morning'. All in all a great afternoon.

The penalty miss did spur Hull on a bit but Blues made several changes and brought some of the kids and Jukey on for the big guns but we held on for a great 2-0 away win, our first at Hull since 2009. This took Blues up to 12th in the table and made our long trip home all that more enjoyable. Blues were 3 points of the playoffs and 6 points off the top. It was brilliant to see the bonding between players and fans at the end of the match when the players came over to sing and dance with the fans. Bacuna revealed his 'Tequila' t-shirt again and it was a nice touch when they pushed a reluctant Harlee Dean to the front and the fans responded by applauding him and singing the 'Harlee Dean, he is a great defender' song. Absolutely brilliant!

The coaches were given a police escort out of Hull and we were back at St. Andrews before 8.30pm to be greeted by the pouring rain. Even the rain couldn't dampen our spirits though. It had been a great day.

I have made 9 trips to the currently named MKM stadium and seen just the one win, 2 draws and 6 defeats with the worst being 6-1 in September 2017. What a day that had been and to say the Blues fans didn't take it well was an understatement as the surprised the home fans who had been taunting us by entering their end from the open outside gates to come up behind them. The look on their faces was priceless when they turned round.

The stadium opened in October 2002 at a cost of £44 million pounds and Hull City have to share the ground with the rugby league club Hull F C. The stadium's capacity is 25,586.

Ground 91 – Hillsborough Stadium – 21st August 2012 – Sheffield Wednesday 3 Birmingham City 2 – Championship

Although I had only got back from America the day before and was feeling really jet lagged Me and Annette got the coach to head to Sheffield Wednesday. I had to take travel sickness tablets to deal with the jet lag before I got on the coach though. We survived the journey but Blues played awful in the first half and our young keeper made a couple of errors and we were 2-0 down by half time.

Blues played better in the second half but lost the game 3-2. Over 2,000 Bluenoses made the trip and the atmosphere was fantastic and we sang throughout the game. Then we had more travel sickness tablets as we got back on the coach to head home. Boss Lee Clarke blamed his use of the 4-3-3 system and Blues were 19th in the table.

I had a great trip to Sheffield in 2018 when the five of us, me, June, Terry, Nigel and Charlie all wore our red away shirts as they seemed to be lucky. We hadn't lost in red all season. I even bought along my flag for the back window of the coach. It was a nice little trip but it was pouring with rain when we arrived at Hillsborough, home of Sheffield Wednesday. We didn't let it put us off though as we all headed to the chip shop up the road. The chips were lovely and we ate them in a sheltered area next to the chippie overlooking the stadium.

We headed into the away end and as usual there was a large contingent of Bluenoses in good voice. Blues played in red again and started off positively. It only took Blues 8 minutes to take the lead when David Davis broke through to put Blues 1-0 ahead. The away end exploded and we celebrated wildly. On 21 minutes it got even better when Jota hit a long range shot that went through the legs of the goalkeeper to put us 2-0 up. More wild celebrations followed in the jubilant away end.

Sheffield Wednesday's Marco Mathias was then shown a red card for an off the ball incident. We all cheered and sang 'time to go, time to go' and waved happily as he made for the changing rooms. We were even happier when Jota got his second goal of the game in 45+5 minutes and sent Blues into the half time break with a 3-0 lead. I really couldn't believe it and I was incredibly happy.

Could it last? Well yes and no as ten men Sheffield Wednesday pulled a goal back after the break to make it 3-1 but then had another player sent off on 68 minutes as their fans streamed out of the stadium in disgust. Unfortunately Blues then went down quite a few gears against only 9 men and just passed the ball around for the last 20 minutes. It was incredibly boring to be honest and we never attacked them at all. It was like we were resting and feeling sorry for our opponents, which was exactly what Steve Cotterill admitted to afterward. We really should have gone out to improve our goal difference as it could cost us at the end of the season. I was really happy with what was a very good away win though and we all headed home happy.

I have visited Hillsborough on 5 occasions and I have seen 1 win, 1 draw and 3 defeats.

Hillsborough was the scene of the Hillsborough disaster on 15th April 1989 when 97 Liverpool fans were crushed to death at an FA Cup Semi Final against Nottingham Forest. I was living in Liverpool at the time and along with two friends and we were planning to attend the semi final in the Leppings Lane end of the ground where the disaster occurred. However, we had all been out the previous evening and one of my friends had a bad feeling and said she would not be going and therefore my other mate agreed with her. I disagreed and planned to go but had a hangover the next day and also decided against making the trip. How lucky that we did not go. We watched it live and it was a very traumatic experience. It took me many years to get over it.

Ground 92 - Autotech Stadium (Solihull Moors FC) – 29th June 2014 – FAWSL - Birmingham City Ladies 2 Manchester City Women 0

My first trip to the Autotech Stadium, which was Home to Solihull Moors FC and Birmingham City Ladies, was against Manchester City Women and I had decided to drive over to Solihull Moors and my sister Annette fancied coming along with me. I had been really looking forward to this, especially as I had not seen Blues Ladies play since I played for them myself in the 1980's. I had never been to Solihull Moors either so it would be a new ground for me. It would seem very strange but hopefully very enjoyable.

I found my way over to Solihull okay and really liked the small homely ground immediately. I went into the club bar which was really nice and welcoming. The ground itself had a small seated stand on one side and another slightly bigger stand behind the goal. Several people stood around the pitch and I saw a few familiar faces from the Blues men's games. There was food, drink and ice creams available and Annette and I had a lovely pork and stuffing bap. The Hollywood Monster mascot, as well as Belle Brummie were wondering around the ground mingling with the fans. There was also face painting going on and the whole atmosphere was friendly and warm. The weather was great too, it was nice and sunny. I loved it all immediately.

The players were warning up on the pitch and it felt really strange because last time I saw Birmingham City ladies I was a Blues player myself. I just wanted to get out on the pitch and kick a ball with them. I missed playing so much! It opened a great floodgate of memories.

I decided to watch the first half standing by the side of the pitch near the corner flag at the end that Blues Ladies would be attacking. The teams came out and Manchester City Women looked quite tall I thought. It was their first season in the Women's Super League after being promoted from the second tier last season. However, like the men's team they had money, therefore they had been able to make some big signings over the summer.

It was an entertaining first half with Man City looking quite physical and getting stuck into our girls. Blues Ladies dominated but went in at half time level at 0-0. For the second half Annette and I walked round to the other side to stand near the corner on the opposite side at the end Blues would be attacking in the second half. Within three minutes of the restart Blues ladies went ahead with a goal from Kirsty Linnet to make it 1-0. Blues were in control but the match was then held up for 12 minutes when the referee went down awkwardly injuring her wrist and needing lengthy treatment before leaving the field. Luckily one of the other officials had the necessary qualifications to take over and the game recommenced.

Eleven minutes from time Kerys Harrop bagged a second for Blues ladies, keeping Blues at the top of the league with a 2-0 win against a Manchester City side that had won their last four games. Blues were now 4 points clear at the top of the table. There was a good crowd at Solihull Moors to witness the win, with 759 in attendance. Very different to the days when I was playing. Overall it was a great experience and a great day and I vowed to attend regularly now that I was living back in England permanently. What better way to spend a Sunday and so far this season Blues Ladies had seen some record breaking attendances at the Moors.

My last trip was with Birmingham City men's team for a pre season friendly in July 2023. Pre season began with a trip to Solihull Moors to play for the annual Arthur Trophy and I was really looking forward to seeing some football again and my beloved Blues. I was also looking forward to seeing the gang again and so it was great to meet up with Terry, June, Harry, Linda and Charlie outside the Moors. It was raining and so we hurried inside once Charlie arrived and we headed into the bar as we were early. Despite the rain it was still really warm and we headed onto the terrace behind the goal once we had consumed our drinks.

We had a good catch up discussing the current squad and our new players. It was a little disappointing that Blues went into the pre season with no new kit yet as once again we lagged behind the all the other teams. I don't think I have ever known Blues start their preseason games wearing training tops with numbers on the back. A bit embarrassing to be honest.

The game kicked off and manager John Eustace put out his strongest eleven for the first half which included some of our new signings. Some senior players were missing completely though and they were Scott Hogan, Tahith Chong and Juninho Bacuna. There was also a trialist by the name of Keshi Anderson from Blackpool and he looked to be quite good. There was rumours that Tahith Chong might be heading to Premier League Luton and I really hoped that it was not true but in honesty I feared it probably was.

Blues dominated the first half and new signing Ethan Laird looked really good and Tyler Roberts was impressive also. It was great to see Ivan Sunjic back and he also had a good game. Overall it was an impressive first half and Anderson crossed the ball over for Lucas Jutkiewicz on 30 minutes to give Blues a 1-0 lead.

Eustace sent our a completely differed eleven for the second half which consisted of the under 23 team and to be honest they played quite well against a strong Solihull Moors second side. There were no more goals and the game ended with a 1-0 win for Blues which saw us lift the trophy in front of 3,633 fans of which around 3,600 were Bluenoses. A good start to our preseason and we all hoped that the next trophy that we lift would be the Championship. Obviously that was a bit of a dream but who knows.

It had been a great day out and I headed home in the sunshine. By the time I got to my moms for dinner there was a full scale thunderstorm. It didn't spoil the day though as it had been brilliant getting back to football again and seeing our Blues family again (although Nigel and Taff were missing).

Obviously I have visited the Autotech Stadium many times when it was the home ground of Blues Ladies but I also visited twice with the men's teams seeing victories on both occasions. With Birmingham City Ladies I visited on 45 occasions and saw 25 victories, 10 draws and 10 defeats. I saw so many great games and watched as Blues came so close to winning the title and a great run to the Champions League semi final. I had some fantastic times and met some special people who became my 'Blues family'.

Ground 93 – Aggborough – 26th July 2014 – Kidderminster Harriers 0 Birmingham City 3 – Pre season friendly

It was a lovely sunny day when I arrived with Steve in Kidderminster and I parked up in the railway station car park and walked to the nearby pub which was full of Bluenoses already. Everywhere I looked there were Bluenoses and for today Kidderminster was blue! We walked to the ground and it was a new ground for me and I thought it was really nice. There were nearly 4,000 inside the ground and the majority were from Birmingham. It was buzzing with loads of new blues shirts on display. Everyone was in a good mood and I saw lots of people I knew.

The game got underway and I soon spotted a large spider on the back of the Blues shirt worn by the fan in front and although I was too terrified to inform him or move, I still managed to get a cracking photo of it and have a little giggle. Blues were totally dominant in the game and went in at half time 1-0 ahead with a goal from Wes Thomas, which was loudly celebrated by us traveling Bluenoses. After the break Blues got a second and from Clayton

Donaldson and then another from Wes Thomas to round off a good 3-0 win and we headed back to the pub for Steve to have a drink before heading to the car to head home. There were Blues fans celebrating everywhere.

I have only visited Aggborough once but I did really enjoy my trip. It was nice to see the old steam train at the station next to where I parked to car. This was my first game back in England after moving back to Birmingham permanently a couple of week before and I was so looking forward to all my new future adventures.

Aggborough has a capacity of 7,000 and was also home to Worcester City between 2013 and 2016 and was originally opened in 1884. It's a lovely little ground and was famous for is pies up until very recently.

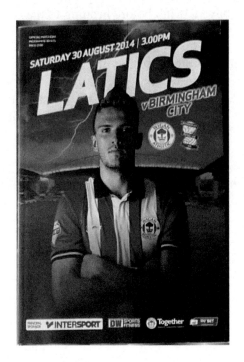

Ground 94 – JJB Stadium – 30th August 2014 – Wigan Athletic 4 Birmingham City 0 – Championship

There was a good away following to Wigan of 1,386 for my first trip to the JJB Stadium but it wasn't a good day to be honest as Blues fell apart and lost the game 4-0 and Blues were down to 20th place. It was a nice new stadium but pretty much the same as all the new stadiums and it seemed to be far too big for Wigan's current supporters. They were quiet despite their win which was in contrast to the noisy away support. It wasn't a great day though to be honest.

My favourite trip came in December 2018. I was excited about the trip to Wigan as there would be nearly 5000 Bluenoses making the journey and I was anticipating a great atmosphere again. We arrived by coach early and headed towards the Red Robin pub only to find that it was already full of Bluenoses both inside and outside and the doormen were not allowing anyone else in. Therefore we headed back towards the stadium and decided to try the bar in Frankie and Benny's which proved to be a good decision as it was not packed and we easily obtained pre match drinks. After a couple of drinks we headed back to the stadium and joined the other Bluenoses in the packed away end. It was brilliant and everyone was in good voice.

The game got underway and Blues were playing in our yellow and blue away kit and looked to be playing well from the off. Che Adams scored on 26 minutes to put Blues in front and the away end exploded in celebration. The singing was non stop and just before half time Michael Morrison scored to make it 2-0 and more celebrations ensued.

The Blues fans made up over a 3rd of the 13,774 attendance and we were making our presence known. We even got to sing 'Jingle Bells - oh what fun it is to see City win Away!' The second half began much like the first with Blues dominating and on 61 minutes Jacques Maghoma scored in front of the away end to make it 3-0 and we went mental! Amazing scenes ensued and 'Garry, Garry Monk!' was belted out. It was brilliant! We were all so happy with a great 3-0 away win. Blues were now 8th in the league.

There was loads of positive feedback on social media from the Wigan fans which included:

'Yeah, Birmingham fans were mad mate!'.

'Them Birmingham fans are something else'

'Aside from the bunch who were booted out early, fair play to the Birmingham fans, amazing support! Wish our fans were that vocal □'

'Fair play to the Birmingham City fans. Normally have a week of the rubbish on the wafc timeline from teams bringing far less than they did today. No rubbish, turned up in numbers, packed the away end and (sadly) probably had a cracking day.'

Garry Monk's verdict was "it was the last thing we said before we left the changing room, that there are 4,500 fans here who have come to support you guys. At this time of year, money can be scarce, we have to give them a performance as we have all season - with some heart and positive front foot football. I think we gave them that. They can have a really good Christmas Day now with three points and the atmosphere on Boxing Day I'm sure will be amazing. We're looking forward to it."

Needless to say once the hoards of Blues coaches left the car park we all had a very enjoyable trip back. We sang and chatted all the way home. It was a very happy Christmas indeed. I have visited the DW stadium, as it is now known, on 5 occasions and I have witnessed 1 win, 2 draws and 2 defeats. The stadium opened in August 1999 at a cost of £30 million pounds and is shared with the rugby club Wigan Warriors. It has a capacity of 25,138 and in UEFA matches it is called Wigan Athletic Stadium due to UEFA regulations on sponsorship.

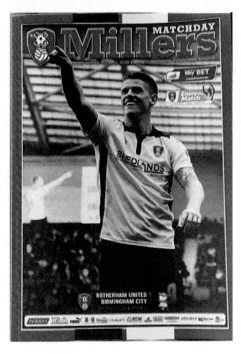

Ground 95 – New York Stadium – 22nd November 2014 – Rotherham United 0 Birmingham City 1 – Championship

It was off to Rotherham in November 2014 to for another new ground and a trip that I enjoyed and Blues took over 2,500 and they were in excellent voice. Although Blues looked poor at times we did hit the post twice before Donaldson scored the winner in the 67th minute to take Blues out of the relegation places. I must admit though, I didn't like playing the lone striker game, I prefer a more attacking style of play but I guessed this was what we would have to get used to under Gary Rowett. Rowett described the game as "the most complete performance we've had since taking over. We played with really good control and good composure". The Rotherham manager thought that "it looked like two poor teams out there".

I had enjoyed the visit despite the poor football on show and the new stadium was very similar to all the new stadiums and Blues had filled the nice away stand behind the goal. Amazingly Rotherham's old stadium Millmoor still remained abandoned not far from the new stadium. It wasn't too far from the town centre either which had meant that we had been able to visit a pub in town before the game.

In April 2019 I woke up really early on the morning of the trip to Rotherham and it was a lovely sunny day. I was feeling really excited about the trip, I'm not sure if it was because of the lovely sunshine or the opportunity to ensure our Championship survival following Blues points deduction. As it was so lovely and sunny I decided on the yellow away shirt and I was soon on my way to St. Andrews to join the others to take our place on the coaches. Blues were taking 7 official coaches and we set up our flag in the back window and we were buzzing all the way to Rotherham. Me, Nigel and Taff had on the yellow shirts and said we reckoned Blues would play in yellow whereas June and Terry wore blue and they were convinced we would play in blue as we always play in blue when we play Rotherham away.

The coaches arrived at the New York Stadium at 1.30pm (we didn't leave till 11.30am) and we immediately headed for the nearby food van where we had hot dogs and pork baps - lovely. Once we had consumed these in the sunshine we headed into the ground where we obtained drinks and discovered Blues were indeed playing in yellow to the delight of me, Nigel and Taff. Twenty minutes before kick off we headed to our seats and June and I had fantastic seats in row A which meant we were standing just to the left of the goal and leaning against the barrier. We had to dodge a few balls in the warm up and the away end looked fantastic with a sea of blue and yellow singing in the sunshine. There was a massive Blues flag which was being passed over the heads of all the Bluenoses.

The teams came out to a wall of noise from the away end and the game got underway. Blues looked nervous and Rotherham looked like they were going to fight for their lives as they needed to win to stand a chance of avoiding relegation. Blues only needed a point. It took only 22 minutes for things to go pear shaped as a Rotherham player handled the ball before firing it into the net and surprise surprise the officials allowed it to stand and Blues were 1-0 down. Blues then played poorly, giving the ball away often and it could have been worse than just the 1-0 score line at half time. To make matters worse the Blues fans became really quiet so I'm guessing that we had a lot of snowflakes here today amongst the 2,573 traveling fans. In previous times Bluenoses would have been singing irrespective of the score and would have got behind the team if they were losing.

Obviously Garry Monk had a word and tweaked it at half time, playing a diamond which brought Jota and Maghoma into the game more. It only took 11 minutes of the second half for Blues to be level as Jacques Maghoma beat a handful of red shirts to fire home and spark delirium in the way end as he ran to the Bluenoses behind the goal. I jumped up and the chain on my handbag broke sending it flying. I carried on celebrating anyway and held aloft my 'we're Birmingham City, we'll fight to the end' scarf as a blue flare landed on the pitch and we were soon engulfed in blue smoke. Seven minutes later Che Adams beat his player and put in a great ball for Jota to calmly fire home and spark amazing celebrations in the away end. The usual songs were being belted out such as 'Keep Right On', 'Che, Che will tear you apart again' and 'Garry, Garry Monk!'.

Rotherham were now desperate to get back into the game and throwing everything at us and we were wondering why it always had to be this stressful. The fourth official held up the board showing 5 minutes of injury time and we all sighed. Then Maghoma broke through and laid the ball to Mbrati who fired home his first goal for the club to spark unbelievable scenes in the away end as Bluenoses spilled over the barrier as they attempted to celebrate with the players. Stewards and security had panic attacks and attempted to grab as many as they could and push others back over the barrier that they were now trying to climb. Meanwhile my handbag had flown over the barrier and I was attempting to get the attention of one of the security guys to pass it back - which I eventually did. It was brilliant! Unfortunately several Bluenoses were escorted out and arrested as apparently its against the law to celebrate and have fun nowadays.

When the final whistle went to signal Blues 3-1 win and ensure our safety and another season in the Championship, the celebrations began as the players came over to join us. They really were unbelievable scenes as both fans and players looked ecstatic. We sang '9 points and we still stay up!' and a really loud version of 'fuck the EFL'. There was also 'you can stick your 9 points up your arse!' It was brilliant. A few of the Blues players threw their shirts into the crowd and Garry Monk made his way over to celebrate with us as well and we sang 'Garry, Garry Monk!' I held my scarf up and ended up on lots of Facebook groups including the Birmingham Mail and official Blues site as the photographers took pictures. Very funny! This took Blues up to 17th place and 10 points off the relegation places so Blues were mathematically safe. There was load of positive feedback from the Rotherham fans too who said:

Jock's Gloves: It was inevitable that they would go on to win. Everyone in the stadium felt it. It did seem like they were celebrating a great victory at the end.

Casper-64-Frank: I don't know what Garry Monk's team talk went like at half time but they came out a different side second half. They dominated that second half especially midfield and marked us out of the game up front. Best team won, Brum were a much better side.

Abbie: find me a better set of fans in the Championship - absolute class every single time.

The Rotherham Advisor (newspaper) reported 'At the final whistle. When he was at his lowest ebb, when a thrilling campaign had finally lurched too far out of the Millers' grasp , Rotherham's manager stayed true to himself. He was hurting yet he stayed hugged to the touchline and waited for the Birmingham players. They were in no rush as they were celebrating long and hard in front of the loudest and best New York away following of the season after making absolutely certain of their own survival.

But he waited.

In time, he shook hands with every single one of them before turning away, taking his despair down the tunnel with him. A leader. Decent man, a good human being, right to the very end.'

I like the trip to Rotherham and I hoped they manage to stay up but I felt they had too much to do and would probably take the 3rd relegation spot.

I have visited the New York Stadium on 5 occasions and I have seen 2 victories, 2 draws and 1 defeat. The stadium opened in July 2019 at a cost of £20 million and has a capacity of 12,021. Historically the land the stadium is situated on was called New York. It is said that the name is inspired by the Guest and Chrimes company who previously occupied the site for nearly 150 years and manufactured a brass stop tsp that was and still is in use in many fire hydrants worldwide. The stop taps are also said to be used in the famous red fire hydrants of New York City.

Ground 96 – Amex Community Stadium – 21ˢᵗ February 2015 – Brighton & Hove Albion 4 Birmingham City 3 – Championship

My first visit to the new Amex Stadium at Brighton was a truly amazing game with Blues playing much better football apart from the moment that Randolph let the ball squirm under him and into the net to give Brighton the lead. Clayton Donaldson equalised for Blues and it was a game of many changes. Blues won a penalty in first half stoppage time but Caddis shot was saved and it proved to be the turning point as Brighton went 3-1 ahead in the second half. Blues then changed to 4-4-2 and brought on Novak and Thomas and they both scored but so did Brighton again and we lost an exciting game 4-3.

I do really like the Amex Stadium as it is lovely and modern and it is possible to walk all the way around the outside of the stadium with no obstacles in the way and refreshments and entertainment available. Once inside it is like the bowl stadiums but with a second tier along one side and the seats are padded and soft. That is definitely what sold it for me.

My favourite game at the Amex came in the July sunshine of 2022 in the Women's Euro Finals.

I was off on my travels again this time by train to Brighton for England Women's second group game against Norway. It was an early start as June and I met Harry at New street station to catch our first train to London Euston. We then had to get the underground to Victoria Station where we got on the Gatwick Express to Brighton and arrived not long after 1pm excited and ready to go.

We walked from the train station to our hotel on the sea front and it looked fabulous! The Jury's Inn was really impressive but we were too early to check in so we left our bags in their safekeeping and headed to a nearby restaurant suggested by the concierge when we asked where we could find the best fish and chips. It was a place called 'English's' and we sat outside at a table in the shade and enjoyed the best fish I have had in a long long time and perhaps the most expensive at £18.50. It was a one off though and we all agreed that it was well worth the experience.

Then it was the short walk to the Pier where we obtained freshly made donuts which were absolutely fabulous. It was really hot though so we went back to our hotel and waited the last 15 minutes in the cool of the lobby before we were able to check in and head to our rooms with mine and Junes room being on a different floor to Harry's. We got into our England gear, put on our face tattoos and wigs and headed down to the lobby to meet Harry. We got quite a few nice comments on our way including a Norway fan who thought we looked great.

Harry was waiting for us and we headed off on our walk to the train station where we caught a train to Falmers station at the Amex Stadium. As we arrived at the stadium we were filmed blowing our horns as we approached and several other press photographers took pictures. I found this amusing and we were also interviewed by a TV crew but I have no idea where this ended up though. My sister text me later that evening to say they had seen us on the ITN news which was brilliant.

The atmosphere around the stadium was fantastic and we saw that the Heineken Beer Bus was again in attendance with England fans enjoying the open top deck already. It was lovely and sunny too as we walked around the stadium and acquired yet more merchandise. We saw Karen Carney and chatted with her for a while and then watched the players arriving to cheers from the waiting England fans.

Once inside the stadium we found our seats and they were really nice (padded) and with a great view. All three of us though that todays game would be our most difficult especially with the talented Ada Hegerberg playing for them and we reckoned it would probably end in a draw and penalties. Hence we were delighted when VAR awarded England a penalty in the 12th minute which was calmly despatched by Georgia Stanway to the delight of the sell out crowd.

The stadium was absolutely buzzing and erupted 3 minutes later when Lauren Hemp scored Englands second. We were on our feet celebrating. This was fantastic. It got even better on 29 minutes when Ellen White made it 3-0 followed 5 minutes later by a Beth Mead goal that made it 4-0 with only 34 minutes on the clock. This was unbelievable and England were totally unplayable. Norway were shell shocked. As were we to be honest.

Four minutes after her first goal Beth Mead claimed a brace as she put England 5-0 up with just 6 minutes remaining before the halftime break. Could Norway hang on. Well no they couldn't as Ellen White completed her brace with 4 minutes to go to halftime and incredibly England went into the break leading 6-0! We were all stunned and in heaven as we celebrated and we were in total awe of England's performance.

I thought England would probably ease up in the second half and make substitutions and although they did make substitutions they definitely didn't ease up and Russo made it 7-0 in the 66th minute. Beth Mead completed her hat trick with 9 minutes remaining and the final score read England 8 Norway 0. It had been an absolutely brilliant atmosphere and a fantastic game! As we headed back to the train station I said to June "that was the dogs bollocks!' to which a nearby women laughed and responded "yes it was'.

We queued for ages to get on the train back to Brighton but we didn't mind one bit as we were so happy. We didn't even mind the late night twenty minute walk to our hotel from the station either and passed several jolly people on our way, some of whom sang '8-0!' We arrived back tired and happy and I fell into my bed exhausted. What a great night. This result meant that England qualified for the quarterfinals and would finish top of the group which meant that they would play in the first quarter final in Brighton. There was still one more group game before that though and I couldn't wait for it.

Ellen White said afterwards: "You could probably see it on our faces in that first half, it was just unreal. Another two goals in the second half - it's just crazy.

The noise and the atmosphere is absolutely insane. We're so thankful for that support. Hopefully we can continue grow as a team but I hope everyone's proud of us."

I have visited the Amex Stadium on just the two occasion so far. The stadium opened in July 2011 at a cost of £93 million and has capacity of 31,876.

Ground – 97 – Vitality Stadium – 6th April 2015 – AFC Bournemouth 4 Birmingham City 2 – Championship

On a lovely sunny Easter Monday we headed to Bournemouth on the official coaches which involved a nice stop on the way down where we could all sit outside in the sunshine with our drinks and lunch before setting off again. We arrived early enough to head into the Wetherspoon's in town where we met Brendan and co and enjoyed a lovely cold pre match drink. Then it was back through the park to Bournemouth's nice little ground and into the away section which was baking in the direct sunlight. No wonder they give this section to the away fans as we roasted throughout the game and the refreshment stalls ran out of water!

Blues began the game well and played the best attacking football that I had seen all season to race into a 2 goal lead against the table toppers and the away end went mental each time and sang we want eight! It could have been 3 had it not been for a missed chance before we allowed Bournemouth to score 2 goals and to go in at halftime all, square at 2-2.

Unbelievably Blues conceded 2 more in the second half and we ended up losing the game 4-2. Paul Robinson had conceded the penalty for Bournemouth's 3rd and was sent off just after they got their 4th goal. Rowett admitted it may have been a mistake resting Rob Kiernan and playing Robinson instead. You just couldn't make it up. We headed home sunburnt and disappointed.

My second visit was a daunting midweek trip to Bournemouth on 9th February 2022 as Blues took on a Bournemouth side who had excelled in the January transfer market. They would also be smarting from a 1-0 FA Cup exit to National League side Boreham Wood, which I admit to having had quite a chuckle about. So, on a cool February afternoon we set off by coach to the south coast with an almost full contingent of our Blues family – myself, June, Nigel, Charlie and Taff. It would be a new ground for Nigel and Charlie and the small stadium looked great as we arrived to see four wonderfully old fashioned floodlights in their full glory. I do love grounds with floodlights as it reminds me of a time when football was fun.

We were early, but not early enough to head for the pub, so we had a nice walk all the way around the ground before heading inside to obtain refreshments. I tried a new cider that I had never heard of before called Inches Apple cider which was okay but not as nice as my usual Strongbow. Not long before kick off we made our way to our seats just in time to see the Bournemouth light show which appeared to be an attempt at a disco on the pitch. "What the fuck is that?" I asked and Charlie said 'I don't know but I like it" I had to laugh.

Lee Bowyer had made a few changes one of them enforced as Marc Roberts had picked up an injury before the game. I thought that Blues started poorly and we were 2-0 down by 31 minutes with Bournemouth also hitting the woodwork. Half time came with Blues still trailing 2-0 but the game changed when Onel Hernandez came on in the 63rd minute as he began to run Bournemouth ragged with his skill and power. He had only been on the pitch for 3 minutes when Bournemouth's Jefferson Lerma hacked him down to receive a straight red card as the away end chanted 'Off! Off,' and then waved him off with 'Cheerio, Cheerio!'

It took a further 120 seconds for Blues to reduce the deficit as Onel Hernandez fired home and the 850 travelling Bluenoses erupted in celebration as we sensed a comeback was on. Minutes later and Jutkiewicz hit a fantastic close range volley which produced an amazing save from the Bournemouth keeper to deny us a deserved leveller. Blues looked the better side by this point but as is always the way with Blues pressing for the equaliser, Bournemouth hit us on the break and some poor defending in the box led to Bournemouth getting a third and putting the game out of reach.

More worryingly, defender Teden Mengi went off, seemingly injured, which left Blues with a very makeshift defence with our two full backs as central defenders. We really did need some new defenders at the club, especially with all our injuries. Another defeat but we were perhaps a bit unlucky against a team currently second in the table. We headed back to the coaches for the long trip home.

So only two visits to the Vitality Stadium so far and both of them ended in defeat. Perhaps our next visit, whenever that may be, could be a little better. A nice little stadium though and I enjoyed both trips despite the defeats.

Ground 98 - Academy Stadium (Manchester) – WFA Cup – 12th April 2015 - Manchester City Women 3 Birmingham City Women 1

On Sunday 12th April 2015 Blues Ladies were in FA Cup action as they travelled to Manchester to take on Man City in the quarterfinals and this was to be my very first Away game with Blues Ladies. The club had arranged coach travel for this game and I was really excited to be travelling with my friends on the coach. When we arrived at the Academy Stadium it was very wet and windy but we still had a walk around the stadium to see what it was like. It was very impressive as it is located just across the road from Manchester City's Etihad Stadium. It holds an impressive 7,500 with seated stands both sides of the stadium and nice terrace areas behind each goal. Also impressive was the fact that the Match day Programme was free along with a free Manchester City key ring. According to the programme notes 'after the first four seasons of the WSL, only arch-rivals Arsenal have won more matches in the league than Birmingham.'

Less impressive was the weather and the result and it didn't help that I had a cold too. The travelling Bluenoses were in good voice though and the home support were suitably impressed according to one of their stewards. However, our verbal support was unable to spur the Blues players on as we slumped to a 3-1 defeat to go out of the Cup. I was disappointed that we wouldn't be in the first ever final at Wembley but it had been a great day out following the Blues. Unfortunately we had to wait ages on the coach in the cold for the players parents to return so that we could head back to Birmingham. When we arrived back at St. Andrews the pub up the road from the ground by the dual carriageway was on fire. I think it had closed down years ago anyway but it was still a shame.

Another great day at the Academy stadium, despite the result, was the League Cup Final 2016. It was a bright morning as we boarded the coaches at St. Andrews which would take us to the Academy Stadium in Manchester for the FA WSL Continental Cup Final. Although Birmingham City Ladies were massive underdogs we were all quite optimistic and looking forward to the day out. It reminded us a bit of when Blues men's team played Arsenal at Wembley in the League Cup – which gave us a bit of hope. Hence the journey went quickly and it was quite lively on the coach as we had a lot to chat about and quite a bit of singing.

Once the coaches arrived in Manchester some Bluenoses headed into the ground but we headed across the road to the 'Mary D' pub. Usually a Man City pub on match days there were already a few Bluenoses inside enjoying a pre match drink or two. Then we headed back to the ground and into the Blues section.

This was really disappointing as Birmingham had been given an allocation of 800 seats in two blocks but there were a few Man City fans amongst us and other Bluenoses were scattered around the ground. It was supposed to be a neutral ground for the final yet Man City had been given the vast majority of the allocation. Would they have travelled as we had in numbers if it had truly been at a neutral ground? I very much doubt it.

There was terracing behind each goal – Man City fans had been given one end and the other was kept closed! The stewards would not let us Bluenoses on there. We were allowed to put our flags up though and the entire terrace end was covered in large Birmingham City flags – a sight indeed! I'm proud to say we completely outdid Man City in the flag department as, despite their large numbers, they only had one flag compared to the many flags we had on display!

The Blues 'singers' (myself included) managed to stand together in the seats and we sang our hearts out. The royal blue contingent stood out as a mass of royal blue and white flags and scarves were waved. We were determined to make up for the unfair advantage of Man City being at home in the final.

The teams came out and we sang 'Keep Right On' loudly. It was a proud moment singing the national anthem knowing our team were in the final. The players looked proud too and as the game kicked off they gave it everything they had against a team consisting of mostly England internationals.

Birmingham's Kirsty Linnett came close to putting Blues ahead with a thunderous 25 yard shot which was inches wide of the post in the 4th minute. But Man City came back at us and our keeper Ann Katrin-Berger made a string of excellent saves to keep Blues in the game. Freda Ayisi was almost through on goal but for a last ditch Man City tackle. Half time came at 0-0 but not before Berger had made another excellent save when Man City's Duggan broke through for a one on one with the keeper.

The second half was much the same as Blues dug in and gave it their all with Berger continuing to make fine saves. Blues started the second half strongly and Freda Ayisi hit a long range shot just wide. With neither team able to break the deadlock the game went to extra time.

In the 104th minute Man City scored the winner as a corner from Duggan was missed by Berger and Bronze looped her header from the far post into the back of the net and our hearts were broken. We continued to sing, including "neutral ground? You're having a laugh!" And "what's it like to buy the cup?" We also sang "you can stick your Arab money up your Arse!"

It was a hard way to lose a final, which had not been very fair from the start, so we felt bitterly disappointed. The Blues players looked heartbroken at the final whistle and we applauded them and sang 'Keep Right On'. Blues had a very promising team at the time and so we had a lot to look forward to. It was going to be very difficult for teams to challenge Man City now with their wealth and ability to attract all the best players with their top wages.

There were some positive tweets from the players about the game and the fans. Man City's Toni Duggan tweeted 'Birmingham you made it tough today... Well played ☐ fans from both teams amazing too!!!!!!☐

Birmingham's Aoife Mannion tweeted 'Wow what a day, gave it our everything!! Cannot believe how amazing our supporters were ☐ together till the very end'

Blues will be back in more finals even stronger as manager David Parker said after the game and will Keep Right On! Us Bluenoses headed back to the coaches somewhat despondent but we were proud of the girls and we still sang on the way home. Despite taking 3 hours due to traffic! We still journey on!

Ground 99 – Macron Stadium – 2nd May 2015 – Bolton Wanderers 0 Birmingham City 1 – Championship

My first trip to the Macron Stadium was the last game of the season away at Bolton and the Blues fans were planning an inflatables party as well as the traditional fancy dress. Blues had been given the entire stand behind the goal and the atmosphere was brilliant. It was a nice new stadium although very much in keeping with all the new modern stadiums. It was originally called the

Reebok Stadium which soon became know as the 'breeze block stadium'. I did like the away end though as it was a two tiered stand in a half moon shape and Blues had been given both tiers for today's game. It was a great view of pitch too.

There was loads of fancy dress costumes and loads had gone as manager Gary Rowett in his traditional jumper and Gary face masks. The best bit was all the inflatables being bounced around - there was Lilo's, sharks, bananas, beach balls etc and it looked fantastic. Many found of these their way onto the pitch and those that weren't returned to the fans were confiscated behind the hoardings by the miserable stewards. The singing was brilliant too.

Thankfully the match was way less dramatic than last years end of season match and when Tesche scored after Gray's shot was blocked on the goal line, the away end went bonkers and the celebrations began. The 1-0 win moved Blues up to 10th place and our highest position of the season. What an amazing season it had been and we all headed home happy and looking forward to the next season under new manager Gary Rowett with a pre season behind him. We would dare to dream again no doubt. It was a great end to my first season back in England as I had moved home permanently following 17 years living in Abu Dhabi in the UAE.

My second visit was in Easter 2018 and I was looking forward to the trip to Bolton on the Tuesday night for the crucial game against a Bolton team just 3 points ahead of us. I had expected about 800 – 1000 Bluenoses to make the trip on a Tuesday night but Blues had amazingly sold our allocation and 5000 of us were heading to Bolton. I was so excited. I was traveling with June on one of the 17 official coaches making the trip. As usual the Blues stewards struggled to organise the boarding of the coaches and as usual we left more than 10 minutes late, which meant we hit the rush hour traffic on the Aston Expressway and it took an hour to get as far as Walsall's stadium on the M6. We arrived at Bolton 3 hours after setting out.

It was buzzing in the away end of the Macron Stadium and June and I were in the upper tier. Once we had downed a quick drink and caught up with various people we knew we headed to our seats. Blues were already singing 'there's more of us than you' to the Bolton contingent. The top tier and the lower tier were singing 'we hate Villa more than you' to each other as they were getting no joy from the Bolton fans. When 'Keep Right On' rang out it was truly epic and echoed around the stadium.

The players came out to cheers and the game got underway. It was a hard fought scrappy game but Blues were up for the fight. 'Garry Monk's blue and white army' rang out. On 40 minutes Blues won a free kick which was floated into the box for the 'Juke' Jutkiewicz to fire into the net to send 5000 Bluenoses into raptures. It was completely mental as blue flares were set off and we bounced around with the blue smoke and the smell of the flares in the air around us. The loudest 'Keep Right On' of the night filled the stadium and Garry Monk punched the air in delight and Blues went in 1-0 up at half time.

The second half got underway and Bolton were throwing everything at us in an attempt to get back into the game. Blues were holding on but on 63 minutes Che Adams received a straight red card for a tackle and Blues were down to ten men. This meant Gary Monk having to make several changes but Blues held firm despite the added 3 minutes somehow turning into 7 minutes as the referee seemed to forget to look at his watch!

When the final whistle sounded the away end erupted in celebration. As 'Keep Right On' rang out the players and staff came over to join in with us and they applauded our fantastic support. It was brilliant to watch Maghoma and Ndoye enthusiastically joining in with us as we sang 'Birmingham, Birmingham, Birmingham!'. Brilliant! Garry Monk applauded us and we sang 'Garry Monk's blue and white army'. It was well worth making the trip with the fantastic night that we had just experienced.

On checking facebook on the way back it was great to see that 'football away days' had put on a photo of the away end at Bolton and had praised Blues fantastic away following on a Tuesday night. Amongst the comments was one from someone from Bolton who said that he lived a mile from the stadium and heard the Birmingham fans singing in his living room. Brilliant. It was also fantastic to see Blues Harlee Dean, in his post match interview say that Blues support was fantastic and he had never seen anything like it ever, coming from Brentford.

One Bolton fan Theo said 'Birmingham City fans loudest that have come this season for sure. Very good support and louder than any club I've ever heard come to the Macron'. Another Bolton fan Sam 'embarrassed to be a Bolton fan today we were shown up in front of the Birmingham fans, could still hear them chanting when we had all left the stadium and were outside- embarrassing'.

What an amazing night, one of those rare occasions that stays long in the memory. Bolton seemed to be a favourite place to visit for us Bluenoses. It also means that Birmingham were now level on points with Bolton, Reading and Hull who were all just above Blues on goal difference and most importantly Blues were 5 points clear of the relegation zone.

At the time of writing Bolton were currently in League One and I had made a total of 3 visits to this stadium having seen two wins and a single defeat. It is a nice stadium to visit and is now called the Toughsheet Community Stadium having been named the University of Bolton Stadium prior to that. It's current capacity is 28,723 and opened in 1997 at a cost of £25 million and a hotel forms part of its stadium with some of the rooms offering views of the pitch. In European competitions the stadium is known as Bolton Stadium due to advertising rules.

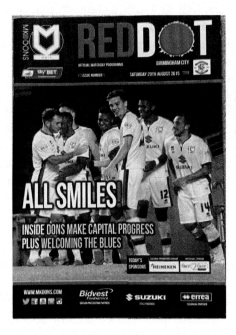

Ground 100 – Stadium MK – 29th August 2015 – Milton Keynes Dons 0 Birmingham City 2 – Championship

There were seven coaches traveling from St. Andrews for my first trip to Stadium MK in August 2015 and we finally got underway about 11.15 am. I was at the back with June, Barry and the lads and we had a somewhat entertaining trip which passed quickly.

We arrived at Stadium MK at 1pm and it looked a really impressive Stadium. Right opposite the away end was a strip of restaurants/ bars with outdoor seating. These included TGI Fridays, Bella Pisa and Frankie & Bennies plus others that I can't remember the names of. Perfect! All the restaurants were already filling with Bluenoses. We all headed into TGI Fridays where Barry got the drinks in and set up a 'tab'. We had a look around and managed to find a table. It was a lovely restaurant/bar and was full of Birmingham fans enjoying the occasion. Lots of people I knew passed by and said hello.

At about 2.45pm we headed across the road and into the Stadium MK. Our seats were in the upper tier and I have to say it was really impressive. Great views and the atmosphere among the 4,500 Birmingham fans was amazing! This was now definitely my favourite away ground to date. It was way too good for the team that currently occupied it.

The Blues fans were in full voice and due to a lack of banter with the home supporters (who were scattered around the stadium), were enjoying an exchange of "we hate villa more that you" chant between the upper and lower tiers. This was really loud and went on for quite a while. There were also renditions of 'Keep Right On' and 'shit on the villa' and then the teams came out onto the pitch.

The first half was forgettable and looked like a Sunday league game. Birmingham just didn't seem to be trying and it looked like a kick about. Gary Rowett later said that it was the angriest he had ever been at half time. I went looking for my other friends at half time and bumped into Brendan and co near the bar. The away section and bar was really quite impressive as it was quite large and had full length tinted windows with a great view outside. Very nice indeed. I saw Barry enjoying a pint with the others and there were some good songs being sang in the bar too.

The second half was a big improvement and Blues took the lead with a fabulous goal from ex-Don Stephen Gleeson against his old team. He paused for a moment before sprinting to the away end to celebrate. The stewards were friendly and sensible (yes I know that's a rarity) especially when a Blues fan made a run for the pitch and was tackled and returned the the Blues end despite him stripping his top off and waving it around in the process. This prompted a chant of "we're Birmingham City. We'll do what we want!" from the Bluenoses.

Stephen Gleeson was then on the receiving end of a tackle that saw him crash into the advertising boards and following lengthy treatment which involved gas and air and a leg splint, he was carried off on a stretcher to applause from both sets of supporters.

Maghoma added a second goal when he was put through by Clayton Donaldson and ran to the Birmingham fans to celebrate. Bluenoses rushed to the front and burst through the barrier gates and passed the stunned stewards to join the celebrating Blues player. It was great! We were all jumping around in delight up in the top tier (as they were also doing in the lower tier). When the final whistle sounded to cheers from the Blues contingent 'Keep Right On' was belted out at full volume and the players and manager came over to applaud us. What a top day it had been as our unbeaten run continued.

Once back on the coaches we watched as loads of Bluenoses headed into the bars of TGI Fridays etc. Then we were escorted out and passed waving MK Dons fans that were obviously impressed by our support. I did wave back as they seemed a friendly lot and then we enjoyed a bit of banter on the way back, including a 'back seat selfie' for facebook. Another great day out watching our heroes.

So far this is my only visit to Stadium MK but I enjoyed my visit very much. The stadium opened in 2007 and as of May 2015 has two tiers and a capacity of 30,500. It also hosts concerts and hosted several of the Women's Euro 2022 games.

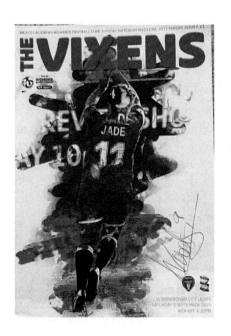

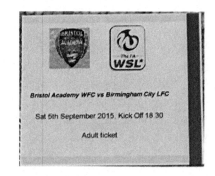

Ground 101 – Stoke Gifford Stadium (Bristol) – 5th September 2015 – FAWSL – Bristol Academy 0 Birmingham City Women 3

Blues were travelling to the Stoke Gifford Stadium in Bristol on Saturday 5th September 2015 for a massive relegation battle with Bristol Academy and due to the international break I was able to travel to Bristol. Linda from Redditch Blues had organised a coach, so I obtained tickets for myself, June and Steve and we were all really looking forward to the trip. Nigel, Terry, Harry and Charlie were also on the coach and when we arrived and headed for the entrance we passed a young Bristol fan with her mom and I heard her say "I wish we could take that many fans on a coach to Away games" as she looked over at us in awe. How nice.

There were even more Bluenoses inside the ground as many had travelled by car and I'm sure we had the majority of the support. It was only a small 'ground' but quite quaint really. The only 'stands' as such were very small sections of terrace behind one of the goals. We stood behind the goal in one of these small covered terrace sections and we sang loads of songs to get behind the girls. There wasn't many Bristol fans really but we created a good atmosphere with our singing.

We were really loud and one of their stewards came over to stand by us and he said we the loudest support they had seen there all season. It was brilliant and Blues won 3-0 and when Karen Carney scored the third she ran over to us to celebrate. At half time we bumped into ex Blues men's team player Chris Wood (he was going out with Blues striker Kirsty Linnett) and I got a photo with him and he signed my programme. I asked him if he'd like to come back to the Blues and he said he'd love to. I wish.

At the end of the game the players came over to chat and Karen Carney said our support and singing was brilliant and it spurred them on. This result would ensure Blues WSL top flight status for another season. I had a fantastic day out and we also had a great trip home as we stopped off at the new services in Gloucester and visited the farm shop. I was late home as the game had kicked of at 6.30pm but I had really enjoyed the trip.

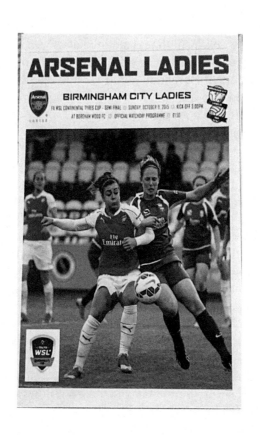

Ground 102 – Meadow Park (Borehamwood) – WLC Semi Final – 11th October 2015 – Arsenal Women 3 Birmingham City Women 1

Blues Women had just one game remaining when we travelled to Boreham Wood on Sunday 11th October 2015 for my first and only visit . It was the League Cup Semi Final and I was really excited as I was travelling on the Blues coach with June, Terry, Steve, Harry and Linda. We had already obtained massive Blues flags for the occasion as well as being decked out in our Blues shirts and scarves.

We had a great journey down south and stopped at the services on the way. We arrived in plenty of time and made our way to Arsenal Women's home ground which was also the home of Boreham Wood FC and opened in 1963. On arrival we immediately headed into the bar and claimed it as our own as loads of other Bluenoses joined us. It was a lovely little bar too. Today's game was being shown live on BT Sport.

We made our way into the ground and purchased a match programme before putting up our flags behind the goal where the other Bluenoses were already standing on the terrace. It was a nice sunny day but a bit cold in the wind. Boreham Wood was a really nice little ground with seated stands on both sides of the pitch and terraced areas behind each goal and had a capacity of 4,502. There was a lovely little refreshment stand on one of the terraced areas behind the goal and Arsenal's mascot was wandering around the ground. They also had a little 'club shop' which consisted of a small table where they sold Arsenal memorabilia such as key rings.

Blues began the game really well and we sang our hearts out to get behind them. It didn't work though, as Blues were 2-0 down by the time they went in at half time. It got even worse on 48 minutes when Alex Scott made it 3-0. We did have something to cheer on 58 minutes when Kirsty Linnett scored for Blues to make it 3-1 and we all celebrated.

I hoped that it might be the start of a Blues comeback but with the Arsenal players diving all over the place and the referee blindsided by them, we had no chance and our Cup dreams were over for another season. Somewhat downhearted we headed back into the bar and we were soon joined by the two teams before we had to board the coach back to Birmingham. As usual Steve got some photos with the players – Arsenal players I hasten to add, and we all teased him for being an habitual groupie.

On the coach on the way home we were pleasantly surprised by the Blues staff who had traveled with us. They gave us all donuts as a thank you. It was a really nice gesture and we were all delighted. Arsenal went on the win the League Cup as they beat Notts County 3-0 in the Final at Rotherham's New York Stadium in front of a crowd of 5,028.

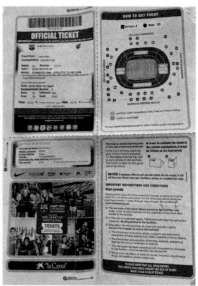

Ground 103 – Camp Nou (Spain) – 27th January 2016 - FC Barcelona 3 Athletic Club 1 – Copa del Ray Quarter Final

My visit to the Nou Camp in 2016 was really exciting and our tickets for the match included free transport to and from the game – very impressive I thought. I was staying in a hotel on Las Ramblas and the coaches were leaving from the Hard Rock Café which was just a ten minute walk up the road. The match was a late kick off, 9.30pm, so the coaches were due to depart from the Hard Rock Café at 7.30pm for the Nou Camp. We got there at 7pm and there were already quite a few people already waiting. The coaches arrived at about 7.10pm just after we had arrived. It was really well organised and we boarded quite quickly and we were on our way.

Traffic was heavy and there seemed to be loads of traffic lights, most of them red! There were also scooters and motorbikes parked everywhere, thousands of them. It didn't take long to get to the Nou Camp though and we parked on a car park about two minutes walk from the stadium. The Nou Camp looked really impressive with all the lights on as we approached. It had a great feel about it. There were lots of stalls selling scarves, flags and memorabilia. I browsed all of them and bought a nice gold stadium badge with the Barcelona crest attached. I wanted a half half Match day scarf but the only one they had that was Barcelona v Athletico Bilbao was dated 30-5-15 from last years final.

We wandered around for a while looking at stalls, taking photos and soaking up the atmosphere. There were lots of tourists about, mostly taking photos on their 'selfie sticks'. I had come to the conclusion that Barcelona was the 'selfie stick' capital of the world! After walking around the stadium to our entrance we headed into the Nou Camp. The first thought that struck me was how much it reminded me of the old Wembley Stadium concourse. I was quite surprised by how old the stadium seemed. I don't really know what I was expecting to be honest.

I was also surprised at the absence of bars as such, although beer could be purchased at any of the many popcorn stalls. Yes, that's right popcorn! There was also hotdogs and crisps available but other than cans of beer no other variety of alcohol was on sale so my craving for a cold cider would not be satisfied. I had to wash my 'Barca' crisps down with a coke instead.

We went up into the stands to look around the stadium and it looked magnificent. There were already quite a few people inside taking photos with the usual selfie sticks! It was quite difficult to find our seats and we had to go down a couple of flights from the turnstiles. When we were in the lower concourse I pointed out a row of seats that were right back inside the concourse and looked awful. As I commented about how bad they were we checked our tickets and it transpired that they were our seats!

I was really disappointed. We sat in them to try them out and the base of the second tier came right over the top of us and went so far down that we could see the pitch but the stand blocked the top/crossbar of the far goal just beneath the stand. A shockingly bad view. This meant we had no view whatsoever of this marvellous stadium so we immediately headed off to find the head steward only to be informed that we couldn't exchange our tickets and could only buy new ones! Therefore we headed back to our crap seats and decided to wait till about ten minutes into the game before moving elsewhere for a better view.

The game kicked off and the Stadium seemed to be buzzing, although there was no real singing like in England. After ten minutes we left our seats and headed up the many stairs to the middle tier and in doing so missed the opening goal scored by Athletico Bilbao. To be honest with you I never heard a sound, no cheer or any noise of note and it was only as I looked at the TV monitor on the second level up that I saw the score line.

At the top of the second tier we found a row of empty seats with a great view of the pitch and the stadium so we sat down to enjoy the rest of the game. We were really high up! I looked around for any away fans but could only see the blue and red of Barcelona everywhere. Behind the far goal was a small section of 'partisan' Barcelona fans who were singing and waving flags. They would bounce and dance every now and then. It was amazing to watch them, they would sing and run from one end of the section to the other end before turning and running back to where they had started and then doing it all again. It looked crazy but funny.

I think my expectations of the Barcelona team were quite high as I was a bit disappointed in their first half performance. Bilbao should have been further ahead in my opinion. I didn't see anything special in Messi, Suarez, Neymar and co and had watched more entertaining Birmingham City performances. Maybe the second half would be better.

I made the mistake of looking for the toilets at half time and despite ending up three floors below I still couldn't locate them and then got lost trying to find my way back to my seat where Steve was. The second half was better and the fans sang the Barcelona football song loudly. Messi was booked for time wasting when Barcelona were leading 2-1 and thousands of white handkerchiefs were waved in the air in disgust. I found this highly amusing as did Steve.

With a couple of minutes to go and Barcelona leading 2-1 (4-2 on aggregate) we decided to head back to the coach before the rush as there were over 69,000 in the stadium. As we were heading out Barcelona scored again to make it 3-1 and we missed it. It is unusual for me to leave early too, as I have never left a Blues game before the final whistle. However, as Barcelona are not my team it wasn't a problem,

The coach was nearby and the walk was nice as I looked back at the stadium with all the floodlights on. There were literally hundreds of coaches from all over Spain and it was so well organised. Our departure was like a military operation as half an hour after the game finished organisers directed one coach after another in a regimented order along roads which had been cordoned off by the Spanish police. We were soon underway and back at the Hard Rock Café in no time at all.

We disembarked and it was an impressive sight as all the 'Barca' fans headed down Las Ramblas. Some, including ourselves, headed into McDonalds which was still open at this late hour. What a wonderful day I had had and I was so looking forward to the Nou Camp stadium experience tour that we were booked on the next day.

Ground 104 – Estadio Heliodoro Rodriguez Lopez – 21st May 2016 – CD Tenerife 3 Real Valladolid 1 – Segunda Division

On the day of the Tenerife game we went to the pick up point in Los Cristianos to get the coach and there were a few others waiting there too and all the group traveling with us were lovely and friendly and made us welcome from the start. Most of the supporters traveling on the coach were British and were in good voice. We were given a free fanzine on the coach and joined in the first and last goal competition taking place. The total journey time would only be about an hour but we had a stop on the way at a lovely café at the service station with a fabulous view of the sea where we all enjoyed a few beers plus supplies for the rest of the journey.

Before long we were arriving in Santa Cruz and we were dropped off at a lovely little bar just down the road from the stadium where other Tenerife fans were already gathered. A few cars honked their horns and waved as they saw us all embark in Tenerife shirts and scarves. We joined the others sitting outside the bar and I admired all the massive banners and flags whilst Steve got the drinks. I chatted to a lot of the Armarda Sur Club and thoroughly enjoyed the experience. The stadium was in view at the top of the road and we headed there about ten minutes before kick off which was at 5pm. We browsed the memorabilia stalls and I obtained a nice silk scarf before we headed into the stadium.

On entrance to the stadium the match programmes were available for free and you could take as many as you wanted. We couldn't really understand where exactly our seats were but everyone seemed to just sit or stand where they wanted so we headed for the main section where the singing was being led by a man on a microphone. The singing was great and continued throughout the game – in Spanish of course. I joined in where I could. There were loads of flags being waved in this section and there was a large banner at the front. It was a completely different (and better) atmosphere than when I visited the Nou Camp recently as these were real football fans here rather than a load of tourists.

I did look around for any Real Valladolid fans but couldn't see any. I think there may have been some in the upper tier at the far end but I couldn't be certain. The attendance was around 8,500 which was probably reduced due to the FA Cup Final being shown live in bars and the game was a mid table affair with Tenerife in 15th place with not more than a very slight chance of reaching the play offs.

Tenerife were playing well and local hero Nano scored two goals to put Tenerife 2-0 up at half time. Nano was only 20 years old and looked an exciting prospect. After the interval Real Valladolid came into the game more and pulled a goal back before Tenerife took control again and had a goal disallowed. Unfortunately Nano had to go off with what looked like a hamstring injury but that didn't stop Tenerife as they grabbed a third goal to seal the points and moved up to 12th and only 5 points behind 6th place and a play off place.

So game over and a 3-1 win for Tenerife and we headed back to the bar for a quick drink before boarding the coach back to Los Cristianos. What a great day out and I met some lovely people.

It had been a nice stadium to visit with mostly terraced steps with seats on them and no roof on the majority of the stadium but with the constant sunshine I doubted that was a problem. The stadium had a capacity of 22,824 which was the 27th largest stadium in Spain and the second largest in the Canary Islands.

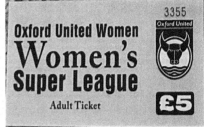

Ground 105 – The Northcourt (Abingdon -Oxford) – WFA Cup – 3rd July 2016 – Oxford United Women 0 Birmingham City Women 2

Sunday 3rd July and Blues Ladies had been drawn away at Oxford United Ladies from the second tier of the Women's Super League in the FA WSL Continental Tyres Cup (League Cup). It was a lovely sunny day as we set off for Oxford.

Oxford United Ladies played their games at Abingdon United's ground which had a capacity of 2,000 and we arrived in plenty of time to see that lots of Bluenoses had also made the trip. The £5 entrance fee, which included parking, was certainly a bargain. The small ground was great, real grass root football supporters heaven.

Alongside the pitch, next to the dug outs was a nice little covered terrace and this was where a lot of the Blues fans were already gathered. Our Blues banner was soon put up at the back of the stand and it was quickly joined by the large Redditch Blues flag. Behind the goal was a nice little clubhouse with outside bench tables (a beer garden) where we were soon sitting with our drinks soaking up the sunshine and watching the teams warming up. It had a nice family atmosphere and there was a nice merchandise stand where I got my match day programme and an 'Abingdon Utd' badge for my collection of grounds I have visited.

The game kicked off and our fans made it a great atmosphere with our singing. Blues Ladies were in complete control of the game and it would only be a matter of time before we scored. The new players were blending into the team well and it was beginning to ease the loss we had felt after losing our three England internationals in Carney, Potter and Moore.

New signings Bella Linden and Andrine Hegerburg were playing well. Linden was unlucky not to score in the 13th minute when the keeper denied the German striker. Andrine Hegerburg then had an effort blocked on the line but it was Hegerburg who gave Blues the lead from the penalty spot after Linden was brought down in the area. Of course we celebrated loudly and waved our flags about.

At half time we headed back to the bar for another 15 minutes of sunshine with a cold cider. Then it was back to the terrace for the second half. Despite Blues possession and our loud renditions of 'Keep Right On', Blues could only add one more goal to our tally as the hardworking Melissa Lawley fired home the second in the 83rd minute. Cue more celebrations around the pitch from the travelling Bluenoses.

The game ended with a 2-0 win for Blues Ladies and a place in the quarter finals of the League Cup. The current WSL Champions Chelsea had been knocked out by London Bees of the 2nd tier of the WSL, on penalties in a shock cup upset the day before. Current league leaders Manchester City Women had beaten Aston Villa Ladies 8-0 (eight!) to also progress.

We applauded the players at the end and following their debrief on the pitch from Marcus they all came over and applauded our support. We headed back to our cars and reflected on a good result. The draw for the quarter final then gave Blues Ladies a home tie against fellow WSL team Liverpool Ladies. I had really enjoyed my visit to this lovely little ground in a lovely setting on a nice sunny day.

Ground 106 – Wheatsheaf Park (Staines FC) – FAWSL – 10th July 2016 – Chelsea Ladies 1 Birmingham City Ladies 1

In July 2016 Blues were away to high flying Chelsea and I was headed to Staines in London for the game against the current Champions who were occupying 2nd place in the WSL just one place above Blues Ladies. It was a long trip down south but it was a lovely sunny day again. We put our Blues flag up behind the goal and it was soon joined by the Redditch Blues flag. The Blues fans were mostly congregated along the side of the pitch near the goal and we were in good spirits.

Wheatsheaf Park was a really nice little ground with a capacity of 3,000 and it had a small club shop just inside the turnstiles which had merchandise for both Staines FC and Chelsea Ladies. I purchased both Staines FC and Chelsea Ladies badges for my collection before we headed into their bar. It was a really nice large bar and as we sat down to enjoy our drinks and read my Programme I saw Marie (Karen Carney's mom) come in and we had a chat about how Karen was finding life at Chelsea.

We soon made our way outside and joined the other Bluenoses along the side of the pitch. There were seated stands either side of the pitch but most people chose to stand and watch the game. The teams came out and we launched into 'Keep Right On' to which some of the Blues players applauded us. Blues Ladies were playing in the new red away kit which was really nice. Chelsea's last WSL game had been a 5-0 away win at Sunderland.

Blues were given quite a bit of credit by Chelsea manager Emma Hayes in her Programme notes as she welcomed Birmingham City as a "big test, as in my view they are the most organised and well drilled team in the division. I didn't for a second think they would struggle this season and if they start scoring more goals there is no reason why they can't challenge for the title."

Birmingham City Ladies were currently unbeaten in 7 games and had not conceded a goal in the last 6 games. There were 1,354 inside Staines to watch a hard fought match that was being shown live on TV and Blues more than held their own. Chelsea were reduced to hitting long range shots on the Blues goal.

In the 48th minute Freda Ayisi shocked the champions with a well taken goal at the end where our fans were situated. I was walking behind the goal at the time and could be seen on TV jumping around waving my flag in celebration. The lead only lasted 4 minutes though as Chelsea scored a soft goal from a Blues perspective to make the score level again at 1-1. As the game went on there were a few hard tackles going in and 10 minutes from the end Chelsea captain Katie Chapman was given her marching orders for bringing down the lively Freda Ayisi as we chanted 'Off! Off!'. She looked over at us as she went off.

The match finished in a creditable draw and Blues Ladies remained unbeaten in 8 games. However, Arsenal Ladies beat Notts County Ladies 2-0 in the other game of the day which meant that Blues dropped to 4th, a point behind Arsenal who moved above us. We sang 'we're gonna win the league' as the players came over to applaud us. Andrine Hegerberg seemed to enjoy this song as she waved her arms in a gesture to us to continue.

We walked back to the car and headed back home in the lovely sunshine. As we were on the motorway by Heathrow airport Steve said "that planes low!" and I looked up saying "what plane" and was stunned to see the wheels of a massive plane which looked to be about ten foot above our car "Fucking hell!" I said as Steve burst out laughing. It had been a really good day and another nice new ground that I had visited.

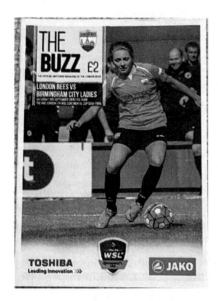

Ground 107 – The Hive Stadium – WLC Semi Final – 3rd September 2016 – London Bees 0 Birmingham City Ladies 4

I was off to another new ground in London in September 2016 and I was really looking forward to the trip. Blues Ladies travelled to London Bees with a place in the final of the Continental Cup (League Cup) at stake and I was looking forward to visiting a new ground. We travelled on the supporters coach down to 'The Hive' in London, which was home to Barnet FC and London Bees of the WSL 2 and had a capacity of 5,100. It was the first time that a WSL 2 team had reached the semi final of the competition and the Bees deserved to be there after knocking out Watford, Chelsea and Sheffield FC.

It was a really nice little stadium with a great club shop that had both Barnet and London Bees merchandise. In fact, I got a lovely London Bees mug and a Barnet badge for my collection of grounds I have visited. So far this was my favourite away ground from the grounds I had visited with Blues Ladies. They had a fabulous bar/ restaurant aptly called The Hive which looked out into the stadium and it had an electronic turnstile into the stand. It was lovely and the food was fantastic. I can recommend the bacon baguette!

There was only one Stand, alongside the pitch, which was open for this game unless a big crowd turned up but that didn't stop us displaying our large Blues flags (4 in total) on the terrace behind the goal. They looked very impressive and there was a large away following armed with Blue's flags and scarves. In fact of the 368 crowd the majority were Bluenoses who were in extremely good voice! 'Keep Right On' was sang many times. A match ticket for today's game was the pricey sum of £1! Shame it didn't entice the locals to come and support their team.

Prior to kick off there was a minutes applause in memory of England Women's U19 player Zoe Tynan who sadly died the week before after being hit by a train at Allerton station in Liverpool.

The game kicked off and what a contrast to last weeks display against Chelsea. Blues Ladies dominated from the start in a totally one-sided game of football and they were a different class from their WSL 2 opponents. Their passing and creativity was magnificent as chance after chance was created and the Bees keeper made several saves. The breakthrough did come though after 26 minutes with a diving header from Kirsty Linnett as she met a cross from Emily Westwood to open the scoring for Blues. We all celebrated loudly amongst a mass of blue and white flags. Despite Blues possession they went in at half time only 1-0 ahead.

In the second half Blues continued to overwhelm the Bees and Kerys Harrop soon headed Birmingham's second goal and we were celebrating again. Such was Blues dominance we were singing "we want three". We were soon granted our wish as 18 year old substitute Charlie Wellings scored the goal of the game with a long range shot that flew over the keeper and into the net to make it 3-0. Cue more celebrations amongst us Bluenoses!

The chances continued to fall Blues way and late on we got our fourth goal when a curling corner from Andrine Hegerberg was diverted into the net by the Bees keeper Davies for an own goal. It was no more than Blues deserved and 4-0 was the final result.

Loud cheers greeted the final whistle and the Blues players came over to the Blues fans as we sang "ka sa ra, sa ra, whatever will be will be, we're going to Man City, ka sa ra, sa ra". A few players came into the crowd to join the joyous celebrations with the fans. This would be the third time in six years that Birmingham City had reached the final having lost to Arsenal Ladies in 2011 and 2012. Hopefully it would be third time lucky!

We all headed back to the bar and we were soon joined by the Blues players and manager David Parker once they had changed. They signed autographs and chatted to us – what a difference from the Prima Dona's of the men's game nowadays. We had a lovely 15-20 minutes with them before getting the coach back home. The team coach was waiting behind ours for them to follow us.

In the other semi final up in Manchester on the Sunday the current league leaders Man City Women beat Arsenal Ladies 1-0 to set up a 'home' final for them at the Manchester City Academy Stadium against Birmingham City Ladies. Now don't get my started on this as I think that it is really unfair that a 'neutral' ground for a final is that of the team playing in the final. It was wrong and should be moved but we all knew that it wouldn't as money talks.

Ground 108 – Pirelli Stadium – 21st October 2016 – Burton Albion 2 Birmingham City 0 – Championship

Apart from it being a night match, I was looking forward to the trip to Burton. As Blues had never played Burton Albion before it would be a new ground for me and it was really exciting. The game was being shown live on TV but it was still a sell out for the Blues end and we were all looking forward to standing on the terraces once again.

We travelled on the official coaches which dropped us on the main road next to the Pirelli Stadium. As we arrived a bit later than usual we headed through the turnstiles once I had been to the club shop to get a badge and a programme (the last one!). Once inside I was delighted to discover a lovely little bar and so me, June and James ordered drinks while Steve went in search of chips which he returned with shortly afterwards and we all pinched a chip. Then it was onto the small but modern terrace, in fact three sides of the ground were terrace areas. I loved it.

The atmosphere was fabulous amongst the Blues fans as we sang our hearts out. There were 1,734 Bluenoses there and our noise filled the small stadium. However, it failed to inspire our heroes as Blues were poor and lost 2-0 to a team near the bottom of the table. Of course ex Blues player Lloyd Dyer scored and celebrated in front of the away end who in return showered him wth abuse and gestures which he thoroughly deserved. He really was a toe rag. It had been a good trip that ended in disappointment. I quite liked Burton's stadium though and it had a nice feel about it.

My second and last trip to the Pirelli Stadium was in August 2017 and another enjoyable trip despite the football.

The 1,715 away tickets for the Burton game sold out by the time they reached bronze members and never even made it to the season ticket holders or general sale. I was lucky enough to get one though as I was a gold member at the time (I have been Platinum for a while now), as were my friends June, James and Steve. So I was really looking forward to the trip. I liked Burton due to the good old fashioned 'terraces' and I relished the opportunity of standing on them amongst a partisan Blues following in full voice.

We travelled on the official Blues coaches and for once (despite leaving late again) we arrived in plenty of time so headed up the road to the away pub 'The Beeches Hotel'. There was also a bar in the pub car park and there were already loads of Bluenoses drinking there. It was a bit cold to be honest so once we had our drinks me, June and James headed inside with Steve following us not long afterwards. There was a bit of singing going on and the cricket was on live from Edgbaston.

It was soon time to head to the Pirelli Stadium for kickoff and we joined the queue at the turnstiles. Once inside we got chips and headed for the already packed terraces. There were loads of Blues fans trying to get on the terraces which seemed full and I just pushed and squeezed my way through as I was used to from the 80's. It was a bit tricky with a tray of chips in my hand but the pre match Thatchers probably helped my quest. We found a spot near the corner just as the teams were out.

The game kicked off with Lucas Jutkiewicz back after injury and Blues started brightly. The Blues fans were in great voice with loud renditions of 'Keep Right On' and 'we've got Redknapp, Harry Redknapp'. They also taunted the home fans with 'your grounds too small for us'. Then in the 29th minute Jacques Maghoma fired the ball home and the away end erupted in celebration. Blues were in control and went in at half time 1-0 ahead (just as I had predicted on FanScore).

I have no idea what went wrong in the second half but we were awful. We let Burton back into the game and it was soon 1-1. Blues just let Burton have the ball, didn't close them down or tackle them and gave the ball away easily. They didn't run or chase the ball and that tosser Lloyd Dyer, who always taunts the Blues fans, managed to score the winner against us yet again! Burton seem to be our bogey team as we had lost every one of the three competitive games we had played against them.

The Blues fans were not impressed with the way some of the players performed in the second half and rightly so. Once again the only bright spot was the introduction of Isaac Vassell who looked fast and dangerous. Blues fans sang 'we've got Vassell, Isaac Vassell I just don't think you understand, he came from Luton Town to send the villa down, we've got Isaac Vassell!'

The game finished in a 2-1 defeat and Harry Redknapp didn't pull any punches afterwards. He said that four or five players went missing in the second half and the team needs surgery and he will bring in more players and these players need not come crying to him when they don't get in the team because they have had their chance and he doesn't care. Harry said the Blues fans are fantastic and deserve better and if it's the last thing he does in management he will give them a good team, he said this team ruined Zola last year. Harry still maintained Blues would finish in the top six. I love this man! Birmingham were now 15th in the table.

So just two visits to the Pirelli Stadium for me and both of them ended in defeat but I enjoyed my visits to a nice little stadium. The stadium was built in 2005 on the site of the former site of the Pirelli UK Tyres Ltd Sports & Social Club and had the land donated to the club by Pirelli in return for the naming rights. The ground cost £7.2 million to build and has a capacity of 6,912 (2,034 seated).

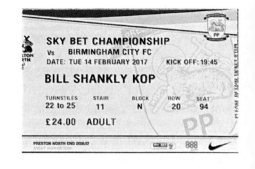

Ground 109 – Deepdale – 14th February 2017 – Preston North End 2 Birmingham City 1 – Championship

My first trip to Deepdale was a midweek game and I was one of 614 Bluenoses amongst a low crowd of 10,233 who spent valentines night in Preston. It was my first trip to the stadium and therefore a new ground for me and I was looking forward to it.

It was a nice stadium with proper floodlights which always makes it feel like a proper football ground to me. It wasn't like some of the new rounded stadiums and was proper square shaped with four nice stands including the away end behind the goal which could be allocated in its entirety to the away club should the following require it. Very nice.

It just didn't go well for Blues though as we lost 2-1 and Craig Gardener was sent off for a foul. Blues were now down to 14th in the table and it wasn't a very good time for us Bluenoses. Zola said he was fed up of talking about luck, he said "the reason we keep losing games like this is not because we are unlucky, at the moment we are very poor, simple as that". It was another depressing trip home on the coach wondering where the next win would come from. To add insult to when we arrived back at St. Andrews our cars had once again been locked in the car park!

Another memorable trip to Preston was in January 2018 and another enjoyable trip this time on a Saturday afternoon. As we arrived in Preston the coaches were met by the police who escorted us to the stadium and we arrived around 1pm. I wanted to see the new Dick Kerr Ladies monument so we headed there, had a look and then went into the nearby Tom Finney's Bar which Terry, Nigel and Charlie were refused entry into. So me and June had a quick drink as it was a 'home bar' and then headed to the 'away pub' called 'The Sumners' which, in contrast, was full of singing Blues fans.

I had hoped to meet up with my old mate Ballie (who I had played football with at Blues Ladies) but she was in a pub by the railway (she had travelled from Liverpool where she now lived) and that was also packed full of singing Blues fans. Ballie said she would try to get to us but didn't manage to, so me and June walked up the road to the ground and got in ten minutes before kick off. The massive concourse was full of singing Bluenoses and there was blue smoke from flares that had been set off below the stands. Even in the toilets you could smell the smoke from the flares. It was brilliant

We had to fight our way up to the stands, it was that packed. Over 2,200 Bluenoses had made the journey and the away end was buzzing. Blues were playing in red again and started brightly, creating several chances. As is always the case though, we conceded a sloppy goal from Preston's only attack when Blues Marc Roberts headed across his own goal to gift the Preston player a goal at the far post. Blues went in 1-0 down at half time but I wasn't too worried as we were playing that well that I thought Blues could get back into the game.

At half time I popped down to the toilets and found Ballie in the concourse so we had that catch up after all, which was great. Blues came out for the second half and played really well. Even Maghoma (man of the match) was working hard and getting stuck into the tackles. Every Blues player was playing their hearts out and Blues completely dominated Preston.

The goal did come too as Maghoma dispossessed a Preston player on the edge of the area and passed to Sam Gallagher who side footed it into the empty net from just inside the area. The away end exploded with noise and celebration which seemed to go on forever. It was no more than Blues deserved and, despite pushing for the winner, had to settle for a point from the 1-1 draw. After the game Preston's manager said that they (Preston) didn't even deserve a point. It gave us all hope though and despite Sunderland winning Blues remained second from bottom as Burton lost 6-0 at Fulham and they dropped to the foot of the table. Blues were only one point off safety.

I enjoyed a very good trip to Deepdale in September 2022 as we again travelled up on the official coaches. It was me, June, Charlie and Taff on coach 3 as we headed to Preston with our flag proudly on display in the rear window. It was a nice warm day too and we actually set off early for once despite being 8 minutes late leaving. We arrived in Preston around 12:30 and headed for the nearby St. Gregory's Social Club. There was a bit of a queue to get in as it seemed that word had got out and there were loads of Bluenoses with the same idea as us. I was nursing a foot injury that I had picked up a few days previously during walking football when another player had trod on my foot and the studs had obviously hurt! Hence I limped to the Social Club.

Once inside we were amazed to see the Bluenoses that we had met in the same club last season and we soon joined them (to get a seat) whilst the lads got the drinks in. It was great and full of away fans. Obviously we all had a laugh and a joke and discussed our chances of coming away from Preston with anything at all. We all went for a Blues win but more in hope than anything else the way things were at the moment.

With kick off approaching and having consumed a couple of drinks we headed back to the stadium and joined the throng of Blues fans in the concourse. We hung back for a few minutes whilst a group of Bluenoses did the Tebily song and performed their beer shampoo and then we passed them at the first opportunity of remaining dry before heading to our seats. Sadly today Blues were nowhere near filling the massive away end where we had previously taken 5,000 but at least we had a very good noisy 2,000 + of us belting out 'Keep Right On'.

Blues looked good in our red away kit (apart from the weird shade of blue socks) and with Kristian Bielik and Tahith Chong in the team we looked quite good. Preston had yet to concede a goal or taste defeat so far this season but I was hopeful that we could change all that and when our wing backs combined to score our first goal as Maxime Colin headed home after 15 minutes the away end went wild. I jumped up and down on my one good foot and we celebrated noisily. This was the first goal that Preston had conceded this season. We just had to keep them from scoring now.

Blues made five substitutions in the second half which I again felt weakened our team but amazingly Blues held out and we achieved a fantastic 1-0 away win at a difficult place but sadly we remained in the relegation places due to other results. Still early days though. At the end of the game the players and manager came over to the fans and it was an absolutely fantastic bonding as the fans sang and applauded loudly and the players responded by joining in and dancing around and applauding us. Manager John Eustace was extremely happy as he thumped his chest out in front of us and pointed to his club crest on his shirt. Brilliant scenes indeed. It was great to have been part of it.

We headed back to Birmingham happy but sensible enough to know that it could just be a one off but hopefully enough to dream that the Bielik/Chong midfield partnership could bring great things.

I have visited Deepdale on 6 occasions and seen 1 win, 2 draws and 3 defeats during this period. The stadium has a capacity of 23,408 and it's a great atmosphere when there is over 5,000 Blues fans in the away end.

324

Ground 110 – The Den (New) – 21st October 2017 – Millwall 2 Birmingham City 0 – Championship

I was looking forward to my first trip to Millwall as it would be a new stadium and I thought that Blues might be able to win this game. Unfortunately it was a 5.30 kick off due to the game being shown live on Sky. Our coaches arrived about an hour before kickoff and we were taken directly to the away turnstiles. Once again it was a sell out away allocation of 2000 and the Blues fans were in great voice.

It was quite a nice little stadium with a capacity of 20,146 and opened in 1993 at a cost of £16 million and replaced the Old Den from which it is about a quarter of a mile away. It a square shaped stadium with four separate stands all with two tiers and it was far from full today. Millwall never give us the lower tier which always remains empty as they prefer to keep us out of the way in the upper tier. For those away fans coming by train there is a specific 'away' station which lead's directly to the away turnstiles.

I don't think the players responded to our support today though as they didn't play at all well. We did have probably the best of the first half though but halftime came with a score of 0-0. Millwall came out for the second half with more hunger than Blues and they went ahead in the 48th minute much to our disappointment. Blues fans responded to the Millwall fans with 'nobody likes you – because your shit'. 'Keep Right On' also rang out in an effort to lift our team but it didn't work and Blues conceded another soft goal on 76 minutes and never looked like getting back into the game. Despite having 16 shots we never seemed to look like scoring.

So a really disappointing 2-0 defeat with the highlight being a text from my nephew Stephen at half time with a photo of me, June and James being shown live on Sky as we pondered the first half. Very funny!

The police kept us locked in the outside away area with the gates closed which led to a bit of a crush and it did kick off a bit. We had to wait over an hour before the coaches were allowed to leave and then we were taken by police escort through central London. It was quite nice really with all the bridges illuminated. We didn't get home till late though and we were knackered.

In November 2018 I was off to London for the midweek game against Millwall at the Den. The coach journey took quite a while and we arrived very early as the coaches had left Birmingham early to avoid the rush hour and the Millwall turnstiles were not even open yet. It was a cold evening so me and June headed to the Millwall cafe to get some chips to warm us up as we waited for the turnstiles to open. My nephew Stephen joined us not long afterwards as he had heard it was pay on the gate and decided to join us from work.

There were over 1500 Blues fans in attendance and it was the only stand that looked pretty full as the other 3 ends of the ground were very sparsely occupied and the stadium looked embarrassingly empty. Us Bluenoses were in great voice though and sang throughout the game. We took the piss out of the Millwall contingent relentlessly including 'nobody likes you - because your shit!'

Blues really needed a good result to get back on track and we hoped the team would pick themselves up and put in a good performance. Blues started really well and on 11 minutes Che Adams hit the post and the ball then hit a Millwall player and went in for an own goal! The away end erupted and a blue flare scorched the pitch as blue smoke filled the stadium. I was jumping around all over the place! Brilliant! It got even better when Millwall had a player sent off on 30 minutes for a bad foul on Mikel kieftenbeld and they were down to 10 men.

Being down to 10 men seemed to inspire Millwall and it became a tough game. Then on 76 minutes Michael Morrison scored and the away end celebrated again. The goal was right in front of the away fans and the noise was tremendous and I again jumped around wildly. A couple of minutes later Garry Monk brought Gary Gardener on for Kieftenbeld which meant that the two Gardener brothers were on the pitch at the same time for Birmingham for the very first time. It prompted a rendition of the 'Toure' song that went 'Craigy, Craigy, Craigy, Craigy Craigy Gardener! Gary, Gary, Gary, Gary, Gary Gardener!' etc and it went on for a while. It was great fun.

The Millwall fans left way before the end to a chorus of 'is there a fire drill?' and the game ended with a fantastic 2-0 away win for Blues . Stephen headed off to catch the train and we headed back to the coaches very happy indeed. It would be a long trip through London and home but it was well worth the trip.

In April 2023 once again in the evening we headed to The Den by coach and we were in good spirits. It was yet another long trip as we boarded the coaches for the Tuesday night game at play off chasing Millwall at The Den. This was always a horrible trip if it was midweek as we had to travel through London and although it was a very picturesque route on the return journey with all the lights, it took ages to get home.

It didn't start well either as there were problems with the wheelchair lift on the accessible coach which led to seats being removed from coach two to accommodate wheelchair users and I ended up with a very irate Barry (who should have been on coach 2) sitting next to me on the back seat (on coach 3). As well as suffering Barry's rants the coaches then left St. Andrews 35 minutes late. I dreaded the rest of the journey and when the young lads in front of us started openly vaping the day only got worse.

Hence it was a long trip and when we arrived at the entrance to the car park at the ground our coach was boarded by 2 or 3 police officers who headed straight down to the rear of our coach and asked two of the young lads in front of them to accompany them to the front of the coach. As our coach continued onward to the away car park we saw one of the lads cuffed and being searched and the other also with the police.

We headed into the ground and Taff got the drinks in just as we were joined by my nephew Stephen and we had a good catch up. It's always great to see him. Then it was up into the stands to join the other Bluenoses who had made the trip. It was a good turnout for a midweek game in London with an 8pm kick off time to suite SKY TV once again. There looked to be over a thousand at least and we were in good voice. It would be a tough game against a Gary Rowett's Millwall that were currently in the play off places and very hard to beat.

Blues looked solid though and the away end exploded when Lucas Jutkiewicz fired home on 28 minutes to give Blues the lead. We sang and danced and generally enjoyed ourselves. Goalkeeper John Ruddy was in inspired form once again but sadly had to go off injured just before halftime but his replacement Neil Etheridge had a great game and made a fantastic double save in the second half to ensure that Blues came away with a brilliant 1-0 win. This took Blues up to 15th in the table.

Blues fans remained behind to celebrate with the players whilst the rest of the stadium emptied in record time. As we headed out after our celebrations we noticed a block of fans in the home end who were still in their seats and Blues fans spotted them and sang 'why the fuck are you still here?' followed by 'time to go'. It turned out they were a group of Americans. I had to laugh and they all got up and headed out after being noticed by the away fans.

We headed back to the coaches and were amazed to find that the young lads who had been detained had come back onto the coach. They were very quiet on the way back though. It was a lovely scenic trip though London but after and hour still in the capital it felt like being in a massive maze that we would never get out of. Our coach finally arrived back at St. Andrews at 2am but the remaining coaches got back at 3am so fair play to our driver who took a difficult route. I got to bed knackered but happy.

Overall I have made 6 trips to the new Den and 3 defeats. Not a pleasant place to visit unless travelling by train but a nice little stadium nonetheless.

Ground 111 – Rossett Park (Marine FC) – 13th May 2018 – FAWSL – Everton Ladies 0 Birmingham City Ladies 3

It was a lovely sunny Sunday as we headed up the motorway to Crosby in Liverpool to watch Blues Ladies play Everton away. This season Everton Ladies had moved from Widnes to a new ground at the Marina Arena, home of Marina FC and it was right near the beach. It did take a long time to get there because of traffic on the M6 – 2 hours 45 minutes to be exact but it was well worth the trip.

It was a nice little ground and I was expecting just a handful of Blues fans to have made the trip but I was amazed to see that there were Birmingham fans all around the ground, in fact it was like a home game with Blues fans being the majority and easily outnumbering the home support! Brilliant! It was great to catch up with all the regular Bluenoses who had made the trip. I had worn my white away shirt (which Blues played in against Chelsea last week) but today the girls were playing in our red away shirt.

It was a really nice little ground with a capacity of 3,185 with just the one seated stand behind the goal near the turnstiles. One side of the pitch had a small covered terrace and behind the other goal was an open terrace which was lovely in the sunshine. This was were all the Bluenoses put their flags on display.

Blues started the game with Charlie Wellings firing wide in the 2nd minute. Charlie was not to be denied though as she hit a spectacular 30 yard shot which sailed over the keeper and into the net to put Blues 1-0 ahead. It was a fantastic goal! All around the ground Bluenoses were celebrating. It certainly made the gruelling journey worthwhile.

At half time I went hunting for the refreshments stall but struck gold instead as I found the club bar with an outside beer garden which was already occupied by some of the Bluenoses I knew. Obviously I joined them in the sun after purchasing a nice cold Strongbow. Lovely!

The second half got underway with Everton making more of a go of it but Blues continued to dominate and Charlie Wellings scored her second of the game with a low shot from the edge of the penalty area. We were now behind the goal with our big flags and we celebrated loudly. Brilliant! Ellen White then got in on the act with 4 minutes remaining when she too scored a spectacular 30 yarder that flew into the net and we celebrated again.

The final whistle signalled a great 3-0 away win and Bluenoses all around the ground celebrated. All the Blues players came over to the fans at the end and I chatted to both Marc Skinner (who had 2 of my BCLFC 50th Anniversary badges) and Charlie Wellings who very kindly thanked me for coming. Then it was off round the corner for a quick ice cream on the beach before setting off home to avoid the traffic from the nearby Liverpool v Brighton (men's) game which kicked off an hour after ours. Happily we made it back to Birmingham in only 2 hours.

Ground 112 – Jonny Rocks Stadium – 21st July 2018 – Cheltenham Town 0 Birmingham City 3 – Pre Season Friendly

Today I was traveling on the 'party bus' and we left St. Anne's at 10.30 and headed to a pub in Tewksbury called the Ember Inn which was only 20 minutes from the ground. We arrived in the sunshine and ordered drinks and a nice meal. There were soon Bluenoses everywhere, especially outside in the sunshine where our flags were proudly displayed on the fences. We had a lovely couple of hours there before heading off to Cheltenham.

As we arrived in Cheltenham there were Blues fans everywhere and I set about waving to them. Due to traffic we arrived at the Jonny Rocks Stadium with about 10 minutes to kick off, having been directed around the stadium once.

We drew the line at the second attempt to send us around the stadium by the stewards and we went about disembarking outside the away turnstiles. There were a lot of Bluenoses inside and we had the end behind the goal and half way along the side.

This was a new ground for me, which doesn't happen often, so it was really nice. It was a happy atmosphere in the sunshine although there wasn't any singing, probably due to it being a friendly game. Garry Monk had pretty much put the kids out, to be honest, apart from Wes Harding, Marc Roberts and Cheikh Ndoye. The players had numbers on their shirts but no names so most of us struggled as to who was actually playing. The programme was of no help either as it gave a list of the Blues players but no numbers. I was disappointed that I would not see the first team players. On the other hand League Two Cheltenham Town fielded their first team.

It was an entertaining game though and Blues went ahead when Charlie Lakin scored on 26 minutes and it remained 1-0 at half time. Blues continued to dominate and Lubala headed home the second from a Lakin corner on 52 minutes. A third goal was disallowed before Blues won a penalty in the 89th minute. The 1,218 (amongst the 2,234 attendance) chanted for NDoye to take the penalty. There were loud chants of 'NDoye! NDoye!' and he looked surprised before gesturing to the bench asking if he should take it and Garry Monk put his thumb up. NDoye then headed towards the penalty spot as the Blues fans continued to chant his name but Lubala put the ball on the spot to take it instead and everyone booed. He did then step aside though and Cheikh NDoye smashed the ball in the net and the away end went wild.

At the end of the game the players came over to applaud us and Cheikh NDoye came over to the fans and I got my photo taken with him. 'Great Goal Cheikh' I said and he replied 'thank you' before high five'ing me and walking away. What a great day. I even managed to get an ice cream before boarding the party bus back to Birmingham.

My second trip to the Jonny Rocks Stadium was another pre season friendly and the start of the 2023 to 2024 season and Blues did not put on any official coaches for the away trip and so we had to make our own way there. We decided to go by car which meant Harry driving and Linda, June and myself travelling with him. We arrived early and parked on the designated away parking area which cost £8 and was part of the community centre next the home end. We parked up in the pouring rain and headed into the community centre which was like a social club with two nice bar areas.

There were already several Blues fans inside and we found a nice table and obtained drinks and sausage baps which were very nice indeed. We had a nice catch up before heading back outside as the rain was easing up. It wasn't far to walk to the away end and we were soon in our seats. There were 1,276 Bluenoses in attendance and they did sing and create a good atmosphere.

Blues looked lively with Jordan James again playing a more attacking role but Cheltenham took the lead against the run of play after 15 minutes due to very poor defending. Here we go again I thought. We really need to work on our defence. In fact, I thought we desperately needed a couple of decent defenders or we could struggle against stronger opposition. It took only ten minutes for parity to be restored when Keshi Anderson fired home to make it 1-1 and we all celebrated in the away end. It certainly looked like Blues fans outnumbered the home supporters.

We again fell behind after more poor defending which allowed a Cheltenham player to shoot from the edge of the penalty area and the ball went in off the post to make it 2-1. I let out another deep sign as I despaired at our ability to defend. Their lead only lasted four minutes this time as Jordan James restored parity when he scored to make it 2-2 and we celebrated again.

Our comeback was complete when Juninho Bacuna scored with a great shot to make it 3-2 just before halftime and we celebrated more wholeheartedly this time. The second half saw more changes but no further goals as Blues achieved their fourth win on the trot and June and I headed for the refreshment stall which amazingly was still serving. We obtained the best Cheesy chips I have ever had and we ate them on our way back to the car. They were lovely!

I popped back into the community centre to use the toilet and bumped into Brendan and sold him a copy of my new book which had just been published – 'Once A Blue, Always A Blue'. Then it was back to the car and back on the road to Birmingham. It had been a very enjoyable away day once again and I was looking forward to the new season.

I was back at Cheltenham a few weeks later when we were drawn to play them in the League Cup and I was looking forward to the journey design being a night game.

For the first time in many years I was actually looking forward to a cup match. I absolutely love the Cup competitions but over the years our managers have used the competition to give the kids a run out and we usually exit to a lower league team at the first hurdle and I absolutely hated that. It was usually poor football and if at St. Andrews it would be played in front of a small and silent crowd with only one stand open. Hence I preferred away cup games.

Tonight would be very different because for once we had a very good squad and even our 'second team' looked very good. Most importantly it would not be our entire under 23 side and there was a sell out away contingent of just under 2,000 heading to Cheltenham. I was really excited. I think most Bluenoses were as well to be honest.

June and I were at St. Andrews for 3.45pm and I headed into the club shop to purchase the new Red away shirt. It was really nice and I had definitely overcome the fact that it was the same colour as last season's away shirt. To be honest it was a different shade of red and each print was different for each one. I was really pleased with it. Today I would be wearing my home shirt though as Cheltenham play in red.

Taff joined us on the coach and our journey began. Obviously the coaches left late again and for some unknown reason they headed towards the M5 via Perry Barr in rush hour. What is wrong with this coach company? Are they deliberately making the journeys longer for us I wondered. None of us were impressed and it took ages to get out of Birmingham. We all agreed that they should have taken the usual route via Hagley Road. It was going to be a long season if they kept this up!

Hence we arrived in Cheltenham with only an hour to kick off. This ruined our plan to have a nice pre match drink in the nearby social club as the queue for the bar was massive by the time we got inside. The club was already full of Bluenoses who had obviously not taken the official coaches. Somewhat disappointed we headed back to the stadium and discovered that we were in the stand along the side of the pitch this time.

On our recent trip to Cheltenham for the pre season friendly we had purchased the best cheesy chips ever and so we had planned to do the same tonight. June was first and we were astonished to see that her chips were just topped with a bit of cold grated cheese which was very swiftly returned in exchange for a pastie. Apparently they had just been taken over and it was a different company but they should have melted cheese again on Saturday. You just couldn't make it up. So I just had a portion of chips which I took up to my seat with me.

John Eustace made eight changes to Blues line up but it was still a very strong team and I was happy. The game got underway and the Bluenoses were in great voice with the away following of 2,000 being half the crowd inside the stadium. Blues dominated from the start and went ahead after 24 minutes when Juninho

Bacuna scored from outside the penalty area and we all celebrated loudly. Bluenoses sang the 'tequila' song which Bacuna showed his appreciation for by applauding the away end.

There were some great songs being belted out and one of my favourites of the evening came when the ball was sent out of the stadium and Blues sang 'just hit my car – got a big dent in the roof' to the tune of the 'we but any car' advert. It made me chuckle. Eight minutes after Blues opener we won a free kick on the edge of the area and Bacuna curled a beauty over the wall and into the net to make it 2-0. Cue another rendition of the 'tequila' song to which Bacuna again showed his appreciation.

Blues were playing really well and Keshi Anderson could well have had a hat trick had his finishing been better. Our new Japanese player was looking really good too. Although there were no more goals in the game Blues had 22 shots with 13 on target. It was fantastic to watch. Blues fans sang 'ka sa ra sa ra, we're going to Wembley' and we generally enjoyed ourselves. It was wonderful to watch and great to be in the draw for the next round of the League Cup.

At the end of the game the players were applauding the supporters and Bacuna was enjoying participating in a rendition of the tequila song as, unbeknown to him, manager John Eustace was standing behind him laughing before waiting for him to finish then congratulating him on his performance. It was a class moment and great to witness. We headed back to the coaches very happy indeed. What a great night.

With all my three visits to Cheltenham ending in victory this meant I had a 100% win ratio here and I had enjoyed every trip very much so far. The stadium is now known as the Completely-Suzuki Stadium for sponsorship reasons and has a capacity of 7,066. The stadium opened in 1927 and has had a variety of names since. It's a lovely little stadium to visit with a great social club nearby.

Ground 113 – Bracken Moor Stadium (Stockbridge Park Steels FC) – 16th September 2018 – WLC – Sheffield United Women 0 Birmingham City Women 2

It was a lovely Sunday morning as I headed off to Solihull Moors to pick up Linda, Terry and Harry for our trip to Sheffield to watch Blues Ladies play Sheffield United Ladies in the Continental League Cup. When I arrived Terry was already waiting and the team were just boarding the team coach to head off. This meant we were able to chat to Marc Skinner the Blues manager and we headed off just behind the team coach. It was a nice day and a nice trip as we took the A38 through Burton and 2 hours later we arrived at the Look Local Stadium – home of Sheffield United Ladies and Stockbridge Park Steels for who Jamie Vardy had previously played for (there is a stand named after him!).

It was at the top of some narrow windy lanes which were very picturesque. The view from inside the ground was lovely too, looking out over the Yorkshire dales and there was a beautiful rainbow. Entrance into the ground was through two small turnstiles and consisted of the seated Jamie Vardy Stand and a small covered terrace behind the goal and this was soon occupied by the Birmingham contingent and the Redditch Blues flag. This lovely small ground had a capacity of 3,500 and was very picturesque. I liked it immediately.

We headed up into the small upstairs bar which had a lovely view out over the pitch as we enjoyed our drinks with all the other Bluenoses who had joined us in there. Lunch was out of the question as the only refreshments on offer consisted of 'boiled sausage' hot dogs or chocolate! Hence my Sunday lunch was a mars bar. Once the match kicked off there were 331 supporters in attendance and around 200 of them were Birmingham fans. It was great!

Blues Ladies played in our away kit of yellow shirts, blue shorts and blue socks and looked really good. Marc Skinner had opted to play mostly our reserve players to give them a chance with many of our first team players on the bench. Somewhat disappointingly Ellen White was absent and we were all concerned as to whether she was injured, rested or something more sinister. Our other England international Lucy Staniforth was on the bench but the team that began the game were playing well. In the first half a Blues shot quite clearly went across the line into the goal and came out again but a goal was not given. We all clearly saw the net bulge just behind the crossbar where the ball went in!

So at half time it was still 0-0 and despite our chances it looked like we would never score! Two second half substitutions made the difference with Lucy Staniforth coming on and scoring on 72 minutes with a long range effort which sailed over the Sheffield United keeper and dipped into the goal and we celebrated around three sides of the ground. Not long afterwards Shania Hayles came on and grabbed Blues second goal from a corner which fell nicely for the lively Shania and we cruised to a 2-0 away win. Blues had been totally dominant and it was no more than we deserved. Needless to say we had a very happy trip back to Birmingham after having a fantastic day out and we had seen our first win in the new yellow away shirts.

I had really enjoyed the trip to a lovely little ground with fantastic views of the Yorkshire countryside. Sadly there were no matchday programmes available for todays game.

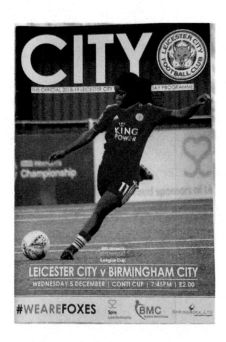

Ground 114 – Farley Way (Quorn FC) – 5th December 2018 – WLC – Leicester City Women 0 Birmingham City Women 6

On a Wednesday night it was League Cup action as we set out for Farley Way - Quorn FC, the home of Championship side Leicester City Women on a cold rainy night. We set out early to avoid the rush hour and arrived at a stadium in complete darkness with the gates locked so we had to head to a nearby pub (a very expensive pub) while we awaited the ground to open.

We headed back to the ground just after six and the gates were indeed open but the car park was in complete darkness with only one small floodlight on. We parked where there was a bit of light and not long afterwards the Blues team coach arrived. The place was still in darkness and then the turnstile opened and we headed into the ground and finally into the clubhouse once it opened. I had a chip cob while the others had burgers and chips and we were soon joined by loads of other Birmingham fans who completely took over the Leicester club house.

It was a nice little ground with a capacity of just 1,400 and the locals seemed friendly enough. There was a seated stand at one side of the pitch which was opposite the clubhouse and was small but really nice. Behind one of the goals was a small covered terrace and there was nothing at all behind the other goal.

We stood alongside the dugouts by the clubhouse for the first half and behind the goal on the small terrace for the second half.

Once outside we put all our Birmingham City flags up and the game got underway with Blues playing in yellow shirts and white shorts so as not to clash with Leicester's all blue kit. It took only 3 minutes for Blues to take the lead as Shania Hayles scored to make it 1-0 and Blues fans all around the ground celebrated. The lead was doubled on 22 minutes when Lucy Staniforth scored and Blues looked classy as they passed the ball around effortlessly. Chloe Arthur then scored a beauty on 31 minutes to make it 3-0 and we celebrated again. Blues were tearing Leicester apart and the lively Charlie Wellings broke through to score and make it 4-0 on 37 minutes and Blues went into the halftime break with a very healthy lead indeed.

Shania Hayles got her second of the game in the 60th minute from a corner to make it 5-0 before Lucy Quinn was fouled in the penalty area, a heavy tackle which we heard from behind the goal and we cringed with the impact. The referee quite rightly pointed to the spot and up stepped Aoife Mannion to coolly despatch into the bottom corner and we celebrated a great 6-0 away win. Blues played such good football and it was such a comprehensive victory that we actually went away disappointed that we didn't get more goals. What a great night and another new ground.

Ground 115 – London Stadium – 5th January 2019 – West Ham United 2 Birmingham City 0 – FA Cup

I had been looking forward to the trip to the London Stadium since the draw for the FA Cup 3rd round paired Birmingham City with West Ham United and we had booked our train travel immediately. Unfortunately I was feeling really unwell with flu like symptoms but I didn't let this stop me and I headed to New Street station with June, James and Steve to get the 8.30 train to Euston. There were already loads of Bluenoses in New Street station and I chatted to Paul Fidler who was also headed to the game with his daughter and mates.

The train journey went quite quickly and our train pulled into Euston at 0955am and we made our way by the London Underground to Liverpool Street and found our way into 'Dirty Dicks' which was really quiet compared to the nearby Wetherspoon's which was packed with Blues. I had already text Stephen (my nephew) to let him know where we were headed and he came into the pub not long afterwards along with several other Bluenoses including MIB Dave and Jeanette.

June and I had to leave to pub early to meet Nigel and Terry who had the extra ticket for Stephen in the Blues end, so we left the others enjoying their drinks while we got the tube to Stratford. Once we disembarked at Stratford it was a long walk to the stadium and I resisted the half half FA Cup scarves as I could not possibly buy a scarf with claret and blue on it! The London Stadium looked good but was spoiled by the claret and blue on it. It took us about 25-30 minutes for us the get to where Nigel, Terry and James were waiting for us and it was then like trying to get into Fort Knox! It began with two searches on the way to the turnstiles and then we had to undo our coats again once we got inside. It was ridiculous and it wasn't a friendly place at all. We were definitely not made to feel welcome.

Once inside I tried to get some hot food but failed miserably and had to settle for a packet of crisps and a mars duo (the chocolate had turned white!) for a total of £3.55 and had to be paid for by 'card only'. It doesn't feel like a proper football stadium, in fact it was totally soulless. We headed to our seats in the upper tier and the view was really good considering we were so far from the pitch. The others soon joined us and the atmosphere amongst the Blues fans was fantastic as 5200 of us belted out 'Keep Right On'. The overall attendance was 55,000 but the only noise came from the Blues fans. At times Blues sang 'is this a library?' as well as 'your support is fucking shit'. The song that really hit home with the West Ham fans was when we sang 'your not West Ham anymore!'

The sound of 5200 Bluenoses belting out Keep Right On was incredible as the game kicked off. It seemed to bounce of the roof and echo around the Stadium - fantastic! Unfortunately Blues conceded after only 2 minutes as Lee Camp only parried a shot which was then headed home by a West Ham player but even their cheer for their goal wasn't loud and was soon drowned out by 'Keep Right On!' Their stadium really was soulless and I was so glad we don't have to play at stadiums like this very often. I felt quite sorry for the West Ham fans who have lost their home ground and have to travel to a soulless pit like this. Blues had a great chance to equalise when Lucas Jutkiewicz had a header cleared off the line by Andy Carroll but we went in at half time 1-0 down but not outplayed.

At half time there was a mascot race as the West Ham mascot 'Hammerhead' challenged the Blues mascot Beau Brummie to a race. Of course Beau Brummie romped home and the Bluenoses sang 'he's one of our own' to Beau and then 'your fucking shit' to Hammerhead. I thoroughly enjoyed that bit of fun as there was no way I was heading back down all them stairs for a half time break! The second half got underway and Blues were playing really well and looked like we could get back into the game. Credit to Garry Monk for playing his strongest team although a a lot of that is probably because we only had 18 fit players at present anyway. Blues just couldn't get the goal we needed though and in stoppage time Andy Carroll scored the second for West Ham and our hopes were dashed.

At the end of the day Blues had not disappointed against a Premier League side and we had all enjoyed a great day out and a new ground to tick off our lists. It got quite tasty on our walk back to the station as the biggest police presence I have ever seen at a football match tried to keep the two sets on supporters separate. A West Ham fan threw horse shit over the bridge at the Birmingham fans and the Birmingham fans set a smoke bomb off (which made me jump out of my skin - along with several coppers) and a blue flare pumped blue smoke into the air. Some West Ham fans stood behind a line of police under a bridge as hundreds of Birmingham fans sang 'your not West Ham anymore!' at them and they didn't look best pleased.

As we walked back to the station the stewards held aloft big lollipops with GO on one side and STOP on the other and most of these had Birmingham City stickers on them which I found hilarious. It took us an hour to get away from the stadium then we headed to Baker Street and into the Wetherspoon's for a drink before catching the train from Marylebone back to New Street. Apart from feeling so unwell and losing, it had been a great day out although I wouldn't be in a hurry to return to the London Stadium.

West Ham fans took to twitter to comment that the Blues fans were the best they have had at the London Stadium this season. I think some of our songs hit the spot though as 'West Ham Transfers' said 'Not many chants by away fans wind me up but when Birmingham fans sang "you're not West Ham anymore" that cut deep. Proper deep'.

Ground 116 – Kingsmeadow Stadium (Wimbledon FC + Chelsea Women) – 27th January 2019 – FAWSL – Chelsea Women 2 Birmingham City Women 3

Birmingham City Ladies were away at Champions Chelsea who had won their last 11 matches including beating table toppers Arsenal on their own ground 2-1 last week and we were heading to London. Chelsea were also unbeaten in their last 13 games but we didn't let this put us off attending and we set out early for the two and a half hour trip to Wimbledon's Kingsmeadow Stadium, home of Chelsea Women FC. Terry, Harry and myself left from Solihull Moors and enjoyed a good catch up on the trip down to London and arrived early just behind the Birmingham team coach.

We parked on their car park and obtained tickets for the terraced area before checking out the club shop (a mobile shop) then heading into the bar as the rain came down. We were joined by loads of other Birmingham fans as well as the Chelsea contingent. One Blues fan had travelled down on his own by train! Somewhat amazingly the sun came out as we made our way onto the terrace behind the goal to enjoy our chips with chilli sauce and we were joined by other Birmingham fans. Despite being right next to the Chelsea 'hardcore' we set up our flags and began singing.

There was a crowd of 2053 with lots of Blues fans scattered around the ground. The Blues fans on the terrace all stood together though and we sang loudly to compete with the Chelsea lot next to us who kept singing 'Chelsea, Chelsea' – yes a truly original song! Each time we sang 'Keep Right On' they tried to drown us out but gave up well before the end of our song as we just got louder. The game got underway with Blues in our lucky yellow away shirts but Chelsea went ahead on 13 minutes. We didn't let that get us down though and we sang 'Birmingham, Birmingham, Birmingham' to get behind our team.

It did seem to inspire Blues and Emma Follis scored on 36 minutes to bring Blues level and we went bonkers! We jumped all over the terraces and taunted our neighbours with 'it's all gone quiet over there' and 'your not singing anymore'. They did the 'Chelsea, Chelsea' bit again and we did 'Birmingham, Birmingham'. Great fun! They sang 'Champions' and we countered with 'you live in the past, just like Villa you live in the past!' I don't think they liked that one much but we had a laugh!

So half time it was 1-1 and I would have been more than happy with a draw. Blues started the second half brightly and Emma's Follis was put through and with a one on one with the Chelsea keeper but she put the ball agonisingly wide. We all sighed and though that was our chance gone but on 60 minutes Lucy Quinn hit an outrageous shot from distance that the Chelsea keeper could only watch fly over her head and into the net for 2-1 Birmingham. We went mental on the terrace and Blues fans all round the stadium were celebrating.

We sang and sang and gave our Chelsea neighbours so much stick. Brilliant! Could we hold out? Well no. Blues gave away a cheap free kick on the edge of the area which evaded everyone and ended up in the bottom corner of the net. We sighed as the Chelsea lot celebrated and sang 'you only sing when you're winning'. We loudly sang 'we're Birmingham City, we'll fight to the end!'

With only 7 minutes left I was really disappointed and hoped we could at least hold on for the draw as Chelsea were now attacking with a vengeance. 90 minutes came and the board went up for 5 minutes of injury time. At least we now had Ellen White back on the pitch having come on as a substitute after months out recovering form a back injury. Could we hold out? In the 93rd minute Blues got the ball to Charlie Wellings who played a lovely ball into the box and there was Ellen White to volley home! Unbelievable scenes on the terraces, around the ground and on the pitch. We sang 'Ole, Ole, Ole, Ole, Ellen White, White, White!' and 'wc only sing when we're winning' just to the wind up the Chelsea lot! A couple of minutes later the final whistle sounded to confirm a stunning score line of Chelsea 2 Birmingham City 3!

At the end we sang a really loud rendition of 'Keep Right On' and all the Blues players headed over to us for high fives.   I high fived every one of the Blues players who were as excited as we were.   Paige Williams said we had been fantastic and our singing had kept them going.   It had been a brilliant day – well worth the trip.   As the Chelsea hardcore trudged past us they shook our hands and said 'fair play!'   Great banter.   We sang 'we can see you sneaking out' to their backs as they departed.

They were definitely not used to losing at home and with a vocal challenge from the away fans.   Was our title challenge back on?   I hoped so.   On our way out of the car park we passed the team coach and saw 'Woody' and shouted 'Come on!' waving our fists in celebration to her.   She roared back at us with arms raised in celebration and a big smile and banged on our car as we passed. Excellent! The trip back was fun as we celebrated and pondered if we could go on and challenge for the title.

It was another nice new ground that I had visited and I really enjoyed the trip. The stadium had formerly been the home of AFC Wimbledon and had a capacity of 4,850 with 2,265 seats. It was built and opened in 1989 with Kingstonian (1989-2017) the first tenants followed by AFC Wimbledon in 2002-2020 and Chelsea Women from 2017.

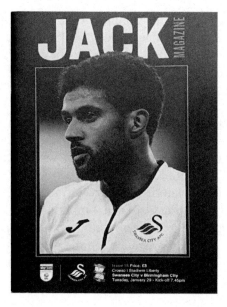

Ground 117 – Liberty Stadium – 29th January 2019 – Swansea City 3 Birmingham City 3 – Championship

Swansea City's Stadium would be a new ground for me as I had only been to the old Vetch Field ground many years ago. It was hard to see the Liberty Stadium properly when we arrived as it was dark and the way that Swansea have their floodlights on the inside of the stadium ensured that it remained dark outside. It did look nice inside but it was just your average new flat pack stadium that they build these days and I didn't think it had any character really. Blues really needed to get back to winning ways although I would have been happy with a draw tonight.

The game kicked off and it was obvious from the start that the referee wasn't going to give us anything. In fact he was shocking, he moved their free kicks so much closer to goal that it was ridiculous and he went about trying to book as many Blues players as he could get away with. I am convinced (along with a few other Bluenoses) that the EFL have spoken to all their referees to give Birmingham nothing. The EFL have well and truly got it in for Blues, which is pretty obvious if you just look at what they keep doing to us.

Swansea went ahead on 22 minutes with a goal that went straight through Lee Camp in our goal but Blues refused to give up and Jacques Maghoma scored a similar goal to equalise on 35 minutes and it was all level again. Obviously the referee didn't like that and decided to send off our defender Kristian Pederson just before half time to ensure that we now had an uphill battle for the whole of the second half. We all though that Garry would sacrifice a striker and take Jutkiewicz off but we were pleasantly surprised to see that he stuck with 2 strikers and went 4-3-2. Brilliant! Just when we thought we couldn't love him any more! Best manager for a long long time.

Blues started the first half strongly but as we were now playing 10 men against 12 (including the referee) it was no surprise when Swansea went 2-1 ahead in the 65th minute. We all sighed and couldn't see a way back but Vassell came on for Jutkiewicz and 2 minutes later we were level from a Jota free kick which was headed by Morrison and fumbled in for an own goal by Grimes for 2-2. We went mental in the away end as we celebrated. Then 4 minutes later the away end erupted again as Che Adams fired a cracker into the corner to give 10 men Blues the lead - 3-2! 'Che, Che will tear you apart again!' we sang to a stunned Swansea! We even sang the national anthem although it didn't have the same effect on the Swansea fans as it does on the Cardiff fans!

A lot of the Swansea fans were heading to the exits and Blues sang 'we can see you sneaking out'. The 90 minutes were up and the board went up to indicate and extra 4 minutes - where did they come from? Oh yes I forgot, we were winning! Blues were giving their all but Lee Camp's kick somewhat surprisingly went out and Swansea came back at us and Wes Harding again allowed a cross into the box which was headed home with 20 seconds remaining to break our hearts. We had to settle for a point in an entertaining 3-3 draw in which 6 cards were shown to Blues players by an awful referee. Not a bad result but it really should have been a win. We now had a very long trip back with work in the morning and we arrived at St. Andrews a little after 1am only to find all the cars frozen!

My favourite game came during the 2022 to 2023 season and was truly memorable. Despite everything I was really looking forward to the trip to Swansea and it was great to see everyone as we boarded our coaches which departed St. Andrews (slightly late again) just after 9.30am. We all presumed that we were leaving early to avoid getting stuck in the traffic that would be heading to the Rugby with Wales playing Ireland in Cardiff. Just our luck really as there always seems to be Rugby on when Blues play in Wales.

It was a pleasant journey though and we got to see some fantastic views in the sunshine on the way there. We arrived in plenty of time and Taff was already at the stadium waiting for us when we arrived. Obviously we headed straight to the nearby Harvester and joined the queue for the bar. Stuart took one look at the queue and decided he was heading into the ground instead. The rest of us persevered though and it was worth the wait as we soon had nice refreshing drinks and we stood in the outside area enjoying the ambiance. We also enjoyed Charlie's KP Nuts with direct hits to Nigel's, mine and Taff's pints. A bit of a laugh and then we headed across to the away end.

We had been saying how much we all enjoy our trips with Blues and the only thing that spoils it is the ninety minutes of football but I predicted that today would be amazing and we would smash Swansea. We all had a good laugh at that but the day was about to turn into one of those memorable afternoons that would be talked about for years to come by those that were there. Today there were over 1,300 Bluenoses although I have to say that it looked to be a lot more than that.

Blues fans were in great voice and the away end was buzzing. There was loads of banter with the Swansea contingent to our left and the atmosphere was great. There were the usual renditions of our National anthem and 'Keep Right On' as well as various other songs. I particularly liked our songs about England knocking Wales out at the recent World Cup and '3-0 on you big day out!' which also referred to the England v Wales World Cup game.

The game kicked off and Blues seemed to be standing off the Swansea players and giving them loads of time to decide what they were going to do and allowing them to knock passes around us. Amazingly though, Blues took the lead on 14 minutes when Reda Khadra was brought down by the Swansea keeper and Scott Hogan stepped up to score from the penalty spot and took his tally to ten goals for the season. We celebrated wildly in the away end and were determined to enjoy the moment while it lasted.

It lasted 7 minutes until Swansea equalised as we continued to stand off them and their player lad time to turn and fire home easily inside our penalty area. Six minutes later and Blues were behind as Swansea easily cut through our defence to fire home from a couple of yards out. Blues were shocking. Bluenoses sang 'get into em!' in a desperate bid to get the players to make tackles. Sadly it failed to inspire them to do so and I said I thought that this must be what the manager had told the players to do and to stand off them. It wasn't working and Blues were lucky to go into the break only 2-1 down to a crescendo of boos from the away end. Blues had only 14% possession in the first 30 minutes. It was like we were just letting them play.

A few bluenoses sang 'your nothing special, we lose every week' to the taunting Swansea fans but by now our support was so stunned by our poor performance that the atmosphere had become very subdued. John Eustace made two changes for the start of the second half with Hannibal Mejbri (why didn't he start?) coming on along with Juninho Bacuna. This did seem to have an impact with

Bacuna hitting a wonderful pass to Chong who sprinted forward and fired past the Swansea keeper into the net on 55 minutes to make it 2-2 right in front of the away end and we exploded in celebration. 'Chong, Chong will tear you apart again!' rang out loudly for the rejuvenated Blues contingent.

We dared to believe again for the next 3 minutes until our goalkeeper John Ruddy sliced a clearance straight to a Swansea player who easily swept it into the empty net and Blues were trailing again. Although a bit of despondency seeped back into the away end we did recognise the improvement in our team and our loud singing continued as we tried desperately to spur our team on. Swansea players were now intent on wasting as much time as they could as player after player went down with feigned injuries for minutes at a time only to get up and jog away easily once the game was disrupted. This practice is poor sportsmanship!

Happily the majority of the Blues supporters remained in the stadium and sang their hearts out despite the taunts from the home supporters. We were rewarded when Lucas Jutkiewicz stooped to score with a diving header in the 89th minute and the away end went completely crazy. The players celebrated right in front of us as the home support looked on stunned. 'Who are ya, who are ya?' was directed at the Swansea fans and people were falling over in celebration. It was mayhem and absolutely fantastic. I couldn't believe it. I was so happy that it was now 3-3 and we might get at least a point from the game and halt our losing streak.

The fourth official held up his board to indicate that there would be 7 minutes of injury time and I immediately started the timer on my phone. I didn't realise that Swansea had made all their substitutions and with one of their players going off injured they were down to ten men. Blues were on fire and going all out for the win but when a shot was cleared off their goal line I suspected our chance was gone.

In the 97th minute Blues won a corner and we roared them on from behind the goal. Rather than the usual time wasting at the corner flag routine, Hannibal opted to cross the ball into the box and Austin Trusty was there to meet it with a header that flew into the net. Queue absolute delirium in the away end with unbelievable scenes of celebration as the players celebrated in front of us. Goalkeeper John Ruddy ran the length of the pitch to join the celebrations and it was mayhem. Non of us could believe it. It was fantastic and I've not seen a stadium empty so fast in my life as the Swansea fans vanished. "Is there a fire drill?' rang out. "We're Birmingham City – We'll fight to the end" echoed around the stadium.

The game restarted and the referee played ten minute of injury time (Swansea players weren't time wasting now!) before blowing his whistle to confirm a fantastic 4-3 win for Blues and the celebrations began in earnest as the players, manager and his team joined us. Absolutely unbelievable scenes and a day and a game that will be talked about for years and one that I will never forget. Everyone was still singing in the car park as we headed back to the coaches.

The trip back was fun as we chatted about the game and we were all in high spirits. We had a laugh when Nigel knocked the emergency window hammer from its holding (an alarm sounds at the drivers cab when it's removed) and Nigel was desperately flaying about trying to fit it in upside down as we roared with laughter. Charlie got his torch out and I directed then to the one on the opposite side and the hammer was then back in its rightful place. I still found it funny though.

Hence I have very good memories from my visits to the Liberty Stadium. I have made 5 trips to this stadium and I have seen one victory, 3 draws and just 1 defeat. Not a bad record really. The Liberty Stadium opened on in 2005 with a capacity of 20,750 which has since been expanded to 21,088. It cost £27 million to build and is also home to the Ospreys rugby team. The stadium became the first Premier League ground in Wales when Swansea won promotion in 2011 and is the third largest stadium in Wales after the Millennium Stadium and the Cardiff City Stadium. In European competitions the stadium is known as Swansea Stadium due to advertising rules.

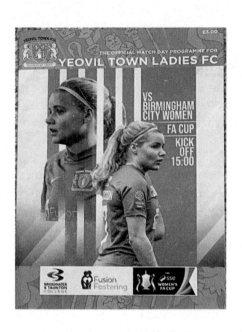

Ground 118 – Avenue Stadium (Dorchester Town FC) – 10th February 2019 – WFA Cup – Yeovil Town Women 1 Birmingham City Women 3

Because of the previous postponement of the Blues Ladies FA Cup tie away at Yeovil Town Ladies due to the weather I was now able to travel to the rearranged game on Sunday 10th February. It was the day after the extremely exciting away trip to QPR as the men had won 4-3 and I was completely drained! However, I was still up early the next day as Harry picked me up at 9am and we headed over to Walsall to pick up Terry. I was really looking forward to the trip and in particular going to a new ground 'The Avenue' home of Dorchester Town FC which was also the home of Yeovil Town Ladies this season. It was a long trip down south with a quick stop at the services and I was surprised to learn that Dorchester is only 7 miles from Weymouth! We did get to see the sea though, as we passed Weston Super Mare.

We arrived at the ground in plenty of time and paid our £2 parking fee and were soon joined by the Redditch Blues who had paid £1 as the parking attendants sympathised with their long trip down! I should have asked for a pound back as we were all decked out in Blues colours – only joking! There were already a few Bluenoses in the car park and we were soon all chatting. It was really cold – despite the sun now making an appearance but we were all wrapped up well and we headed to the turnstile. Once inside we headed into the bar and after obtaining drinks we watched the Man City Women v Chelsea Women game which ended in a Desmond (tu tu – 2-2). This meant that if Blues won our game in hand we would move up to 3rd place.

I had to persuade Terry to have a beer as it was that cold he was thinking of a hot drink! The bar was full of the usual Bluenoses and I was impressed by the amount of Bluenoses that had made the long trip on a cold day. I brought a Dorchester Town FC badge to add to my Collection of grounds I have visited and we headed onto the terrace to put my flag up as Harry and Terry got chips and curry sauce from the nice little snack bar – the chips looked lovely too and both of them seemed to enjoy them. The rest of the Blues contingent sat together in the seated stand at the side of the pitch and there looked to be 50 or more of us that had made the trip amongst the 523 attendance. I had been hoping that they would all stand on the terrace with us so that we could sing as our usual singers Alex, Carl and Nigel were absent so that just left me! I did try to get them all going but to no avail. Harry, Terry and I stood on the little terrace behind the goal where I had my Blues flag on display.

The game got underway and Blues were playing in our 'lucky' yellow shirts and we were dominant from the start. Blues created several chances but when we did get the ball in the net the linesman flagged for offside. I was beginning to think it was going to be a difficult afternoon until Charlie Wellings was fouled in the area on 38 minutes and a penalty was awarded. Terry, Harry and I looked a bit worried as Aoife Mannion stepped up to take the penalty as she had missed a few this season but we needn't have worried as she calmly fired the ball home and it was 1-0 at half time. I took this opportunity to get some chips and curry sauce which were lovely! Proper chip shop chips and they were the best chips I have had at any football ground!

The second half got underway following our halftime trip to the bar and Blues continued to dominate and with only 2 minutes gone the lively Emma Follis scored to make it 2-0 to Blues. We were looking sharper now and on 58 minutes Charlie Wellings got Blues third goal and we all celebrated and began to relax. It began to get a bit scrappy and Yeovil brought on their 16 year old substitute Erin Bloomfield who scored with her first touch of the ball from a cross which our keeper came for but the Yeovil player got there first and headed into an empty net. Very disappointing as it was Yeovil's only chance and was not a fair reflection of the game.

The final whistle sounded and it was a good 3-1 win which ensured that Blues progressed to the 5th round of the FA Cup where we would meet Reading away on Sunday 17th February. It was a long trip back from Dorchester but it had been a great day out and very worthwhile. I arrived home at 8.30 feeling tired but happy – great fun following the Blues.

The Avenue stadium was built in 1990 at a cost of £3 million pounds and has a capacity of 5,009 (710 seated). It was a really nice little ground and I really enjoyed my visit there.

Ground 119 – Rush Green Stadium (West Ham United) – 15th September 2019 – FAWSL – West Ham United Women 1 Birmingham City Women 0

The weekend was a doubleheader down in London as I traveled to the Charlton game on the Saturday with the men's team and I drove to Rush Green on the Sunday for the ladies game with West Ham. It was a long drive and we had to stop and ask a West Ham fan, who was washing his car, directions to West Ham's training ground as we got close. He gave us directions and we wished him well on his trip to the Vile tomorrow night telling him we hoped West Ham thrashed them. When we arrived the West Ham stewards were arseholes and wouldn't let us park on their car park quite obviously because we were Blues fans! This meant we had to drop Terry off and go and find parking on a road nearby.

It was a roasting hot day and there was a crowd of nearly 1,300 in attendance with a small following from Birmingham. West Ham's ground was a bit small to be honest but they did have a little club house and a club shop selling merchandise. Amazingly the capacity was supposed to be 1,000 which did leave me a little puzzled as today's attendance was nearly 300 in excess of that. There was a small seated stand along one side of the pitch and a small terrace on the other with a very small roof which we tried to stand under to get a bit of shade. We were right behind the dugouts which were made of clear Perspex and the substitutes looked like they were roasting!

It was great to see the usual Bluenoses in attendance and we all stood together near the two Blues Redditch flags and cheered our team on. The game got underway and it was the same story as the previous week as Blues played some good football but fell a goal behind. The second half saw Blues play better and dominate a game that had to be stopped on several occasions for water breaks as it was so hot. Despite hitting the post and missing chances Blues just couldn't find an equaliser although one shot from Lucy Staniforth hit the post and looked to have crossed the line before their goalkeeper clawed it out with a resigned look on her face but it wasn't given!

So the game ended in another 1-0 defeat and we all remarked that it is going to be a long hard season. At least we were not bottom of the league as Liverpool had that honour with a worse goal difference than us. We waited for the traffic to ease then headed back on the long journey home.

The small stadium was the home of West Ham United Women and remains the home of West Ham United U23 and is situated in Romford in London.

Ground 120 – Technique Stadium (Chesterfield FC) – 26th January 2020 – WFA Cup 4th Rd – Sheffield United Women 0 Birmingham City Women 3

The last weekend in January 2020 was WFA Cup weekend and Blues ladies had been drawn away at Sheffield United in the fourth round. I was off work for once and I was excited about our trip to Chesterfield to see the Blues in FA Cup action. It would be a bit of relief from the awful season we were having in the WSL at the time and it would also be a new ground for me to visit. Sheffield United were playing their home games at the Proact Stadium (now called the Technique Stadium) which is the home of Chesterfield FC.

We set off early from Solihull Moors with me, Linda, Terry and Harry making the trip with Harry being the designated driver and we arrived in plenty of time so we headed into the nearby KFC for mega boxes. Once inside the stadium we met up with lots of other Bluenoses who had made the trip and got chatting to a pleasant Sheffield United fan. It was a really cold day but we were suitably wrapped up and headed into the stand to join other Blues fans. It's a nice new stadium with a capacity of 10,400 all seated and pretty standard for the new smaller stadiums. They only had the one stand open which was the stand situated at one side of the pitch and behind the dugouts.

There were more Blues than Sheffield fans. Amazingly there were two Manchester United Women's flags hanging up at the back of the stand. I had absolutely no idea what was going on and presumed that they must have been left from a prior game? Weird. Lynda arrived and put their large Redditch Blues flag on display.

It was a good game which Blues totally dominated and we should have been 2 or 3 up at half time but we went into the break level at 0-0. It took only 10 minutes of the second half for Blues to make their dominance pay when Harriet Scott- the pocket rocket - scored with a header before Lucy Staniforth made it 2-0 with 59 minutes on the clock. Blues continued to attack and looked really good throughout and Harriet Scott scored her second in injury time with yet another header to make it 3-0 and a comfortable journey into the fifth round. We all danced about and celebrated despite the cold conditions and debated who we would get in the draw. I watched the 5th round draw live as Blues were drawn away to Sunderland. A bit of a way to travel but a good draw as I fancied our chances of progressing.

It had been a very good trip and I liked the stadium which is now known as the SMH Group Stadium and has been home of Chesterfield FC since the start of the 2010-11 season. The stadium was built in 2009 at a cost of £13 million pounds and is an all seater stadium.

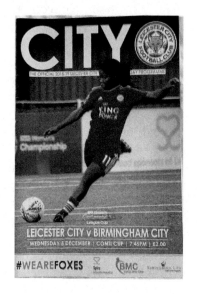

Ground 121 – King Power Stadium – 4th March 2020 – Leicester City 1 Birmingham City 0 – FA Cup

As usual the official coaches left late at 5.15 pm and we all knew that we would be in the rush hour both in Birmingham and when we arrived in Leicester. Of course this proved correct and as happens for all Blues midweek away games we arrived really late just 15 minutes before kick off along with 20+ other Blues coaches. This meant massive queues to get in that were very badly managed by both the stewards and the police as they insisted on searching everybody one at a time along with sniffer dogs. Premier League eh. As kick off approached people got agitated and started pushing from the back and the police formed a line by the turnstiles to ensure that the majority of us were getting crushed. Fabulous. It took 32 minutes to get into the stadium which meant that we had missed 17 minutes of the game by the time we got inside to find there were already people in our seats. As all the 5100 Bluenoses were standing we just found gaps nearby to stand in. Even the aisles were full.

It was a brilliant atmosphere amongst the loud Bluenoses and happily it was still 0-0 when we finally got inside. I think most of us would just be happy not to be humiliated against the third best team in the country at the time and Blues were more than holding their own against a full strength Leicester team. The atmosphere amongst the Bluenoses was fantastic and we never stopped singing throughout the entire game. In contrast the Leicester support was silent as Blues sang 'your support is fucking shit'. Each half of the Blues support sang 'we hate Villa more than you' as we were getting no joy from the home support. It felt like Blues were at home to be honest. We sang 'shall we sing a song for you?' to the silent Leicester fans and 'is this a library?'.

Amazingly Blues were the better side in the first half as our boys played out of their skin - I was so proud of them. Leicester manager Brendan Rodgers must have had a few words at half time as Leicester came at us much more in the second half but Blues bravely held firm until 8 minutes from time when Leicester grabbed their winner with a headed goal that just beat Lee Camp in our goal. This inspired Blues and we attacked them with gusto as the Blues fans roared them on. Unfortunately we just ran out of time and I am convinced that had we had 5 or 10 more minutes then we would have got back into it but it wasn't to be and despite our narrow defeat we were all very proud of our team.

As the Blues players came over to applaud our support at the end of the game 'Keep Right On' rang out loud and proud as blue and yellow smoke (we played in yellow) filled the air. On a funny note one of the blue smoke bombs was thrown so high that it landed on the inside of the roof and blue smoke poured down from the roof. It looked really funny. We all headed back to our coaches in good spirits despite our defeat.

It was a nice, fairly new stadium and I have visited it 4 times in total but unfortunately it has not been a happy hunting ground as I have the misfortune to have witnessed 4 defeats including Blues Women's defeat to Leicester Women in December 2021. The stadium was previously named the Walkers Stadium from 2002 to 2011 and has a capacity of 32,261. It opened in July 2002 at a estimated cost of £35-£37 million.

Ground 122 – Shenley Lane Community Association – 10th October 2020 – Northfield Town 1 Boldmere St. Michaels 3

I was really missing going to live football so much following lockdown and now I was having to watch Blues on TV due to the top (lockdown) tiers having to play inside empty stadiums. I had being hoping to get to a local non league game and in particular to my closest team Northfield Town but their fixtures kept clashing with Blues games until the international weekend when Blues were without a game and Northfield Town were at home. I decided I would get myself down to Shenley Lane to watch their match against Boldmere in the Midland Division Two. My mate June said she would come too but on the day of the match as the rain poured down June had too much to do at home therefore I would have to go alone.

I though twice about going myself due to the heavy rain but I got my coat on, jumped in my car and headed to the ground. I had intended walking but the rain put paid to that. I parked in their car park, put on my Birmingham City face mask and headed into the ground via their social club and had a temperature check on the way in. Amazingly the rain stopped and the sun came out. I was pleased to see other Bluenoses who had come to cheer on their local team just as I was doing.

It was a nice little ground – well a pitch really with dugouts and a small stand, which was beginning to fill up with some fans bringing their drinks with them from the bar. It was the smallest ground I had visited so far with a capacity of 1000. There was well below that today, probably less than 100. It was nice and cosy though with a beer garden behind the goal and the small covered stand had an area containing bench seats and an area for standing. I stood along the side of the pitch and the view was amazing of trees and a lovely big green hill with a couple of big houses sitting at the top. Really pretty.

Northfield Town played in all blue (royal blue) with yellow socks and I was happy to be cheering on a team playing in blue. Boldmere were in red and black stripes with black shorts and socks and it seemed an evenly matched game to me although Northfield Town edged it in the first half and probably just deserved their 1-0 first half lead. I overheard a regular supporter telling his friend that last year this game was a top of the table game. Not this season though. Of course it was nowhere near the level of football I have been used to watching following Blues but it was interesting to watch. Boldmere were awarded a penalty in the second half – I don't know what for as it was too far away to see at pitch level and they scored to make it 1-1. Boldmere then scored twice more to make it 3-1 and that was how it ended when the final whistle sounded.

It was cold and I was definitely ready to head home but I had really enjoyed the experience and it was another new ground for me.

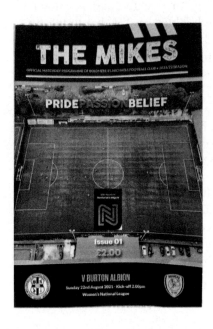

Ground 123 – Trevor Brown Memorial Ground – Boldmere – 25th October 2020 – FA Women's National League – Midland Division – Boldmere St Michaels Women 10 Burton Ladies 1

With the pandemic ruling out visits to any top flight games I decided to venture across the city to Boldmere to watch Boldmere St Michaels Ladies play Burton Ladies. It also meant that I would get to see Terry again, one of my 'Blues family' as he was always helping out down at Boldmere St Michaels and I had missed my friends so much since lockdown in March. With the help of my satnav I survived spaghetti junction and found my way to Boldmere and parked up outside the clubhouse.

It was a really nice little ground with a capacity of just over 2,000 and a lovely social club attached to the stand behind the goal. There was a seated area along one side with lovely bench tables resembling a beer garden next to this stand. On the other side was the new modern changing rooms with a gym etc. It all looked really nice. I was soon catching up with Terry and giving him a couple of copies of my new book 'Forever Blues' which he happily showed to his friends. Then I made my way outside to watch the game. I was pleasantly surprised by the level of football on display and I though Boldmere Ladies played some really good football and they scored quite early on. In fact I missed the first 3 goals as I turned to listen to Terry and then Alan the Villa fan.

Boldmere St Michael's Ladies used to be Birmingham and West Midlands Ladies until quite recently when they moved to Boldmere to play and changed their name. Birmingham & West Midlands, who compete in the FA Women's National League, would play under the banner of Boldmere St Michaels FC as of the 2020/21 season. At the start of the 2019/20 season, Birmingham & West Midlands Ladies entered a partnership with Boldmere St Michaels which saw the club change their training and home games venue from Castle Vale to the Trevor Brown Memorial Ground, home of Boldmere St. Michaels FC.

At halftime Boldmere St Michaels Ladies were winning 5-1 and after enjoying chips with curry sauce I headed into the clubhouse for a coke. I was back out for the second half as Boldmere continued to play well and they scored some cracking goals as well as hitting the crossbar. The match ended with a 10-1 win for Boldmere and I had really enjoyed the experience. It was great to be out watching football again amongst real football fans. After the game I was chatting to one of the Boldmere Ladies players and when I asked if they were at home next week she said no, they were off to play Redditch Ladies in the WFA Cup. That planted a seed. The attendance was 55 so it was really nice to see people enjoying a day out watching football again. I headed back across the city feeling refreshed and happy.

I have been back quite a few times since and I have watched Boldmere St. Michaels Women play on eleven occasions and I have seen 6 wins, 2 draws and 3 defeats. I have really enjoyed each of my visits and I now play for Boldmere St. Michaels walking football team 'The Mikes Women'.

Ground 124 – The Valley Stadium – Redditch – 1ˢᵗ November 2020 – WFA Cup 3ʳᵈ Qualifying Round – Redditch United Women 1 Boldmere St. Michaels Women 2

The following Sunday I decided to head to The Valley Stadium to watch Boldmere St. Michaels Ladies play Redditch Ladies in the WFA Cup. I would be flying solo this trip as no one I knew wanted to join me. Even Redditch Lynda had plans. I was not to be put off though as I was keen to see some football and to visit another new ground.

I got the satnav out again and google maps said it was only a 25 minute drive so I set off at 12.45 for the 2pm kick off and despite my sat nav sending me to a farm gate not far from the ground, I eventually found my way there. It was a bit of an overcast day as I made my way to the turnstiles but I was really impressed by the nice traditional entrance and ground. It was only £2 entrance fee and once inside it looked really nice. I was disappointed not to get a team sheet due to the pandemic but I was not disappointed by the ground. It had a capacity of 5,000 and was home to Redditch United men's team who played in tier 7 and Redditch United Ladies who played in West Midlands Regional Women's League Division One South. In the past the ground had been home to Birmingham City Ladies FC.

The ground had a larger seated area at one side of the pitch next to a nice little beverage section with a serving hatch were I obtained a lovely Chips with curry sauce but they also had a selection of breakfast rolls. Unfortunately they only had sausages left which is why I had the chips. There was a small seated area on the other side of the pitch behind the dugouts but I was mostly impressed with the lovely terraced area behind the goal with a small roof at the back. This was were I headed and I stood just under the roof near one of the crash barriers. Brilliant. It was a good job too because not long into the game and the rain came pouring down.

There was only a small crowd with the vast majority supporting Redditch Ladies. I would estimate between 50-100. I was neutral but had developed a bit of a soft spot for Boldmere. Today Boldmere were playing in their Away kit of green shirts which Terry informed me was not what they had ordered. They had ordered fluorescent green but this darker green kit had been sent instead from the supplier but they just kept them as it would have been too much hassle to change them. I doubt this would happen in the men's game.

It was a tight game between two good teams and it was Boldmere St. Michaels who opened the scoring and they went into the halftime break leading 1-0. Boldmere were attacking the goal I was was standing behind in the second half and I had a great view of their second goal from a corner to make it 2-0. This inspired a response from Redditch as they began to attack relentlessly which woke up the crowd who got behind their team and were quite impressive to be honest. Redditch thought they had scored from a cracking overhead shot which was surprisingly disallowed and pulled back for a Redditch free kick. Redditch did eventually pull a goal back though and their fans were roaring them on. Good support, I thought, but the comeback they yearned for was not to be and Boldmere St. Michaels progressed to the next round with a hard fought 2-1 win on a day when the 2020 FA Cup Final was played which saw Manchester City beat Everton at Wembley.

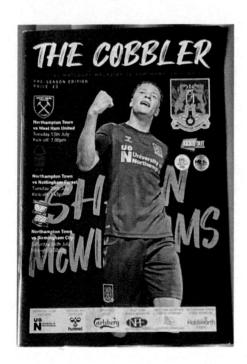

Ground 125 - Sixfields Stadium – Northampton – 24th July 2021 – Friendly – Northampton Town 3 Birmingham City 2

Saturday 24th July 2021 finally arrived and I was so excited to be heading off on another Blues adventure after over a year of not being allowed to do so because of the pandemic. It was a lovely sunny day and it was me, June, Harry and Linda who were heading to Northampton by car as Blues were not putting on coaches for today's game despite over 1,700 Bluenoses making the trip. June made her way to my house and Harry picked us up before we went on to pick up Linda and we were soon on the motorway and on our way. It was great to catch up again.

We arrived in plenty of time at Northampton's ground and parked across the road on the TGI Fridays car park and headed into their restaurant for some lunch. It was great and we had a lovely meal and a nice drink as the place filled up with arriving Bluenoses. We spotted the team arrive in two coaches which I guess was because of the Covid precautions and we hoped they would put on a good show today for us travelling Blue army.

We headed into the ground and it was great to see familiar faces and to watch the away end filling up with happy Bluenoses. I had a new flag that I got for my birthday with Weoley Castle on and Four Blues crests and me and June put it up at the back of the stand where our seats were. Blues fans had one stand behind the goal and half of another stand along the side whereas the Northampton fans were scattered about in the other stand along the side with the remaining stand behind the other goal being left empty. There were way more Blues fans than home supporters.

The Blues fans were already in full voice and singing their hearts out and after all this time it sounded absolutely wonderful. The players looked impressed with our support as they came out onto the pitch and Lee Bowyer said after the game that they had goosebumps when they came out and heard our singing. It was brilliant. 'Keep Right On' was belted out along with various other songs, some of which were directed at the lack of support from the home fans. Lee Bowyer got a great reception from the Blues support and he acknowledged us with a wave as we sang 'Bowyer, Bowyer give us a wave' which was soon followed by 'let's all wave at Bowyer'. It was all good stuff.

It was a nice new little ground which was a bit different from some of the new flat pack stadiums currently springing up and had a capacity of 7,653. The stand along the side of the pitch which was occupied by the Bluenoses looked as though it could be expanded by adding an upper tier as the roof was high and there were stairways at the rear that went up to a second level. Perhaps they were already in the process of building this second tier.

Right behind the empty stand stood a tall embankment/hill with a massive funfair at the far end, which I must say, looked very impressive. The hill was much higher than the stand and was currently occupied by several people eager to watch the game without paying. It looked like they had a good view too. Amused Blues fans sang 'who's the wankers on the hill?' I found this quite funny to be honest.

Blues looked good in our new yellow and blue away kit and we took the lead after only 4 minutes when Ivan Sanchez danced passed several Northampton players before firing Blues in front and we all celebrated. Unfortunately we then gifted Northampton two goals with the second being a howler as our keeper spent too long on the ball instead of clearing it and was easily dispossessed by a Northampton player who then had an empty goal and the simplest of tap ins. Disappointing to say the least. Blues were dominating though and were soon level when Lucas Jutkiewicz headed home to make it 2-2 at half time.

The second half saw Blues continue to dominate and as well as having shots blocked and saved we also hit the post a few times. I couldn't believe that none of these efforts went in and I was dismayed when Northampton scored with their only shot of the game to take a 3-2 lead. Blues really should have had about eight goals but ended up losing 3-2. Disappointing but it was only a friendly and we had played really well. It had been a great day out and I had missed following Blues so much and I headed home happy. I don't think I will ever take it for granted again.

Sixfields Stadium opened in October 1994 at a cost of £6 million and it's current capacity is 7,798 and was expanded in 2014. The ground was also home to Coventry City between 2013 – 2014.

Ground 126 – The Tottenham Hotspur Stadium – London – 4th September 2021 – FAWSL – Tottenham Hotspur Ladies 1 Birmingham City Ladies 0

On the Saturday Blues Ladies season was due to begin and their first match saw Blues away to Tottenham Hotspur Ladies and would be played at Tottenham's new stadium where the men played. As soon as it had been announced that The Tottenham Hotspur Stadium would be the venue for this game, we had all been very excited at the prospect of visiting the new stadium and had booked train tickets in anticipation.

I had been unwell but I was feeling better on the day of travel although still tired but I was excited about the trip. It would be me, June, Harry and Nigel making the trip and we had all spent the previous day sorting out our Covid passes (required to be shown at the stadium) and they were now proudly stored on our phones ready. June and I got a taxi to Moor Street station where we met up with the others and boarded our 09.14 train to Marlybone Station in London.

We arrived at 11.13 and decided to head to Arsenal's Emirates stadium, at the suggestion of Nigel, to have a look around as he had not been to this stadium (neither had I to be honest). So we jumped on the underground and went and had a look around the Emirates stadium. We then had to find a nearby underground or overground station to head to Tottenham for our match and I must admit to struggling a bit as I became breathless with all the walking. At least Harry hung back with me as I lagged behind the others.

After finally arriving at Seven Sisters station we discovered it was a 30 minute walk to the stadium. I was knackered and time was knocking on which meant we had to pop into McDonald's on the way to pick up a take out which we ate on the way. As the stadium came into view I was absolutely amazed by the size and presence it had. It looked absolutely gorgeous with all its modern twists and turns and big screens on the outside showing the Tottenham crest as well as both the men's and the women's players.

It was so unlike the modern 'flat pack' stadiums that had no character. The Tottenham Hotspur stadium had character in abundance and we took loads of photos as we rushed towards the stadium in our, now hurried, quest to find the away end. There were lots of fans milling around with quite a few Birmingham fans amongst them. It took us a little longer than we hoped to find the away turnstiles which were the other end of the stadium to where we arrived and there were stewards and security metal detectors at every entrance.

Having gone to so much trouble to download our Covid passes we were somewhat disappointed that nobody checked them and we were soon inside the away concourse. I have to say that the away concourse was absolutely amazing with a massive poster on the wall with the Birmingham City crest and a message welcoming us and thanking us for 'travelling the 118 miles to be here'. The bars were also amazing and the toilets were like those seen in 5 star hotels – absolutely unbelievable. Sadly there were no programmes available for the away fans which I found very disappointing.

We headed quickly inside as kick off was approaching and we saw loads of Bluenoses that we already knew. The inside of the stadium was just as amazing as the outside with massive screens around the stadium with both the Blues and Spurs crests on display. Three sides of the ground had 3 amazing tiers with lots of executive boxes in between and above them and LED advertising going around the stadium. The other end had a massive stand with the seats in a curve at the top and the gold Tottenham cockerel taking pride of place at the top.

The away section was extremely comfortable and had barriers in place ready to implement safe standing when it returns, hopefully later this season in some stadiums. A totally impressive stadium! My only criticism would be that all the seats were grey with no crest or club name factored into the seating and so the whole effect was that it looked really bland. A real shame in such a fabulous stadium. I did like the way a new hotel next to the stadium was joined by a fabulous twisty bridge/corridor to the stadium.

The match was not much to write home about as Blues Ladies looked totally overawed by the stadium when they came onto the pitch and it effected their performance. Blues did hold their own but failed to defend a corner and conceded the only goal of the game to lose 1-0. There were around 100 Bluenoses in the 5,000 crowd and we made a lot of noise but I can only imagine the atmosphere had it been 5,000 of us in a full stadium watching the men's team play. I can dream!

Despite being quite breathless at times I did have a great day out and it was brilliant to get a new ground in and such a fantastic stadium at that. It was definitely my new favourite away ground. We headed home from a closer underground station to Marlybone and were back in Birmingham by 9pm. Great day out.

The Tottenham Hotspur Stadium has a capacity of 62,850 and is the 3rd largest football stadium in England and the largest is London. It opened in April 2019 and cost £1 billion to construct. The stadium also hosts NFL games and features the world's first retractable football pitch which reveals a synthetic turf field underneath for the NFL games and other events. It is a very impressive stadium.

Ground 127 – Weston Homes Stadium – 18th September 2021 – Championship – Peterborough United 3 Birmingham City 0

We arrived in Peterborough and we headed to the ground to have a look around and to get some food. We bumped into Stuart and Liam as we disembarked and had a quick chat before heading to the chip shop/kebab house near the stadium where I obtained doner meat and chips and enjoyed them on our way back to the turnstiles. I purchased my usual club badge from the club shop and we headed to our entrance.

There were over 4,000 Bluenoses in attendance today and we had been given the entire stand behind the goal and over half of the stand along the side at the right of the away end. It was an impressive sight and a mass of blue and white. This was my first time to Peterborough United's stadium and it was a nice little ground although it only had two floodlights on one side as the opposite side was a new stand. The new stand did look impressive with POSH spelt out in the seating and I do love a ground with good old fashioned tall floodlights, even if it did only have two. It did have a nice family feel about it too.

The Bluenoses were in exceptional form today and there was already blue smoke in the air and lots of singing. The blue smoke bombs continued throughout the game and the atmosphere was brilliant but sadly the team let us down on the pitch with an absolutely shocking performance against the divisions worst team. Blues were thrashed 3-0 by a team that couldn't score goals or win games but the worst of it was the awful performance by our players. Everyone agreed that this was the worst performance of our season so far.

Despite the result we still had a nice journey home as we shared banter on the coach but Blues dropped to 11th in the table. Early days yet though.

My second trip was for a pre season friendly game in July 2023. There was only one coach going to Peterborough despite Blues selling around 1,200 tickets and it was me, Charlie and Taff making the trip as June was away on a mini break in Oxford. I would miss my mate. I got to St. Andrews early and went in the club shop to take my new books in and to get the new shirt. It was really busy in there as loads of people were also looking to purchase the new home shirt. I got mine and managed to join the queue before it stretched around the shop.

I headed back to the KOP car park and met Charlie and we laid our flowers at the tribute to Trevor Francis. It was an beautiful sight with so many tributes. There were so many scarves and shirts and amazing items all laid out in front of the lovely massive tribute canvass erected by the club. We spent a while paying our respects and taking photos then we met Taff in the club shop before heading round to Tilton Road to get on the coach.

Stuart was already on the coach and we joined him towards the rear of the coach and we were soon joined by Liam also. It was a nice journey to Peterborough as we all had a nice catch up. As there was only one official coach it was the accessible coach which meant that we were dropped off right outside the ground and we immediately made our way to the nearby chip/kebab shop. It was nice and sunny but as soon as we sat outside with our food it started to rain and so we had to make our way back inside to stay dry.

We were soon joined by the giant rabbit called 'Peter Burrow' the Peterborough mascot who swaggered into the shop swinging a giant carrot. He took a moment to survey the clientele inside the shop as the guy behind the counter informed him that 'it's all Birmingham fans in here mate' and he slowly made his exit again. The rain had stopped and we headed back outside and made our way towards the away turnstiles as we concluded that we didn't have enough time to head to the pubs by the river.

Once inside the lads purchased beers/ciders at £5.50 for a bottle! I decided on a bottle of coke at only £2.50 before we headed up to our seats in the stand. They offered a surprisingly good view and there were a lot of other Bluenoses present and in good spirits. There was a special presentation for Barry Fry and he was greeted by rapturous applause from the Blues end which Barry fondly acknowledged by raising his arms in the air to us and telling us to 'Keep Right On!'

Before the game there was a minutes applause for Trevor Francis which was amazing and the Blues end (containing the majority of the support inside the stadium) sang 'There's only one Trevor Francis!' really loudly for the entire minute whilst also applauding. It was amazing and sent a shiver down my spine. Trevor was the best player I ever saw play and he will always be our king and never forgotten.

The game, however, did not live up to expectations as the final preparation for the new season. We were stunned as the Blues defence caved in time after time and we were 3-0 down with only 15 minutes on the clock. We were stunned and it wasn't too long before fed up Bluenoses left for the pubs in an attempt to rescue something from their day out.

It was disappointing to be honest but Blues pulled a goal back before halftime when Scott Hogan was put through and a one on one with the keeper saw Scotty made it 3-1. The second half was a bit better but it wasn't brilliant. Jukey scored a consolation in the last minute when Keshi Anderson set him up and we enjoyed a bit of a half hearted celebration behind the goal. The game finished in a 3-2 defeat and we headed for the exits. It didn't give us much faith for the first match of the season against Swansea next Saturday. Especially as Swansea battered Reading 4-0 in their last preseason friendly. Oh well.

Weston Park Stadium, which is also known as London Road Stadium, has a capacity of 15,315 and was built in 1913.

BIRMINGHAM CITY
SUNDAY 10TH OCTOBER 2021
3:00PM · £2

Ground 128 – Chigwell Construction Stadium (Dagenham and Redbridge FC) – 10th October 2021 – FAWSL – West Ham United Women 1 Birmingham City Women 1

It was nice traveling to London by train on a Sunday as it wasn't too busy and before we knew it we were arriving at Euston Station. We discovered that we only had to change once on the underground and out second train took us all the way to Dagenham and took about 30 minutes. It was nice because the train was almost empty and it was both underground and overground (Wombleing free – if you know, you know). We disembarked at Dagenham East station and made our way outside to look for somewhere to get some lunch.

There was a nice looking pub just across the road that was advertising Sunday Roasts but Harry seemed to prefer the nearby café so we headed in there. There were several West Ham fans in there and it looked quite popular so we decided this probably meant that the food would be good. We were correct in our assumption as we both enjoyed sausage, mash and onion gravy, which I have to say was wonderful and set us up for the day.

So, fully fuelled again, we headed in the direction of the ground which wasn't too far at all and we were soon stood outside the Victoria Road stadium which was home to Dagenham and Redbridge along with West Ham United Women. The stadium had a capacity of 6,078 and it was a really nice little ground. It was a lovely sunny day too.

We opted on tickets in the away end behind the goal as we thought this would be were the other Blues fans wound be and we headed into the ground after looking round the small club shop. It looked nice inside with a lovely little terrace along one side of the ground and a small terrace behind one of the goals but neither of these were open for todays game. There was a seated stand behind the goal where we were currently situated and two seated stands along the side separated by a small gap that seemed to suggest that one of the stands was added at a later date.

I looked around for the Blues contingent but in all honesty there was only about ten of us and everyone was spilt up between the stands. We did see Sharon and Lyndsey and went over for a chat with them. Sharon had her Blues flag with her and Harry and I were sitting a few rows back behind them for the game.

There were over 1,000 in attendance and most of them were West Ham fans but they were very quiet. The game started and Blues had been struggling this season having lost most of their players with hardly any recruitment and it showed. With only one point achieved so far and only one goal scored this season most of us didn't hold out much hope today but we lived in hope.

West Ham took the lead in the first half with ex-Birmingham City player Claudia Walker scoring from distance and I let out a sigh. I never gave up hope though and I was rewarded when Louise Quinn scored right in front of us to make it 1-1. I was the only one in the stand that was jumping around in celebration. I didn't really care if I upset the West Ham fans, I was enjoying celebrating a rare Blues goal.

I turned to Harry who remained glued to his seat and asked him why he hadn't celebrated and he replied that he was in shock at seeing a Blues goal. He did look a bit concerned about me winding up the West Ham fans though. It was great as the Blues players looked amazed to see a lone Bluenose loudly celebrating amongst the home support. Excellent.

The game finished 1-1 and we headed back to Dagenham East tube station happy and still in one piece. It had been a really enjoyable day our at a lovely little stadium which was another new ground for me. All in all I had a great time and enjoyed the atmosphere in the stadium.

The stadium is actually the Victoria Road stadium but is currently known as the Chigwell Construction Stadium for sponsorship purposes. It was opened in 1917 and is located in Dagenham, Greater London.

Ground 129 – Rowheath Pavilion – 21st November 2021 – Crusaders Women FC 1 Boldmere St. Michaels Women 8 – Birmingham County Cup

In November 2021 Harry and myself headed over to Rowheath Pavilion to watch Boldmere St. Michaels Women take on Crusaders Women in the Birmingham County Cup. The small ground consisted of a few football pitches near to a lovely old fashioned Pavilion which housed the teams dressing rooms as well as a lovely little café that looked out onto a very picturesque lake. It was literally only 5 minutes from my house and was very close to Cadbury's in Bournville (Birmingham).

It was a freezing cold day and we immediately headed into the little café where we obtained refreshments from the counter having failed to navigate the online ordering. As kick off neared and having explored the surrounding area we headed over to the pitches and found the one that was being used today when the teams came over. We met a couple of other Boldmere fans and got chatting to them.

The game got underway and we spent a lot of our time collecting balls each time it went out of play. I had to duck once to avoid it hitting me in the face. It was an entertaining game of football which Boldmere dominated against the lower tier Crusaders but it was freezing cold. I had dressed warmly but Harry's coat wasn't especially thick and he was literally shivering so we went back to my car at halftime and out the heater on to warm him up,

It worked a treat and we headed back across to the pitch for the second half which Boldmere continued to dominate. Despite the weather it was lovely being outdoors watching a football match again after the recent pandemic and it was enjoyable as Boldmere won the game 8-1. We both headed home cold but happy and looking forward to getting warm again once in our warm homes.

Rowheath Pavilion is a not for profit community centre with a community café and church. It is a really lovely little place to visit.

Ground 130 – RICOH Arena – 23rd November 2021 - Coventry City 0 Birmingham City 0 – Championship

Blues were away to Coventry City on Tuesday night 23rd November 2021 and 4,000 Bluenoses made their way to Coventry for the game and it would be my first visit to thr RICOH Stadium. We met the others at St. Andrews and got the coach to the RICOH stadium and I wore my new third shirt, which was good as this was the kit the Blues played in today.

It was buzzing in the away end and the 4,000 Bluenoses made a lot of noise. Blues played well against a Coventry side flying at the moment as they occupied 4th spot in the league table. Once again the referee was shocking and Ryan Woods received his marching orders and for the second game running Blues were down to ten men. 'You're not fit to referee!' rang out as well as 'Fuck the EFL' and I wholeheartedly agreed with both these statements. Blues came away with a very credible 0-0 draw but the point saw us drop to 17th in the table.

It was a very nice stadium and looked good from outside and inside. It had been a great atmosphere in the away end and I had enjoyed the trip. That was until we attempted to return home. The motorway was down to only one lane on the way back with 3 lanes closed and this caused absolutely awful traffic congestion that saw us get back really late at 23.30. Due to the fact that there was only one (3 carriage) train back to Birmingham the majority of fans were on the motorway and it made you think that this was either deliberate or some people are completely stupid. By the time I got home I had a sore throat and felt unwell.

I had an enjoyable trip to Coventry to watch England Women play in the Arnold Clarke Cup in February 2023 which England went on the win for the second time in a row and set a record attendance for the stadium. Harry, June and I headed to Coventry for the England Women v Italy Women game in the Arnold Clarke Tournament. Today the match was being played at the RICOH Arena, home of Coventry City and we had seats at the very back of the home stand behind the goal. Harry was driving and we had been advised to park at the nearby Coventry Rugby club as it takes ages to get off the official car park (which has to be pre booked).

We arrived at 12.00 and mistakenly ended up parked on a Gypsy site near to the Rugby ground but it turned out to be okay as it meant we got away really quickly after the game straight onto the motorway. I was really excited heading towards the stadium as there were loads of merchandise stalls on the way to the stadium and I got a half/half scarf, an England hat and a tournament programme. Brilliant. We headed straight into the fan zone which was in a large covered section attached to the stadium and contained a mini fair, food stalls, bars and a giant pic and mix sweet stall – the biggest one that I have ever seen!

On our way into the fan zone we were given free sunglasses, giant hands and paper england flags. The yellow sunglasses and giant hands had Arnold Clarke on them and the sunglasses came in very handy as we were bathed in sunshine during the game. Whilst in the fan zone we obtained foot long hotdogs and a lovely cold cider to wash it down with. June got a massive bag of pic n mix.

It was a good game despite manager Serina Wiegman playing mostly reserve players and England won 2-1 in front of a record crowd for the RICOH of 32,128. Happily England would go on the retain their trophy with a 100% record having won all three of their games in the tournament. It was a good journey home and a very enjoyable day out.

I visited twice in 2023 with both games ending in defeat. In April 2023 June and I went in fancy dress. The last away game of the season was upon us and it was away at nearby Coventry City and tradition meant that many would go as fancy dress, June and I included. The lads refused to participate but June and I got ourselves dressed up as Hippie Chicks and I must admit we did look cool. June's outfit was black with flowers and mine was purple and pale green with flowers and a cool headband. June arrived at mine early to apply my face tattoos which were two hearts on one cheek and a purple butterfly on the other cheek. They looked great!

Then we were off to meet the lads in Morrisons for a breakfast before heading over the get the coaches from St. Andrews. There were five coaches heading to Coventry and it didn't take us long to get there but it took ages to get on the car park and to disembark. I purchased a programme, put it on the coach and then we headed into the away end. We obtained drinks and admired the rest of the fancy dress in the concourse. The Bluenoses were already in good spirits and they were singing and bouncing around the concourse.

Having consumed our drinks we headed up to our seats amongst the 4,500 travelling Bluenoses and the atmosphere was fantastic. The Coventry fans were also in good voice and todays crowd was over 30,000. I wondered where the Coventry lot had been up to now. The North stand had been closed from the 2014/2015 season due to low attendances and only reopened to fans again this season. The place was rocking today though and I couldn't help but be impressed.

The game got underway and Blues made a disastrous start by conceding a very poor goal after only 3 minutes. While we all sighed in despair the Coventry lot were in full voice and very excited. Bluenoses responded with 'where were you when you were shit?' very very loudly. It didn't deter them for long and they continued to sing abuse at us until Blues loudly reminded them that 'we saved your club!' which resulted in a respectful silence for a short while as they knew this was true and without our help they wouldn't be here now.

Sadly we were once again playing against 13 men as the officials were very anti Blues and gave every decision to those is sky Blue including ignoring a clear offside in the lead up to Coventry being awarded a penalty for a cruel and contentious handball by Jordan James. Coventry made it 2-0 from the spot and manager John Eustace was sent off at halftime when he confronted the referee over the penalty decision.

Second half and Blues tried but failed to get back into the game. The Blues squad had all been hit by a sickness bug that had being doing the rounds and a few looked like they may still be suffering the after effects. Tathith Chong had to be stretched off in agony after being hacked down by a Coventry player who didn't even get a talking to let alone a card. No surprise there though. He was off to hospital for an X-ray. So Blues lost the game 2-0 and the Coventry fans enjoyed their big day out.

We headed back out to the coaches where we were kept behind for ages afterwards as the police and stewards refused to let us leave. It gave me chance to admire all those in fancy dress and there were some great costumes including a blue Elvis, Spiderman, Superman , Ali G, Super Mario, a dinosaur and my favourite was a mom and son Umpa Lumpa. They were brilliant!

It had been a lovely sunny afternoon but when we arrived back in Birmingham many roads were flooded. That was a bit of a shock, especially the flooding on Spaghetti unction which caused a tailback of traffic which added to the already long journey back. Blues remained 17th in the league table.

I have visited the RICOH stadium on 4 occasions and seen 1 draw and 2 defeats for Blues and a victory for England Women. The stadium is now named The Coventry Building Society Arena with a capacity of 32,609 (40,000 for concerts). The facilities include a 6,000 square metres exhibition hall, a hotel and a casino. It was built in 2005 and expanded in 2010. The construction cost was £113 million and was also home to Wasps Rugby Club.

Ground 131 – Central Ground (Sutton Coldfield FC) – 20th March 2022 – Women's National League North - West Bromwich Albion Women 2 AFC Fylde Women 2

It was on a lovely Sunny March afternoon when I headed over to Boldmere to meet Terry and Harry. Harry and I left our cars at Boldmere and Terry drove us the short distance to the Central Ground, home of Sutton Coldfield FC to watch West Bromwich Albion Women play AFC Fylde in the Women's National League North. We paid our £1 entrance fee and obtained great matchday programmes, also only £1 each then headed into the clubhouse where I obtained a 'Sutton Coldfield FC' badge for my collection. It was a really nice clubhouse with views out to the pitch and large TV screens showing the Crystal Palace v Everton FA Cup quarter final game.

I was feeling hungry by now, so we headed out to the refreshments stall where I obtained chips with curry sauce, a cold Pepsi and hot drinks for the lads which we then took back into the bar area. Terry knew a few people who he chatted to and one of the Boldmere regulars that I knew came and sat with us for a chat whilst I ate my chips, which I have to say, were really nice. It was soon ten to two and nearly time for kick off so we all headed outside to watch the game.

It was a really nice little stadium with two very small seated stands on either side of the pitch. We took up our places standing near the half way line in the bright sunshine which meant that we didn't feel the slight chill in the air and had a great view. This would be the first time that I had seen Albion Ladies (apart from a preseason friendly against Birmingham City Women a few years ago) and I checked my programme for information about their league and current position.

Albion were currently in the Women's National League North and were playing AFC Fylde Women who were several places above them in the table. Albions local rivals Wolves currently topped the table and looked favourites for promotion at the end of the season. AFC Fylde wore a lovely zesty yellow away kit with thin black stripes at the front which reminded me of the new car I was currently awaiting which is a similar colour and I really liked the kit. Obviously I was a neutral today and I had my Birmingham City shirt on under my coat (which I had proudly displayed in the bar). Harry remarked that I would be the death on him! I had to smile.

The game proved to be very entertaining and well worth the one English pound entrance fee and I'm sure the rest of the 84 fans in attendance would have thoroughly agreed. AFC Fylde took the lead in the first half which they held until halftime. Albion grabbed an equaliser early in the second half before scoring a cracker to take the lead not long afterwards. This seemed to please the majority of the fans until AFC Fylde scored to level the game at 2-2 and the game ended all square but I have to say it was very entertaining.

I had thoroughly enjoyed my day out in the sunshine watching a very good game of football and catching up with friends and other football loving people. It was genuinely nice being outdoors and visiting a new ground to add to my growing list. This is what life was all about.

Ground 132 – Illey Lane – (Previously Bartley Green FC) – 22nd March 2022 – Bustleholme FC 1 Tipton Town 4

On most days I check my Futbology app to see what local games are taking place in case I fancy going to a game and as I checked on the Tuesday morning I saw there was a non league game only 4 kilometres from where I live. I text Steve (my sister's boyfriend) to see if he fancied going as he lived close too. I love being outdoors at football games and it would be a new ground for me so I picked Steve up and we headed to the Black Horse pub in Illey for a drink beforehand.

The floodlights for the ground could be seen from the pub and I was looking forward to the adventure. Once we left the pub and headed down the road I saw the small entrance lane on the right and set about manoeuvring around the many large pot holes on the long one lane track to the ground. I use the word ground loosely as it was basically a pitch with a couple of sheds which housed the 'refreshments' and the one toilet. The car park was the grassed area behind the goal, protect by some netting. It was very quaint though.

Getting out of the car I was immediately hit by the stench of cow dung! Boy was it strong! Although I think my nose became a bit 'nose blind' by the end of the game, it was completely overwhelming throughout my time there. Steve noticed it too, despite spending a lot of his time on his phone describing the ground to his mates. We made our way up to the pitch and despite it being dark now it looked really nice surrounded by trees and with a tiny shed like stand at one side of the pitch. It wasn't much bigger than a shed either.

I spotted a cow behind the dugouts and I use the word dugouts loosely too as they contained what looked to be old 'school chairs' for the manager, players and officials to sit on. Steve was really amused by the sight of the back end of the cow and took some photographs to record the moment. We took a position not too far from the halfway line and it was good to see that there were quite a few other people who had also come to watch the game. I reckoned there were around 50 people there in my opinion.

The first team out were Tipton Town who were playing in all blue and they were soon followed by Bustlehome FC who were in a kit similar to Norwich City, yellow tops and green shorts. The 'football ground' itself belonged to Bartley Green FC who sadly folded near the end of the 2013-14 season but still had a vibrant social club and there were a few teams who now used the pitch to play their games on. They had been in existence since 1948.

Bustlehome FC were a team from Rowley Regis, formed in 1975, who moved their home games to Illey this season, according to the lady serving the refreshments to Steve when he went to get a coffee to warm himself up. I must admit that it was getting cold and I retrieved my hat from the car to keep me warm. The game was being played in the West Midlands (Regional) League Division One. Tipton Town were formed in 1948 and had briefly shared their home ground with Bustlehome FC for a while before Bustlehome moved to York Road prior to their move to Illey this season.

It was an entertaining game to watch and I thought that Tipton Town looked the stronger team and they were 2-0 up by halftime. It was amusing to see the ball flying into the bushes or trees and having to be retrieved by the players as the bemused fans looked on, although occasionally a supporter would head into the bushes to retrieve the ball. This source of amusement had worn off long before halftime. I survived the halftime break and the second half saw more goals as Tipton Town extended their lead to 4-0 before Bustlehome pulled a goal back to make the final score 1-4 with the visitors taking the points.

As soon as the final whistle sounded we headed to the car to get out of the cold and to get away before the other cars also parked on the grass. Obviously the pot holed lane had to taken extremely slowly in the pitch black but it had been a very entertaining evening which I had thoroughly enjoyed.

The ground is now home to AFC Birmingham and they were given the old dugouts, tunnel and some seated sections from St. Andrews (Birmingham City FC) when the new owners of Blues completed the Stadium improvements at St. Andrews. I have yet to visit again yet to see all of this although I have seen the photos on the AFC Birmingham Twitter page.

Ground 133 - Dickens Heath Sports Club (Birmingham) – 24th April 2022 – Leafield Athletic Ladies 1 Boldmere St. Michaels Women 0

It was great to be heading to a new ground again and it was a cold but sunny Sunday April afternoon. I always think that it is wonderful to be outdoors at a football game on a Sunday afternoon. Today Harry was picking me up and we drove the relatively short distance to Solihull, although it was more Earlswood side, and discovered the small ground called Dickens Heath Sports Club which was the home of Leafield Athletic Ladies FC.

It was just past Shirley Town FC and tucked away just off the road. There was a fair sized car park where we easily found a space as we were early. We would have been even earlier had Harry's Satnav not taken us to another Leafield

Athletic (where there was a youth game in progress) 5 minutes away near Highgate United's ground. There did seem to be a few little football grounds in the area and it was really nice.

We soon found the lovely little clubhouse/changing rooms with a really nice little balcony/terrace and large outdoor table area all over looking the two pitch's. It was really quaint and had a 'Leafield Athletic Ladies' sign on the front. It only cost £3 for me and £1 for Harry as a senior, well worth the afternoon out. Inside there was a nice little bar and a small cafeteria where they were starting to prepare food. I was starving and ready for either a hotdog or a burger. The pitches and clubhouse were surrounded by trees on all sides and it was a very picturesque sight.

Terry arrived not long afterwards with some of the Boldmere people and we then obtained food and we sat inside out of the cold wind to eat it. I had finally decided on sausage and chips whilst Harry declined any food as he was having a roast dinner later and Terry had hotdog and chips. I even got to enjoy a Thatcher's Gold with mine.

Today Leafield Athletic Ladies would be playing Boldmere St. Michaels Women in the last match of the season which would see Boldmere crowned champions of the FAWPL Midlands Division One (4th Tier of Women's football) irrespective of today's result. I had been told that the Leafield team would be giving Boldmere a guard of honour when they came out but sadly I missed this as I was still enjoying my food.

More friends arrived just before kickoff, Alan and Anne and I had also been introduced to Heidi who was was starting up the Boldmere St. Michaels Womens walking football team, to which I had been invited to join. The man in a suit, from the FA, arrived looking very smart and ready to present the league trophy after the game.

Sadly the game did not live up to expectations and Boldmere looked below par whilst Leafield Athletic looked extremely keen to beat the Champions elect. It wasn't a great spectacle and was won by Leafield Athletic by the only goal of the game, scored in the second half and inflicted a rare defeat on Boldmere St. Michaels. The highlight had been when we spotted the arrival of the league trophy, just before the final whistle, by the FA man and it looked very impressive indeed with purple and white ribbons and shining in the sunlight.

Once the game was over we were made to wait (as was the man from the FA who looked very bored) for the team to finish their debrief before collecting the trophy and celebrating with bottles of champagne on the pitch. I was disappointed to see the Leafield Athletic players heading to the changing rooms before the presentation as I thought it would have been a mark or respect to applaud Boldmere.

So next season Boldmere would be playing in the third tier of womens football and playing the likes of West Bromwich Albion, Burnley and Middlesbrough. I wish them luck and I'm sure I will get to see some of their games when I get the chance. It was another good afternoon out.

HOME CLUB HEDNESFORD TOWN FC — **PREMIER DIVISION** — **AWAY CLUB** BIRMINGHAM CITY FC XI

	Home			Away	
Colours	Shirts White		Colours	Shirts Blue	
	Shorts Black			Shorts White	
	Socks White			Socks Blue	

Date 2nd July 2022   Attendance

Competition (if other than a League Game) First Half Team = Pre-Season Friendly

Referee G Rollason   Assistant (Red) R Stott
Assistant (Yellow) M D'Aguilar
Fourth Official

Lewis Gwilliams	1	Oliver Basey
Josh Webb	2	Josh Williams
Harry Manton	3	Finn O'Brien
Taylor Byrne	4	Remi Walker
Lewis Ison ©	5	Luke Carsley
Luke Rowe	6	Chris Ogor
Cameron Ebbutt	7	Odin Bailey
Todd Parker	8	Finlay Thorndike
Riley O'Sullivan	9	Josh Andrews
Numair Rashad	10	Kyle Hurst
Joe Cuff	11	Adan George
	Subs	
Harvey Portman	12	Eng Oduka
Kyle Bennett	14/13	Brad Mayo
Chay Tilt	15	Ini Ono
	16	Josh Homes
	17	Keke Symmonds
	18	Rico Patterson
	19	Kieron Wakefield/20 Josh Beeson

OWN GOALS TO BE CLEARLY MARKED

FINAL SCORE

CHECK TO GOAL TIMES SHOWN

Ground 134 – Keys Park – 2nd July 2022 – Pre season Friendly - Hednesford Town 3 Birmingham City 5

Thanks to my Futbology app I discovered that Blues had a friendly coming up away at Hednesford Town on Saturday 2nd July and I made plans with some of the others to make our way there. There was no mention of this game on the Blues website so we presumed that it would be the Blues youth that would be playing. It didn't matter though, we would just be happy to see some football and go to a new ground – for me and June at least.

Harry and Linda made their way to mine and I then picked up June and drove us to Keys Park the home of Hednesford Town FC. We arrived early as I was keen to get a parking space and explore the stadium. It wasn't open when we arrived and Terry was already there and waiting for us as he had made his way over from Walsall. Terry and Harry sat chatting while me, June and Linda attempted to get in the bar but had to settle for a wander around outside when we failed to get past the doormen.

The turnstiles were late opening but once inside I quite liked the traditional little ground with its floodlights and terraces. There was a nice little food outlet/burger van selling lovely food. June and I had our eye on the pork, chips and gravy but the pork wasn't ready yet so we had no choice but to head upstairs to the bar for a drink. It was a really nice bar too in a big room with large round tables and a cracking view of the pitch and of the inside of the stadium. We saw Martin O'Connor sitting just outside the windows and he looked around and waved at us. The bar was now full of Bluenoses.

We decided to head back outside to get some food and me, June and Linda all had the pork, chips, gravy and stuffing and it was wonderful. The best food that I have had at an away ground. Very impressive. We walked around inside the ground to the seated area behind the goal as Terry said this was the most sheltered part and it certainly seemed to be really cold and windy despite the occasional burst of sunshine. Terry said that it was always cold at Hednesford as it was near a big lake and the wind was indeed, freezing. I wished I'd put a thicker coat on.

I took in my surroundings and admired the two terraces, one narrow terrace running along one side of the pitch and the other behind the opposite goal. This appeared to be the main home end as this is where the large home flags were already in place. There was another seated stand in the middle of the opposite side to the narrow terrace and this housed the bar at the top of the stand. There was also an outside bar area with picnic type tables but it was closed today, understandably so as it was cold.

There were already loads of Bluenoses already in the ground with the majority in the stand alongside the pitch but several others were scattered about with some in our stand and some on the home terrace. As kick off approached I could see a coach pulling into the car park and it turned out to be the Blues party bus and they were soon pouring into the stadium and the singing began. The handful of young home fans behind the goal tried to compete but they had no chance against so many passionate Bluenoses. The official attendance was 641 and I'm betting 600 of them were Birmingham fans.

The Blues youngsters basically fielded a different team in each half and played some nice football and we were 4-1 ahead at half time. Our goalkeeper looked really good against a strong Hednesford team and made some good saves. It was when he was changed in the second half that Blues conceded another couple of goals but all in all it was a good entertaining 5-3 win for Blues and nice to have something to cheer about.

Ground 135 – Estadio Antonio Dominguez Alfonso – Las Americas, Tenerife – 9th October 2022 – CD Marino 1 UD Villa de Santa Brigida 2

While I was on holiday in Playa Las Americas in Tenerife I found that the local football team nearest to where we were staying were playing at home on the Sunday. I decided that it would be a great way to spend a couple of hours after visiting the market in Los Cristianos and it was only 1 kilometre from our apartment. I walked from our apartment to the stadium where it took me a couple of minutes to find the entrance which meant I missed kick off by a couple of minutes. It was a 12.00 midday kick off and it was already very hot with the sun blazing down.

I purchased my match ticket for 8 Euro's and made my way into the stadium and I purchased a Club Deportivo Marino scarf just inside the entrance. It was a really nice little stadium despite the large athletics track that ran around the pitch. There was a nice covered stand to one side of the pitch with a roof that offered shade from the sun and I decided that was where I was heading.

CD Marino were playing in their nice blue home kit and the away side UD Villa de Santa Brigida were in all yellow. There were around 300 to 400 people in the stadium all of whom were sitting on the concrete steps in the shade of the roof or standing at the back. I took a walk along the top of the steps and stood at the back to watch the game. Although there was only one stand it did curve around part of one end behind the goal and the rest of the open area looked out to the mountains and it really was stunning scenery. The other two sides were lovely grassy banks with the teams name made up of plants etc and a small score board at the top to the bank.

I popped into their cafeteria near the entrance at the top of the stand where I obtained water and a marathon (snickers to the youngsters) and I watched as the barman serving beer to a fan stopped to take a swig from his bottle of beer. Nice little café and there were outside tables if you wished to watch the match whilst enjoying your drinks/food.

Todays game was between two teams in the third tier of Spanish football and although it wasn't amazing football it was enjoyable to watch and I enjoyed my afternoon. CD Marino took the lead and I was hoping that the home team might go on to win but the away side equalised from a corner in the second half to make it 1-1. Despite CD Marino looking the better the side it was the away team who grabbed a late winner and a couple of the home players looked broken when the final whistle sounded.

I had enjoyed my afternoon and headed back to our apartment in the afternoon sunshine to grab a late lunch and chill out for a couple of hours.

Ground 136 – The Bolt New Lawn – Forest Green Rovers 1 Birmingham City 2 – FA Cup – Tuesday 16th Jan 2023

It was a cold day as we boarded the coach for the trip to Forest Green that was due to leave at 3.45pm. There were only 2 official coaches today although the away allocation of just over 1,000 was sold out and I suspected that a lot of Bluenoses would be travelling on the party buses. Today would be a new ground for the four of us and that was why we were looking forward to the trip so much. Sadly the football of late had been really poor and I suspected it would be even worse if our manager decided to play a reserve side as seemed to be popular in the Cup competitions.

It was a decent enough trip to Gloucester although it was real shame that it was a night game as we never got to enjoying what would have been a scenic trip in the daylight. The coaches stopped at the Gloucester services or 'Farm Shop' on the way and this is definitely my least favourite of all the motorway services. I call it the 'telly tubby services' due to its resemblance to the homes of the Telly Tubbies'. This was difficult to envisage in the pitch black and therefore my description was lost on Nigel who was visiting the services for the first time. It was only good for a comfort break (toilets) as the farm shop was way too expensive (£8 for a sausage roll) and didn't stock the sort of food and drinks that we were looking for. I was gasping for a can of coke but there was nothing like it to be found. Not even normal lemonade so we left empty handed. Luckily I had brought a bottle of water with me.

We arrived at the Forest Green Rovers ground in plenty of time and reflected on how nice the views from the top of the hill, where the stadium was situated, would have been in the daylight. There were some lovely little houses to be seen on our way up the hill. Although the ground was new it was small and this would be the last season that FGR would play there before moving to yet another new stadium. The current stadium had a capacity of just over 5,000 and on a cold night like tonight I wondered wether the home fans would achieve that capacity. I knew of lots of Bluenoses who had tickets for the home section for tonight's game though.

When we arrived I headed into the little club shop to purchase a badge for my collection and had the pay the small amount of £3.00 by card as the stadium was cashless. This is something that makes me sad as I am a big believer in using cash as currency and it is steeped in history and a cashless society is soulless. How can it truly feel like you are earning and spending money when it's all on a card or phone? Truly sad.

Another disappointment was the fact that there were no programmes as they were 'online'. Who wants a programme that is online? The main reason for purchasing match programmes (as well as a good read) has always been as a momentum or keepsake that you have been to the game and to add to your collection. I know I wasn't the only one to be disappointed but I'm sadly getting more used to it this season.

My next stop was the outdoor bar area where we purchased cider (in can's that didn't even come close to filling the plastic pint glass) at £4 each and headed into the nearby tent to consume it. We bumped into a few people we knew in the tent including Redditch Pete and Pete who sits by me on the KOP. It didn't take us long to finish our drinks despite the cold and we headed off to find the away entrance.

It was a nice walk round to our entrance along a pathway bordered by trees which was really nice. We arrived at our turnstile to find a queue, despite being early, which was due to the fact that the new modern turnstile would not accept tickets that were dated 7th January when today was the 16th of January due to the previous postponement. Modern technology eh!

Finally the stewards gave up on the turnstiles and opened a nearby side entrance which they then personally manned and removed ticket stubs the good old fashioned way. Disaster averted. Once inside we noted a very small refreshment stand to our left but as none of us fancied vegan sausage rolls or pies we decided to find our spot on the terrace. Then we spotted the really big trays of nice looking chips (many with gravy on) that people were buying but sadly we then decided that the queue was way too long to join.

We found a spot at the back of the terraced area near the halfway line and had a good look at the stadium in front of us. Blues had the open terrace that ran the entire length of the pitch which was narrow and lacked a roof. Opposite us was the home seated area and behind each goal were home terraces. One end was mostly empty whilst their main end hosted a fair few who sang on the odd occasion, mostly to point out that our support was "fucking shit". They had a very good point too as, despite being a sell out, we had failed to bring any singers on this occasion and when they did make the effort (16 minutes into the game) the acoustics were poor due to the lack of a roof. Nigel and myself tried on several occasions to start the singing but mostly failed.

John Eustace had made wholesale changes to the team including Neil Etheridge, Jordan James, Jordan Graham and Emmanuel Longelo being in the starting lineup. Despite the changes it should still have been a strong team against a poor Forest Green Rovers team who currently propped up League One. However, Blues started poorly and lacked passion and fight and the League One team looked like they wanted it more than us. We had no heart and FGR were first to all the first and second balls.

I don't think it came a surprise to many of us when FGR took the lead with only 8 minutes gone when one of their players lashed home a long range shot after our players failed to put in a block. My heart sank and unless we started playing with some fight and passion I couldn't see any way back and we would be out of the FA Cup in the 3rd round once again.

The second half saw John Eustace make his changes and on came Chong for Longelo, Maxime Colin for Jordan Graham and Alfie Change for Jordan James. This seemed to made a difference and it took only 5 minutes for Lucas Jutkiewicz to score to make it 1-1 and it was game on again. Although we were still poor we were much improved and the young Alfie Chang looked really lively and was full of the passion and fight that the others lacked. He could actually pass the ball too which had been a problem before he came on with Blues hitting poor passes across the pitch.

I was busy worrying about a potential replay if the scores remained the same especially as it would be on my birthday the following week and I obviously had plans, although June informed me that I would have to cancel them. Happily I didn't have to ponder this for too long as Kevin Long lashed home from a corner and Blues took a 2-1 lead. We celebrated accordingly and the singing began. There was a couple more substitutions but the game finished 2-1 despite our poor performance and Blues were into the 4th round of the FA Cup and a trip to Blackburn beckoned.

It was back to the coaches and off down the steep hill and back on the road to Brum with most of us in good spirits. Goalkeeper Neil Etheridge had pulled off a fantastic triple save when the scores had been 1-1 and it was very 'Gordon Banks' and I predict that a save like that must surely mean our name was on the trophy. Everyone laughed. I'd no idea why.

The Stadium is currently known as The New Lawn and has been the home ground of Forest Green Rovers since 2006. It was also home to Gloucester City during the 2007-07 season.

Ground 137 – Cadbury Recreation Ground – Cadbury Athletic 3 Bolehall Swifts 0 – Saturday 7th October 2023

Somewhat unusually I had a free Saturday during the football season as my club Birmingham City had played West Bromwich Albion the night before, and beaten them 3-1, and so I decided to go to visit a local team. I briefly considered going to watch AFC Birmingham play at Illey where they now had the old dugouts, tunnel and seats donated from Birmingham City when they updated the stadium recently.

Then I discovered that Cadbury Athletic FC were playing at home at the Cadbury Recreation Ground and I had been keen to visit this ground for quite a long time but the opportunity had not presented itself until now. I had seen Cadbury Recreation Ground in a couple of books about the greatest stadiums and this had grabbed my interest and I was keen to add it as a new ground.

Happily Cadbury Recreation Ground is only a few minutes from where I live and I managed to persuade Steve to join me as June had pulled out the day before. It was a lovely sunny day and I managed to find street parking easily just a minutes walk from the entrance to the ground. It only cost a few pounds for entry and a programme and we made our way to the steps at the side of the pitch and admired our surroundings.

It looked great with a lovely old pavilion type building behind one goal that housed the changing rooms and a little room selling refreshments. Behind where we were standing was the very impressive old Victorian factory buildings that housed Cadbury. They looked fabulous and I thought back to how it must have been in the past when my Grandpa worked there. Cadburys had always looked after their staff and we always had bags of Cadbury chocolates in our house that had come from the staff Cadbury shop. No wonder my dad went off chocolate when he was young. I never went off it though and I proved this with my halftime Wispa from the little café.

It was a good game too with Cadbury Athletic playing in purple (like Cadbury chocolate wrappers) against Bolehall Swifts who looked like Norwich City in yellow tops and green shorts. The sunshine was fabulous and Cadbury won 3-0 and the small crowd went home happy. I did wonder how they would get on when the dark nights draw in though as there were no floodlights but I really enjoyed my day and it was a great experience and a lovely unusual new ground. I would definitely visit again if my own team were not playing.

Epilogue

From March 1973 up to May 2024 I have visited 137 football grounds over 7 countries and it has been an amazing experience. Some grounds I have visited only once whereas others I have been to on many occasions. I have been to 1287 football matches during this time with 1148 of these involving Birmingham City and the rest being mainly Birmingham City Women and England (men and women) with a few random games along the way.

I had a period of time whilst I was living in Abu Dhabi in the UAE for 17 years when I was only able to get to games when I was back in the UK visiting family and therefore limiting my football during this time. I have been back living in Birmingham again since 2014 and I am having enormous fun travelling home and away with my beloved club Birmingham City and it is like a rollercoaster.

Over the years I have many many great memories and perhaps too many to share in this book with my favourite away games being Blues trips to Wembley, especially our League Cup win over favourites Arsenal in 2011. Our trip to the Millennium Stadium in 2002 when Blues won promotion back to the top flight was also amazing. Other amazing away days were Huddersfield on the last day of the season in May 1995 when Blues won 2-1 to clinch the Second Division Championship and promotion back to Division One.

Another amazing day out was my trip to The Dell , which is now demolished, to see Blues win 1-0 against Southampton, when Mick Harford scored, on the last game of the season in May 1983 to escape relegation. Highfield Road, also demolished, was another great last day relegation escape when Blues won 1-0 at Coventry with a very late Mick Harford goal on a lovely sunny day in May 1982. I could go on and on with all the good and bad memories that I am lucky enough to have accumulated.

Obviously my favourite ground is my home stadium of St. Andrews and my beloved Birmingham City. It is difficult to have just one favourite away ground but my favourite away trip has to be Fulham with its lovely location on the Thames and the charming character of the ground. I love stadiums with character, which can be sadly lacking these days, and I love grounds with floodlights which probably remind me of days gone by when you could see a stadium from some distance with the four floodlights towering in the distance.

Sadly my beloved Birmingham City were relegated to League One at the end of the 2023-24 season but with fantastic new owners I am hoping for a great season in the third tier and I will be looking forward to being able to visit several new stadiums. These could include Cambridge United, Crawley Town, Exeter City, Lincoln City, Mansfield Town, Stevenage, Shrewsbury Town (I visited their old ground), Stockport County and Wrexham. So I am already looking at the positives and daring to dream again. I have other stadiums on my bucket list too which includes nearby Halesowen Town as the little stadium is listed in two of the greatest grounds books that I have. It is never ending and incredibly interesting travelling around the country/world visiting new stadiums and a quest I don't think I will ever get bored of.

I am also lucky to have a very loving and supportive family and a fantastic group of friends who frequently travel with me and I consider them my Blues Family. Currently these are my best mate June along with Charlie, Nigel, Taff, Harry and Linda and on occasions I am also joined by Stuart and Liam and several others. They all know who they are.

So take my advice and get out there and follow your team around the country and enjoy the joys and sorrows and the great outdoors. You will meet fantastic people on your travels and have some great laughs along the way. You may even bump into me along the way. Remember to 'Keep Right on' and 'Still Journey On!'

I hope you have enjoyed my memories and that you may be inspired by them. Thanks to everyone who has been a part of my journey (and my book).

402

Printed in Great Britain
by Amazon

42390234R00225